MODERN COURTSHIP AND MARRIAGE

E. E. LeMasters
Professor of Sociology
Beloit College

The Macmillan Company
New York

MODERN COURTSHIP AND MARRIAGE

THE MACMILLAN COMPANY
NEW YORK · CHICAGO
DALLAS · ATLANTA · SAN FRANCISCO
LONDON · MANILA
IN CANADA
BRETT-MACMILLAN LTD.
GALT, ONTARIO

THIS BOOK IS DEDICATED
TO THE MEMORY OF MY
MOTHER AND FATHER.

PREFACE

In writing this book, the author was dedicated to the proposition that a marriage text should do more than aid the student with his personal adjustment—it should also help orient him to the societal problems related to modern courtship and marriage. In almost every chapter, social issues related to the modern American family are posed for thought and discussion.

In addition, the book attempts a more complete analysis of the American courtship system than the other texts in this area. It is believed that this is the most complete study of the American courtship system yet published. In devoting approximately one-third of the analysis to courtship, it was hoped that the student might be able to function more effectively in the system if he had some insight into its nature. The aim here, of course, is that of preventing unfortunate marriages rather than attempting to salvage them later. The book also contains a more systematic analysis of modern folklore related to courtship and marriage than has been customary.

Theoretically, the analysis is oriented toward "functionalism" as originally employed by the anthropologists Radcliffe-Brown and Malinowski. Essentially, this approach demands that we always see social behavior as part of a total pattern of social organization. With this approach, it is possible to use the marriage course to help the student gain some insight into the total culture of which the courtship and marriage systems are a part. Since a great many students who enroll in marriage courses are not social science majors, this broader objective appears to have some merit.

The reader may wish to know something of the author's qualifications to write a book of this nature. In addition to fifteen years' experience teaching marriage and family courses at the college level, the writer has had professional training and experience as a family case worker, has been a Dean of Students, and has served as a personnel counselor in naval aviation during World War II. He has also taught parent education classes, lectured widely to youth and parent groups, and has maintained a private marriage counseling practice for several years.

In large measure, this book is based on material organized at the University of Wisconsin while the author was serving as Visiting Lecturer during the academic years 1952–1953 and 1953–1954. We are grateful to Professor Howard Becker, then Chairman of the Department of Sociology and Anthropology, for the invitation to lecture at the University.

We are also indebted to the teaching assistants who worked with us at Wisconsin: Everett Dyer, Robert Herman, Walter Shea, Robert Witt, Charles Wanninger, and Robert Friedrichs. Many of the ideas presented in this text were first developed in discussions with this group.

We also wish to thank the following persons for stimulation and/or assistance in planning and writing this text: W. Fred Cottrell and Read Bain, of Miami University (Ohio); Edwin Lemert of the University of California; Robin M. Williams, Jr., of Cornell University; John Gillin, now at the University of North Carolina; C. W. M. Hart of the University of Wisconsin; Charles Curtis, our associate in Sociology at Beloit College; Ruth Cavan of Rockford College; Robert Winch of Northwestern University; Reuben Hill of the University of North Carolina; and Evelyn Duvall, of Chicago.

To Dean Ivan Stone and President Miller Upton of Beloit College, we are indebted for their interest and support.

Mr. Vaile Deale and staff of the Beloit College Library were

extremely courteous and helpful in locating elusive reference material.

We are indebted to Professor John Winget of the University of Cincinnati for reading and criticizing the first draft of the manuscript.

Thanks are due Mrs. Joan Fiese for typing two complete versions of this text.

The wives of textbook writers are a long-suffering group—only they know. I wish to pay homage to my wife for her patience while being initiated into that sacrificial body.

To our sons, Bill and Gary, we say: "Look, Daddy is home again!"

E. E. LeMasters

Beloit, Wisconsin

CONTENTS

PART I

PERSPECTIVE

CHAPTER I

THE SCIENTIST STUDIES COURTSHIP AND MARRIAGE

Introduction

In most human societies, courtship and marriage behavior are regulated by tradition, and enforced by gossip and community pressure. In American society, however, rapid social change has minimized the usefulness of tradition alone. Parents, and young people themselves, have increasingly felt the need for outside help in thinking about courtship dilemmas and preparation for marriage. To provide this help, high school and college courses have been organized, and a new group of specialists, known as "family life educators," has emerged.

In the 1920's, when these courses were first organized, there were relatively few research data available on the topics discussed, which meant that the instructor, and the textbook itself, had to rely largely on personal observation, supplemented by case studies and historical material.

As the social science movement grew in the United States,

more and more effort was directed toward applying the methods of scientific research to courtship, marriage, and family life. This has resulted in a mass of research material being published, most of it since 1930.

Many persons have questioned whether the social scientist can make any significant contribution to the understanding of behavior as personal and intimate as courtship and marriage. Is it not true, these persons ask, that people are "too complicated," especially when "they're in love," for the scientist to study them with any profit?

The reply of the social scientist is simply this: that science is essentially a *method* for studying phenomena, and that the scientific approach can be applied to *anything,* whether it be rocks, protons, or people. He may admit, however, that at any given moment the methodology available to the social scientist may be inadequate for the solution of certain problems, or that the studies to date in a certain area may be inadequate to answer certain questions. For example: the writer believes that the data available now are inadequate to explain why certain persons in our society never marry. But this does not mean that the social scientist will never be able to explain this group; the studies have simply not been made as yet. In other areas, however, such as what attracts individuals to each other, the problem may be more complicated, possibly necessitating a new research approach. Recent studies by Winch and associates,[1] * as a matter of fact, seem to indicate that we do need a new approach to unravel the dynamics of mate selection.

The social scientist is not as bothered by the complexity of humans as is the nonscientist. As a general rule, people live in groups, and these groups evolve patterns or systems of behavior. In Part II of this book, for example, you will find a rather complete description and analysis of the American courtship system; yet most Americans are probably not aware that there is a courtship

* References throughout the text will be found at the conclusion of each chapter, not in footnotes.

system as such. Regardless of whether the general public knows it or not, there is not only a highly structured courtship system, but an American marriage system as well, also described and analyzed in this book.

In essence, the social or behavioral scientist is dedicated to the proposition that courtship, marriage, and family systems can be studied in the same way that economists study economic systems, or political scientists analyze political systems.[2] Our methodology may still be crude, and our studies are undoubtedly incomplete, but it is believed that these deficiencies will be reduced, given time, trained personnel, and money.

It is not always recognized that the social scientist does not have to be 100 per cent accurate to be helpful. If he can predict marital adjustment, for example, even 20 per cent more accurately than the nonscientist, he could still be very useful in our society. If he could develop a marital prediction test that would prevent 10 per cent of the divorces in America, that in itself would be a valuable contribution. It is not necessary, therefore, for our knowledge to be perfect or infallible: it only has to be better than the information available from other sources. The rather heavy enrollment in high school and college marriage courses, plus the increasing use being made of the marriage counselor, seem to indicate that Americans have already become convinced that the scientist has something worthwhile to say about "love" (or the lack of it) in modern courtship and marriage.

At the end of this book, the student will be in a position to decide for himself whether or not the efforts of the social scientists in this area to date have borne any fruit. All we ask is that an open mind be maintained until the evidence has been examined.

Limitations of the Scientific Approach in Studying Courtship and Marriage

Even though the writer believes that considerable progress has been made since 1930 in the scientific analysis of courtship and marriage in the United States, the fact remains that we should not idealize this approach. As Locke points out clearly,[3] most of our findings, of necessity, relate to statistical *probabilities,* and may or may not hold true for any given couple. For example: most of the major studies indicate that a short courtship (less than six months) is a hazard in our society. This seems reasonable and most persons will accept the principle, yet a friend of ours, a college chaplain, married his wife after a whirlwind courtship of two weeks and "has loved happily ever since," as he puts it.

Does this mean that the research data on this point are in error? Not necessarily. It could still be true that our ministerial friend's marriage is atypical and that a *relatively* high proportion of marriages following brief courtships are unsuccessful. In other words, the principle could be sound but there would still be exceptions.

It may also be, of course, that the length of the courtship is not as important as its *intensity,* with some couples accomplishing in two weeks what takes other couples several months. As yet, however, the research is not refined enough to measure the relative speed with which different couples determine marital compatibility.

Actually, the courtship and marriage research data are essentially similar to the life expectancy tables used by life insurance companies in computing premium rates for different age groups. The actuarial scientists do not know *who* will die in any given year, but they can predict rather accurately the *rate* for any given group. It may turn out that a particular man of seventy may outlive another man of thirty, but this exceptional event does not invalidate the principle that *most* men of thirty will outlive *most* men of seventy, thereby justifying a lower annual premium rate for the younger men.

Operating on the same statistical principle, a marriage counselor might advise a young man that marriage outside his own social class is usually more hazardous than marriage within one's own socioeconomic group, but this should not be taken to mean that interclass marriages do not often succeed in our society. The differences here, in other words, are *relative* and not *absolute*.

It also needs to be admitted, quite candidly, that the research on many items still leaves much to be desired, that modesty and caution must constantly accompany any attempt to apply general findings to any specific case. The writer will try hard to remember this in the chapters ahead, and the reader should be careful to do likewise.

Objections to the Scientific Study of Courtship and Marriage

A few years ago one of our students in the marriage course— a very attractive girl from Sweden—reacted negatively to the quantitative studies of courtship and marriage. In her belief, "love should not be studied with an adding machine. Every person is unique, and every love affair is unique. Why can't the scientists leave love and marriage alone?" (this last with feeling). Interestingly enough, this girl was a political science major and believed in the scientific study of political and economic behavior, her resentment being confined to the invasion of personal or *intimate* areas of behavior by the social scientist.[4]

The writer believes this resentment to be fairly common, even among intelligent and educated persons (as this girl certainly was). In some ways, this hostility seems to be greatest toward the IBM or quantitative studies of intimate behavior, and this could be a factor in the rather general resentment expressed against the Kinsey research. Case studies, in particular, do not seeem to arouse equivalent hostility. It may be that students, as well as the general public, feel that the impersonal, quantitative methodology tends to dehumanize social science research, "turning people into numbers," as one student expressed it. It might even be that the average student's fear of mathematics itself is related to this reaction. The writer confesses that he too resented being regarded as a number while serving in the armed forces during World War II.

When all the above is admitted, however, it is still essential to remember that modern social science is becoming increasingly quantitative in nature, whether the general public likes it or not. And since the research findings reflect this mathematical approach, it is impossible to avoid statistical analysis in a courtship and marriage course.

Actually, there is nothing essentially inhuman about quantitative science: Albert Einstein, one of the most humane figures of modern times, worked almost exclusively with mathematics and statistics all his life. We are faced, therefore, with bias or prejudice in this resentment of quantitative research on courtship and marriage.

Gunnar Myrdal, in his classic study of the American Negro, *The American Dilemma,*[5] points out that anti-Negro feelings are deepest when personal or intimate behavior is involved—eating together, intermarriage, etc. The same dynamics may be related to the resentment of some persons to the scientific study of sex, courtship, love, and marriage. It is essential to recognize that a bias of this nature may be encountered in reading and/or discussing some of the data to be presented in this text.

Why Study Courtship and Marriage?

Not everyone, of course, agrees that courtship and marriage *should* be studied—at least not in the classroom. On some college campuses, certain professors will be found who view with alarm the development of marriage courses. Nevertheless, a great many people in our society believe these courses to be highly worthwhile. Why?

There are several reasons advanced by the advocates of these courses: (1) Americans are concerned about the rather striking increase in divorce in our society since World War I; (2) these persons believe that the best approach to the divorce problem is to prevent unfortunate marriages—in other words, to focus our efforts on guidance before marriage rather than on counseling after marriage; (3) it is believed by this group that marital choice is probably the most crucial decision the average American is ever called upon to make, and that young people need help in thinking about this decision; (4) that parents, because of the rapid and sweeping social changes in our society, no longer feel completely adequate to help their sons and daughters resolve all the problems of courtship and marriage; and (5) that only an organized high school or college course, taught by a professionally trained person, can deal adequately with the mass of research material being published in our society on courtship, marriage, child-rearing, and family relationships.

Rightly or wrongly, high school and college students are increasingly interested in such courses, and more and more schools and colleges are offering them.

It is true that we have no conclusive evidence as yet that marriage courses prevent unsuccessful marriages. Is it not also true, however, that American education in general has never been scientifically evaluated? The writer, for example, took four years of Latin in high school, on the assumption that this would help make him an educated man. But what is an educated man and precisely what ingredients go into the product? College faculties have been debating this issue for generations, without reaching a clear-cut answer.

Certainly, no competent family-life educator would presume to think that a single course in courtship and marriage will automatically admit the student to that select circle of happily married couples in our society. We do believe, however, that a course of this nature should be helpful to most students in thinking about and preparing for marriage.

But My Parents Are Divorced . . .

It occasionally happens that students from unfortunate or traumatic family backgrounds are disturbed by some of the material presented in a course of this nature. We all tend to apply the data presented to our own lives, and in some cases this can make us uncomfortable. The author can remember his days as a graduate student in psychiatric social work, when most of the students became disturbed sooner or later as the result of applying psychiatric material to their own personalities. To some extent, this happens in marriage courses also. The textbook or the instructor may be describing a courtship problem, for example, not knowing that one of the students in the class is facing this problem at that very moment. If the topic happens to be divorce, it is extremely likely that at least one member of the class has come from a home broken by divorce, or may, in fact, be experiencing a divorce in his family at the present time.

If there are married students in the course—and there usually are these days—it is not unlikely that some of them are faced with some of the problems discussed in the course. A few years ago the writer was reviewing Terman's data related to sexual climax in married women, not realizing that one of the married men in the class was experiencing this exact difficulty with his wife. A few days later, when this student came in to see us, he said: "You probably didn't realize it, but almost everything you said on Friday applied to our marriage. In fact, it seemed almost that you were describing our sexual problem. I was really sweating during that lecture." The instructor, of course, was not talking about any particular married couple, and in fact was unaware that this married student was having any sexual adjustment problems. At the same time, the material was so close that the student was disturbed by the discussion.

When this sort of situation develops, the student should ask for a conference with the instructor. In this way, the problem can be analyzed, misunderstandings can be clarified, and it may be that the instructor can be helpful, or can refer the student to the proper source for help. In the case above, the married student came in, unburdened himself of his marital worries, and we were able to make several suggestions that eventually helped him and his wife improve their sexual adjustment.

It has been the writer's experience that a marriage course can be made a constructive experience even for the student from the most traumatic family background, but this is not always achieved without individual conferences at some point during the course. It is the responsibility of the student to inform the instructor if he feels the need for such discussion.

Functions of This Text

In planning this book, several basic objectives have been kept in mind. It may help the student if these are made explicit at this point:

1. *A relatively complete description of the American courtship and marriage systems.*

All of us have some knowledge of dating patterns and marital practices (including some malpractices). Nevertheless, few of us have anything like a complete or systematic understanding of the total American courtship and marriage systems, including the various subsystems. For example: have you ever analyzed the role of parents in our modern courtship system? Are you aware that their role differs considerably from one social class level to another? Do you have any clear understanding of the part played by the peer group in modern dating practices? Do you know how our system of engagement is changing? It is the function of this text to help you see modern courtship and marriage in a much more complete (systematic) way than you have ever seen it before. If the book does not do this, it will have failed in one of its basic functions.

2. *An analysis of modern courtship and marriage.*

This means that we not only intend to describe American courtship and marriage patterns but also to subject them to *analysis*. Perhaps this can best be illustrated by taking a specific characteristic of our courtship system, such as the "romantic complex."

To analyze this complex, a series of basic questions must be posed: is this romantic approach to marriage peculiar to American society, or is it found in other marriage systems? Has it always been a basic feature of American marriage, or is it a relatively recent development? What factors in our society seem to be related to the romantic complex? What are the problems or stresses posed by the complex? And, finally, what are its strengths: for example, why is it so widely accepted?

It should be evident that the answers to these questions can only be obtained by persistent digging, by probing into the history of American and Western civilization in general, by socio-logical analysis of the interrelationships between our marriage system and our other basic institutions (religious, political, and economic), supplemented by an attempt to understand the emo-tional and spiritual needs that couples are attempting to satisfy through marriage. In a very real sense, then, our examination of courtship and marriage will involve us in a broad-scale study of people and their social environment in modern American society.

3. *To summarize the research on courtship and marriage.*

In recent decades, a vast amount of research material related to courtship, marriage, and family life has been published in the United States. Table 1, based on a survey by Foote and Cot-trell,[6] gives some indication of the mounting volume of these studies.

Obviously, the average person, no matter how intelligent or well-read, has very little chance to obtain even a slight under-standing of this research unless it is summarized for him in some convenient form. It is true that many newspapers and magazines have attempted to present the findings of some of these studies— usually the more striking ones—but the fact remains that only the surface of this research is touched by these articles. It becomes necessary, then, for books and courses of this nature to help the student understand the basic findings of these research studies.

TABLE 1.

COURTSHIP AND MARRIAGE RESEARCH, 1945–54

1945	74
1946	88
1947	82
1948	81
1949	107
1950	103
1951	120
1952	139
1953	101
1954	136
Total	1,031

It is true, of course, that not all the research material can be included even in a book of this kind; a series of books would be required. But the major studies, at least, can be presented, analyzed, and discussed.

4. *To structure the discussion of basic questions.*

Almost all of us have sat in on discussions that never got anywhere, or were essentially aimless. As a rule, this sterility has resulted from the fact that the basic issues were never identified, or were avoided. One of the functions of this text is to uncover the basic issues involved in modern courtship and marriage and expose them for discussion and analysis.

Perhaps a case illustration will make this point clear: a girl asks whether or not persons of different religious faiths can be successfully married in our society. The text analysis of interfaith marriages indicates that the following questions would have to be answered in analyzing this problem: (1) What do we mean by "successful" marriage? (2) What are the basic factors that seem to determine marital success in our society? (a review of the data); (3) Of what relative importance are these factors? (4) Is it true that marriages between persons of the *same* faith seldom fail? (5) Is it "religious faith" or *degree of devoutness* that is crucial? etc.

Eventually, this line of analysis will lead us to see that this question can be answered intelligently only by exploring the total persons who will be involved. This does not deny the role of religion in modern marriage, but it does focus attention on other aspects of the marriage that will also be crucial: sexual compatibility, family background, personality needs, economic factors, and so on.

If this text can achieve the four functions analyzed above, it seems to us that it will have served its purpose.

Plan of the Book

It may be helpful to the student if the general plan of the book is explained at this point. Part I, Perspective, is designed to give the reader an over-all view of the American family today, its major characteristics, and its recent changes. Part II, The American Courtship System, is an attempt to give the student a comprehensive understanding of the dating process and mate selection. Considerable space is devoted to this analysis, on the assumption that insight into the courtship process may help the young person participate in it more intelligently. Part III, Marriage in Modern Society, analyzes the major factors involved in marital adjustment, including the presence or absence of children.

At times, as individual factors in courtship and marriage are considered, it may seem to the reader that we are regarding human beings as though they were made up of unrelated segments of behavior, economic, psychological, etc. This is not really the case, even when it appears so. The fact is that human beings as such can hardly be analyzed as complete entities until we have seen what components go to make up the total person. If you attempt to understand your roommate, for example, you will soon find yourself discussing his or her family background, religious convic-

refer to *Western* culture—that complex of behavior, such as Christianity, which has been common to the area.

The student should remember that culture is amazingly variable and that it apparently is not based on biological instinct. Human sexual behavior, to cite one instance, has a biological base, but the manner of behavior taught and permitted varies greatly from one culture to another.

2. *The concept of subculture.*

In this book extensive use is made of this concept,[8] because of the tremendous diversity of our behavior. Basically, a *subculture* is simply a distinctive set of behavior patterns adhered to by a subgroup within a large and heterogeneous society, such as the United States. Thus, there is a Catholic subculture in our society,[9] a rural subculture,[10] a Southern subculture,[11] etc. It must be understood that subcultural groups, such as the Catholics, share most of the basic culture patterns of their society, but in certain areas—birth control, for example, in the case of the Catholics—their behavior is relatively distinctive.

3. *The concept of social class.*

In recent years the research of Warner and others on social class in the United States has had extensive impact on American social and behavioral scientists.[12] Many nonprofessionals, as well as some within the profession, show a tendency to reject this research, perhaps because they believe it is "unAmerican" or "undemocratic" to think of social class groups in our society.

It may help the student to accept and use this conceptual tool if it is explained at this point that *all* human societies are stratified one way or another. The Soviet Union, for example, has a social stratification system,[13] and so did the America of our forefathers. There is nothing incompatible between a social class system as such and the basic values of our society, such as freedom and equality. The only requirement is that position in the class system be *achieved* and not inherited or *ascribed at birth*.

Viewed in this way, the American social class system becomes a fruitful area for research, largely because it has been discovered that all the various socioeconomic layers tend to possess a distinctive subculture or way of life. The use of nursemaids and governesses to rear children, for example, is a part of the subculture of the upper class in our society and produces a child-rearing system for that group that is relatively characteristic. At the other end of the status system, at the bottom, the rather typical outside employment of the mother, as Frazier has shown,[14] produces a different child-rearing system. Whether it is food preferences, voting patterns, or love-making techniques, there seem to be relatively distinctive behavior patterns at the various social class levels in the United States. The research to support this statement seems rather impressive.[15]

Although income is the basic variable determining social class membership in our society, the student should remember that other factors are involved as well. A Roman Catholic bishop's income, for example, may be relatively modest in the United States, but he associates on an equal plane with the highest ranking groups in the community. A racketeer, on the other hand, may have a very high income but be unacceptable socially to persons far below him in the economic structure. College professors, like members of the clergy, usually occupy status positions somewhat above what their income would warrant.

In addition to income and occupation, such items as length of residence in the community, ethnic background, racial membership, and clique associations affect social class membership. The interested student will find this clearly explained in the volume by Warner cited in the references at the end of this chapter.

As the term "social class" is used in this text, it refers essentially to the subculture or way of life characteristic of the several socioeconomic levels in modern America. The author recognizes that these overlap and that the differences between the various levels are relative and not absolute. It should also be made clear that the various subcultures are not being evaluated in this text:

it is simply being argued that they are *different*—and that these differences must be taken into account in analyzing modern courtship and marriage.

Most of the patterns analyzed in this text are those of the middle-class groups, although some attempt is made to point out social class variations where the data are available.

Since most college students are, or soon will be, members of the middle class, it seems justifiable to focus largely on the subculture of that group. An even more urgent reason, however, is that most of the research to date on courtship and marriage has utilized middle-class samples. Hence there is not too much choice.[16]

4. *The concept of rapid social change.*

In almost all analyses of American society by social scientists, repeated reference is made to "rapid social change." This conceptual tool refers to the fact that ours is a culture subject to unusually fast and pervasive transformation, whereas some cultures appear to alter themselves relatively slowly.[17]

Not all parts of our culture, however, change at the same rate of speed, and this has produced what Ogburn has called "culture lag," a state of affairs in which parts of the culture are out of adjustment, one part having changed while a related part has failed to change, or has changed very little.[18]

All through this analysis, it will be necessary to use rapid social change as a conceptual device.

5. *The concept of culture conflict.*

In our culture, and perhaps in most complex cultures, there are deep conflicts within the system.[19] Divorce, for example, is hardly compatible with the "until death do us part" clause in our marriage vow. Whenever the individual man or woman in our society runs into one of these basic conflicts, there is no easy way out: one value has to be sacrificed to realize another. This concept of culture conflict will be useful at various points in our analysis.

6. *The concept of social system.*

In recent years, the term "social system" has become increasingly common in sociological analysis.[20] Basically, this concept is used to point up the fact that most human behavior is not haphazard but is *organized* and *structured*. Thus, it is no accident that an overwhelming proportion of adult Americans have one husband or one wife at a time instead of two; this is the result of a marriage *system* known as monogamy. Similarly, the fact that most young Americans "go steady" sooner or later is not the result of chance. It is a feature of the American courtship *system.*

The untrained observer is apt to overlook the existence of these social systems, feeling that people are free to do "as they please." To some extent, of course, this is true, but it usually "happens" that most people do about the same thing. If they did not, complex societies could not function because too much behavior would be unstructured and hence unpredictable. Social systems never specify all of a person's behavior; they only assure that certain crucial acts will fit into the pattern. The American system of marriage, to cite an example, allows a man a choice of blonde or brunette, but he cannot marry his *sister,* regardless of her hair color. This is what is implied in the concept of social system.

7. *The concept of neurotic.*

Anybody writing about human behavior needs a term to describe the person who is somewhere between normal and abnormal. The term "neurotic" has been developed in our society to describe such individuals. They are not considered to be mentally ill—at least not in the legal sense—and yet they are psychologically and emotionally different from most people. They are apt to be more complex than most of us.[21]

It may be that the term "neurotic" has come to be practically meaningless in our society, a catch-all phrase to describe your enemies or your relatives, but if it is discarded, a similar concept

· will have to be developed to take its place to describe the group of persons it originally referred to.

These, then, are a few of the basic concepts we will rely on in our analysis. You will find the material much easier to handle if you make these tools of the trade a part of your working vocabulary.

Conclusion

In this first chapter we have indicated some of the logic (we hope) behind this book and some of its methodology. We are now ready for Chapter II, an analysis of the American marriage system.

References

1. See "The Theory of Complementary Needs in Mate-Selection," by Thomas and Virginia Ktsanes, in Robert F. Winch and Robert McGinnis, *Selected Studies in Marriage and the Family* (New York, Henry Holt & Co., Inc., 1953), pp. 435–453, for a summary of this new approach to analyzing the dynamics of mate selection.

2. See George Peter Murdock's classic study of the human family, *Social Structure* (New York, The Macmillan Company, 1949) for an impressive illustration of the analysis of marriage and family patterns as *systems* of behavior.

3. See Harvey J. Locke, *Predicting Adjustment in Marriage* (New York, Henry Holt & Co., Inc., 1951), pp. 5–6, for an excellent statement of this point. .

4. Reuben Hill has a penetrating discussion of this point in his classic study, *Families Under Stress* (New York, Harper & Bros., 1949). See Part One: "Sharing the Sanctity of the Home," pp. 3–7.

5. Harper & Bros., 1944.

6. See Nelson N. Foote and Leonard S. Cottrell, Jr., *Identity and Interpersonal Competence* (Chicago, University of Chicago Press, 1955), pp. 231–290, for a review of this vast literature.

7. For a detailed analysis of the concept "culture," see Melville J. Herskovits, *Man and His Works* (New York, Alfred A. Knopf, Inc., 1949), chap. 2.

8. For a detailed analysis of the concept of "subculture," see Albert K. Cohen, *Delinquent Boys: The Culture of the Gang* (Glencoe, The Free Press, 1955). We are indebted to this work in our use of this concept.

9. For the classic analysis of Catholic subculture in the United States, see John L. Thomas, *The American Catholic Family* (New York, Prentice-Hall, Inc., 1956).

10. An excellent analysis of rural subculture in our society is to be found in Charles P. Loomis and J. Allan Beegle, *Rural Social Systems* (New York, Prentice-Hall, Inc., 1950).

11. See Howard W. Odum's classic, *Southern Regions of the United States* (Chapel Hill, University of North Carolina Press, 1936).

12. For a brief and readable summary of this voluminous research, see W. Lloyd Warner, *American Life* (Chicago, University of Chicago Press, 1953).

13. See John F. Cuber and William F. Kenkel, *Social Stratification in the United States* (New York, Appleton-Century-Crofts, Inc., 1954).

14. E. Franklin Frazier, *The Negro Family in the United States* (New York, Dryden Press, 1951).

15. See Warner, *op. cit.*, also Cuber and Kenkel, *op. cit.*, for a review of this mass of research.

16. For an analysis of family subcultures according to social class membership, see Robert F. Winch, *The Modern Family* (New York, Henry Holt & Co., Inc., 1952), chap. 4. A more detailed analysis may be found in Ruth Shonle Cavan, *The American Family* (New York, Thomas Y. Crowell Co., 1953), chaps. 5, 6, and 7.

17. For a brief and readable analysis of the sweeping changes in our society in the past fifty years, see Frederick Lewis Allen, *The Big Change* (New York, Harper & Bros., 1952).

18. See W. F. Ogburn, *Social Change* (New York, B. W. Huebsch, 1922).

19. One of the best analyses of culture conflict is to be found in Robert S. Lynd, *Knowledge for What?* (Princeton, Princeton University Press, 1948). The student will also find rewarding the famous article by Read Bain, "Our Schizoid Culture," *Sociology and Social Research*, 19 (1935), 266–276.

20. See Loomis and Beegle, *op. cit.*, chap. 1, for a concise description of the social system concept.

21. The classic analysis is Karen Horney, *The Neurotic Personality of Our Time* (New York, W. W. Norton & Co., Inc., 1937).

Suggested Readings

1. "Editor's Introduction: Scientific Method and the Study of the Family," *Selected Studies in Marriage and the Family,* edited by Robert F. Winch and Robert McGinnis, (New York, Henry Holt & Co., Inc., 1953), pp. 1–17.

2. "The Family as a Closed System," *Families Under Stress*, by Reuben Hill (New York, Harper & Bros., 1949), pp. 3–7. See also his Preface, pp. vii–x. This study is highly recommended for book reports.

3. *Families in Trouble* by Earl Lomon Koos (New York, Columbia University Press, 1946) provides the average student with an excellent illustration of the modern attempt to study the American family systematically. This monograph is highly readable, interesting, and relatively short (128 pages). Chap. 1, "The Methodology of the Study," pp. 1–22, applies particularly to the material covered in the first chapter of the present text.

4. *Social Structure* by George Peter Murdock (New York, The Macmillan Company, 1949), is an excellent study for the better student who wishes to explore the cross-cultural study of marriage and the family.

5. John L. Thomas, *The American Catholic Family* (New York, Prentice-Hall, Inc., 1956). This is very good for book reports, also as a study in subculture.

6. Frederick Lewis Allen, *The Big Change* (New York, Harper & Bros., 1952). A beautifully written analysis of the rapid and deep social changes in our society in the past fifty years.

CHAPTER II

THE AMERICAN MARRIAGE SYSTEM

Introduction

The basic purpose of Part I of this text is to provide the student with some perspective, or over-all view, of our courtship and marriage system. The assumption is that one can move about in the system more intelligently if it can be viewed, as it were, from a distance, as in the movies when the camera is set for a long shot; once this perspective is attained, we will move the camera up closer and take a careful look at the system in all its fascinating detail.

In our own teaching of this course, we have sometimes found that some of the students become restless or impatient during this part of the analysis, wishing to plunge immediately into the discussion of dating, sexual behavior, or marital adjustment. While this is understandable enough, it seems to us that the later material will be more fruitful, and have more point, if the class has this general picture of the system at the beginning. This chapter, then, is devoted to that purpose.

24

Basic Features of the American Marriage System

1. *Ours is a monogamous system.*

We might as well begin with the obvious and point out that ours is a monogamous type of marriage system. This means, essentially, that our moral code, as reflected in our Judeo-Christian religious values and our forty-eight state legal codes, do not approve of a man or woman having more than one spouse *simultaneously*. Note, however, that this is not actually lifetime monogamy but is really a form of serial monogamy. In a sense Americans have taken monogamy and have adapted it to their own purposes, just as they did with capitalism and democracy. Modern American monogamy, then, is not the same system that the early settlers brought with them from Europe. The modern version is different in that both divorce and remarriage are permitted in all our forty-eight states (there are no federal laws in this area, marriage and divorce being completely left to state control).

As a matter of fact, the American marriage system is much more complex than this, for about 30 per cent of our population are Catholics, and the Catholic church does not approve of divorce and subsequent remarriage. Thus, we have a large segment of our population (most Protestants and Jews) accepting serial monogamy, while another large group (most Catholics) does not accept it.[1] This is what makes American society complex, the fact that it is not as homogeneous or monolithic as some others, but is a mixture, a sort of cultural mosaic, with diverse elements in close juxtaposition.

And even this is not the whole story concerning monogamy in the United States, for the Protestants and Jews are not enthusiastic about divorce and remarriage either, and some congregations, such as the Episcopalians, are opposed to the remarriage of a divorced person. Furthermore, the groups that *tolerate* serial monogamy (divorce and remarriage) do not idealize it. Even for these groups, lifetime monogamy is the ideal. As a matter of fact, divorced persons are still in the minority in our society, so that lifetime monogamy still functions as a marriage pattern for the majority of our adults. If it is true, as the writer will attempt to establish in another chapter, that divorce is still regarded as a personal tragedy in our society, then this supports the notion that lifetime monogamy, and not serial monogamy, is still the basic goal for most Americans.

At this point, it should be made clear that monogamy is not the only type of human marriage by any means. Most of the scientists working in this field identify three basic combinations of males and females in marital union: monogamy, polygyny, and polyandry. The first of these, monogamy, should be clear enough to the student. In the second pattern, polygyny, a man is permitted more than one wife, if he can afford it; and in the third type, polyandry, two or more men are expected to share a wife. Ralph Linton has even described what he considers to be a fourth system, called group marriage, in which several men share several wives.[2] But Murdock, one of the authorities in this field, questions the existence of this fourth variety.[3] There can be no doubt about the other three systems, however, for they have all been recorded by numerous observers in various parts of the world.

Most Americans, we believe, tend to assume that monogamy is the most common type of marriage, but this is not necessarily so. Murdock, for example, in his interesting book, *Social Structure,* took a sample of 250 societies from the major culture areas of the world, and found the distribution shown in Table 2.[4]

TABLE 2

FREQUENCY OF MARRIAGE SYSTEMS IN SAMPLE OF 250 SOCIETIES

Type of Marriage	Number of Societies
Monogamy	43
Polygyny	193
Polyandry	2
Group Marriage	0

You and I, of course, tend to regard monogamy as being natural or instinctive, but this is by no means as clear to the scientists who have studied the matter at length. We suggest that persons interested in this question consult the Murdock study, also the appropriate chapters in Ralph Linton's classic volume, *Study of Man*.[5] There is also some interesting material in Ford and Beach, *Patterns of Sexual Behavior*.[6]

It is understandable that you and I should regard monogamy as natural, for this has been the ideal in Western civilization for a long time, but this should not lead us to the false conclusion that monogamy is instinctive, or in-born, for we know that it is learned behavior. The fact that polygyny is the preferred type of marriage in several major culture areas of the world, such as Africa and the Middle East, seems to prove that man is not born monogamous or nonmonogamous. Both men and women seem to be capable of adjusting to at least three types of marriage, assuming that the child is conditioned from birth to expect this as the approved marital pattern for his society.

It might help us to remember that polygyny was once practiced in the United States by the Mormons, who justified the system by reference to the Old Testament. This means, it seems to us, that marriage patterns are subject to more variation than most of us are inclined to think.

Murdock does conclude that monogamy is probably the most common type of marriage in this sense: that most men in polygynous societies are unable to obtain more than one wife, because of economic reasons and the lack of surplus women, so that most marriages in polygynous cultures are actually monogamous.[7]

As a matter of fact, monogamy is permitted in all polygynous societies, but it is not the preferred pattern. Thus we see that these people actually recognize two types of marriage, whereas monogamous cultures, such as our own, recognize only one.

It could be argued, with some logic, that American legal structure also recognizes two types of marriage: lifetime monogamy and serial monogamy. Both are permitted by law, even if one of them is not accepted by all our religious groups.

It probably is true that all the three basic types of human marriage have their advantages as well as their disadvantages. Since polyandry is rare, we might assume that it has a great many more disadvantages than the other types, but we can hardly make the same assumption about either monogamy or polygyny, for both of these systems have been reported for culture areas which encompass literally hundreds of millions of human beings. Hence, it seems, we must recognize that humans are capable of either monogamous *or* polygynous marriage. It is important to recognize that neither one of these systems will satisfy all the needs of all the adults in any given society at any given time, including the United States. For this reason, if for no other, all human societies have had to work out alternate patterns of some sort for men and women unable to adjust to the preferred system of marriage. In polygynous societies, for example, it seems to be recognized that some men would prefer to have more than one wife, but at the same time monogamy is permitted for those men who are unable, or unwilling, to take plural wives. The catch, of course, is that women are not given the same choice.

In our own society, our state legal codes recognize that not all persons are capable of living all their lives with one spouse, and these codes permit a switch of partners, provided certain legal requirements are met. This does not mean that our society encourages men and women to terminate their marriages periodically; it only means that the law recognizes that *alternate* patterns must be provided for those individuals unable to adjust to the preferred pattern, which is still lifetime monogamy.

It might be well to point out that the human sex ratio (the number of males per 100 females), being relatively equal in most societies, tends to favor monogamy. The sex ratio limits the number of plural marriages that can exist at any time in a society, and, furthermore, too many plural marriages would mean that some males and/or females would be prevented from contracting a normal marriage at all, a situation hardly conducive to social order.

This has been a rather long-winded discussion, but the American version of monogamy is complex and it seems important to gain some insight into its complexity at this point.

2. *Ours is a semipatriarchal system.*

If we look at marriage from the point of view of *power* distribution, it is possible to identify three basic types: patriarchal, in which the male is dominant; matriarchal, in which the female tends to be powerful, although not necessarily dominant; and equalitarian, in which the two sexes are relatively equal in power.

Historically, Western societies have been patriarchal. Christianity, for example, originated in a patriarchal culture area, and male symbolism is still dominant in our religious structure (God is symbolized as the *Father,* Christ is the *Son,* the Pope is a man, and so forth). The Roman husband-father has been cited by Zimmerman and others as having been in an extremely powerful position,[8] and since Roman law became the basic model for English law, which in turn was the prototype of our American laws governing marriage and the family, it follows that our patterns were originally male-centered.

As a matter of fact, a woman had no legal status in the early English courts and could only initiate legal action through a man: either her father, her husband, or her legal guardian. Thus, she had the same legal status that children have today in our society. This male-centered nature of our culture can be seen very readily when it is remembered that women were not permitted to vote in the United States until near the end of World War I. This may seem incredible to young people today, but it is there in the history books. Frederick Lewis Allen describes it vividly in his fine volume, *The Big Change,* which is an analysis of the basic changes in our culture during the past fifty years.[9]

But, you say, isn't this mere history today? Don't we have a

completely equalitarian system of marriage now? It is our contention that we are still in transition from a patriarchal pattern to
an equalitarian relationship between husbands and wives. Godfrey,
for example, in a study of farm families in Illinois, was able to
identify patriarchal authority patterns in a significant proportion
of her sample.[10] Koos also reports the survival of these traditional
patterns among modest income families in New York City.[11]
Komarovsky also found them as late as the 1930's in an urban
sample of unemployed men.[12]

It seems likely that the transition to the equalitarian marriage system has been most rapid in the urban middle and upper
classes, with strong survivals in certain ethnic groups, such as the
Italians, in such religious sects as the Amish of Pennsylvania and
Ohio, and in low-income groups. Since most college students come
from urban, middle-class families, they tend to discount or overlook the patriarchal remnants in our culture.

For the record, let us list a few of these male-centered
survivals:

A. **The marriage vow:**   The basic marriage vow taken by
women in our society includes the phrase: "love, honor, and
obey." It is true that some ministers have dropped the word "obey"
from the vow, but it is still included by the Catholics and by
numerous Protestant and Jewish congregations. This, it seems to us,
represents a survival from our patriarchal past.

B. **Residence after marriage:**   When a young couple establish their residence after marriage, it is customary, even now,
for the girl to move to the community in which the husband is
employed. She may have a job herself, but she must resign her
position, and leave her friends, to join him. This is a male-centered
pattern. It forces the girl to find a new position, to develop new
friends, to adjust to a new community. In a completely equalitarian
system, the couple would be free to decide which one should give
up his or her job and move. We grant that some couples actually
do this today, but in the majority of cases the girl has to make the
move.

In some cases, as a matter of fact, domestic court judges have held a wife to be guilty of *desertion* for refusing to resign a professional position in order to follow her husband to a new community. Call it what you will, this is a patriarchal pattern.

C. The married couple's name: Let us suppose that John Dumple should marry Grace Rockefeller (two hypothetical names, we hope). Do they take the Rockefeller name for themselves and their children? No, they become Mr. and Mrs. John Dumple. The wife, of course, in order to cash in on her illustrious ancestors, will probably sign her name as "Grace Rockefeller Dumple," and they very likely will use "Rockefeller" for their children's middle name. But why don't they just decide to use her last name to begin with? Because ours has been a patriarchal family system and it is still so as far as the last name of the married couple is concerned.

Actually, we would need some form of hyphenated name, such as "Mr. and Mrs. Smith-Jones," to fully express our equalitarian marriage ideals. But hyphenated names seem odd to Americans, so we continue to have the girl give up her surname and adopt that of the husband. Note that the children take his last name also, another illustration of the male-centeredness of the system.

D. Men initiate courtship: In the early colonial family, according to Calhoun,[13] the young man was required to ask the girl's father (but not her mother) for permission to "keep company." Note that the whole matter was to be settled *between the men*. This does not mean, of course, that the girl and her mother had nothing to say about the decision, but the formal structure was patriarchal in that it was channeled through *men*.

Today, of course, this all seems very quaint and "out of this world," but notice that we still expect the young man to ask for the date, to initiate the dating relationship. Girls, of course, learn how to maneuver in situations when the boy seems reluctant to take the first step, but the very fact that the girl has to *maneuver* reveals how male-centered the system still remains. In a fully equalitarian system, either sex would be completely free to initiate dating.

There has undoubtedly been a great change in this since your grandmother's day, but there is still a long way to go.

E. The girl gives up her job to bear children: We admit, at the outset, that nature has not designed husbands very well for the bearing of children, but once the child is born, why does it always have to be the wife who must give up her job or profession and stay home with the baby? In the case of breast-feeding, the point is clear enough, but most mothers today do not nurse their babies at the breast.

The answer, it seems, is that historically the man has been the breadwinner, while the woman has been the homemaker and the rearer of children. This division of labor has altered greatly in recent decades in the United States, but some of its traditional features remain.

In the case of some highly trained middle-class women, this forced retirement from their profession can be very difficult, and for these women, it still seems to be "a man's world." We have often wondered what men would think, or how they would adjust, if they had to give up their work to become fathers. We, for one, would not like it very much.

F. We still have a "double standard" sexual code: There seems to be little doubt that young men in our society enjoy greater sexual freedom than do young women. Girls are still condemned, or at least censured, if they become pregnant before marriage, but their boy friends escape with relatively mild punishment. Girls are more closely supervised than boys, at least in college, with the girls being required to sign out, be in at certain hours, and so forth, while college men are permitted absolute freedom in coming and going. Some colleges will not permit girls to live in sorority houses, even with a housemother in attendance, but these same schools usually permit men to live in fraternity houses. The reputation of a girl is considered to be more vulnerable than that of a boy, so she must be careful. Otherwise, "people will talk" about her.

Whether we consider premarital intercourse or extramarital

sex relations, it seems clear, if we may rely on the Kinsey research, that men have had more sexual experience than women in our society.

A great deal of this seems to be a carryover of the old double standard of sexual morality of the eighteenth and nineteenth centuries, by which it was all right for a boy to do something but immoral for his girl friend to do the same thing; or it was perfectly proper for a husband to have an extramarital affair but a horrible sin for his wife to have a lover.

Here, again, there seems to be movement toward an equalitarian standard, but it is by no means an accomplished fact as yet. Perhaps we should add that a great many persons in our society hope that women *never* adopt the sex code of men, on the ground that this would constitute a lowering of female moral standards.

In concluding this discussion of the semipatriarchal nature of our courtship and marital patterns, the reader should keep in mind that we are viewing the American family in the process of change or adaptation, and our thesis is that the traditional male-centered characteristics of our courtship and marriage system have not yet completely disappeared. It seems likely that they will eventually disappear, as they already have to a large extent in some of the subcultures of our society. But, in general, the process of adaptation to modern equalitarian norms seems to be far from complete.

3. *Ours is a very romantic type of courtship and marriage.*

In the United States, we take romance very seriously. In a sense, love is the dominant theme of our culture. It is the core of the Christian system of values; it pervades our most popular music; most of our films are based on love or its absence; our mass magazines devote most of their fiction to romantic love and its complications; our young people spend a considerable portion of their time in high school and college in the pursuit of love; and our psychiatrists do a thriving business with persons who are not loved or who are unable to love. In a nutshell, Americans seem to be in love with love.

It is no accident that the only real justification for marriage in our culture is that we are in love. Persons in other societies may marry for money, or power, or the sake of convenience, but not Americans.

"He adores her."

During the late 1930's, when the now Duke of Windsor was King of England and wished to marry Wallis Simpson, a divorced woman, it was interesting to observe the deep sympathy Americans felt for the King. "After all," they would say, "he's in love. And he ought to have the right to marry the woman he loves." One could detect the same sympathy two decades later for the Princess Margaret as she struggled to marry "the man she loves."

The interesting thing about all this is that royal families have never been free to marry whom they wished, unless they wished to give up their royal prerogatives. The marriage of such persons has always been considered a matter of governmental concern and not simply a private love affair. This is repugnant to Americans, for they believe that marriage must serve one basic purpose: the satisfaction of deep personal needs, such as affection, security, emotional warmth, companionship, and sexual satisfaction.

In the writer's marriage counseling experience, the greatest sin a husband or wife can commit is to be psychologically cold, or unresponsive. This is even worse than sexual coldness, judging from our counseling experience.

Interestingly enough, courtship does not stop at marriage in our society, in the sense that a man can stop being attentive to his wife just because they are married. The ideal husband is the one who kisses his wife in the morning, sends her flowers and gifts on the right occasions, holds her coat for her, opens the car door, and does not take his sexual life for granted. This type of man, at his best, continues to make love to his wife until "death do us part," just as the marriage vow says he should.

The wife, in return, is duty-bound not to get fat, this being one of the great sins for middle- and upper-class wives; to retain her youth and good looks; to respond with ardor to her husband's sexual overtures; to dress well; to laugh at his jokes; and in general to be a good sport, a real man's woman.

It is not meant that these patterns are to be found at all levels in our society. We doubt that low-income married couples observe all these niceties, and we suspect that this romantic version of marriage is largely a product of urban subculture and is much less dominant among the rural segments of our population. But since the urban middle class seems to be widely imitated in the United States, these norms are very likely going to diffuse to other groups.

Ralph Linton, in his *Study of Man*,[14] has questioned whether very many men and women are capable of being this romantic, and this seems to be a legitimate question. It may be,

of course, that the patterns described above are *ideal* norms to
which most of our men and women are not actually held. In our
religion, for example, we have moral standards that large numbers
of our men and women cannot practice on all occasions, but this
does not destroy the validity of the norms. Rituals have been
developed for the forgiveness of error and sin, and the values remain
as a sort of goal toward which persons may strive.

In a sense, this seems to us to be the function of the romantic
norms in our courtship and marriage: not that we expect *every*
man or woman fully to achieve the pattern, but to work *in that
direction*. If this functional analysis is correct, then it may be that
some of the most severe critics of the romantic complex have missed
the point.

We think it interesting that Somerset Maugham, one of our
most successful authors, in his autobiography, *The Summing Up*,[15]
says that he has never married for a simple reason: he never met a
woman for whom he cared that much.

It is possible, we believe, that this deep and abiding love in
American marriage sets an extremely high standard of personal
compatibility, perhaps higher than that to be found in most human
societies. If this is true, it might be one of the reasons why the
American divorce rate has been relatively high. If so, it should be
possible to lower the divorce rate by reducing the level of expectation, but this does not seem likely. Such an approach would be
similar to reducing the amount of sin by lowering our moral
standards, a solution that most Americans would consider to be no
solution at all.

4. *Our young people are on their own.*

In the Italian courtship system of the nineteenth century,
a girl of the middle or upper classes was never permitted to be
alone with a suitor until they were betrothed. To some extent, this
was true of courtship in very proper families in colonial New
England. A student of ours who served in Latin America during
World War II reported that he went with an attorney's daughter

for six months before he was permitted to be alone with her; up to that point, a younger sister was always present. A similar pattern has been reported for rural France by another student of ours who dated the daughter of a French Catholic middle-class family.

These practices seem fantastic to young Americans, for our young couples go almost anywhere unchaperoned. It is true, of course, that high schools and colleges still require chaperones for social functions, but this type of supervision is limited to the building in which the affair is being held, and everyone recognizes that couples can leave the building if they wish to avoid supervision of their behavior.

If we look at this feature of the American courtship system carefully, it will be seen that it indicates a lot of faith in young people by parents and other adults; it also demands at a relatively early age a degree of self-control which many societies, such as those cited above, would consider impossible or dangerous. In some ways, it is amazing that so many of our young people, especially those at the high school level, manage this freedom as well as they do. Whether people realize it or not, this part of our courtship system is most unusual.

This freedom from immediate supervision in dating is in line with another basic feature of our marriage system: the final responsibility for choice of marital partner rests upon the slender shoulders of the young persons themselves. With our ancestors, parents usually had to give their approval, and in many societies, whole kinship groups have to approve such a grave step. But not so in the United States. We have eliminated the matchmaker, or the go-between, and this function has been assumed by the peer group itself. Our research is not adequate enough at present to determine which generation makes the wiser decisions in matchmaking, the youngsters or their parents, but the question appears to be largely academic, for there are no indications that this pattern will be changed in the near future.

After marriage, our young couples prefer to live by themselves, preferably a considerable distance from all their relatives.

This neolocal residence system is unusual, for in most human societies it is felt that the young couple should reside either with or near the groom's family (patrilocal residence), or near the bride's family (matrilocal residence). But with us they should live *alone*.

It is true, however, as Sussman points out,[16] that parents in our society actually do aid their married children in many different ways, but this behavior is essentially unstructured or informal. The parents are not *required* to give such aid, and the married couple are not required to accept it.

It might almost be said that the role of parents, siblings, and other relatives toward young people in our society is this: they stand by, prepared to help if the youngster gets into a "jam," but it is taboo to force help on the young person, or couple; they must request the aid.

Perhaps enough material has been presented to indicate the extent to which the younger generation is on its own in the United States. This point takes on more significance if the student has some cross-cultural perspective, which may be attained by reading some of the selections given at the end of the chapter.

5. *Our sexual standards for marriage are restrictive.*

In some societies, such as premodern China, it was acceptable for economically successful men to have concubines; in France, at least up through the nineteenth century, a middle- or upper-class man was permitted to have a mistress, provided he was discreet about it and did not create undue scandal.

In the United States, however, we expect husbands and wives to be sexually faithful. It is known, of course, through the work of Kinsey and others, that a significant proportion of our married couples—a minority, however—does not achieve full sexual loyalty, but this does not mean that they are not *expected to*. In other words, we recognize that complete sexual monogamy is not achieved by all, but this does not alter the basic norm itself.

It can be argued that Americans are attempting to enforce

sexual norms between married couples that are more restrictive than those to be found in most human societies. The male, in particular, has been expected to focus his sexual interest on his wife more exclusively than he is in most culture areas of the world. In China, Japan, Africa, Latin America, Spain, France, the Middle East—all these societies have granted men sexual privileges denied women.

It seems clear that the romantic type of marriage idealized in our culture requires sexual loyalty by both partners. Failure to achieve this usually poses grave problems for the marriage itself.

6. *The child-bearing role of women is less dominant in our marriage system.*

A few years ago, it was announced in the public press that the King of Egypt had divorced his wife because of her inability to bear him a son. In some societies the failure of a wife to bear children, regardless of whether it is her fault or not, constitutes grounds for divorce. In rural Ireland, even today, a wife is considered a failure if a child is not born within a year or so after marriage.

None of these situations seems to prevail in modern America, except possibly in some subcultures, such as the Amish. It is true, of course, that most young couples wish to have children, but we do not necessarily consider a marriage a failure if children are not one of its products. Nor can we divorce a wife or a husband for this reason. In some states, an annulment of the marriage could be obtained if it could be proved that one of the partners knew he or she was sterile *before* the marriage took place and concealed this fact from the other person, but this action is based on *fraud* rather than sterility.

As a matter of fact, if a married couple should prove to be sterile in our society today, we do not assume, as they did in colonial America, that it is the wife, and not the husband, who is sterile. This in itself reflects the equalitarian nature of modern marriage in the United States.

The 1950 census reveals that the average American couple today has about three children, and this is an increase of about one child over the pattern of the 1930's. Although this is more than adequate to maintain our population, it is not impressive if judged by world-wide birth rates.

Without taking the space to analyze why our birth rate is relatively low, it must be indicated that there are some important implications of this American birth rate. For one thing, it means that American women are much more independent than their great-grandmothers, who averaged between five and six children. There is an old folk saying to the effect that "a pregnant wife doesn't leave home," and there seems to be a grain of truth in this. And since the critical period for American marriages is the first five years, the time when they have fewest children, it can be seen that childbearing would not prevent too many of our wives from leaving an unsatisfactory husband, especially middle- and upper-class women.

On a more positive plane, this modest birth rate has made it possible for American mothers to make outstanding contributions to our community life, to participate in political activities, to work outside the home, and to give each child unusually good physical care and an education superior to that of his parents. Whether this small family has also resulted in superior psychological care of the child seems to be still a matter of debate.

In summary, it can be stated bluntly that the childbearing role has been de-emphasized in our culture at the same time that other roles of women have been expanded. Whether this is good or not depends upon one's basic values. We will return to the matter in our discussions of courtship, marital adjustment, and child-rearing.

7. *More and more of our wives work outside the home.*

Women, of course, have always *worked,* so that the only thing new about this trend is that they are increasingly working *outside* the home. As of 1950, between 25 and 30 per cent of American wives held full-time positions in the economic system. The research on these employed women appears to be inadequate, so that it is difficult to appraise the full meaning of this trend.

Figure 1: Employed Women in the Labor Force, United States, 1940–1955.*

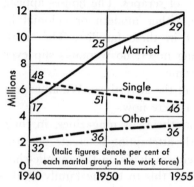

These figures tell the story of the rapid increase of married women in the labor force since 1940.

* Source: Table courtesy of *Fortune* Magazine.

It seems obvious, at least to us, that such women are more independent economically; that this may make them more independent in other ways too (in their marriages, for example); that their families enjoy a higher standard of living than families that have only one breadwinner; that these women carry a heavy schedule, adding their breadwinner role to their child-rearing and homemaker roles; and, finally, that there is a deep and pervasive difference, or set of differences, between the women who accept employment temporarily and the women who plan on permanent outside jobs.

Since a separate chapter is devoted to this topic, it should be sufficient at this point to merely indicate that the two-breadwinner type of family unit seems to be a basic new pattern in American families, and it seems to be here to stay.

8. *Our marriage and family norms are taken from the middle class.*

Our movies, our television shows, our mass magazines, almost invariably portray middle-class married couples or families, and upper-middle-class groups at that. The men all seem to have white-collar jobs; they seem to be doctors or lawyers or business executives. Their wives are slender, well groomed, and attractive (for some reason, they are usually portrayed as being smarter than their husbands). The children, usually a boy and girl, are talented and bright, even if they do get into a lot of scrapes. The houses appear to be substantial and comfortable, either modern or colonial in architecture. Nobody ever gets fat in these families. The small children never seem to have running noses; no woman's slip ever shows; the men are tall and handsome.

This is the never-never land of the advertisers. We all expect to live there some day, if we are not there now.

It should be recognized that the mass magazines, in their advertising programs, are consciously attempting to create patterns of consumption for the future. Their emphasis on the middle-class family is no accident, for they believe this to be the family of the future—that is, the family that will set the norms of tomorrow.

Space will not permit analysis of all the implications of this characteristic of our marriage system, but they should not be ignored. For example, it may be difficult for fathers and mothers who are not members of the middle class, such as lower-class parents, to serve as effective models for their children. In fact, since the norms are based almost exclusively on *urban* life, it may also be difficult for *rural* parents to serve as effective models. It is also possible that both the courtship and marriage systems work better for middle-class persons than they do for lower- or upper-class persons. In other words, the systems are based on middle-class subculture, hence are more functional for persons born and reared in that subculture. As an analogy, we might point out that Hollingshead, Havighurst, and others seem to have discovered that the average public high school is designed primarily for the children of middle-class parents, and works best for that group.[17] If this should prove to be an accurate analysis of our public school system, is it not possible that the same thing will be found to be true of our courtship and marriage institutions? We believe this is a distinct possibility and propose to examine the matter in more detail in later chapters, especially those on courtship.

Some General Observations on the American Marriage System

In the preceding section, some of the dominant characteristics of our marriage system have been discussed. In the balance of the chapter, a few general comments on the system are offered for what they may be worth, not as established facts or conclusions, but as hypotheses for consideration or discussion. These will be presented as a series of questions.

1. Is it possible that we may be overloading the psychological burden of the marital relationship? In other words, could it be that we are expecting marriage to meet too many of our basic needs? It may be, for example, that our mobile, competitive, impersonal social order deprives us of deep satisfactions in our nonfamilial relationships, such as our work. If this should be the case, it would tend to channel a very large portion of our deepest needs through the husband-wife relationship, and this might help explain why so many of our marriages fail: they cannot carry such a heavy load. Under such a set of circumstances, even ordinary marriages would not be good enough to stand the strain.

2. Are we expecting too much of our young people in courtship and/or marriage? They decide, for the most part, when and whom they will marry; they move off to be by themselves after marriage; and they are gradually getting married at an earlier age. Persons with a great deal of cross-cultural perspective, such as Margaret Mead, seem to believe that we have gone far in the direction of depriving young couples of family guidance and support as they move into marriage.

3. Can the husband-wife relationship be absolutely equalitarian? Most societies, it seems, have seen fit to emphasize one sex or the other. Is it possible to operate a marriage and family system in which males and females are on exactly the same power basis? We know, for example, that most businesses have to have

a president or manager. Isn't this true of the family as a collective enterprise? Or is it?

4. Have we gone too far in de-emphasizing kinship obligations after marriage? Ours is known as a "contracted kinship system," with the main relationships being restricted to husband or wife and their children, the so-called "nuclear family." Even our parents may feel neglected once we marry and start a family. Grandparents, uncles and aunts, and all kinds of cousins have very poorly defined relationships to the newly married couple, or, later, to their children. Even our contacts with brothers and sisters seem to become relatively anemic after marriage. All these vary tremendously, of course, from one family to the next, but this variation itself testifies to the *unstructured* nature of the relationships.

5. Is the American family committed to too high a standard of living? Are too many mothers working outside the home, and losing the opportunity to be with their children, in order to buy bigger and better appliances for the home? We recall an article in a so-called "home magazine" which concluded that "every family needs an electric dishwasher." We wondered whether a good vacation for the whole family, or for the mother, wouldn't be a better investment. As a child, our most personal talks with our own mother took place while we were drying the dishes for her in the evening. We suppose that today such conversations take place while driving to the supermarket, as one mother told us, or perhaps while trying to fix the dishwasher when it won't work, as another mother told us.

It seems to us that married couples today need a sound sense of values; otherwise the "appliance men will get you if you don't watch out."

Summary

In this chapter we have been taking a good look at the American marriage system. As we have seen, some of it is quite new, and this newness seems to bother some people. It may help us understand the system if we realize that it is part of a larger social system, our total societal pattern, and that the basic parts of this total system have to be adapted to one another. Viewed in this way, it may be realized that Americans *had* to develop a different type of marriage system to fit the "American way of life."

The other basic parts of our civilization or "social structure," as some social scientists prefer to call it, consist of our economic system, our political system, and our religious system. It seems obvious, at least to us, that the deepest values of these social institutions have been incorporated into our courtship and marriage system. Note the following list:

Free enterprise	Equality
Free competition	Value of love
Rights of the individual	The individual's worth
Democracy	

Are not all these values to be found in the American courtship and marriage system? Could it be otherwise? We think not.

In this Part I of the text, entitled Perspective, we are viewing courtship, marriage, and the family in American society from a distance, as it were, trying to see it as a *social system,* or a combination of systems, in which behavior is patterned or structured and is not necessarily by chance, although chance plays a part. If our conceptual system is any good, the system should begin to seem less mysterious, less accidental, but not necessarily less attractive. After all, the economic activities in our society constitute an economic system, and this has been analyzed in detail by economists without destroying the excitement of playing the stock market or making a million dollars. We suggest that the same set of circumstances prevail in courtship and marriage, and that the chase will be no less fascinating just because social scientists are subjecting the system to systematic analysis.

References

1. For an excellent and objective analysis of the Catholic point of view on divorce and remarriage, see John L. Thomas, *The American Catholic Family* (New York, Prentice-Hall, Inc., 1956).

2. Ralph Linton, *Study of Man* (New York, Appleton-Century-Crofts, Inc., 1936), pp. 181–182.

3. See George Peter Murdock, *Social Structure* (New York, The Macmillan Company, 1949), pp. 24–25.

4. *Ibid.*, chap. 2.

5. *Op. cit.*, chaps. 10 and 11.

6. Clellan S. Ford and Frank A. Beach, *Patterns of Sexual Behavior* (New York, Harper & Bros., 1951), chap. 6.

7. *Op. cit.*, p. 27.

8. See Carle C. Zimmerman, *Family and Civilization* (New York, Harper & Bros., 1947).

9. Frederick Lewis Allen, *The Big Change* (New York, Harper & Bros., 1952).

10. Eleanor P. Godfrey, "A Construction of Family Types and Their Initial Empirical Validation," unpublished Ph.D. dissertation, Radcliffe College, Cambridge, 1951.

11. Earl Lomon Koos, *Families in Trouble* (New York, Columbia University Press, 1946).

12. Mirra Komarovsky, *The Unemployed Man and His Family* (New York, Dryden Press, 1940).

13. Arthur W. Calhoun, *A Social History of the American Family* (Cleveland, Arthur H. Clark, 1919).

14. *Op. cit.*, chap. 11.

15. William Somerset Maugham, *The Summing Up* (New York, Doubleday, Doran, 1938).

16. Marvin B. Sussman, "The Help Pattern in the Middle-Class Family," *American Sociological Review*, 18 (1953), 22–28.

17. See Robert J. Havighurst, *Human Development and Education* (New York, Longmans, Green & Co., Inc., 1953).

Suggested Readings

1. Francis L. K. Hsu, "Chinese and American Marriage Practices," in Marvin B. Sussman, *Sourcebook in Marriage and the Family* (Boston, Houghton Mifflin Co., 1955), pp. 8–12. This excellent comparison of two

quite different marriage systems is taken from Hsu's study, *Americans and Chinese* (New York, Henry Schuman, Inc., 1953).

2. John Sirjamaki, "Culture Configurations in the American Family," also in Sussman's *Sourcebook*, pp. 1–7, is an excellent analysis of American family patterns. This appeared originally in *The American Journal of Sociology*, 53 (1948), 450–456.

3. Robert Winch's *The Modern Family* (New York, Henry Holt & Co., Inc., 1952) has a good cross-cultural analysis of family systems in chap. 2, "Vignettes of the Family in Other Cultures," pp. 19–46.

4. Ruth Nanda Anshen (ed.), *The Family: Its Function and Destiny* (New York, Harper & Bros., 1949). Chap. 1, "The Family in Transition," by Anshen is excellent for the material under discussion in this chapter. There are many other worthwhile articles in this collection for the interested student.

5. Margaret Mead, "The Contemporary American Family as an Anthropologist Sees It," in Judson and Mary Landis, *Readings in Marriage and the Family* (New York, Prentice-Hall, Inc., 1952), pp. 1–9. This originally appeared in *The American Journal of Sociology*, 53 (1948), 453–459.

CHAPTER III

FOLKLORE ABOUT MARRIAGE IN OUR SOCIETY

Introduction

In complex social systems there may be no one, not even among the so-called "experts," who has a complete understanding of how the entire system operates, or even its subsystems. Thus, on purely theoretical grounds, we might hypothesize that no one completely comprehends the system of marriage now in effect in the United States.

For example, let us ask this relatively simple question: do we still have monogamy, or have we evolved a new type of marriage? The answer, if you think about the matter, is not simple. We might reply that, for the bulk of our population, we still have what could be described as lifetime monogamy, even though divorce and remarriage are now permitted by all our forty-eight states. But, for a sizable minority of our adult population, at least 25 per cent, we have a new system of marriage sometimes referred to as serial monogamy (a system that permits one mate at a time).

Thus, it can be seen that we actually practice two versions of monogamy in the United States. The picture, however, is more complex than this, for our Catholics, who now include about thirty per cent of our population, do not accept serial monogamy and consider this to be a sin against God and natural law. Jews and most Protestants, however, accept divorce and remarriage under

Figure 2: Urban and Rural Population of the United States, 1850–1950.*

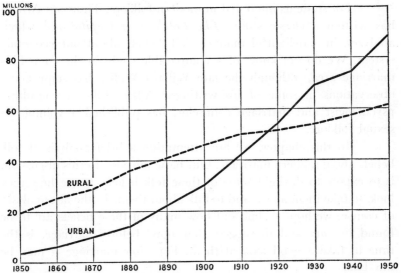

This chart reveals the rapid increase in the urban family characteristic of modern American society. This is one reason why the family has changed so much in recent decades.

* Source: *Statistical Bulletin,* Metropolitan Life Insurance Company, September, 1951.

certain circumstances and consider serial monogamy to be completely moral. But at the same time, these groups deplore divorce and do all they can to limit its incidence. Yet, as we have seen, divorce and remarriage are completely integrated in our formal moral structure, namely, the laws of our several states. And our federal legal structure takes no position on divorce and remarriage, leaving the matter entirely to state control.

In view of this complexity, it is not hard to understand that a considerable body of folklore (or folk belief) has accumulated about the nature of marriage in modern America. Indeed, it is an axiom among social scientists that folklore, superstition, and mythology tend to develop about parts of a social system that are complex, poorly understood, and not subject to complete control. We would say that all three of these conditions are characteristic of marriage in the United States.

For students interested in modern folklore, Thurman Arnold has written a classic study, *The Folklore of Capitalism,*[1] which analyzes, in a delightful manner, folk beliefs about our economic system. We do not know of a comparable study in the courtship-marriage area, although the late Willard Waller has some acute observations in some of his writings.[2] Albert Ellis, a consulting psychologist and marriage counselor, has published a volume on sexual folklore.[3]

In this chapter, we are attempting a brief analysis of folk beliefs about modern marriage. Our basic purpose, in this discussion, is to expose to daylight some of these folk beliefs, to see how they look, to take them apart, and to talk about them. In the last analysis, of course, we hope to find out how many of these beliefs are to be found in *you,* and to suggest that now, before marriage, is the time to take a good look at them. For after marriage it may be too late.

We have been collecting clichés and folk sayings about marriage, and in this chapter we are giving you a look at our private collection. It may be that you would like to start a collection of your own. It is an inexpensive hobby and relatively harmless.

Now we are ready for the analysis. Our plan of attack will be to state the belief as it is usually worded in everyday language, then to restate it in more technical terminology, and then to analyze the assumptions and implications of the belief.

Folk Beliefs About Marriage

1. *"After all, you don't marry the whole family."*

Have you heard this one? It is not rare but is found all over the United States. Usually, in our experience, this folk belief is resorted to by persons planning to marry someone whose family, or parts of it, they find unacceptable. Realizing—or sensing—their predicament, they fall back on this folk belief for moral support.

In our collection we have seldom if ever heard this one from married persons, who seem to know better. Hence this is basically a part of the subculture of the unmarried in our society.

Essentially, this bit of folklore assumes that a human being, such as a future husband or wife, can be "abstracted" or isolated from father and mother, brothers and sisters—all that complex of deep emotional and physical network that sociologists designate by the term "family."

Is this possible? With perhaps a very few exceptions, the answer is in the negative: it is improbable. But, you ask, why do we say this? There are several reasons:

A. Modern psychology, psychiatry, and sociology tell us that you and I are, to a very great extent, the product of our families. What we believe, how we feel, our total emotional and intellectual make-up, reflect, almost every minute of our lives, what happened to us in our families. The human infant is born plastic and receptive, without any elaborate built-in social behavior, *and the family gets us first.* Furthermore, the family has us more or less exclusively for the first five years of our life, and these are perhaps the most impressionable years of all.

Thus, even if you could separate your future husband or wife from his family *physically,* they would still be in your house every minute, because they are part of your husband or wife, for good or for bad.

B. In another sense, we marry the family also, for our children will carry one half of their biological inheritance from the family we marry. Unfortunately, the research on human genetics does not seem adequate at the moment for us to assess objectively the implications of this biological heredity, but it obviously is important.[4] Such characteristics as intellectual capacity, physical attractiveness and longevity seem to be clearly related to biological ancestry, but other characteristics, such as mental health or emotional stability, are very likely related to genetic background also.

Hence, when you pick out a husband or wife, you are also choosing half of the genetic inheritance of your children. And in this sense, obviously, we do marry the family.

C. But, you say, what about situations in which the person has left his or her family and no longer has much contact with them?

This is a very good question. The answer is that such a person is still very much affected by his family, but in a negative rather than a positive way. As a matter of fact, such an individual tends to be complex and can only be understood by a clear knowledge of his family. In other words, if you would understand such men and women—and they are not rare in our society—it is absolutely essential that you have insight into what they are *running away from*. Otherwise, you will never grasp what it is that they are groping for or seeking.

Actually, the families of such individuals will be living with you each day in absentia, as the lawyers put it. In a very real sense, you marry the family in this type of situation *even more* than you do when the family environment has been pleasant and satisfying.

D. In all human societies, according to anthropologists, there is an incest taboo prohibiting marriage within the immediate kinship group, and this makes in-laws inevitable. Thus, in our society, as well as in all others, each new marriage represents a sort of merger or alliance of two kinship groups, both of which have a good deal at stake. For this reason, if for no other, we almost always are a part of two families after we marry. This will be dealt with in more detail in Chapter XV.

Does this convince you of the utterly unrealistic assumptions of this particular folk belief?

We do not mean to imply, however, that you should rush out of class and cancel your engagement because of problems in the other famliy. All we mean is that you should be mature enough to *face* the problems and not assume that you can ignore them after marriage.

2. *"I think her problems will take care of themselves once she is married."*

We always shudder when we hear this one. It seems to assume that marriage is a cheap form of psychotherapy. Thus, if you are a neurotic, or a seriously maladjusted person, all you need is a willing partner (victim) and a wedding license.

In the most flagrant case of this sort we have ever witnessed, analyzed elsewhere in this book, a confirmed homosexual took a wife, hoping to solve his problem.

In another situation known to us, a chronic alcoholic found himself a willing woman and married, hoping thus to settle down. In this case, unlike the one above, the treatment worked, but it required fifteen years to bring the miracle about. Need we describe what this young wife went through during the interim? We have discussed the experience in detail with her and she does not recommend reforming alcoholics as a very pleasant way to spend your life. It is true, however, that she now has a loving and devoted husband. But the price was very high.

Essentially, this folk belief assumes that living in marriage is easier on personality complexes than is living alone, an assumption with which we believe most psychiatrists, psychologists, or marriage counselors would not agree.

It is true, of course, that some of us can stand up to life better with a mate at our side, but to a very great extent this depends upon *who the mate is*. In other words, this folk saying tends to assume that our maladjusted friend will make a good choice of marital partner. But is this a reasonably safe assumption? Are persons with rather pronounced personality problems in a good position to make good marital choices? In the case of the alcoholic cited above, he admits that he was very lucky in that he stumbled upon (almost literally) a good woman—that is, one who was herself reasonably stable and who did not get discouraged easily. But how common are such marital partners?

Actually, modern marriage is so complex that even the so-called "well adjusted" persons often find it difficult.

Unfortunately, we do not have adequate research data on this sort of question. We do know, of course, that all of us have personality problems of one kind or another, most of which are amenable to marriage. In this discussion, we have in mind the more difficult type of problem person, the so-called "neurotic." These often comprise the chronically ill (the psychosomatic invalids), the alcoholics, the sexual deviants, those who can't hold a job, etc.

About the most one could say for marriage in these cases, it seems to us, is this: *assuming a good marriage,* the relationship will often help the person manage his or her complexes *better*. It will not, however, remove them. Extensive psychotherapy is normally required for this.

The big question in these cases, we think, is this: *what price* will the other member of the marriage have to pay? That was the way the wife of the reformed alcoholic put it to us.

3. *"I think we'll work that out after we get married."*

Well, many do, but there is a sizable assumption in this statement: namely, *the belief that marital adjustment does not begin until marriage occurs.* Actually, this very likely is not the case at all. In a very provocative study by Locke,[5] it was found that the well-adjusted married couples in the sample had apparently already achieved adjustment in major areas *before marriage took place*. If this study is valid and reliable, then the statement at the beginning of this discussion would have to be modified to read: "I think we'll work that out *during our engagement*."

As a matter of fact, we tend to be critical in general of the assumptions made about adjustment in marriage. For our money, that marriage is best which demands the least adjustment, although there may be some exceptions to this. It is true, of course, that most humans can adjust (get used to) almost anything or anybody. Indeed, this adaptability is one of the distinctive human qualities. But is all adjustment good for us, either in marriage or elsewhere?

4. *"Don't you think most marital problems will take care of themselves if there is a good sexual relationship?"*

It seems to us that here again we are dealing with a trait of the subculture of the unmarried adult, for most married couples, we believe, know that a good marriage has to have more than sex to hold the couple together for fifty years.

The reverse of this folk belief is probably a lot closer to the truth: that you cannot have a really good marriage *without* sexual compatibility, but you can have a poor marriage *with* sexual compatibility.

This is true for the simple reason that for men, at least, sexual behavior is essentially *segmental* and does not involve the total person. Male conversation about sex reveals this very clearly, as can be seen by anyone who cares to read such realistic novels as *From Here to Eternity*[6] and/or *The Naked and the Dead*.[7] Kinsey also reveals this rather thoroughly in his second volume, in which he compares male and female sexuality in our culture.

Most men, whether you and I like it or not, are capable of making love to women whom they do not love—and by "love" we mean that they would not be capable of living in marriage harmoniously with these women. For this reason, many husbands can enjoy their wives sexually and still not enjoy being married to them.

It is generally supposed that women in our society are different from men sexually, in the sense that they respond with much more of their total being. In other words, they do not *localize* or *compartmentalize* sexual behavior nearly as much as men do. Kinsey has an extensive analysis of this in his volume on the female, and, in general, he supports the belief about this in our culture.[8]

It may well be true that *sex is enough to sustain courtship,* but not marriage.

For these reasons, we would suggest rewording this folk belief as follows: "Don't you think most *courtship* problems will take care of themselves if there is a strong sexual attraction?" Our answer would probably have to be in the affirmative.

5. *"I think they would get along better if they had a baby."*

For the baby's sake, let's hope so. Whether they will or not, however, is very debatable.

We must admit that this belief has more reality content than do most of the ones analyzed so far. It is true, for example, that childless couples have a somewhat higher divorce rate than do couples with children, but what this proves we are not at all sure. For example, divorce rates are highest in the first three years of marriage, which is the period when a good proportion of our couples have not yet started their families. For this reason, it seems to us, the basic variable responsible for the relatively high divorce rate for these couples might be the newness of their marriages rather than the absence of children. It would be interesting to know, for example, whether separation rates (as distinct from divorce rates) are higher for lower-lower-class couples *without children* than for lower-lower-class couples *with children.* We use Warner's "lower lower" class here because they have the highest separation rates, and because many family social workers have had the impression that separation is often associated with the presence of numerous children in the marriage.

It is interesting to note also that children, since World War II, seem to be losing their power to hold couples together, judging by the increasing proportion of divorced couples who now have children.

Another odd and somewhat perplexing fact is that the highest adjustment scores made in several of the marital prediction studies *were made by childless couples.* This seems to indicate that the *absence* of children might even be associated with extremely good marital adjustment, at least in middle-class subculture, from which most of the samples for these studies was drawn.

It still seems to be true, however, that children tend to hold married couples together. But do they make marriages any *happier*? Or is it simply that couples with children are willing to put up with more? We hesitate to say this, but our own belief, based on twenty years of professional experience, is that the latter statement is closer to reality.

Why? Because rearing children in our society is not an easy matter, and because the child can make a marriage worse just as often as it can improve it.

We would be the first to grant, however, that for some couples, where the relationship is potentially good but suffering from a sort of marital anemia, the arrival of a baby often gives the marriage greater depth and significance. We think it unwise, however, to deduce from this that *all* unhappily married couples should expect parenthood to resolve their marital conflicts.

For those who think we are too extreme in this matter, let us point out the following: social workers who specialize in evaluating potential adoptive parents will rarely approve a couple if the worker believes that the basic motivation to adopt is based on a desire to save the marriage—judging by the writer's experience in family social work. This attitude, we believe, is based on a deep conviction on the part of these workers that a child does not necessarily solve marital problems.

In the last analysis, it seems to us, this folk belief rests upon a romantic notion of child-rearing, and is essentially unrealistic.

6. *"The trouble today is that young people take their marriages too casually."*

It seems to us that this sort of belief is based more on newspaper accounts than on actual experience with young couples. It is obvious that some of our Reno habitués can hardly be heartbroken about the failure of their latest great love, but we must be extremely careful in drawing any conclusions about the general population from such an unrepresentative sample. As a matter of fact, Leo Rosten, in his magnificent sociological study *Hollywood*,[9] found that marriage was not even taken lightly in the film colony itself, contrary to popular belief. Rosten thus tends to support the findings of Waller, who believed divorce to be traumatic for the couples in his small nonrandom sample.[10]

In a much later study of divorce by Goode,[11] using a more representative sample than Waller or Rosten, divorce appears to have been a difficult experience for the majority of the wives studied (he did not study husbands). None of these studies of divorce supports the notion that American couples take their marriages (or their divorces) casually.

There are, of course, deviants in our society who regard marriage as a sort of joke, just as there are deviants who commit murder casually. But we do not believe that the research to date has demonstrated that the so-called "average American" couple, old or young, take their marriage lightly. We conclude, therefore, that this particular belief is an example of modern folklore.

7. *"I know that someday the right person for me will come along."*

This belief represents an extreme form of the romantic complex and, as such, may not be found too widely in the general population. If we may believe Burgess and Wallin, the young engaged couples in their sample were not blinded by romance, but had considerable insight into the realities of courtship and marriage. Because of this finding, it is not clear, at least to the writer, just how much of the romantic complex actually survives in modern America. We do feel, however, that enough survives to warrant analysis of this aspect of it.

Basically, our critique of this belief is based on its two fallacies: first, the idea that the right person *will come along*. This, we feel, implies a passive approach to courtship that seems to us to be unrealistic, even for girls. The American courtship system is a free enterprise system, which means that it relies heavily on competition as a sorting device. The greatest rewards in this type of courtship system, just as in our free enterprise economic system, go to those who *compete*—in other words, to those who participate in the system.

If we conceptualize the courtship system in these terms, then it seems clear that the right person may never come along unless we take an active part in the courtship system. As our banks like to say in their advertisements, "the future belongs to those who plan for it."

The second fallacy in this folk belief is the assumption that there is *only one person* for us in the whole wide world. This notion is deeply imbedded in the symbolism of our popular songs, although we are not convinced that young people take these completely at face value.

On purely theoretical grounds, it must be admitted that there may be one person in the world best suited to share our life in marriage. That is, if we accept the idea, which appears irrefutable, that all of us are unique personalities, then it seems to follow that somewhere there must be another unique personality who would fit with us better than anyone else. As we say, on purely theoretical grounds, we are inclined to concede that the popular songs are right. Our fellow sociologists will no doubt consider this to be treason on our part, since it seems to be the fashion in texts of this nature to take a dim view of the romantic complex. If our colleagues react in this fashion, we will have to plead with Patrick Henry: "If this be treason, make the most of it."

Once we leave the realm of pure theory, however, and descend to mundane reality, it becomes obvious that few of us, if any, will ever have much chance to search for the perfect mate. Of the millions of potential partners in the world, or in the United States, we will, at best, get to know only a few. Since we can hardly choose from persons we do not know (although some married couples seem almost to achieve this), it follows that our real problem is to choose *the most compatible person available to us.*

How big is this group of eligibles? For most of us, not very large, as the following will demonstrate. In 1946, the author studied 85 Senior girls at Cornell University, in an attempt to learn two things: (1) How many different young men they had dated, and (2) How many of these men they had ever considered marrying (whether or not a marriage proposal had been made). The most popular girl in the group had dated about seventy different boys, starting in the eighth grade and continuing up to her last semester in college. Of this number, she had considered five of them as good marital prospects, and of this group, three had proposed. Of the three, one had been rejected because of religious differences, leaving two. Of these, she had been engaged to the first during her second year at college, the engagement being terminated by mutual agreement the next summer (we do not know why). When our study was made, she was engaged to the third man, of those who had proposed, and they were to be married when she graduated in June. She was looking forward to what appeared to be a good marriage, but looking back on her nine years of dating, and her seventy different dating partners, she was amazed to learn how small the group of eligibles had actually been. In fact, until this study was made, she had been unaware that her ultimate choice had been made from such a restricted group.

Let us remember that this girl had been unusually active (or mobile) in the courtship system. The statistics on the least active girl in the group are very different. This girl began dating in the Junior year of high school and, by her last term in college, had actually dated only seven different boys. Of this group, she had considered marriage with only one, the boy to whom she was currently pinned. Whether or not they would ever marry, she was not sure. Thus, in a sense, her range of choice so far had been limited to *one*.

In the total group of 85 Senior women in this study, the median girl had "gone with" three young men she considered to be potential marriage partners, two of whom had proposed, and to one of whom she had been either pinned or engaged.

Returning now to our original discussion, it seems clear that our actual marital choice, even for very active daters, and in spite of the relative freedom in our courtship system, is made from a very limited range of persons. For this reason, we feel that the idea of a right person is fallacious, even though we concede that on theoretical grounds the notion can be defended.

8. *"Don't you think they are terribly in love?"*

We're sorry, but we do not, unless the comment is made about an elderly married couple holding hands as they walk across the campus. We can admit that young couples may be, and usually are, "terribly infatuated" or "awfully thrilled" with each other, but we hesitate to apply the word "love" to such untested relationships. It seems to us that the earlier Americans had a point in their belief that the marriage ceremony marks the *beginning* of true love and not the *culmination* of it.

Let us illustrate what we mean. As a child of seven or so, we were in the room when our maternal grandmother, a woman of eighty-four years and fifteen children, died. As she neared the end of a long and active life, she sank into a sort of coma. At this point, our grandfather entered the room and approached the bed. As he took her hand, his presence seemed to arouse her and she opened her eyes. After a few minutes, her hand slipped from his and she was gone, thus ending sixty-eight years of marriage. Don't you think they were "terribly in love"? We do.

Here is another illustration of a couple we consider to be "terribly in love." We recently visited a new and beautiful "County Home for the Aged" in one of our more progressive states. At this home there is an elderly couple, both in their seventies, who always hold hands as they walk down the hall or enter the dining room. As they look at each other, after all these years, they seem to glow with warmth. Their relationship has impressed the staff so much that a newspaper reporter was invited to interview the couple, and this resulted in a widely reprinted feature story about them.

We do not deny that young couples are capable of deep

affection, but it does seem wise to think of married love as something that grows, deepens, and is gradually built into a more and more significant relationship. The most happily married couples we know seem to reflect this developmental type of marital bond.

Conceptualized in this way, we do not *fall* in love, we *achieve* it. This is in line with the opinion of marriage counselors that good marriages are not an accident: they are an achievement, the result of two human beings learning to live together happily and constructively.

For these reasons, we believe the statement under discussion to be fallacious. It implies a sort of static concept of love, of something completely achieved *at the beginning* of marriage. It might be compared with the belief that graduation is the *end* of our education, whereas wise people prefer to think of it as only the *beginning*. This was the point of view of our old professor who came up to shake our hand when we received our Doctor of Philosophy degree. "Well," he said, "now that all the required courses, the term papers, and the grades are over, you can concentrate on educating yourself."

For young married couples we might put it this way: "Now that all the fun and commotion of courtship are over, you can concentrate on getting to know each other and building your love."

For a good portrait of the young couple "terribly in love," see the film *This Charming Couple,* produced by McGraw-Hill for courses of this sort.

When a young couple walk across the campus holding hands, beaming at each other, most of us are pleased to learn that the new generation is not too different from the old. But how much more impressive it is to see *middle-aged* couples hold hands as they take their walk in the evening, or to catch *them* sneaking a kiss in the park! This, we say, is *really love.*

9. *"You know, I really don't think they have ever had an argument."*

In this folk belief, there is the concept of the perfect marriage as one in which the man and wife appear to be exact duplicates of each other, hence no differences, no arguments.

It may be that some couples, although not very many, settle their differences through *discussion* and, in this sense, avoid *argument,* but this implies more self-control than most of us are capable of over the span of several decades.

Actually, it is fallacious to conceive of the perfect marriage as one in which the husband and wife are as much alike as possible. If we are to grow in marriage, then we must learn from each other, and this requires differences between the spouses. As Waller and Hill [12] point out, the trick for married couples to learn is not to *avoid* argument, but rather to learn how to argue constructively.

We would make the same observation about engaged couples. As a matter of fact, we are always concerned when an engaged person tells us, with pride, that "we never argue about anything." We immediately wonder whether their engagement is accomplishing anything.

In conclusion, it seems to us that this folk saying should be reworded as follows: "I really don't think they have ever had a *destructive* argument."

Summary

This has been a brief look at our collection of folk beliefs about marriage in our society. We have not been able to show you our entire collection, but it may be possible to slip a few of the less glittering ones into some of the other chapters.

We suggest that you and your dating partner start a collection of your own. Or perhaps your marriage class would like to work on a collection as a group project.

Keep in mind that folk beliefs of this sort tend to develop

about parts of a social system not well understood or easily controlled, conditions that seem to apply to both courtship and marriage in our society and, perhaps, in most societies.

Remember, too, that folklore, from a functional point of view, may operate to prevent rational analysis of behavior, or to provide the individual with a feeling of false security.

It may be true, as Linton suggests in his *Study of Man,*[13] that all courtship and marriage systems, including our own, contain a sizable percentage of nonrational belief and behavior, but this does not mean that we should not attempt to *reduce* the amount of folklore and myth in American courtship and marriage. This, in a sense, has been the aim of this chapter.

Having taken this somewhat brief look at the American marriage system in perspective, we are now ready to examine in detail our courtship system and the process by which the individual man or woman moves toward—and into—marriage. This will be the purpose of Part II.

References

1. Thurman Arnold, *The Folklore of Capitalism* (New Haven, Yale University Press, 1937).

2. Willard Waller, *The Family, A Dynamic Interpretation* (New York, The Cordon Company, 1938).

3. See Albert Ellis, *The American Sexual Tragedy* (New York, Twayne Publishers, 1954).

4. A good summary of this material may be found in Amram Scheinfeld, *Women and Men* (New York, Harcourt, Brace & Co., 1953).

5. Harvey J. Locke, *Predicting Adjustment in Marriage* (New York, Henry Holt & Co., Inc., 1951), p. 358.

6. James Jones, *From Here to Eternity* (New York, Charles Scribner's Sons, 1951).

7. Norman Mailer, *The Naked and the Dead* (New York, Rinehart & Co., Inc., 1948).

8. Alfred C. Kinsey, *Sexual Behavior in the Human Female* (Philadelphia, W. B. Saunders Co., 1953), chap. 9.

9. Leo C. Rosten, *Hollywood* (New York, Harcourt, Brace & Co., 1941).

10. Willard Waller, *The Old Love and the New* (New York, Liveright Publishing Corp., 1930).

11. William J. Goode, *After Divorce* (Glencoe, The Free Press, 1956).

12. Willard Waller and Reuben Hill, *The Family* (New York, Dryden Press, 1951), pp. 309–312.

13. Ralph Linton, *The Study of Man* (New York, Appleton-Century-Crofts, Inc., 1936), chaps. 10 and 11.

Suggested Readings

1. Thurman Arnold, *The Folklore of Capitalism* (New Haven, Yale University Press, 1937) is a classic analysis of folklore in modern society. It is excellent for book reports. The first three chapters illustrate his method of analysis.

2. Geoffrey Gorer, *The American People* (New York, W. W. Norton & Co., Inc., 1948), chap. 4, "Love and Friendship." This is a delightful version of love and marriage in the United States as it looks to a British anthropologist.

3. Denis de Rougemont, "The Crisis of the Modern Couple," in Ruth Nanda Anshen (ed.), *The Family: Its Function and Destiny* (New York, Harper & Bros., 1949), pp. 322–333.

4. Ruth Benedict, "The Family: Genus Americanum," in Anshen, *op. cit.*, pp. 159–169.

5. Ralph Linton, *The Study of Man* (New York, Appleton-Century-Crofts, Inc., 1936), chap. 11, "Marriage."

PART II

THE AMERICAN
COURTSHIP SYSTEM

CHAPTER IV

THE AMERICAN COURTSHIP SYSTEM

Introduction

Although it may seem to the casual observer that courtship activities in our society are random or unstructured, this is far from the truth. If we reflect for a moment, it becomes obvious that complete anarchy and chaos would prevail if young men and women were left completely to themselves during the courtship period.

It may be remembered that in Chapter I the position was taken that human groups always tend to organize their behavior, and this produces *social systems,* patterns of behavior which are observed by most (not necessarily all) members of the society.[1] This *structuring* of behavior accomplishes at least two broad purposes: 1) it produces at least a minimum level of social order and thus facilitates the operation of the larger society; and 2) it defines the situation for the members of the society, thus reducing confusion and insecurity.

Regarded in this way, then, we may assume, purely on

theoretical grounds, that there is an American courtship system, just as the economist assumes that there is an American economic system. Our problem, then, in this chapter, is to delineate the basic characteristics of this courtship system and to give the reader some insight into its general operation. In the succeeding chapters, we will focus intensively on segments of the system and analyze them in detail.

Obviously, it is being assumed that knowledge of the system and its operation will aid the student as he or she participates in the system. In view of the power of "love" in our culture, this may seem to be a dubious assumption, that courtship will always consist of just "doing what comes naturally." We believe that all liberal (nonvocational) education is forced to make the same assumption that we make in this chapter: *that knowledge is good,* both as an end in itself and as a tool for achieving goals. It certainly seems, at least to us, that a student might benefit as much from the study of the American courtship system as he would from, say, the study of paleolithic man—and this is not meant as a reflection on stone age man, for whom we have a lot of respect.

At any rate, this is the frame of reference from which this chapter and the others in Part II have been written.

Some Definitions

For our purposes, courtship may be defined as the process by which the individual moves from the single status of the adolescent to the married status of the adult. Thus, as we use the term "courtship," it includes random dating as well as the more marriage-oriented types of heterosexual social relationships. In this sense, we take the position that *all* dating experience is essentially preparation for marriage, hence we feel it should all be considered as courtship. We are aware that Willard Waller and others following him have considered random dating as a dalliance relationship, an activity that was an end in itself.[2] We do not deny that such dead-end dating relationships exist in our girl-boy social system, but it seems to us that dalliance itself has to be included *as part* of the total American courtship system. For this reason, the broader definition of the term "courtship" is preferred in this analysis.

The phrase "courtship system" merely points out that this behavior is not random or unstructured but falls into patterns of behavior, some of which are highly normative (enforced by group pressure), while others are permissive or optional.

It is *not* implied that there is only one courtship system for all Americans. It is recognized that there are subsystems within the system, based on religion, age, social class, urban-rural residence, etc. Although some of these variations will be touched on, it is probably true that the system we describe is largely that of the urban middle-class subculture.[3] Perhaps the reader can add to the analysis on the basis of his or her background. Class discussion may also help to make the description more complete.

Some General Observations

From a functional point of view, all human societies have to have some organized way of getting young males and females from childhood into adulthood, from single status into some type of marriage. To accomplish this, some type of courtship system will be found in any human society, although its nature and its prominence will vary greatly from one society to another. For this reason, it is fallacious to assume that the courtship patterns of our society are very old or very widespread in human society. In many ways they are new and unique, at least in part.

Furthermore, we must not assume that the system is static or fixed, for it seems to be in a constant state of change and adaptation. We know that our courtship system is intimately related to the other basic social structures in our culture—our religious institutions, our economic system, etc., and it may be assumed that the courtship system changes as the other parts of the culture are modified. How much time lag there is in this adaptation of the courtship system to new social conditions is not clear, although it can be assumed that some lag would be inevitable. Thus to some extent the system, or part of it, is always outmoded.

It may be that no one completely understands how the system works. This seems to be a reasonable possibility in view of the complexity of American social organization. Furthermore, since the descriptions of the courtship system are usually written by middle-aged persons, it may be that their analyses themselves represent a sort of time lag: the two or three decades that have elapsed since the observer participated in the system. It is true that we are getting an increasing amount of empirical data about the system, based on reports from young persons themselves, but these are, at best, inadequate for an analysis of the total courtship system.[4]

If the preceding observations are valid, there seem to be several sources of error in any particular description of the system:

1. The limited experience of the observer, since no one participant can hope to have been exposed to the total system. Most of us, for example, have been limited to one social class, at least during our courtship period. Some persons—perhaps most—have dated on more than one social level, but that does not mean that such persons have acquired an intimate insight into dating practices of young persons *born and reared* on that level. The author, for example, had one date with an upper-class girl during his courting days. But this hardly qualifies him to make any general statement about the dating practices of upper-class young people. For this reason, students also must use some caution in assuming that they know what modern courtship practices are.

Even the college professor who studies the courtship system through his students has to remember that college classes practically never constitute a cross section of American society.

2. Another source of error is to be found in the fact that the system has changed since the observations were made. Even a study as late as Burgess and Wallin's *Engagement and Marriage*, published in 1953, is soon threatened by time and rapid social change, for almost twenty years have sped by since they began collecting their data (1936).[5] And it is almost ten years since

they completed gathering their material (1946). In the meantime, the devastating depression of the 1930's and the war of the 1940's have undoubtedly left deep marks on the courtship system, some of which were probably not fully developed in the couples old enough to be in the Burgess-Wallin sample. This means that we are not sure that their findings still hold true—and this in spite of the recent publication date of their work.

3. A third source of error must also be admitted: the norms of the culture itself tend to prevent our seeing it clearly. If a group of students are asked such a question as: "What qualities do you look for in a good date?" the answers are very apt to reflect the qualities they think they *should* look for. But a detailed study of their dating companions for a selected period might reveal that they do not *actually select* dates the way they say they do. In other words, their verbal responses reflect cultural norms but their actual behavior may deviate from these norms.

The following illustration will show how this works. After World War II, the Chrysler Corporation asked consumers what they would like to see in the new postwar car. A large proportion of the sample replied that they would like smaller cars that would be easier to park, also cars that used less gasoline. On the basis of this study, Chrysler brought out a smaller Plymouth, one that consumed relatively modest amounts of gasoline. *This car did not sell.*

During this same period, General Motors, operating on a different analysis of consumer desires, increased the size of its cars, emphasizing *appearance* and *power* (as opposed to convenience and economy). *These cars swept the market.* As a matter of fact, Buick, with its very high gasoline consumption, has been one of the best sellers of the postwar era.

The point is this: car buyers may say one thing when asked to describe the car they *should* buy, but this doesn't mean that this is the car they will *actually* buy. As a matter of fact, one could probably assume just the reverse: that most of them will buy the *opposite* of what they know they *should* buy. In a recent report of car-buying habits (1955), it was reported that Chicago dealers were having difficulty selling the *less expensive* models because most purchasers wanted "the works." [6]

All through this discussion of courtship, we will have to be alert for the cultural blinders that may prevent our seeing the system *as it is* and not as *it should be.*

With these introductory matters disposed of, let us sketch in the broad contours of the system.

Major Characteristics of the American Courtship System

1. *The system is competitive.*

In many ways, our courtship system resembles our economic system: it is based on free competition and, at least theoretically, all members of the system are equally eligible to participate. In our economic system we are free, at least in theory, to work where and for whom we choose; to start a business; or not to work at all. Similarly, in our courtship system, we are free to date persons who attract us, to go and come as we please, subject to some parental guidance; we are even free not to date at all, if that is our pleasure.

Actually, this is a very romantic view of our courtship system, just as most descriptions of the economic system are also romantic. Persons are free to date anyone, as long as they stay within their own group, as the saying goes. We are not usually free to date members of other races; our families usually do not approve of dating someone whose economic position is vastly below ours (they are not as critical if the date is *above* us on the economic ladder); there are rather definite religious lines that tend to limit freedom of courtship in America; and there are also fairly stiff age limits, so that most of our young people date within their own peer group (that is, their own generation). It is true, of course, that all these boundaries are not ironclad, and that all of them are occasionally crossed over. But these unusual cases should not confuse us into thinking that the competition in the system is *unrestricted.* There are actually a great many limits to what one may do or may not do, most of them unwritten or unofficial. But they still exist and do regulate dating. The real freedom to compete in the system is almost always *within* our own social world, as we shall see as we analyze the system.

It is almost impossible for Americans to realize how unusual this competitive nature of our courtship system is. Traditionally, in Western societies, parents, relatives, or professional matchmakers shopped around for a suitable marriage partner for a boy or girl. Arensberg and Kimball found this system in rural Ireland to be prevalent even in modern times.[7] As a matter of fact, it may still be found in the United States in disguised fashion, through our lonely hearts clubs and similar organizations.[8]

In a very real sense, American parents prepare their sons and daughters for the courtship market: we have their teeth straightened, move into "nice" neighborhoods or suburbs, send them to "good" schools and colleges, buy them a decent wardrobe, supply a car for the boy, teach them the social graces, and then send them forth to seek their husband or wife.

Actually, the above description is very similar to, if not identical with, the way in which we prepare young people to compete in the economic system.

One of the advantages of this competitive courtship system is that it dovetails neatly with our economic, political, and religious structures, all of which also stress competition to a considerable extent.

It must not be assumed, however, that there are no disadvantages resulting from this emphasis on free competition. Actually, any social structure involves a certain price that has to be paid to realize the advantages of the system—in other words, "you can't have everything" in social systems any more than we can in individuals. There are gains and losses in all of them. What, then, are the problems created by the competitive nature of the American courtship system?

For one thing, the system favors the aggressive person, which means that the less aggressive man or woman is at a real disadvantage. These gentle people may make excellent marriage partners (as we believe they do), but their chances of success in the courtship market are not good.

The system also tends to emphasize a host of superficial personality attributes that seem to have relatively little to do with marital adjustment. In girls, these include a good figure (curves in the right places), being pretty, skill in facial make-up and dressing, etc. In boys there is a premium for being tall, slender, knowing the latest dance steps, having a car, being expert at parlor tricks, etc. Blood, in a recent study, has questioned whether such things as physical appearance are really basic in modern campus courtship.[9] His data were obtained by having students check items on a questionnaire, a procedure that seems to us somewhat dubious in studying courtship, for the simple reason that the responses are most likely to indicate what the students think they *should* do rather than what their actual practices *are*.

In a general way, one might compare the problems of the American courtship system with those of the American radio and television broadcasting system. In the latter, we know that there has been a heavy emphasis on crime and comedy because "that is what the public wants," as the broadcasters put it.[10] As a result, some of the programs of a cultural or educational nature are forced off the air for lack of a sponsor. Thus the public gets what it wants but not necessarily what would be good for it.

In American sports, which are intensively competitive, there is an elaborate set of rules designed to assure fair play, with a referee or umpire (sometimes several of them) usually present to punish players who violate the code. This is also true, to some extent, in our competitive economy, with Better Business Bureaus, Chambers of Commerce, and courts of law which attempt to maintain some sort of fair practices in business. There are also Industry Codes and other devices for controlling competition.

In the courtship system, however, there appears to be no effective police system to enforce the rules, such as they are. It is true, of course, that the peer group itself can, and does, function to punish flagrant violations of the code, but it is an open question as to how effective this control is.

In earlier decades the court of law, through breach-of-promise suits, used to handle the most severe cases, but such suits have become rare in recent years. Also in days of old, parents and older siblings used to function to prevent abuse of courtship privileges. Thus a man who had "kept company" with a girl for several months without committing himself to marriage would be asked to declare his intentions by the father or an older brother. This sort of practice is rare today, although a student of ours has found it among the French-Canadians of Montreal.

It is undoubtedly true that parents still act in severe situations to maintain some sort of fair play in dating, but one wonders how effective this is in modern urban communities.

There is an old saying that "all's fair in love and war," and this seems to be essentially the case in modern courtship. In the economic system this is called *caveat emptor*, which Webster translates to mean: "Let the purchaser beware" (that is, he buys at his own risk). One would not have to stretch this principle too far to make it fit the courtship system as well.

Purely on theoretical grounds, one would expect to find a great deal of confusion, conflict, and personality damage in any social system where competition is intense, the rules are poorly defined, with no adequate referee or umpire, and where the stakes are high. If this is a fair description of the American courtship system, then we would expect a sizable proportion of the contestants in the game to get hurt, either physically, emotionally, or both. It is our belief that this is actually the case, although we admit not having the data to substantiate the charge. Information of this nature is not easy to obtain, since most of us prefer to keep our love wounds secret. As the analysis of the courtship system and its product, marriage, proceeds, the reader can judge for himself the positive and negative effects of the system.

2. *The system is youth-centered.*

In some societies, according to Ralph Linton and others,[11] the process of selecting marriage partners is essentially *parent-centered*. That is, the main concern in arranging the marriage focuses on how this new union will affect the family and its kinship group. The Chinese, for example, in their traditional marriage system, would be concerned that the daughter-in-law be a good choice for the son's mother, and this might take precedence over the value of the girl for the son himself.[12] This is taboo in America. The primary concern in marriage—perhaps the *only* legitimate concern—is the happiness of the bride and groom. And this attitude pervades the entire courtship system. Parents must not interfere because they might "ruin their daughter's life." She may be planning to marry a man whom they feel positive will never make her a good husband, yet they are often helpless to alter the course of events. Indeed, they often do not even try, on the theory that "it's her life."

Perhaps we are overstating the case at this point, but there is certainly some truth in the proposition.

The system is youth-centered in its lack of any real chaperonage, thus permitting young people to run the system themselves, at least in large measure. It is true, of course, that almost all high school and college social affairs have official chaperones, but this hardly disproves the point. These social wardens are under no illusion that they are actually *controlling* behavior, not with the automobiles parked outside. The real purpose of the modern chaperone is to protect the good name of the school or club by seeing that no scandalous behavior takes place *on the premises*. And, of course, it seldom does.

It seems clear that a youth-centered system of this sort has evolved to prepare people for an urban impersonal social order in which the individual will inevitably be on his or her own in all sorts of social situations. The system, in order to work well, requires child-rearing of the highest order, for the only real parental control consists of *internalizing* moral and ethical norms so that they will operate in the absence of adults. And this internalization can only be achieved if the child respects the parents and has a positive relationship with them (at least one of them). This seems to create problems for the child reared in a disorganized family—and this seems to be true of a large proportion of our male and female delinquents.

Furthermore, the system requires *very rapid maturation* if the boy or girl is to avoid difficulty. This seems to be especially true of youngsters from the lower-income groups, those who do not go to college but often marry during or soon after their high school years. Thus it may be that the American courtship system works best for middle- and upper-class young people, in that they tend to postpone marriage until after college, thus having an additional four years of maturation before making a marital choice. If it is true that marriage instability rates (including desertion as well as divorce) are highest at the low-income levels, as some students believe,[13] then it may well be that our courtship system is dysfunctional (not well designed) for that group.

3. *Courtship in America is an elaborate process.*

For that segment of our population that goes through college —and this is increasingly true of high school graduates—the courtship process appears to extend over about an eight-year span, beginning about the last year of Junior High School (if not earlier), continuing through high school and college. In a survey by the author, using the graduating class of a Middle West liberal arts college, approximately one third of the men and women were engaged or pinned (almost the equivalent of engagement) by June of their Senior year. Two thirds of these men and women still had some serious courting to do, it would seem, so that our estimate of an eight-year courtship period may be too conservative. Ten years might be more accurate for college graduates. Whatever the exact figure, it seems obvious that our middle- and upper-class young people spend about a decade of their lives in premarital dating, another term for courtship.

Actually, in a very real sense, this long courtship period produces its own way of life, what we refer to as a subculture, with its own codes, norms, recreation patterns, clothing styles, etc. There is a coke joint subculture in our society so elaborate that Mary Ellen Chase, the author of *Harvey*, has written a play about it called *Bernardine*.[14] The main theme of this play is that young people, the single adolescent, live in a world of their own, a world that no adult can understand. These behavior patterns might be referred to as "teen-age subculture" but this limits the age group too severely. It seems to us another possible term is "adolescent subculture" but not

Figure 3: Median Age of Bride and Groom at Marriage, by Previous Marital Status: 19 Reporting States, 1954 *

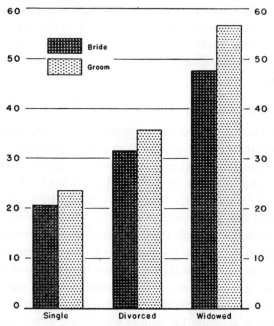

In this chart we see that courtship involves all age groups—not just the young —if we include the divorced and the widowed.

* Source: National Office of Vital Statistics, Special Reports, vol. 44, number 6.

all persons engaged in dating can be labeled "adolescent." Actually, the most accurate term is "courtship subculture," and it is not limited to young people, although they comprise its main creators. The writer has studied middle-aged and elderly widows and widowers in the process of remarriage, and these persons exhibit some of the traits of the subculture: for example, attending movies rather often, frequenting taverns or restaurants, necking, etc.

When it is remembered that young persons in our urban society have relatively few economic or other adult responsibilities, it is easy to understand why courtship subculture in America is so elaborate: it represents almost the only part of our civilization that young single persons are permitted to create and mold to their own purposes.

Students of the family, with the exception of the late Willard Waller, have not described this courtship subculture very adequately, and it appears that the best analysts have been the writers of short stories, novels, and plays. We do not propose to attempt a complete analysis in this text, for that would require a volume in itself. An attempt will be made, however, to describe this "way of life" where it seems relevant.

4. *The system still has a double standard of behavior.*

Oddly enough, although our society seems to favor complete equality of the sexes, judging by our legal code, this is far from attainment in courtship. This is well illustrated on the college campus, where the girls are locked in their dorms or sorority houses each night while the boys are permitted to roam the streets all night (and often do). There is scarcely a college in the United States that does not enforce curfew hours for undergraduate women; yet we know very few that follow the same practice for male undergraduates (except possibly for Freshmen).

Boys still pay most of the checks during courtship, and they still are expected to initiate dating relationships.

It seems clear that the system still reflects our patriarchal background, just as our marriage system does. In some ways, however, it seems to us that marriage in the United States is being *equalized* more rapidly than is courtship. Space does not permit us to pursue this line of thought but it would be a good topic for class discussion.

It may well be, of course, that we do not want complete

equality between the sexes in courtship, or in marriage, but some of the current practices, such as not permitting girls to initiate court-ship (except on very special occasions) seem to be outmoded.

5. *Ours is a very romantic courtship system.*

Since this has been discussed elsewhere in the text, only brief reference will be made here. The basic features of the "romantic complex," as it is called, are these:

A. Love *precedes* marriage rather than develops after mar-riage (as the early American colonists believed it would).

B. Love (personal compatibility) is the *only* justification for getting married. This rules out *money, convenience,* or *parental wishes* as justification.

Our popular songs illustrate the complex better than any sociologist can. Listen to them.

6. *The system is flexible.*

If we could only visualize the American courtship system, it would resemble our vast network of highways, by means of which one may choose alternate routes in traveling from one city to another. The ultimate destination, marriage, is the same for everyone, but the routes leading to the destination are varied.

One girl will continue random dating for years, with perhaps a few lapses into going steady, before she meets her husband. Another girl will find her dream in high school and scarcely ever look at another boy. A third will be engaged and disengaged several times before finding the one she really wants (and who wants her too). Another will hardly date at all through high school or college and then, perhaps on her first job, she meets her future husband.

As we shall see, there are almost endless variations in the American courtship system, and this seems appropriate in a society as diverse and complex as ours. It may be, of course, that some lose their way in this richness of variety, but on the whole this seems to be one of the virtues of the system.

7. *The system is democratic.*

Democracy, it seems, is always relative, not absolute, being essentially a seldom-achieved vision of how people *might live.* It is in this qualified sense that the American courtship system may be said to be democratic.

Its democracy derives from the permissiveness of the system in regard to dating across religious, ethnic, economic, and racial boundaries. Except for the last of these, race, there undoubtedly is a great deal of cross-cultural dating, at least in the random dating stage, the point at which parents are least anxious. How permissive the system is at the point of going steady or engagement is debatable, although there are some studies that we will review in the later chapters of this part of the text. It seems clear, however, that the freedom *to date* across social barriers is not the same as freedom *to marry* across such barriers. This is not to condemn the system, since freedom always seems to have limits of some sort.

8. *The system involves the progressive commitment of the individual.*

If we examine the design of the American courtship system carefully, it will be seen that the system contains a graduated or progressive series of stages, each one of which brings the individual a step closer to marriage. These steps or stages are:

(1)	Group Dating	(4)	Pinned
(2)	Random Dating	(5)	Engagement
(3)	Going Steady	(6)	Marriage

Thus there are five stages in the system, if we include pinning, which is found in the courtship system of most American colleges. Each of these stages actually can be broken down into substages as well. Going steady, for example, can be subdivided into two types: marriage-oriented and not-marriage-oriented. Since each of the stages will be analyzed intensively in the next few chapters, we are interested at this point only in commenting on the total system.

If the five stages are studied carefully, it will be observed that the first one (group dating) permits wide freedom in the choice of dating partners—if there can be said to be a partner at that point —and involves only the most superficial and temporary involvement of the individual. At this stage, religious and economic barriers would be at their lowest point, and the exposure of the self would also be at a minimum. The next stage (random dating) also permits wide latitude in dating partners and relatively little revelation of the self. It seems that it is largely these two stages that give the impression that the system is permissive in choice of dating partner.

Once the young man or woman reaches Stage Three (going steady) the parental pressures increase and continue to increase through Stages Four and Five. All this might be diagramed as follows:

Figure 4. Schematic Drawing of the American Courtship System

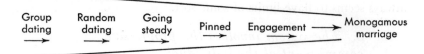

In this drawing, the lines on the outside indicate freedom of choice and movement, so that what starts out as an extremely free dating and courtship system gradually leads the individual into rather deep and permanent commitments, and these in turn finally lead him or her into marriage.

The flexibility of the system makes it possible to enter or leave the system at any point. One could, for example, meet a person on a blind date and get married the next day (except in states requiring a waiting period). One can skip or bypass stages, such as moving directly into marriage from a going steady relationship. Furthermore, one can back up in the system and start over again. Thus a girl might break her engagement and return to the random dating stage. Even marriage, as a matter of fact, does not terminate courtship for a sizable segment of our population, those who divorce, separate, or desert. If we include the widowed among those who marry more than once, it becomes clear that the average American works his way through the courtship system more than once. Indeed, Burgess and Wallin found that most of their engaged couples had been *engaged twice* before they married.[15] If their urban sample is at all representative, and if we add their data to the couples who marry more than once (for all reasons), it seems clear that most Americans have more than a nodding acquaintance with the courtship system. Some of them, as a matter of fact, are in and out of it all their adult lives.

In view of this, plus other observations earlier in the chapter, it seems clear, at least to us, that courtship is a major experience for most Americans, comparable to the other major experiences of their lives: their school years, their work experiences, etc. We agree with Willard Waller that one can never really understand an American marriage until the courtship preceding it has been analyzed.[16] We might even go a step farther and say that one can never really understand an *American* until his or her courtship experiences have been comprehended.

This may be obvious if we are talking about adolescents and college students, but it is much less obvious when we are trying to understand married couples—and it is then that we must remember that courtship experiences do not disappear magically on the wedding day, nor do they cease to be a part of the individual. If the poet's statement is true that "I am a part of all that I have met," then this certainly includes our years of dating before marriage.

When it is remembered that the average middle-class person —that is, those who graduate from college—spends at least eight years in the courtship system, it seems that the system is well designed to prepare the individual gradually for marriage. More will be said about this as we attempt to evaluate the system.

The System Seen in Cross-cultural Perspective

It sometimes is useful to compare our own way of life with that of other societies. Space does not permit us a very elaborate

cross-cultural portrait of human courtship systems, so we will have
to be content with just a few comparisons. Interested students will
find some excellent readings on the subject at the end of the chapter.

In describing the traditional courtship system of Puerto Rico,
Reuben Hill characterized the system as follows:

> Contacts between girls and boys from puberty on were carefully
> limited and supervised through a system of chaperonage. To enter
> courtship boys had to meet criteria of acceptability authored essentially
> by the girls' parents. In effect, mate selection was really "parental
> choice," by veto rather than "free choice" by the young people them-
> selves since parents determined so carefully who would be permitted
> to enter courtship with their daughter.

> Once courtship began, couples were rarely permitted to be alone
> until the wedding night. Thus it was possible to insure that girls came
> to the altar virginal and properly dependent upon their husbands for
> tutelage in matters of sex and reproduction.[17]

Hill points out that Puerto Rican Spanish has no word for
"dating without serious intentions." Indeed, random dating is
pounced upon as a sign of fickleness. Here we see a courtship system
fairly typical of Catholic cultures, and a system unlike the present
one in the United States. If your ancestors or your parents came
from Italy, Spain, or other Catholic cultures in Europe, or from
Central or South America, this was the courtship system they were
reared under.

In their description of courtship in rural Ireland in modern
times, Arensberg and Kimball emphasize the impossibility of a son
or daughter marrying without parental approval.[18] Unless they
choose to migrate from the community, as large numbers of them
have, girls cannot hope to get a husband unless their parents pay a
sum equivalent to the cost of a good farm, the money being used to
buy the farm of the boy's parents. This permits them to retire and
gives the young couple a farm to operate. Even then, the boy's
parents reserve the West Room (a sort of parlor) as their living
quarters for the rest of their lives.

Under this cumbersome and expensive dowry system, a man will often be in his forties before he can marry, and most of the young people cannot hope to marry at all in the local community, since most parents can only manage one marriage under this system. Obviously, parents are in a position of almost absolute control over courtship and marital choice. As in Puerto Rico, virginity is a requirement for the girl, and the system seeks to assure this by reducing casual or random dating to a minimum, also by a strict chaperonage system.

In premodern China marriages were usually arranged by a professional *matchmaker,* who consulted with families having eligible sons and daughters, arranged introductions between sets of parents, and in general served as a marriage broker.[19] The young couple might meet once before the final agreement to see if they had violent objections to the marriage, but for all practical purposes, it was an agreement *between two families.*

A summary of the cross-cultural view

In summarizing this brief cross-cultural view of the American courtship system, the following features of our system seem to be most striking:

1. The elaborate development of *random dating* and its complete moral acceptance.

2. The almost complete elimination of any effective chaperonage.

3. The minimizing of the role and the power of parents to supervise and control courtship.

These American inventions (and they really are inventions) are undoubtedly related to a host of norms and patterns in the total American culture: our urban pattern of life, our industrial economy, our Christian concern for the individual, our democratic values, our free enterprise economic system and its emphasis on competition, etc. As our analysis of courtship and marriage continues, we will have more to say about these.

Some Problems of the System

1. *The diversity of the groups it has to serve.*

As a melting pot society, the United States has included within its population—and still does, to some extent—a great variety of racial, religious, ethnic, and cultural strains, some of which have been and are highly incompatible. What happens today, for example, if a boy from an orthodox Jewish family falls in love with a girl from a liberal Protestant denomination? What courtship practices will be acceptable to both families? Or supposing a Puerto Rican boy in New York City begins dating the daughter of an Irish Catholic family, what will their families be able to agree on in the areas of dating, engagement, and marriage?

The stock reply to such questions is that youngsters from such diverse backgrounds *usually* do not date each other. But it *does* happen, as every high school and college counselor knows. How often, and with what complications, is not very clear.

Perhaps an even greater difficulty resides in the fact that the system must serve extremely diverse economic groups, each of which has its own subculture. We have already suggested that the system works best for middle-class young people, including all persons, regardless of their class of origin, who go on to college. It might be argued, of course, that we have described only the middle-class courtship system and that there are other dating patterns for lower- and upper-class groups. We are prepared to grant this criticism up to a point, but to push this line of analysis too far is hazardous, it seems to us, because of the fact that we live in a *mass society* in which the mass media (movies, television, magazines, etc.) reach almost the entire unmarried youth group, and the dating practices portrayed by these media are almost exclusively middle class.

If it is granted that there are subsystems of the American courtship system—and we readily concede the point—there still remains the question: Which is the *parent* or *dominant* system? We argue that the middle-class system is dominant, or that it is in the process of becoming dominant. Why? Because it *is* the system portrayed vividly and *often* by the mass media; also because social customs in the United States seem to *filter down* rather than rise from the bottom.

Actually, with the exception of pinning, all the elements of the system as we have described it are to be found at the *high school level*, and that assures its dominance, it seems to us.[20]

If there are various courtship subsystems in the United States, then it seems that some of our young persons would *overlap* two or more of them and that some problems would be inherent in that fact. In other words, the person is exposed to more than one behavior system, and to that extent is what sociologists call a marginal person. As a matter of fact, this is probably what happens to the lower- (or upper-) class child who attends high school: a courtship system incompatible with the way of life of their economic group is presented to them and they struggle to adapt themselves to it. In a sense, these young persons live in two different social worlds, the one of their parents and the one they encounter at high school.

2. *The roles of parents are inadequately developed.*

Except for their responsibility of internalizing cultural norms, it is difficult to see where parents fit into the modern American courtship system. They pay the bills, of course, and serve as counselors in some cases, but they do not seem to carry very great responsibility for supervising or controlling what goes on. In the parent education classes taught by the writer, it seems to be clear that a great many parents feel inadequate in their courtship role, if it may be so described. They seem to feel that they should have more to do during this period of parenthood but just *what* they should do, or *how* they should do it, seems to be a mystery. It is the opinion of the writer that this is one of the basic weaknesses of the system.

3. *Incompatible values in the system.*

In the analysis of social systems, we often find conflicts between parts of the system. Karen Horney, the psychoanalyst who has paid a great deal of attention to culture and social systems, has pointed out that within the basic values of American society there is a conflict between the *humility* emphasized by Christianity and the *aggressive* competition stressed in our economic system.[21]

Within each of us, on the level of personality analysis, there are conflicts very similar to those existing in the culture. Thus a college student might be torn between the desire to make high grades and the desire to be a heavy-drinking fraternity pal, values usually not compatible.

Getting back to the American courtship system, there seems to be a very real conflict between the value of feminine chastity and the value of almost unlimited freedom in courtship. As we saw in the Puerto Rican courtship system, societies that value chastity usually erect elaborate social structures (chaperonage systems) to assure that end. In the American system, the chaperonage controls have essentially been discarded without discarding the chastity ideal (we are, of course, referring to female chastity; none of the socie‑ ties referred to in this chapter have attempted to enforce male chastity).

In this modern American courtship system, the only controls that might preserve female chastity under the free courtship pattern would have to be *internalized* in the girl herself: in other words, in what is usually termed the conscience or superego, to use the Freudian term. In some ways, it is amazing that so many of our young women do enter marriage chaste, for societies such as Italy or Puerto Rico would have thought this impossible without very rigid chaperonage. These societies seem to view the sex drive as an irresistible impulse, one likely to explode the instant a man and woman are left alone.

If these Latin peoples have overestimated the strength of the sex drive, it may also be true that we Americans have underestimated it. The data on engaged couples, for example, indicate that perhaps half of those studied have had sexual relations during the engagement period.[22] And since these couples were predominantly middle class, whose sexual norms are relatively conservative, according to

Kinsey, it may very well be that the national average is higher than 50 per cent.

It may also be that the concept of feminine chastity has been retained as an *ideal* but not one that most Americans expect to find attained very often. In this respect, it may be similar to some of our other Christian ideals, such as "turn the other cheek" when someone strikes us.

There are other conflicts in the system also, one of which is the retention of certain patriarchal features, such as the male right to initiate dating, in a society dedicated to almost complete male-female equality in marriage. The age-old custom of having the male pay the costs of courtship seems to be in conflict with the economic equality prevailing between men and women in modern marriage. A survey by the author's students on a Middle-Western liberal arts college campus revealed that about a third of the men reported that they had to restrict their dating because of the cost—and this on a campus where the girls complain of lack of dates! [23] This situation becomes even more ludicrous when it is known, as it is on this campus, that the girls come from higher economic levels and have more spending money than the boys. Here, it seems to us, is a clear illustration of nonrational behavior resulting from traditional practices not being adapted to new social conditions. The student should remember that *all* social systems contain a certain percentage of nonrational elements, so that our courtship system is not unique in that respect. The problem is to keep the nonrational elements *at a minimum*, and this involves the courage to discard old customs and the creative ability to develop new and better ones. In the field of dating, this task is largely the responsibility of young people themselves.

Summary

In this chapter an attempt has been made to sketch in the basic features of the American courtship system, on the theory that the student will be able to participate in the system more intelligently if he or she knows something about it. It is recognized that the system is not uniform in all segments of American society, but the system described shows some signs of becoming dominant.

If you doubt the value of this analysis, it might help to remember that we study geology, biology, economics, and other bodies of knowledge on the same theory as the one implicit in this chapter: that knowledge is valuable, either as a means of achieving certain ends or as an end in itself.

We are now ready for the intensive analysis of the various parts of the system. This discussion will take on added significance if the reader will relate it to his or her personal observations of the system. As a participant-observer in the system, you should be in a good position to compare your findings and those of your friends with those of the writer. This will also help you contribute more to class discussion. It would be especially helpful to the class if you bring to its attention variations in the system, if you have observed any, also new developments in the system.

References

1. For an excellent analysis of the concept "social system," see *Rural Social Systems* by Charles P. Loomis and J. Allan Beegle (New York, Prentice-Hall, Inc., 1950), pp. 3–7.

2. This idea is analyzed in Willard Waller, *The Family* (New York, The Cordon Company, 1938), pp. 230–235.

3. Some social class differences in adolescent subculture may be found in August B. Hollingshead's classic study of a high school stratification system, *Elmtown's Youth* (New York, John Wiley & Sons, 1949).

4. Examples of this empirical approach to courtship analysis may be seen in Robert O. Blood's article, "A Retest of Waller's Rating Complex," *Marriage and Family Living*, 17 (1955), 41–47; also in Robert D. Herman, "The Going Steady Complex: A Re-Examination," *Marriage and Family Living*, 17 (1955), 36–40.

5. Ernest W. Burgess and Paul Wallin, *Engagement and Marriage* (Philadelphia, J. B. Lippincott Co., 1953), Preface.

6. News story in Chicago *Tribune,* Financial Section, April 25, 1955.

7. C. M. Arensberg and S. T. Kimball, *Family and Community in Ireland* (Cambridge, Harvard University Press, 1940).

8. For an interesting discussion of "lonely hearts" clubs in our society, see Lee R. Steiner, *Where Do People Take Their Troubles?* (New York, International Universities Press, 1945), chap. 5.

9. See Robert O. Blood, "Uniformities and Diversities in Campus Dating Preferences," *Marriage and Family Living*, 18 (1956), 37–45.

10. For an excellent discussion of this, see Charles A. Siepmann, *Radio, Television, and Society* (New York, Oxford University Press, 1950).

11. Ralph Linton, *The Study of Man* (New York, Appleton-Century-Crofts, Inc., 1936), chaps. 10 and 11.

12. Francis L. K. Hsu has a very good comparison of the American and Chinese courtship and marriage systems in his study, *Americans and Chinese* (New York, Henry Schuman, Inc., 1953).

13. For data supporting this point of view, see William J. Goode, *After Divorce* (Glencoe, The Free Press, 1956), chap. 4.

14. Mary Ellen Chase, *Bernardine* (New York, Oxford University Press, 1953).

15. *Op. cit.*, pp. 134–137.

16. *Op. cit.*

17. Reuben Hill, "Courtship in Puerto Rico: An Institution in Transition," *Marriage and Family Living*, 17 (1955), 26–35.

18. *Op. cit.*

19. Hsu, *op. cit.*

20. Hollingshead, *op. cit.*

21. Karen Horney, *The Neurotic Personality of Our Time* (New York, W. W. Norton & Co., Inc., 1937).

22. This statement is based on the data in Lewis M. Terman, *Psychological Factors in Marital Happiness* (New York, McGraw-Hill Book Co., 1938) and Burgess-Wallin, *op. cit.*

23. This study, as yet unpublished (1956) was made by Janet Layman and Barbara Van Epps.

Suggested Readings

1. Ernest W. Burgess and Paul Wallin, *Engagement and Marriage* (Philadelphia, J. B. Lippincott Co., 1953), chap. 2, "The Study of Modern Marriage."

2. Lee R. Steiner, *Where Do People Take Their Troubles?* (New York, International Universities Press, 1945), chap. V, "Rendezvous for Lonely Hearts."

3. Charles P. Loomis and J. Allan Beegle, *Rural Social Systems* (New York, Prentice-Hall, Inc., 1950), chap. 1, "The Nature of Social Systems." The better student will find this discussion extremely worthwhile.

4. Reuben Hill and Willard Waller, *The Family* (New York, The Dryden Press, 1951), chap. 6, "The Cultural Background of Courtship."

CHAPTER V

RANDOM DATING

Introduction

Random dating is one of the unique features of the American courtship system. Basically, the "random dating complex," as it might be termed, involves the right to date numerous members of the opposite sex, once or as often as one wishes, without any permanent commitment whatsoever, either party being free to terminate the relationship at any point. Furthermore, several different persons may be dated simultaneously—not the same evening (although late dates are not unknown), but during the same week, or the same month. This is not considered cheating, since random dating partners have no exclusive privileges. Also, this is not thought to be fickleness, as it would be in the Puerto Rican dating system, according to Hill's analysis.[1] Nor is it regarded as promiscuity, as it would have been in colonial New England.[2]

Actually, random dating can best be compared to American shopping practices: it is literally a form of shopping around. The couple take a superficial look at each other with no obligation to buy (continue the relationship). If they both like what they see, another date is agreed upon. If they do not, the relationship is ended. Eventually, one of these shopping trips will lead into something, usually a going steady relationship, but sometimes an engagement or even a marriage results.

Random dating has its own ethical codes, as will be shown later in the chapter. It also has a substage that we call "group dating," which we will analyze at this point.

Group Dating

There is a point in the maturation process, somewhere about the Junior High School level, at which boys and girls are not quite ready for complete paired-off dating—either the youngster does not feel secure enough with the other sex or his parents will not permit normal dating—and the solution to this problem seems to be what we call "group dating." In this pattern, boys usually come to the social event in groups, as do the girls, so that both sexes have the moral support of their own kind, which seems to be necessary at this stage of the game. Obviously, group dating gives moral support to the parents also, equally vital at this point of the parent-child developmental sequence.

Some persons may question the existence of this courtship stage, for some youngsters apparently bypass it, entering the courtship system at the random dating or the going steady stage.

In a 1954 survey of 120 parents by the writer, 84 per cent reported that their adolescents had passed through a stage which was best described as group dating.[3] Most of these fathers and mothers, members of PTA study groups, were of middle-class economic status, and it may well be that this pattern does not exist at lower social class levels. Students of ours from upper-class backgrounds definitely report the prevalence of group dating at that level.

Activities at the group dating level include school dances, picnics, movies, coke joint sessions, and parties at the homes of the youngsters. Necking seems to be very mild, possibly because of the lack of privacy.

What is the function of group dating? It seems clear that its place in the total courtship system is to provide a relatively painless transition from the nondating one-sexed "gang" stage of social maturation to the two-sexed dating stage. All young people do not need group dating, nor do all parents, apparently. But it fills a real need for those who do need it.

The Functions of Random Dating

Random dating, including group dating, appears to have the following functions in the American courtship system:

1. *It serves as the point of least resistance to enter or re-enter the system.*

Some way must be provided for getting into any social system; furthermore, there has to be a point at which entrance into the system is relatively easy. This can be illustrated in urban sociology by reference to the function of the slum in the history of the American immigrant: he seldom had any money or credit, so he entered the system at the bottom, at its point of least resistance. Then, gradually, he worked his way up. This is, essentially, what random dating does for the courtship system and its participants: it provides a point of relatively easy entrance into dating, and if we have broken off a more serious relationship, it also provides a way of "getting back into circulation." These are both important and indispensable functions for the successful operation of the courtship system.

In the Herman study of "The Going Steady Complex" at the University of Wisconsin, he found that going steady is now the *preferred* dating relationship for high school students, but this does not negate the crucial role of random dating.[4] After all, not everyone can be fortunate enough at any given moment to have a steady boy or girl friend, which means that random dating must always be there for the dating beginner or for the person temporarily out of luck. It is interesting to note how closely this resembles the role of the slum in the modern city: no matter how prosperous the American economy becomes, nor how much people prefer the suburb, the slum continues to exist: not only that, but it also sports a "no vacancy" sign most of the time. Random dating may not be preferred by modern Americans but some of them have no choice, and for them it is random dating or no dating at all.

2. *Random dating serves to anchor one end of the courtship continuum.*

It can readily be seen that engagement functions as a relationship for the person ready for marriage and having someone he wishes to marry. But the vast majority of young persons on any given day are either not ready for marriage or have not found the persons they wish to marry. For these people random dating provides a sort of happy hunting ground until they are ready and able to move on in the courtship system. In the Herman study cited above, he found that going steady serves this purpose also, as going steady is not marriage-oriented for most high school students planning to go to college. At this point, it seems that random dating and going steady overlap. In a sense, this type of going steady is a modified form of random dating.

3. *Random dating performs a dalliance function.*

A large proportion of American youth have hopes of rising in the economic system, and marriage is often conceived, rightly or wrongly, by these persons as a handicap or barrier to their economic ambitions. For this reason, these people often wish to make sure that marriage will not take place during the first few years of dating. To achieve this end they have their choice of either not dating at all or of dating different persons, and the second choice is less frustrating than the first. It is true that going steady, if properly controlled, is a third choice for such persons, but one that seems to be more hazardous.

Often parents, for various reasons, are opposed to what they call early marriage, and such parents tend to encourage random dating rather than more intimate dating relationships.

4. *Random dating serves a variety of learning functions.*

These include the social graces, such as eating in public restaurants, dancing, card-playing, drinking, polite conversation, and the like. Some preliminary knowledge of the opposite sex, including mild necking and its control, is an important part of this learning.

On a much deeper level, and one not seen by many persons, random dating plays an important role in forming conceptions or images of the self: What am I like? Am I pretty or handsome? Do people find me interesting? Am I popular? Thus, we gradually acquire through random dating new perceptions of ourselves: what kinds of people we like, what sorts of things we like to do, etc. It is this *learning about ourselves* that is crucial in all stages of dating, not just during random dating, for it is only by knowing *ourself*, our needs and interests, that we can make an intelligent marital choice. Often, it seems to us, young people think of dating as a means of getting to know what *other* people are, and this is a legitimate and important function of courtship, but insight into *ourselves* should be thought of as being even more important.

5. *Random dating serves parents in various ways.*

For one thing, it gives parents a period to get used to dating and its ramifications without the added worry of marriage, for marriage seems far off at this point.

Actually, random dating marks the beginning of the real emancipation process, and as such is a crucial stage for both the parents and the child.

During the random dating period parents get their first opportunity to see what sort of persons their son or daughter will choose to associate with, and for parents with insight these choices can tell a great deal about their son or daughter.

6. *Random dating serves as a free enterprise dating market.*

Probably at no other courtship period are the socioeconomic barriers as low as during random dating. Economic, ethnic, religious, racial, and age differences are at their minimum level at this point. In some ways, this period gives us a chance, if only for a brief period, to escape our own social group and learn something about other facets of modern America. One of our students illustrated this in a term paper when she wrote: "As a member of a closely knit and devout Catholic family, I always knew that I would eventually marry a Catholic boy, but all during the random dating stage I dated Protestants most of the time. In this way I got to know Protestants quite well—something that I might have missed had I dated Catholic boys during this period." She went on to say that she was now engaged to a Catholic.

In this discussion we have been analyzing the functions of random dating. It may be true, as Herman argues,[5] that going steady has become the most popular type of dating, but random dating still seems to play a basic role in the courtship system.

The Stranger as a Dating Partner

The very nature of random dating makes it inevitable that the dating partners will often be relatively unknown to each other, if not actually complete strangers. This is seen most clearly in the pick-up date, where a couple meet at a dance or a tavern and go home together, usually knowing only the other person's first name, and perhaps never seeing each other again. But even when the date is prearranged, the couple normally have only a slight knowledge of each other, especially in the larger community. This is less true in the small community, but Americans do not live in small communities for the most part.

All this means that in random dating a great deal of the experience is related to getting along with strangers—that is, learning how to keep the conversation going, putting our best foot forward, being warm and friendly but not revealing our true emotions, learning to discount "the line," controlling our sexual impulses, and so forth. It can readily be seen, it seems to us, how useful all these skills are in our urban, mobile type of society, where *most* people we associate with are essentially strangers.

We believe that Waller and his followers have tended to overlook the value of this type of learning in their criticisms of random dating.[6] Most of this criticism seems to assume that the only function of courtship is to prepare young people for *marriage,* whereas we argue that this is only one of the functions of courtship. From this point of view, random dating may not train the person for marriage, as Waller contends, but it certainly seems to train him for life in modern society. Lowrie stresses this learning function of random dating in his penetrating study.[7]

Looked at from the parents' point of view, however, the stranger as a dating partner presents many problems. Night after night, they see their sons and daughters, their most precious possessions, go out with dating partners more or less completely unknown to the parents. Where will they go? What will they do? How fast will they drive? Is he a "nice boy"? Is she is a "nice girl"? Who are the parents? Do we know them? And so on into the night.

A father once said this to us: "When a new young man comes to take my daughter out, I am not so concerned about his morals as I am with his driving habits. I feel that N——— can take care of herself and my fear is not that he will attack her but that he may kill or maim her with his reckless driving." This father is expressing only one of the fears that parents often harbor as they see their youngster go out with a person about whom they know practically nothing, if that.

It is true that many parents require their daughter to introduce the new boy friend before going out on the first date, but this does not tell the *boy's* parents anything about the girl, nor does it really tell the girl's parents much about the boy. We agree that it is a nice practice, and one to be encouraged, but let us not deceive ourselves about its effectiveness. Like the modern chaperone, this practice looks nice but does not accomplish too much.[8]

In the last analysis, it seems to us, parents have to rely on the judgment of the son or daughter in modern courtship, for the simple reason that the parent cannot effectively supervise courtship in our urban social world. This, of course, makes the basic parent-child relationship of crucial importance.

To our knowledge this phase of modern courtship, the role of the stranger, has never been adequately studied, but in our discussion groups with parents it comes up for frequent comment.

The Evolution of Random Dating

In discussing random dating with college students of today, it seems clear that there are really two types: (1) consecutive or sequential random dating in which a couple date each other for a week or so and then move on to someone else; and (2) simultaneous random dating in which a person dates several different persons during the same time span. Our students seem to believe that the first type is dominant today but that the second type was dominant when their parents were dating in the 1920's and the 1930's. Our impression is that this is correct. Essentially, it seems to us, the two systems are qualitatively similar, but the second type may have some quantitative advantages: you can run up a higher score that way, it would seem.

The Codes Governing Random Dating

In any type of social behavior, there have to be codes or norms of behavior to define the situation; otherwise, behavior becomes highly individualistic and unpredictable. Let us see if we can identify the codes governing random dating.

Some years ago, the late Willard Waller sketched in some of the code as he had observed it on a state university campus.[9] Some of his "rules" were:

1. Always try to appear very busy and popular, as if you are rushed to death. This applies more to girls than boys, of course, but popularity as a date does not hurt boys either.

2. Don't accept last minute dates, because this proves that you aren't really busy at all.

3. Don't accept blind dates, since this also is a reflection on your popularity.

4. Don't accept dates from persons who do not "rate"—that is, persons at the bottom of the dating totem pole. This rule implies that no date is better than just *any* date at all.

5. Don't neck too much on the first date (this one intended for girls), because this will give you a bad reputation.

6. Be polite to your date, even if he or she is a bore, for he will talk to his friends and you may find yourself on a black list.

These six rules or code principles represent the gist of the "rating and dating complex," as Waller called it. Recently, in a study at the University of Michigan, Robert Blood failed to find much evidence that Waller's rules still exist. He concludes: "However valid Waller's picture may have been in 1929–30, it seems doubtful that it should any longer be assumed to be typical of rating and dating on American campuses." [10]

It seems to us, however, that there is a serious discrepancy in methodology between Waller's and Blood's method of gathering data. Waller used essentially his *observations* of the dating system, supplemented by discussions with students and their term papers, whereas Blood is using a *questionnaire* technique in which male and female students are asked to check the norms they perceive to be in operation. The problem, it seems to us, is that people do not always behave the way they say they do. We know, for example, that a man may check an item such as this: "People should all be treated equally regardless of race," yet the same man may be actively engaged in his business or personal life in discriminating against certain racial groups.

Our point is this: Waller and Blood may *both* be correct, because students may *think* they behave one way when actually they behave quite differently. It is well known that a great proportion of human behavior is nonrational, and certainly courtship would be no exception. Yet the participants usually consider their behavior to be rational. In this sense, we are not at all sure that young people are in the best position to describe and analyze their dating behavior, and for this reason we are not too convinced that Waller was wrong in 1929–30.

Here is a good case illustration of what we mean. We recently interviewed a student who had had only two regular dates in her four years on the campus (she had dates at home during vacations, however). This girl is charming, full of life, and interested in all sorts of things. She likes men and is puzzled why they do not like her. Our theory, which we did not state as bluntly to her, is simply this: she is *homely*. Physically, she is not pretty, or feminine, or attractive. We believe she would make an excellent wife and a good mother, but not one man on the campus had taken any serious interest in her for four years. Now we submit that some sort of nonrational code is in operation when girls of this sort go dateless on a college campus. And part of the male code is this: a homely date is worse than no date at all. So is a fat date. The truth is that physical appearance plays a tremendous role in random dating; in fact, it is often the only thing we know about the person, and this is especially true of the male code.

Now let us ask this question: has any of the research on marital adjustment ever demonstrated a relationship between the physical appearance of wives and the marital satisfaction of their husbands? We do not know of any such finding.

One of the nicest men we knew as a college undergraduate had a badly disfigured nose, giving his face a rather unattractive appearance. In every other way, he was a fine person. Yet in four years he never had a date, partly because of his perception of how much emphasis the dating system placed on physical attractiveness.

For several years the writer served as a Dean of Students, in which capacity we met weekly with the directors of the various residence halls. The housemothers of the girls' dormitories frequently remarked that some of the "nicest" girls went dateless week after week. These older women could never understand what standards the men on the campus were using in choosing their dates. Can you?

Our own observations of random dating and its codes, based on several hundred interviews with students, parents, college counselors, and residence hall directors, are as follows:

1. *The criterion of selection of partner in random dating is extremely superficial.*

This emphasizes such things as clothes, physical shape, smile, hair style, and the like. Actually, this is inevitable because of the very nature of random dating: the relationship, by definition, is casual and the participants are not in a position to make choices on any deeper set of values.

Notice how this is revealed by the comments made after a casual date: "He's a lot of fun"; "She bores me"; "He's not much of a dancer"; "She's very pretty"; etc. None of these comments goes very deep, nor could they, by the very nature of the relationship.

It was in this sense that Willard Waller and Reuben Hill considered random dating to be dysfunctional (have a negative relationship to preparation for marriage).[11] Their position was simply this: that random dating does not prepare for marriage because it emphasizes values not related to sound marriage. In other words, it does not prepare young people for marriage, it only prepares them for more random dating.

The error in this analysis, it seems to us, is in the assumption that random dating is *supposed* to prepare young people for marriage, a function which we believe should not be expected of random dating. Our position is that preparation for marriage is a function of going steady, pinning, and engagement, whereas the function of random dating is to prepare young people for courtship—that is, to launch them into the dating system. If this analysis is correct, then most of the critiques that have been written about random dating are irrelevant.

Returning to the superficial values that dominate random

dating choices, it seems obvious that many very fine persons would
be overlooked in this system, while many others would be vastly
overrated. We all know this to be true. And it *is* too bad, but it
seems to us to be one of the prices that have to be paid for our competitive courtship system. After all, similar prices have to be paid
for our competitive economic system—such as the "singing commercial"—so why must we assume that a competitive courtship
system will not exact its toll also? After all, you can't have everything, as the saying goes.

2. *Random dating is intensely competitive.*

The only protection the individual has is his (or her) ability
to compete. In some ways random dating closely resembles interscholastic or intercollegiate athletic competition in which each boy
is pitted against every other candidate for a particular position. And
the boys who cannot compete do not play.

Obviously, in any highly competitive social situation, somebody has to lose, and this means that somebody has to get hurt. This
happens every day in our economic system when one business fails
while its competitor across the street prospers.

In most competitive systems, however, there are certain built-
in mechanisms or structures by which the less successful competitors
can protect their personalities from ego damage. For example, a boy
who gets hurt and cannot play football may become the manager or
the team trainer; another boy takes up the saxophone and becomes
the most popular musician in school; another one forgets about
athletics and becomes an honor student. Actually, in high school or
college, there are a number of routes through which young people
may meet their basic needs, only one of which is represented by
dating. All of us know busy and happy young men and women who
have had very few, if any, dates during their school years. And on
the adult level we all know adult men and women who have
achieved happiness and success without ever marrying. If these alter-
natives were not in our competitive society, the system would not
work, because too many people would get hurt.

In random dating, the ones who suffer ego damage are those who cannot renounce dating as a basic goal, or those who cannot give up a particular person as the desired dating partner—that is, who "carry a torch" for someone not interested. These persons are too inflexible to utilize the alternate means of achieving status and satisfaction. Such persons are poorly equipped for successful participation in any competitive social system. Their plight is unfortunate, but what can be done to help them is not clear. Good counseling may be helpful in some cases, while in others the person seems to have to "grow out of it"—that is, to suffer until he gradually acquires insight.

3. *Random dating is essentially trial and error.*

By this we mean that intelligent or rational planning of effort is at a minimum. Dates are usually not accepted with persons known to be incompatible, but this is not usually known until a trial and error date has been experienced. Thus, by its nature, the random daters are doomed to some rather dull and frustrating evenings. This is one of the obvious advantages of going steady: we can predict in advance the sort of evening we will have.

Some of the trials can be rather severe as most of us know from personal experience. A young woman once told us of a harrowing experience she had during World War II. She met a handsome officer on a train and it happened that he was stationed near the city where she worked. He asked if he might take her to dinner the next week end and she agreed. They had a delightful dinner and then went for a drive in his car. When the car stopped, the girl was expecting a mild attempt at necking, but instead the man became almost violent as he attempted to make love to her. Finally, she found a large flashlight in the glove compartment and hit him on the head with it. At this point, the man seemed to regain his self-control and drove her home.

Not all the trials are of this nature, but some of the long boring evenings can be memorable in themselves. We once spent about three hours listening to a blind date describe her recent appendectomy. She went into such detail that by the end of the evening we felt that we could perform the operation ourselves.

"I don't exactly understand what you do as an electronics engineer. Could you explain it in dollars and cents?"

THE SATURDAY EVENING POST

It should not be assumed, however, that such experiences, harrowing as they may be, are without value, for in this way we gradually learn with what kinds of people we are compatible and vice versa. It may be a hard way to learn but it seems to be effective.

4. *Random dating involves relatively little parental supervision.*

Since marriage seems so far off, and since they hardly know the dating partners, parents tend to exercise very little control at the random dating stage. Certain hours will be specified, and some nights may be designated "no date" nights, but the supervision hardly goes beyond this. In the smaller community, parents may have a "black list" of certain boys and girls they do not approve of as dates, but this is not always effective in these days of the automobile and the drive-in theater.

Some parents, however, do go beyond this. One of our students from a devout Jewish family told us that his parents had always required that he date only Jewish girls. His parents reasoned that he might fall in love at any time and thus it would be safer if even his casual dates were Jewish. Interesting enough, the boy accepted this point of view and was willing to co-operate. He did report, however, that as long as his dates were Jewish his parents did not exercise any additional supervision.

There is a certain obvious danger in parents permitting young people to date outside of their own cultural group during the random dating stage. It could happen, and it *does* happen, that they might meet a person with tremendous appeal, and then the parents would have to decide whether to oppose the relationship or let it run its course. From the cross-cultural studies we have seen, most societies do not permit courtship between persons considered ineligible to marry each other.[12] Our society, however, is in a very peculiar position in this matter, because *theoretically* all our various ethnic, religious, and economic groups contain legitimate marriage partners.[13] The marriage laws support this proposition, as do our basic democratic and Christian values. This means that the role of parents as dating censors is not an easy one, and in the last analysis their best chance of getting a marriage they approve of is to rely on the long years of family conditioning the girl or boy has experienced, as Bates has shown in his valuable study of the role of parents in courtship.[14]

However, there seem to be numerous cases in which random dating outside the social world of the family does eventually lead to marriage, much to the discomfort of the parents. We suspect that in most of these cases the basic parent-child relationship is not very good, but we have no research data to support this theory.[15]

5. *Random dating sexual standards are relatively strict.*

Persons unacquainted with American courtship customs might get the impression that American young people neck and pet rather indiscriminately, since they date so many different persons, but this would be erroneous. The fact is that the *more* persons the average boy or girl dates the *less* necking and petting they engage in, at least in regard to *extent*. The necking and petting problem in American courtship is not located primarily in the random dating stage but occurs in the later stages: going steady, pinning, and engagement.[16] It is not difficult for the normal American girl to resist the advances of a casual date whom she scarcely knows; only a "promiscuous" girl would engage in heavy necking or petting on a random date. The real problem arises when a girl gets to know a boy well, becomes fond of him, perhaps thinks she is in love with him. But the very nature of random dating tends to eliminate feelings of this sort.

Parents seem to sense the sexual safety of random dating; at least they usually oppose young girls seeing the same boy too often. Their policy seems to be that there is safety in numbers.

When we say that the sexual standards of random dating are relatively strict, it is not implied that necking is taboo at this stage. Perhaps the first date may be more or less "neckless," but later dates tend to show a progressive amount of necking (kissing and embracing); however, a taboo still operates on petting in the random dating stage.

As the couple get to know each other better, there comes a stage in their relationship when they are in a sort of twilight zone between random dating and going steady. When a decision is made to go steady, a new and deeper relationship usually develops, and it is at this stage that necking sessions become prolonged and more intensive. For some persons, petting may develop at this point also, although more conservative couples would reserve petting for pinning and engagement. Kinsey does not give us data of this nature and we know of no research to date (1957) that does. Our analysis is based largely on data from middle-class college students, but the Kinsey research indicates deep social class differences in sexual norms, with the lower-income groups reaching complete sexual relations at younger age levels.

Basically, necking and petting codes specify that *what* is permitted depends upon *whom* one is with: in other words, how *deep* the relationship is.[17]

6. *Random dating is a recurring experience.*

By this we mean that it is not a dating stage one passes through once and never experiences again, as is often the case with pinning or engagement. The reason for this is that random dating constitutes a sort of dating pool, containing all those persons not committed to a dating partner at the moment. In this sense random dating is like our families: we can always return there when we have no place else to go.

As a learning situation, then, random dating has several chances to influence most of us, and at different stages of maturation. A girl of sixteen, for example, may engage in random dating for a few months, then begin to go steady, after which she may return to random dating temporarily. By this time, she is a year or so older, has had considerable dating experience, and is in a position to view herself in random dating in a new perspective. This is also true of going steady, of course, but is less true of pinning and engagement. Because of this recurring nature of random dating we are inclined to attach considerable importance to it as a part of the individual's total dating experience.

7. *Random dating is usually the individual's first real experience with dating.*

In the Herman study cited before, an attempt was made to construct a dating profile for the high school years, using a sample of 192 state university students. The findings were as follows:

TABLE 3
GOING STEADY IN HIGH SCHOOL

	Going Steady	Total Sample—192
Freshman Year	29	
Sophomore Year	50	
Junior Year	97	
Senior Year	131	

In these totals, we have taken the liberty of combining two of Herman's categories, the one labeled "Often dating the same person" and the other "Going steady." But even after this combination, going steady does not become numerically dominant until the Junior and Senior years of high school. In other words, random dating seems to be the *first* dating experience for most of these young people. Of course, a good many of them (104) "rarely dated" in their Freshman year, and a good proportion (52) were "rarely" dating in their Sophomore year, but it still seems that their first encounter with the courtship system is at the random dating level.

If our analysis of this point is correct—and this would make a good question for class discussion—then it seems to follow that these first or early dating contacts have unusually strong impact. Psychiatric theory of personality development stresses the early years of life, perhaps unduly so, and it may also be true that the first few *dates* (not years) may have repercussions far beyond those of a year or so later. There is no systematic research on this point, to our knowledge, but case studies indicate that there may be some truth in the above proposition. If so, this too indicates the importance of random dating in the individual's total courtship experience.

In summarizing this part of the discussion, we have been attempting to point out the basic nature of random dating, why it is the way it is, and its role in the total courtship system.

We are now ready for a few more basic points before bringing this analysis to its conclusion.

Skills Essential in Random Dating

The student has a natural interest in learning how he or she can improve his or her success in the courtship system (this is purely of academic interest, we trust, to the married students). For this reason, a few observations are made below which may or may not be helpful. They are based primarily on fifteen years' experience in courtship and marriage counseling rather than systematic research.

1. *Emotional self-control is most essential in random dating.*

Some persons do not have this ability to control emotion; they fall very easily, and they reveal their feelings readily. Thus, in a dating stage that resembles a poker game, they are at a disadvantage with most of their opponents (dating partners). They are often exploited and hurt.

Notice that emotion, even deep emotion, is appropriate in the later stages of courtship, but it is out of place in random dating. Girls who are dropped suddenly by boys while random dating will often find that the basic reason was that the boy felt that the girl was becoming too serious, or that the relationship was getting too involved.

We recall the sad story of a Freshman girl who fell "horribly in love" (as she put it) with a Senior boy with whom she had had a few casual dates. This particular Senior was a well known character on the campus, so much so that none of the Senior women would date him at all.

This girl lost weight, lost sleep, couldn't study, and finally flunked out of college—and all this as the result of a few dates with a young man whom she scarcely knew. To the girl this all seemed to have the air of a tragic love affair, but to other persons it seemed only to be a foolish one.

2. *The person who cares least will dominate the relationship.*

Many years ago Waller pointed this out in his analysis of what he called "the principle of least interest." [18] According to this principle, the party who is *least involved* (cares less) is in a position to dominate and possibly exploit the other party. This applies at all stages of courtship, but it seems to be especially applicable to the early stages of dating such as random dating or going steady, for at these stages there seems to be a greater likelihood of one person being only superficially involved. Thus, in the engagement stage we expect both parties to be deeply involved emotionally, so that the chances of one person being in a position to dominate or exploit the other should be at a minimum, because both have so much at stake. In random dating, however, one expects the level of involvement to be less equal than in pinning or engagement.

It should be admitted, however, that *complete equality* of involvement is probably rare in human relationships, so that Waller's principle may operate to some extent in *all* dating relationships. If this is true, we would only add *more so* in the case of random dating.

Participants in the courtship system (also married persons) need to regard this "principle of least interest" seriously. If you find yourself involved in a relationship in which you seem to be the only one who cares, then watch out, for that is how people get hurt. Ask yourself these questions: How much am I being asked to give as the price of continuing the relationship? And is it worth it?

3. *Ability to interpret behavior correctly is essential.*

In random dating, more so than in any other dating stage, things are said and done that do not mean what they seem to mean, as every intelligent participant in the system knows. It is like the elaborate joking relationship found in some preliterate societies by the cultural anthropologists. There is the type of patter known as "the line" or "the approach," and it is a highly developed art in our society. It might be compared to the elaborate techniques of the confidence man as described in modern criminology.

In using the line the main goal is to make an impression, to interest the other person, so that further dates can be arranged. In this type of conversation, a person may say, "I think you're a wonderful dancer" when he may actually think just the opposite.

One male student studied by the writer used this approach: he concentrated on Freshmen women and told them glorious stories of his combat experiences in the Marines, although he actually had never served outside the United States. Sometimes he told them that he had contracted an incurable tropical disease while serving in the Pacific and that he only had a few years to live. But his most effective technique was to give a young girl a terrific rush for a week or so and then propose a trial engagement. If the girl accepted the proposal, the pact was sealed with a Marine Corps ring which he said was given to him by a dying buddy.

Does this sound "corny"? Would you think that college girls would fall for this line? Well, they did—at least *some* of them did, for this chap was engaged to three girls simultaneously, one on our campus, one at a nearby teachers' college, and one in his home community.

In this case, admittedly not typical, the ultimate goal was sexual exploitation, and the "trial engagement" device was apparently successful in achieving this goal. In addition to sexual needs, there also seemed to be an enjoyment of the pure thrill of the chase in this young man. In other words, he liked to "live dangerously," and juggling his relationships with three fiancées simultaneously was exciting—as indeed it must be!

In discussing this case with a clinical psychologist who also knew the student well, it was our belief that this man was the type who has a need to victimize women, who enjoys hurting them, psychologically if not physically.

It is not implied that this case is the normal pattern in our society but notice how beautiful the set-up is for such a neurotic or psychopathic personality. It would be hard to design a courtship system better suited to the needs of such individuals.

In the "confidence game," referred to earlier, the victim is often a middle-aged or wealthy widow, with marriage held out as the bait. *The Saturday Evening Post* reports that the national champion in this field was illegally married to 55 women within a few years.[19]

To return to our basic point: the maneuverings, verbal and otherwise, in random dating may be compared to those of a poker or chess game, in which the opponents attempt to conceal their true moves from each other. There is excitement and thrill in the pure art of the game, and only those get hurt who do not know the rules.

During the war, when the writer was serving in England as a personnel counselor in United States Naval aviation, it was obvious that the English girls were not very experienced at playing the American version of random dating. In several cases in which the writer was consulted about courtship problems, most of them involving pregnancy, some very fantastic "lines" had been extremely successful, so that the English girls believed marriage to be assured, when actually the relationship had hardly progressed beyond random dating or going steady by American standards.

4. *In random dating flexibility is of vital importance.*

By this we mean that one must be prepared to give up unobtainable partners, to drop relationships that threaten to become destructive, to switch tactics when old ones seem to be futile. And last but not least, one must realize that dating popularity is but one of the satisfactions of the high school and college years. If you are not handy at random dating, concentrate on other rewarding activities and let the dates come when they will.

Is Random Dating Actually Courtship?

In his classic article, "The Rating and Dating Complex," published in 1937,[20] the late Willard Waller, the pioneer student of the American courtship system, argued that a great deal of dating activity was not courtship at all but a type of "dalliance" relationship, the main object of which was to *prevent* marriage. To some extent, Waller's theory was based on the economic conditions prevailing in the 1930's, when marriage was financially impossible for most college students. There have been deep socioeconomic changes in American society since the 1930's, however, and these seem to have reduced the frequency of the pure dalliance relationship.

Waller defined courtship as follows: "Courtship may be defined as the set of processes of association among the unmarried from which, in time, permanent matings usually emerge." [21] Modern random dating, as we see it, can be considered courtship by this definition, for most random dating partners eventually do marry (but not necessarily the current random dating partner).

Actually, most of the recent studies of courtship in America do consider random dating as real courtship—that is, as a learning experience which eventually leads to marriage. This is the point of view of Lowrie,[22] Blood,[23] Cuber,[24] and Burgess-Wallin.[25] We think Cuber puts it well when he writes: "To be realistic in our day, one must study formal courtship and pre-courtship as one continuous process." [26]

It is perfectly true, as the Lowrie study points out,[27] that a great deal of modern dating is an end in itself, really a new form of mass recreation. But this should not blind us to the underlying goal, which is still *marriage*.

Summary

In this chapter we have been analyzing random dating, in which we have included group dating patterns of the Junior High level. It has been argued that random dating, for better or worse, is one of America's gifts to the modern world, that it remains a basic and important part of our courtship system, and that it is often misunderstood, even by its inventors. Nobody knows how many youthful egos and hearts are banged up in the random dating process, but they probably are numerous. And yet such learning constitutes a basic part of growing up in the United States.

References

1. Reuben Hill, "Courtship in Puerto Rico: An Institution in Transition," *Marriage and Family Living*, 17 (1955), 26–35.

2. See Stuart A. Queen and John B. Adams, *The Family in Various Cultures* (Philadelphia, J. B. Lippincott Co., 1952), chap. 12.

3. This material has not been published as yet.

4. Robert D. Herman, "The Going Steady Complex: A Re-Examination," *Marriage and Family Living*, 17 (1955), 36–40.

5. *Ibid.*

6. Willard Waller, "The Rating and Dating Complex," *American Sociological Review*, 2 (1937), 727–734. See also his text, *The Family* (New York, The Cordon Press, 1938), p. 235.

7. See Samuel H. Lowrie, "Dating Theories and Student Responses," *American Sociological Review*, 16 (1951), 335–340.

8. In John Bartlow Martin's study, *Why Did They Kill?* (New York, Ballantine Books, 1953), it is pointed out that the teen-age boy who committed the murder in this case was "well thought of" by the parents of the various girls he dated.

9. See "The Rating and Dating Complex," cited above.

10. Robert O. Blood, "A Retest of Waller's Rating Complex," *Marriage and Family Living*, 17 (1955), 41–47.

11. See Reuben Hill and Willard Waller, *The Family* (New York, The Dryden Press, 1951), pp. 217–220.

12. We have in mind here Linton's discussions in his *Study of Man* (New York, Appleton-Century-Crofts, Inc., 1936), and George D. Murdock's analysis in his study, *Social Structure* (New York, The Macmillan Company, 1949).

13. August B. Hollingshead has an excellent statement of this point in his article, "Cultural Factors in Mate Selection," *American Sociological Review*, 15 (1950), 619–627.

14. See Alan Bates, "Parental Roles in Courtship," *Social Forces*, 20 (1942), 483–486.

15. Bates seems to believe that this is the case too although his study was not focused on this point. *Ibid.*

16. This statement is based on extensive material from our own students which has not been published to date.

17. This point is stressed in a study by John F. Cuber, "Changing Courtship Customs," *The Annals* of the American Academy of Political and Social Sciences, 229 (1943), 31–34.

18. See his 1938 text, cited above, pp. 275–276.

19. Robert M. Yoder, "A Way with Women," *The Saturday Evening Post,* May 7, 1955.

20. *Op. cit.*

21. *Ibid.*

22. *Op. cit.*

23. See Blood's article cited above, also a more recent study of his, "Uniformities and Diversities in Campus Dating Preferences," *Marriage and Family Living*, 18 (1956), 37–45.

24. *Op. cit.*

25. Ernest Burgess and Paul Wallin, *Engagement and Marriage* (Philadelphia, J. B. Lippincott Co., 1953).

26. *Ibid.*

27. *Ibid.*

Suggested Readings

1. Willard Waller, "The Rating and Dating Complex," *American Sociological Review*, 2 (1937), 727–734. Reprinted in part in Robert F. Winch and Robert McGinnis, *Selected Studies in Marriage and the Family* (New York, Henry Holt & Co., Inc., 1953), pp. 371–380.

2. John F. Cuber, "Changing Courtship Customs," *The Annals* of the American Academy of Political and Social Sciences, 229 (1943), 31–34. Reprinted in Judson T. and Mary G. Landis, *Readings in Marriage and the Family* (New York, Prentice-Hall Inc., 1952), pp. 57–60.

3. Samuel H. Lowrie, "Dating Theories and Student Responses," *American Sociological Review*, 16 (1951), 335–340. Reprinted in Landis and Landis, *op. cit.*, pp. 71–79.

4. Reuben Hill and Willard Waller, *The Family* (New York, The Dryden Press, 1951), chap. 9, "Bargaining and Exploitative Attitudes." This remains the classic discussion of this phase of American courtship.

CHAPTER VI

GOING STEADY

Introduction

According to the Herman study, going steady has become the preferred dating pattern at the high school level.[1] If this is true, then it seems to follow that going steady would also be the dominant pattern at the college level, and research by the writer indicates that this is the case.[2]

The late Willard Waller believed that random dating was the preferred type of dating when he first began to study the system in the 1920's.[3] Although Waller's observations were based largely on college students, it has been generally believed that random dating was also the preferred pattern at the high school level in the 1920's.

To test Waller's thesis, the writer has explored somewhat intensively the dating experiences (or at least the *memories* of such) of parents who have been members of study groups taught by us over the past five years. Most of these persons support Waller: that random dating was the dominant pattern in their high school and college years. They do report that high school Seniors were apt to

120

be found going steady, but not the younger students. At the college level, according to these informants, going steady was likely to be dominant at the Junior or Senior year.

In the dating system reported by these parents for the late 1920's and the 1930's, a girl's popularity was based on *how many* boy friends she had, with some qualitative factors involved, of course. If a girl went to a dance, for example, the success of the evening was based on how many *different* fellows were on her dance program—and these programs became treasured possessions, to be looked at in later years and sometimes to be shown to grandchildren as proof that grandmother was a belle in her day.

At dances today, couples going steady often, or perhaps usually, dance all evening together, joining their friends between dances. If they exchange dances, this is apt to be the exception rather than the rule. The success of the evening, in this system, is determined by how much enjoyment the couple derive from dancing with each other, plus the other events of the evening, but it definitely is not determined by how many fellows ask the girl to dance.

It is interesting to hear the reactions of parents to these modern dancing customs. One mother exclaimed to us: "My heavens! They go to a dance these days and dance *with the same boy* all evening! Why, in my day, a popular girl had a different fellow for every dance. Of course, you had to save the first and the last dance for your date, but that was all. I can't see the way they do it now." This mother was about forty years of age and was upset because her daughter, a Junior in high school, was going steady.

In this chapter we hope to answer the following questions: Why has going steady become the preferred dating relationship? Is this an improvement upon or a decline from the random dating system of former decades? What is the modern going steady pattern? What are the functions of going steady? And, finally, what are the problems related to going steady?

Description of the Going Steady System

The following characteristics seem to be the major essentials of the present-day going steady system.

1. *It begins earlier than it formerly did.*

This means that going steady is experienced as a relationship today much earlier than in the 1920's or the 1930's. High school Sophomores and Juniors go steady, and even Junior High students report some going steady experience.

It is this change that seems to have disturbed parents. They cannot understand why a girl sixteen years old wants to have a steady boy friend.

2. *It is the preferred dating status.*

In other words, this is the goal for most high school and college students, with random dating being relegated to the status of second choice.

In the Herman study, going steady was not actually achieved by the majority of the sample until their Junior year in high school, but this fails to show that the younger persons *wanted* to go steady.[4]

This is another change difficult for parents to grasp because in their courting days random dating was the preferred pattern. The plaintive "But *why* does she want to go steady?" often heard from mothers can be answered best by the reply: "For the same reason that you wanted to date a lot of different boys: it is the dominant dating pattern, the thing to do."

As a matter of fact, students today often report that they have *no choice* about going steady. As one girl told us: "In my high school you either went steady or you didn't go. After a few weeks of maneuvering in the fall, everybody paired off for the year. Sometimes there was a reshuffling at the end of the term, especially if some boy got kicked out of school or joined the service. If you went out with a fellow more than twice in one week, everybody thought you were his steady and nobody else would ask you for a date. Most of the couples broke up for the summer, but come fall we all chose up sides again."

3. *Going steady today is not marriage-oriented.*

In a study of 565 Seniors in an Eastern suburban high school, Daly found that 80 per cent of the group had gone steady at one time or another. About half had started going steady as Juniors and were still dating the same person at graduation. But of this latter group, *only eleven* said they expected to marry this person.[5]

In the Herman study of going steady, using a University of Wisconsin group of students, it was very clear that going steady at the high school level is *not* oriented toward marriage for the vast majority of persons planning on attending college.[6] Since college attendance is becoming increasingly the norm in the United States, it appears that high school going steady is not usually oriented toward marriage.

Unfortunately, parents don't know this. If they did, their blood pressure might be lowered considerably on occasion. Most parents, at least those known to the writer, still seem to fear that every going steady affair will lead straight to the altar.

It is true, of course, that a very small percentage of them *do,* which is one of the reasons why parents can never be *sure* their daughter won't fall in love with her latest boy friend. As one mother told us, with her eyes flashing: "It may be true that only a small percentage of them get married, as you say, but when *the small percentage is my daughter,* your statistics don't do me much good!" To that we could only reply, *"touché!"*

4. *Modern going steady is a combination of going steady and random dating.*

In other words, it is a new type of dating relationship, an invention of the modern era. This is true because it no longer corresponds to the marriage-oriented going steady pattern of earlier decades, and yet it is not random dating either. It is essentially a combination of the two types of relationships.

It sometimes seems to us that the term "random going steady" might describe the new pattern fairly well. The dating is "random" in the sense that almost any "nice" person will do as a partner: very elaborate standards need not be met because marriage

Jerry Marcus

"If this is the way you're going to act every time another man looks at me, I'm glad I found out before we got married!"

is not under consideration. Thus, almost any pleasant person met on a date could serve as a temporary going steady partner, and often does.

At the same time, the pattern is "going steady" in that, for the moment, the relationship is exclusive, with other dating partners being taboo. It is not clear how rigidly this exclusive feature is adhered to; we are all familiar with late dating, for example, in which somebody else comes after the steady has gone home—but at least it is *supposed* to be an exclusive relationship. And yet the system permits other persons to be dated simply by switching partners: one boy terminates his relationship with a particular girl and becomes the steady boy friend of another girl, with a relatively short interval, if any, in between.

These "switches" should not be too painful, as a rule, because the dating partner is not usually perceived as a potential marriage partner, at least not at the high school level. As we shall see later, this is not necessarily the case at the college level, where the going steady complex is somewhat different.

To summarize, it seems to us that these four basic characteristics contain the essence of the modern going steady pattern. Before analyzing the functions of going steady, let us pause briefly for a short comparison of high school and college going steady practices.

Going Steady on the Campus

So far, most of our discussion has focused on going steady at the high school level. What about going steady in college?

It seems that the following general statements can be made about going steady at the college level: [7]

1. Going steady in college is much more likely to be oriented toward marriage than is the case in high school. This is the result of the older age level of the college student and his approach to full adult status in the society.

2. Parental opposition to going steady is much less prevalent at the college level, although it is by no means rare. Some parents object to Freshmen going steady even in college, although we suspect that this is often a cover-up of their disapproval of the particular steady.

3. Going steady in college tends to overlap with pinning, especially so on campuses with widespread fraternity membership. On some small campuses with strong fraternity participation, pinning may displace going steady almost completely.

4. Going steady, combined with pinning and engagement, represents the dominant or preferred type of relationship in college, with random dating serving only to tide one over from one steady relationship to the next.

On campuses with unequal sex ratios—usually more men than women—this dominance of going steady severely handicaps the men in getting any dates, as the pool of women is kept at low ebb. This problem is especially noticeable at state universities, such as Ohio State, where the men usually outnumber the women by a vast proportion.

If one had detailed case studies, it might very well be found that there are two distinctly different going steady patterns for high school and college. Basically, it appears that the high school variety is a dalliance relationship,[8] at least for middle- and upper-class groups, whereas the college type is marriage-oriented.

Functional Analysis of Going Steady

From the basic theoretical orientation of this book, we are especially interested in analyzing the functions performed by going steady. In other words, we would like to know what part going steady plays in moving individuals from single status to marriage, and also what is the place of going steady in the total American courtship system.

As we have seen, there are really two types of going steady, that oriented toward marriage and the purely temporary or dalliance type. Let us consider the marriage-oriented pattern first.

Judging by the work of Daly and Herman cited earlier, this type of going steady appears to represent only a small minority of high school going steady relationships for students planning on a college career. Such young persons are not considered to be ready for marriage, either by themselves or their parents. Their academic plans take precedence over marriage, and this tends to force them into dalliance or temporary dating relationships. To be sure, there is a trend for students to marry while still in college, but except for veterans of military service, the trend is still very weak.

In a few situations, however, going steady *does* become marriage-oriented among middle-class and upper-class youngsters. The writer has analyzed a number of these "deviant" situations and has arrived at the following hypotheses concerning them:

1. Going to college, or pursuing the career suggested by the parents, has no real meaning for the boy or girl or both, so that they are not actually college- or career-oriented but are *marriage-oriented*. Usually, it is the parents who are college-oriented and not the boy or girl. Viewed from this perspective, these young people are very similar to those from lower-income levels: high school graduation marks the height of their educational ambition and they consider marriage the next step.

2. The basic relationship between the young person and one, or both, of the parents is not very good. In these cases, the boy or the girl may wish to marry early in the hope of escaping an unpleasant home situation; or to marry early to spite the parents; or be anxious to marry to fill an emotional void created by disturbed family relationships. This type of situation seems to be rather common, judging by our counseling records.

3. A very deep and significant love relationship develops that survives all obstacles, whether it be parental opposition or long delay. We once interviewed a couple, then happily married for many years, who said they had "fallen in love" at the tender age of fifteen. Both families, members of the upper class in their community, had regarded the affair lightly, considering it a case of "puppy love." But it survived all through prep school and two years of college, at which point the parents decided that maybe this was "the real thing" and approved the marriage. Today, almost two decades later, this couple seem to have been "made for each other." Their friends consider them to be an unusually happy married couple.

4. The boy is well known to the girl's family, unusually

well thought of by them, so that a marriage-oriented type of relationship is not seriously objected to. In some of these situations, the two families have known each other for years, so that both families find the relationship easy to tolerate.

It seems to the writer that the four types of situations described account for most of the marriage-oriented going steady relationships among middle- or upper-class young people in high school. For this group, going steady serves the same functions that pinning does on the college level: it is a sort of "engaged to be engaged" relationship, testing whether or not the couple are compatible enough to consider marriage.

At lower income levels, going steady appears to lead rather directly to marriage, seeming to serve the functions of engagement. A large proportion of these young people are not able to complete high school, either for economic or other reasons, and they assume adult roles in the community at an early age: they enter the economic system early, they marry early, and they become parents early. For these low-income young people, the courtship system described in this book hardly exists. It becomes just another part of our civilization that they experience largely by means of the movies, television, and the pulp magazines. To our knowledge, no adequate studies have ever been made of courtship at these "lower lower" class levels, except by novelists such as James T. Farrell in his Studs Lonigan series of novels.[9]

In the second type of going steady, that of a dalliance nature, the relationship is not intended to lead to marriage. It usually results in another going steady affair, and *eventually* one of these relationships will produce an engagement. There is no limit to the number of times one may go steady, nor is there, apparently, any real limit to the length of time a going steady affair may be allowed to run. At a panel discussion on dating, the writer heard a high school girl, a Senior, report that she had gone steady with a boy all through high school but that they had no particular plans for marriage. The audience seemed to think this a bit too long for such a relationship but the girl defended herself vigorously.

Just because these relationships are not oriented toward marriage, one should not assume that they are nonfunctional in the courtship process. On the contrary, they perform a whole series of functions, all of which are important both to the individual, his family, and the larger society.

Since this type of going steady is really a combination of random dating and going steady, it follows that the functions tend to overlap those of random dating. It seems logical to assume, however, that the learning process in going steady is more *intensive,* although less *extensive.* For example: one would not get to know as many different members of the opposite sex while going steady, but the ones known should be experienced on a deeper and more complete level. It is for this reason that some of our keenest students of American courtship, such as Evelyn Duvall and Reuben Hill,[10] have contended that a few going steady experiences are better preparation for marriage than a host of random dating relationships. These observers believe that random dating is too superficial to teach us much about people.

The writer has already presented a defense of random dating in the preceding chapter, so it only seems necessary to point out here that each stage of courtship involves a different type of learning, both about ourselves and other people, and that each stage has a contribution to make toward our preparation for marriage and adult life.

Basically, going steady represents the first tentative step toward marriage—a very short and uncertain step, to be sure, but one nevertheless. It involves a somewhat deeper exploration of the other person as a human being, of his family, his unique set of characteristics, his hopes and dreams. In this exploration process, we are exploring ourself too: what I am, how my family differs from his, etc.

The necking process illustrates this exploration well—perhaps too well. The couple begin with a superficial kiss, and then gradually, as they get better acquainted, they acquire more detailed knowledge of what the other person is. A girl will find that some boys offend her with their love-making attempts, whereas another boy makes it seem enjoyable.

Unfortunately, in some going steady relationships this is about the only kind of mutual learning that seems to take place. But in the more constructive situations, the systematic exploring covers much more than just the human anatomy.

At its best, random going steady seems to have the following advantages over pure random dating:

1. It reduces, at least temporarily, the competitive pressure in dating, thus producing a more relaxed dating atmosphere.

2. It assures the partners of a date at all times, reducing the insecurity prevalent in random dating.

3. It permits the partners to get to know each other much more realistically than random dating usually does.

4. It provides some training in the norms required later in monogamous marriage: loyalty, faithfulness, honesty, etc. This may be idealizing going steady, but at least these virtues seem to get more use in going steady than they do in random dating.

In summary, our functional analysis of going steady indicates that this represents one of the basic innovations of the American courtship system, and that it plays an integral part in preparing the individual, not only for marriage, but for adult life in general.

Case Study of Going Steady: The following case has been under observation by the writer for several years. Most of the persons involved have been interviewed by us at least once. It is our belief that this case illustrates many of the problems, and also the values, of going steady today.

In this situation, the girl, whom we shall call Helen, began going steady with a boy, whom we shall call Ralph, in the second year of high school, much to the discomfort of the girl's mother. The couple continued to date all through high school, but not always on a going steady basis.

Helen's mother struggled, in a quiet and refined middle-class way, to break up the relationship, or at least keep it from being exclusive of other boy friends. When we asked her why she objected to the relationship, she replied: "Oh, Ralph is a nice boy, it isn't that. But Helen is too young to be going steady. We think she should wait until college for that." When we pushed her for more details, she admitted that she was not convinced that Ralph was "the right boy" for Helen.

The daughter's strategy in handling her mother, with whom she had an excellent relationship, was to laugh at the mother's fears and take the position that she and Ralph were just good friends.

Helen's father never seemed much concerned about the matter one way or another.

We did not have an opportunity to discuss the situation with the boy's parents, but they seemed to approve of the courtship.

Finally, high school was over and Helen went off to college, much to the mother's relief, because she felt sure that the daughter would "meet someone" at the University.

Ralph had not planned on going to college but decided to join the United States Air Corps, hoping to find a career there.

When Helen left for college, she and Ralph said "good-by" and went their separate ways. Helen told her mother that the affair was "all over—we parted good friends." The mother reported this to us with obvious relief. During the next few weeks we received from the mother glowing accounts of the boys Helen was dating in college. We learned later that Ralph also visited the campus twice that year, just for "friendly visits."

The first summer after her Freshman year at college, Helen worked at a summer resort where she met "lots of boys," but none of them seemed to have made much of an impression. When we talked with her at the end of the summer, she seemed to have very little enthusiasm for her college work, nor did there seem to be any new "love interest" to replace Ralph.

In September Helen returned to college and seemed well settled in her college career. But one week end late in the fall her parents received a telephone call announcing that she was married —to whom? Ralph, of course. Helen announced that she was dropping out of school to "make a home" for Ralph, who had just been selected for officer training by the Air Corps. The couple seemed to be tremendously happy.

The end of the story is this: the couple now have two children and both of their families are very pleased about the whole thing. The young couple are regarded by their friends as ideally suited for each other. The girl's mother is now enthusiastic about Ralph as a son-in-law. The father, as usual, has no comment.

Discussion of Case Study: It seems to us that the following observations are relevant to this case.

1. This is one of those rare going steady relationships that survived three years of high school and over a year of college, even though the young people came from middle-class families and at least one of them was planning on college. This is what really concerns parents about these youthful going steady affairs: you never know when one of them will become serious. Even though only a very small percentage of such affairs survive until marriage, the fact remains that *some* of them do, and this requires that parents regard each going steady relationship with a critical eye.

2. Why was the mother so critical of this relationship? After all, the boy came from a respectable family, had a good reputation in the community, and was very fond of Helen, as she was of him. In view of the mother's present delight in the son-in-law, why all the fuss earlier?

The writer believes that a social class variable was operating in this case, for the girl's father was a physician, whereas the boy's father was a skilled mechanic with a large firm. In a sense, the girl was dating a boy *below* her in the social status system of this community, and girls usually don't do that in our society. The work of Hollingshead, for example, reveals that Americans girls usually marry *slightly above* their own social position.[11]

Ask yourself this question: if Ralph had been the son of the town banker, or even the son of a prominent attorney or physician, would the mother have been so concerned? We think not. What she really meant when she said, "We are not sure Ralph is the boy for

Helen," was this: she was not sure that Ralph had a very promising career ahead of him.

3. Down underneath, the mother had great ambition for Helen: she was to have a brilliant career at the university, perhaps continue on to graduate school, and eventually marry a distinguished man. And it is true that the daughter *could* have had such a career, judging by her high school record, which was brilliant.

Note, however, that this was essentially the mother's ambition and not Helen's. Actually, Helen's goal was to get married, have a family, and assume an adult role in society. She told us that she considered college to be too much like high school. Furthermore, she felt that through her father and mother she already had the essentials of a good education and that she could continue it herself —an opinion which we shared with her.

4. This mother, in spite of an excellent relationship with the daughter, failed almost completely to understand her. For one thing, she did not see that Helen really had very little interest in college or an academic career. The mother was actually *projecting* this ambition onto the daughter unconsciously.

In addition, the mother was blind to the fact that Helen and Ralph were really very well suited temperamentally for each other. Helen was the big and strong type of woman, the kind that likes a man she can "mother" to a certain extent. Ralph, although strong enough to hold Helen's respect, fitted in well with her needs. They make a good team.

It may be that the mother was confused by some rapid social change in this case, for girls today seem to be increasingly interested by marriage and parenthood, much more so than their mothers of the 1930 era. Helen, for example, hopes to have four or five children, a figure that strikes the mother as "astronomical." Parents are always faced with rapid social change in attempting to understand their children in our society, and this case is no exception.

5. Notice that it was the *mother* who was concerned in this situation. Why the mother? Why not the father? In a recent book

called *In-Laws: Pro and Con,* Evelyn Duvall points out that it is *usually women* in our society who get involved in problems of this sort.[12] Why? The theory is that this is due to the division of labor between mothers and fathers in rearing children in our society. Since the mother spends a greater part of her life taking care of the children, she has more of her life *invested* in the children and hence has more at stake in what happens to them. According to this theory, it is her parental role rather than the fact that she is a woman that gets her involved in courtship problems and other crises affecting the children.

6. And last, but not least, it is interesting to note that this going steady relationship has a happy ending, even if it is not the ending originally planned by Helen's mother. Let us ask the question: *why* did this situation turn out well? We believe the answer may be found in the fact that Helen had a good relationship with both of her parents, and having this, she had absorbed their basic values, so that her courtship was essentially on a sound basis. She *knew* that they would learn to love Ralph, just as she had, because she was their daughter. To her, it was as simple as that. And she turned out to be right.

Problems Related to Going Steady

Perhaps it has been implied in our discussion so far that going steady presents few if any problems. Let us try to balance the analysis by looking at the negative aspects of the modern going steady complex.

Parental Opposition

We might as well face it: most parents do not approve of youngsters in their teens, or even later, going steady. This opposition is strongest—"most violent" would be a better description—at the high school level, but it also appears at the college level, especially when the girl or boy is a Freshman.

Rightly or wrongly, parents are more enthusiastic about random dating at the younger age levels than they are about going steady.

The writer has investigated this parental opposition rather thoroughly during the past several years while teaching parent education classes. At its deepest level, this opposition is based on fear that certain things will happen to the son or daughter. These fears seem to be as follows:

1. *Pregnancy.*

Parents are worried about the sexual problems created by going steady, being firm in their belief that random dating is far safer from the sexual point of view. They often describe the case of some "nice" girl who became pregnant and then add: "That would never have happened if she hadn't gone steady for two years."

2. *Son or daughter will marry the "wrong" person.*

Parents fear that the youngster will not "look around" enough; that he will fall in love with "the first person he goes with"; that he will "marry too young"; that he might marry somebody "not suited for him."

It is our belief that often the parents are not so opposed to going steady as they claim to be but that they actually disapprove of the particular going steady partner. The following case illustrates this point. A certain mother complained to us that her daughter, a Freshman in college, was going steady. We asked why this was considered a problem. "She's much too young. Her father and I think she should date different boys for at least another year or so." The parents did not try to prohibit the girl's seeing the boy— middle-class parents are more subtle than that—but they used various devices, well known to young lovers, to discourage the relationship. But a few months later, after the affair had been broken up, the mother reported, with obvious joy, that the daughter was going with "the most wonderful fellow!" "Not *going steady?*" we replied.

The mother said yes, they were going steady. She seemed immensely pleased.

Now, in all fairness to this mother, it must be admitted that of the two boys (both known by the writer), the second is a much more impressive person and much easier to contemplate as a prospective son-in-law. But our point is this: these parents were actually not opposed to going steady but lacked enthusiasm for the particular boy friend.

Here is another illustration: we recently led a discussion of dating problems for a Junior High group and were somewhat surprised to find a fifteen-year-old girl, daughter of a very prominent family in that community, to be going steady. Futhermore, she had already dated this boy steadily for a year, having begun in the eighth grade.

At this point we made the following comment to ourselves: that this girl's parents would have permitted such a relationship at this age only if the boy came from a prominent family also, and that probably the two families knew each other well.

Further discussion with the girl confirmed this analysis. The boy's family was even *more* prominent than the girl's, and the two families had been friends and neighbors for years.

We believe this case, as well as the preceding one, tends to show that parents are not primarily opposed to going steady itself but are basically concerned about *who* the going steady partner is.

If one continues this line of analysis far enough, it is impossible to escape the conclusion that *alert parents are forced to consider every going steady partner as a potential son-in-law or daughter-in-law.* This seems ridiculous in view of the fact that most of these dating partners will soon disappear, never to darken the door again, but since one of these going steady partners will eventually *have to be* the future in-law (unless the son or daughter never marries) who can tell which one it will be? And for this reason, is it not true, say the parents, that *every* going steady partner must be taken seriously by intelligent parents?

We must confess that the parents seem to have a point here.

It might help if young people would give their point of view some consideration instead of scoffing at it.

Other Problems Related to the Going Steady Complex

1. *Reduction of dating pool.*

It seems clear that the prevalence of going steady reduces the chances of persons least able to compete in the courtship market of having any dates at all. These persons do not score high enough in the dating competition to achieve a steady boy or girl friend, yet their chances of getting even an occasional date are minimized by the prevalence of going steady. In other words, "feast or famine" is the norm.

2. *Limitation of variety in dating partners.*

One of the main advantages of random dating in earlier decades was the great variety of the opposite sex that one could "sample" in a few months of intensive effort. Today, in schools where going steady has become almost compulsory, this variety has been sacrificed. Parents in particular regard this as a real loss but we do not get the impression that their sons and daughters do.

It must be admitted, however, that going steady *does* limit one's opportunity to date very many persons, and it should also be admitted, we believe, that this does have a destructive effect on some young people. The following case from the writer's marriage counseling experience will illustrate how this can happen.

This married woman, still in her twenties, consulted us about divorcing her husband. They had now been married five years, had one child, and she felt that their marriage was basically a failure. There was nothing "horrible" about the marriage, she said, but it just didn't "add up to much." She had lost much of her respect for her husband, their sex life had become routine, and she felt depressed when she looked forward to spending the rest of her life "with this man."

As the story developed, it became clear that this girl had

done what parents worry about so much: she married the first boy she ever went steady with. They had begun dating back in high school, had gone steady all through high school and college, and finally married.

It seems that her parents had always "taken a dim view" of this boy, even back in their high school days, and had urged her to date other boys, all to no avail. They felt that the boy had no ambition, that he did not suit the daughter's personality, and that in general he was a "drip" (to quote her father's words). After the marriage, the son-in-law never did anything to change her parents' opinion of him, and now the wife had come to think he was a "drip" also. She now felt that her parents had been right and that she should have dated other fellows in high school and college.

In a recent study of the courtship experiences of a group of Senior college women conducted by the writer's students,[13] over half of the Seniors interviewed felt that their parents had been correct in their opposition to going steady at the high school level. This finding interests us because it seems to be customary to think of parents as always being wrong in courtship matters.

One Senior girl was explicit about it: "I wasted two years in high school going with a boy I could never possibly have married. My father and mother tried to break it up but I kept going with him until I came to college. Now that I look back at it, I think I was silly for wasting two years on him. All we had in common was a lot of necking." She went on to explain that she felt the two years had been largely wasted because she hadn't "learned very much about men by sticking to one boy that long." In other words, it wasn't that she hadn't *enjoyed* the two years; the regret was that they had not been more fruitful in terms of her maturation in the courtship process.

3. *Sexual problems.*

These have already been touched upon from the parents' point of view. Judging by our discussions with students, it appears that the parents are correct in their analysis, and that going steady does produce more sexual problems than does random dating. To our knowledge there are no good research studies of this question at the present (1956).

Basing our analysis on case material and student papers, it appears that the sexual defenses of the average American girl, the so-called "nice" girl, work best against casual dates and are less effective against boys she knows well. In other words, she can cope well with the advances of the stranger, but her friends are much harder to resist.

It seems that sexual conquest with a "nice" girl is a matter of gradual involvement: each night, each week, each month, the relationship becomes a little more intimate, until finally the possibilities are more or less exhausted. If this analysis is even half correct, it can readily be seen that some severe necking and petting crises could be reached in a long going steady relationship. Burgess and Wallin, as well as Terman, have shown that this *is true* for at least half, and probably more, of our engaged couples.[14] It may very well also be true of at least *some* of our going steady couples. It should be made clear that we are not implying that this *has* to happen. The argument is merely that the *chances* of its happening appear to be greater in going steady than they are in random dating.

Summary

In this chapter the argument has been advanced that the going steady complex has displaced random dating as the preferred dating relationship for American young people, both at the high school and the college level.

It has also been argued that this modern going steady is really a new type of dating pattern, combining certain features of random dating and the older version of going steady.

Although this development has not been without its problems, the writer has supported those observers who believe that this change represents essentially an improvement in the American courtship system.

References

1. Robert D. Herman, "The Going Steady Complex: A Re-Examination," *Marriage and Family Living*, 17 (1955), 36–40.

2. This statement is based on approximately 200 student papers describing courtship at the college level during the period, 1950–56.

3. See his classic article, "The Rating and Dating Complex," *American Sociological Review*, 2 (1937), 727–734.

4. *Ibid.*

5. Maureen Daly, *Profile of Youth* (Philadelphia, J. B. Lippincott Co., 1951), p. 30.

6. *Op. cit.*

7. The following statements are based largely on the student papers cited above.

8. In our use of the term "dalliance," we differ with Waller's use in that we consider these nonmarriage-oriented relationships as true courtship, that is, as part of the total process leading up to marriage. For Waller's point of view, see the article cited above.

9. James T. Farrell, *Studs Lonigan* (New York, Modern Library, 1938).

10. See Evelyn Millis Duvall and Reuben Hill, *When You Marry* (Boston, D. C. Heath & Co., 1953).

11. See August B. Hollingshead, "Cultural Factors in Mate Selection," *American Sociological Review*, 15 (1950), 619–627.

12. Evelyn M. Duvall, *In-Laws: Pro and Con* (New York, Association Press, 1954).

13. This study was made by Janet Layman and Barbara Van Epps. Their sample was a randomly selected group of Senior women at a private coeducational liberal arts college in the Midwest.

14. See Ernest W. Burgess and Paul Wallin, *Engagement and Marriage* (Philadelphia, J. B. Lippincott Co., 1953), chap. 11 for a review of this data.

Suggested Readings

1. Maureen Daly, *Profile of Youth* (Philadelphia, J. B. Lippincott Co., 1951). This excellent study contains data on approximately 1,500 high school boys and girls from the major regions of the United States.

2. Robert D. Herman, "The Going Steady Complex: A Re-Examination," *Marriage and Family Living,* 17 (1955), 36–40. The writer served as faculty adviser of this study while teaching at the University of Wisconsin.

3. James H. S. Bossard, *The Sociology of Child Development* (New York, Harper & Bros., 1948), chap. 21, "The Role of the Peer Groups." Although this is not primarily a discussion of dating, it is an excellent analysis of the role of the peer group in modern society, and that is very pertinent to our problem.

4. August B. Hollingshead, *Elmtown's Youth* (New York, John Wiley & Sons, 1949). Part II, "The Social Scene," and Part III, "The High School Students," make excellent readings for most students, and the material is closely related to our discussion.

CHAPTER VII

PINNING

Introduction

It has been observed in an earlier chapter that the American courtship system provides an amazing variety of dating relationships. In this chapter we are going to examine "pinning," a dating stage in which the couple are neither going steady nor engaged but somewhere in between.

The "pinning complex" may not be highly developed on all college campuses, and is usually not very prominent at the high school level, but in its fully elaborated state, it exists as a basic and integral part of the courtship system.

As far as the writer can discover there has been very little, if any, systematic research on pinning. In the magnificent study of engagement by Burgess and Wallin, for example, covering 819 pages, there is scarcely a mention of pinning,[1] and this seems surprising in view of the close relationships between these two stages of the courtship process. In view of the lack of research data on the subject, it will be necessary to rely on case studies and descriptive material for our analysis.

Description of the Pinning Complex

In its purest form, pinning is a courtship status that is best described as "engaged to be engaged." As such, it is designed for couples too involved for a mere going steady relationship and yet not ready for a formal engagement. The pinning part of the complex refers to the fact that the girl consents to wear the boy's fraternity pin as a symbol of their relationship. On some campuses, usually the smaller ones, the event is noted in the society column of the college newspaper and very often the girl is serenaded by the young man's fraternity brothers. Thus one can see that there is an actual pinning complex, composed of a rather elaborate set of behavior patterns.

As described above, pinning seems to be limited to those college men who belong to Greek letter societies but this is hardly the case. The fact is that any number of "sacred" objects can be used to symbolize a pinning relationship: varsity athletic awards of various kinds, class rings, keys and pins awarded for membership in honorary societies or other organizations, etc. The main requirement of any object used for pinning is that it should have deep significance for the owner, so that his willingness to allow the girl to wear it indicates how much he thinks of her. During and after World War II, it was a common experience to see girls wearing military symbols to signify a sort of pinning relationship, the "wings" worn by pilots being ideally suited for this purpose.

At this point it should be clear that pinning may be found at the high school and prep school level also. When the writer was a high school student, several centuries ago, a girl was especially honored if she could persuade some athlete to allow her to wear his varsity athletic sweater, and when this was accomplished, they were considered to "be in love." Since they were not formally engaged, it appears that this was essentially a pinning relationship.

Some high schools and prep schools, of course, have fraternities and sororities, and in such schools the pinning complex appears to resemble that of the college campus.

One of our students who attended a high school in which fraternities were prominent has described the pattern as follows:

In our high school, fraternities and sororities dominated the social life of the school, just as they do on this campus. All, or almost all, of the prominent students belonged to Greek letter societies. We had pledges, "hell week," dances, and all the rest of it. Some of the groups even maintained club rooms in town, although this was against school regulations.

At this school, a fellow always "planted" his fraternity pin when he thought very much of a girl. Usually, this just meant that they were going steady, but sometimes they had a secret understanding and considered themselves engaged.

We didn't have serenades because the cops wouldn't stand for it—the singing was too bad, I guess—but we did have a ceremony to celebrate a "planting." This consisted of the fellow and his girl, plus a lot of his fraternity brothers, going to our favorite hang-out, where the pinning was announced and the fraternity "treated" the house. That was always a big night.

In a pinning relationship, both partners are supposed to enjoy exclusive dating privileges in a manner similar to that of engagement: it is considered a rather serious offense to be caught dating anybody else, more so than in a going steady relationship. In some cases it seems to be customary for the girl to consult her parents before accepting a pin, but our observations lead us to suspect that this is most often the case of Freshmen or Sophomore women.

Pinned couples appear to spend a lot of time together: they often study together, meet between classes, and attend social and athletic events together. In all these respects, their behavior resembles very closely that of engaged couples.

It would seem that pinned couples would tend to form their own social groups, just as married couples on the campus do, but the writer has been unable to confirm this.

There is every reason to assume that pinning develops its own necking and petting norms, but nobody seems to know what is "par for the course," as one of our students put it. On purely theoretical grounds, based on what we know about engaged couples, one would expect to find intensive necking, supplemented by some extensive petting, but not much beyond that.

There are almost endless local college folkways associated with pinning. At some schools, for example, there is a ceremony by which the boy's fraternity pin is "chained" to the girl's sorority pin. This, apparently, makes the tie more binding.

On another campus, according to one of our students, the exact position of the boy's fraternity pin on the girl's blouse or sweater signifies the depth of their pinning relationship; his pin is normally worn below her sorority pin, but on this campus the girl would wear his pin at the same height as her pin if they were *engaged*.

There are undoubtedly other local and regional practices related to pinning of which we have no knowledge.

Different Types of Pinning

In a panel discussion devoted to pinning on the college campus,[2] the group agreed that there are actually *four* different types of pinning relationships: "random" pinning, going steady, engaged to be engaged, and engaged. Each of these will be discussed briefly.

1. *Random pinning.*

This is pinning at its worst and means essentially nothing, except that either the girl or the boy is being exploited. This type of boy seems to carry an ample supply of pins or rings in his pocket and "plants" one every time there is a full moon, if not more often. His aim may be sexual exploitation but in some cases he is attempting to meet certain emotional needs of an immature nature.

Girls who participate in this type of casual pinning may be trying to justify liberal necking and petting practices, or they may be trying to impress their associates.

Needless to say, this type of pinning can seldom serve any constructive purpose, although it may be useful for other ends.

2. *Going steady.*

In this type, pinning merely represents a going steady relationship that has been symbolized by a pin or other object. Most likely, this would be more common at the high school level but it also is found on college campuses.

There are no particular problems in this type of pinning as long as the dating partners define the relationship correctly; but if one or both of them are confused about the nature of their dating status, numerous problems could develop.

3. *Engaged to be engaged.*

In this, its purest form, pinning has come into existence as an intermediate stage between going steady and engagement. As such it seems to the writer to meet a real need, as will presently be shown.

4. *Engaged.*

In this fourth type, pinning is often a cover-up for a secret engagement, usually in situations in which one or both sets of parents are not willing to approve a formal engagement. In a sense, pinning then becomes an informal type of engagement and serves to supplement the formal engagement system.

Functional Analysis of Pinning

From a functional point of view, pinning has evolved as a form of trial engagement, an engagement less formal and less rigid than the traditional engagement, and one especially well suited for young people of college age. As more and more of American youth have gone on to college, pinning has developed as part of the collegiate subculture, defining a new stage in courtship between going steady and engagement. As such, it enriches the courtship system by making it possible to define dating relationships not adequately defined by going steady or engagement.

Case Study of Pinning

In this situation, the young man was a Junior in college when he met the girl, who was then a Sophomore. They went steady for one semester, at the end of which they seemed to be deeply in love. At this point they wanted to become engaged but both sets of parents were opposed to this step at that time. The girl's parents felt very strongly that she was too young to be formally engaged (she was nineteen), but they had no objection to her being pinned to this boy, whom they liked very much. The young man's parents were reluctant to see him become engaged until graduation, partly because he was a premed student with several years of postgraduate training ahead of him.

The final compromise was this: they would become pinned until the boy graduated, at which point they would be free to become engaged if they still wished to. The girl's parents felt very strongly that she should not be married until graduation, at which point they would be happy to accept the young man as their son-in-law. Thus their courtship pattern will be somewhat as follows: about six months of going steady, approximately a year of being pinned, and one year of engagement.

The boy's parents like this plan because they feel that it will give the son a year to get adjusted to medical school before he tackles marriage.

In some ways such a long courtship may be a hardship on the young couple, but the plan has certain advantages, one of which is thorough testing of the relationship before marriage rather than after. The other advantage, of course, is the preservation of close and pleasant relationships with their parents, a goal very important to both of these young people.

As we see it operate in this case, the pinning complex has evolved as a device for resolving some of the conflicts of middle-class parents and their children, namely, the desire of the parents to prevent early or hasty marriage, and the desire of their children to move toward marriage when they reach physical maturity, which they have already attained by the time they enter college.

On the deepest level, the conflict resolved by pinning is a conflict between the physical maturation process of the human and social maturation: boys and girls are physically mature at eighteen but are not considered socially mature by middle-class or upper-class parents. And so pinning represents a sort of compromise between the desires of the children and the demands of the parents. In a later chapter on sex and courtship, it will be seen that this same conflict is evident in that area of behavior.

Advantages of Pinning

At its best, when it functions as a type of trial engagement, pinning serves the following purposes:

1. It reduces the frustration level of young people whose parents are unwilling to sanction a formal engagement. It does this by moving the couple out of the going steady stage and into a trial engagement status, thus giving them the feeling that they are one step closer to their goal, which is marriage.

2. It reduces the anxiety level of the parents because they can feel that "after all, they're not actually engaged; they're only pinned."

3. Pinning permits a serious relationship to be tested with less fuss and fanfare than does formal engagement. For one thing, it is not announced by the parents, as an engagement is, nor is it published in the society page of the hometown newspaper, as an engagement usually is. Thus, if it doesn't work out and has to be broken, there is less public reaction, at least on the home front, if not on the campus. In the social world of the school or college,

however, the relationship *is* publicly defined and there are usually repercussions or reverberations when the pin is "lifted" (if the boy asks for it), or "returned" (if the girl requests him to take it back).

It seems obvious that a true pinning relationship cannot usually be terminated without some emotional strife, or without some reaction from the peer group, but the price to be paid for breaking a pinning should be much less than that exacted for dissolving a formal engagement.

4. Pinning, being basically a college dating structure, has the advantage of seeming to be more adult than mere going steady, thus helping the college student to feel that he or she is growing up or becoming more mature. This may seem silly to some readers but this function has been obvious in many of our discussions with pinned couples, who tend to think of going steady as "high school stuff."

Actually, one of the basic needs of the postadolescent or college student is to feel or know that he is moving toward adult status in the society, and anything that serves this purpose constructively is worthwhile. Pinning seems to accomplish this purpose for some couples.

Problems of Pinning

Most of these revolve about the fact, pointed out at the beginning of the discussion, that a pin (or ring or whatever the symbol is) may have *four different* meanings: (1) a random or casual relationship; (2) a going steady relationship; (3) a trial engagement; and (4) an engagement. This ambiguity opens up all sorts of possibilities for confusion, conflict, exploitation, and heartaches.

On the basis of our observations on five different campuses where we have taught for the past fifteen years, it is the writer's belief that pinning produces more courtship problems than does any other type of dating relationship, for the simple reason that it is the least clearly defined. It may mean one thing to the girl and something else to the boy. Furthermore, it may be defined differently by the boy's friends, the girl's friends, by his family, or by her family. The possibilities for confusion and difficulty seem almost unlimited.

Pinning would appear to lend itself beautifully to the male for sexual gain. It is less costly than engagement (he already owns the pin), and it is a lot easier to get out of. Yet it often carries the same necking and petting privileges as engagement, which research has proved to be considerable.[3]

Here is an illustration: while an undergraduate, the writer knew intimately a campus "big wheel" who always planted his fraternity pin on a new girl each fall. Come autumn, his fraternity brothers knew a serenade would be coming up soon. Now, in this case, pinning meant simply this: that this fellow had found a sexual partner for the year. In other words, he would not pin a girl unless she was willing to be intimate with him. In his three years as an upperclass man, he was pinned to three different girls, none of whom he eventually married, but with all of whom he had a sexual affair.

It is interesting to note that in each of the three cases the girl ranked considerably below the boy in the social world of the campus—that is, he was a well-known campus personage and she was not (at least not until she became pinned to him).

It is not implied that this is a typical case of pinning, but neither can it be said that this use of pinning is rare.

Let us suppose that an engagement ring meant four different things: we are *not* engaged, *perhaps* we are engaged, *one* of us is engaged, and we *are* engaged—wouldn't that create havoc? And yet that is exactly the case with a fraternity pin or similar pinning symbol.

Or let us suppose that a wedding ring had four different meanings: we are *not* married, *perhaps* we are married, we are *going to be* married, and we *are* married. What could be more ridiculous? But pinning is in exactly that state in many cases today.

Conclusion

It seems that several observations and suggestions can be made about the pinning complex as it operates today at the college level.

1. It is poorly defined and ambiguous much of the time, thus producing confusion and difficulty. If you are pinned, or about to be, try to "pin down" what the relationship means to you and your partner. And then find out if your friends and your families define the relationship the way you do.

2. Pinning probably works best when it means "engaged to be engaged," or a trial engagement. It could also be called a *pre-engagement*. Unless it means this, it will overlap with going steady or engagement and create confusion.

3. Pinning has very real possibilities for sexual exploitation or for other types of exploitation, and one should be alert to this possible use when pinning is proposed.

4. Pinning is most highly developed in the subculture of college campuses on which Greek letter social groups are prominent.

5. Properly defined and used, pinning meets a real need and serves as a valuable part of the American courtship system.

References

1. See Ernest W. Burgess and Paul Wallin, *Engagement and Marriage*, (Philadelphia, J. B. Lippincott Co., 1953). There is no reference at all to pinning in the index of this volume.

2. This panel discussion of pinning was part of the 1955 Marriage Conference at Beloit College. Four undergraduates participated.

3. See Burgess and Wallin, *op. cit.*, also Lewis M. Terman, *Psychological Factors in Marital Happiness* (New York, McGraw-Hill Book Co., 1938).

Suggested Readings

1. Ernest W. Burgess and Paul Wallin, *Engagement and Marriage* (Philadelphia, J. B. Lippincott Co., 1953), chap. 4, "Going Together." Part of this discussion is concerned with the pre-engagement stage of courtship.

2. Robert F. Winch, *The Modern Family* (New York, Henry Holt & Co., Inc., 1952), chap. 10, "The Adolescent and His Parents." At the point of pinning, the average young person in our society has entered the final stages of the emancipation process, which Winch analyzes very well.

3. Reuben Hill and Willard Waller, *The Family* (New York, The Dryden Press, 1951), chap. 7, "The Sentiment of Love." Since most young persons will be attempting to define love as they move from going steady toward pinning and engagement, this discussion fits in well at this point. It has become a classic in the literature.

4. Ruth Shonle Cavan, *The American Family* (New York, Thomas Y. Crowell Co., 1953), chap. 12, "Social Relationships Preparatory to Marriage." This has an excellent summary of social class differences in dating.

CHAPTER VIII

ENGAGEMENT

Introduction

Our analysis of the American courtship system has now reached the last stage, having traced the dating process through group dating, random dating, going steady, and pinning. In this discussion we shall wish to pose questions such as these: How does engagement differ from the other stages of courtship? What are the functions of engagement? Has the American engagement pattern changed in recent decades? What are the problems involved in modern engagement?

Fortunately, many research data on engagement have been published in the last twenty years and this will be of great help in our analysis.[1] As a matter of fact, engagement is the only stage of the courtship process adequately studied by social scientists to date.

Description of the Engagement Complex

In Western civilization there has existed for a long time a system of betrothal, now called "engagement" in the United States, whereby a contemplated marriage is announced to the community. In Europe, and even in parts of modern America, there has also been a custom of posting the banns, a church notice of intent to marry.

Historically, this public announcement has served a number of useful purposes: it signified the approval of the families concerned, defined the courtship status of the girl and boy, and also gave injured parties (such as other lovers) a chance to take action. Furthermore, it has always carried some protection for the girl in the event of pregnancy, not an uncommon event for engaged couples.

In modern America, with its secular culture, the banns are not necessarily posted in the church, but engagements are announced in the public newspapers, at least for the more prominent families. Almost every Sunday one can read an announcement something like this in *The New York Times* society section: "Mr. and Mrs. Richard Harrison Smyth, II, of Old Westbury, Long Island, and Miami Beach, announce the engagement of their daughter, Anne, to Mr. Roger M. Heldman, III, son of Mr. and Mrs. Roger M. Heldman, of Greenwich, Connecticut . . ."

In large cities the newspapers have room for only a few such announcements and they naturally limit them to prominent persons, but in small towns one can still read the news of most of the engagements taking place.

In addition to the public announcement, which is normally a part of an engagement, it is customary in the United States, even at modest income levels, for the man to give the girl a diamond ring, even though he has to purchase it on credit (which he usually does). Thousands of young wives have had to help complete the payments on the engagement ring after they finished paying for the honeymoon. As a matter of fact, one jewelry store consulted by the writer reports that about 90 per cent of their engagement rings are sold on credit, and amazingly enough, they also report that about *half* of the payments are made by the girl. We suggested to the manager that perhaps the boy gave the girl the money and she simply brought it to the store, but the manager rejected this theory. His theory, incidentally, is that the average girl has always wanted a diamond ring and is perfectly willing to pay for it; all she needs is an excuse to buy one, and this is provided by the engagement.

This store reports that lower-class persons are more apt to splurge on the engagement ring, and that on this level most of the final payments are made by the women themselves.

These patterns are not usually found on middle- or upper-class levels, according to this jeweler, it being customary for the man to visit the store alone, select the stone and the setting, and present it to the woman at a dinner or some other special occasion.

At the lower income levels, according to our informant, the couple usually come in together to select the ring.

In any event, it is a very big day for the average American girl when she can show off her new diamond ring to the girls in the dorm or down at the office. It is a fine old custom, at least for the women, and they usually make the most of it.

Oddly enough, the girl does not give the boy any sort of engagement ring, yet male wedding rings are popular. We are surprised that some enterprising jeweler (of the credit variety) has not dreamed up some sort of engagement ring for the masculine finger.

After the engagement is announced, whether by word of mouth or by the newspapers, or both, it is customary to set a date for the wedding, if this has not been done before, and at this point the girls' friends begin to plan a series of parties to celebrate the happy event and to "shower" her with gifts for her new home. Some of these presents may be on the humorous side, such as the traditional rolling pin with which to discipline her husband, but most of them are eminently practical: sheets, pillowcases, towels, cooking utensils, and the like. We were surprised recently to read in a newspaper an account of a "canned goods shower" for a girl about to be married. This was a new one on us. In our day, there was an old-fashioned idea that the married couple could at least provide their own food if the relatives and friends provided the utensils, but apparently this has changed.

As the time draws near for the wedding, there are more and more parties for the bride, usually extending right up to the eve of the wedding. Sometimes the women play cards at these affairs but a great deal of the activity centers about the engaged girl.

Interestingly enough, very little of this sort of shower or party can be found in the subculture of the male. In some circles, probably the higher-income levels, it is customary to have a "bachelor's dinner" at which the groom says good-by to his single status, but this is actually not very common as far as we can discover.

It is amazing that men have not developed a more elaborate set of "rites of passage" for the engaged man. Judging by the vast male subculture centering around sports such as hunting, fishing, or golf, one can certainly conclude that men are capable of creating all sorts of ceremonies when it suits their purpose. Why, then, haven't they evolved a more impressive set of social events to celebrate engagement and the forthcoming marriage of one of their brothers?

One theory is that marriage means more to women, that it represents the center of their universe, the core of their existence, whereas for the man it is a peripheral interest, secondary to his work or career. If this theory is correct, and we believe it has a great deal of merit, then the elaborate social calendar of the bride is simply the result of the importance attached to the event.

In the case of the man, the banquet celebrating his winning a letter in football or his initiation into a fraternity is usually much more impressive than any affair resulting from his engagement.

Once the engagement has been announced, the new courtship status of the couple produces new attitudes toward them on the part of their families and their friends. For example, the girl's family will now permit the boy to stay later (if this is possible), to give the girl more intimate gifts, and so forth.

In a sense, the engaged couple occupy a sort of twilight zone or "no man's land" in the eyes of the community: they are *almost* married but *not quite*. This produces certain sexual problems for the engaged couple, as we shall see later in the chapter.

Some engaged couples begin to consolidate their financial resources long before the wedding takes place. They may purchase an automobile together, begin payments on furniture they have selected, open a joint savings account, or even begin building a house. In these and other ways it is clear that the behavior patterns of the engaged couple are relatively distinct from those of the pinned or going steady couple. Actually, it seems that the behavior of engaged couples tend to resemble those of newlyweds more closely than anything else.

This, then, is a brief description of what we like to call "the engagement complex." It is undoubtedly somewhat different at the various social class levels, and one suspects that the complex scarcely exists at the lower income levels, where young couples appear to move directly from going steady into marriage. There are also some differences related to ethnic and religious backgrounds, although the writer believes that the main differences are more apt to reflect social class levels.

Functional Analysis of Engagement

From a functional point of view, engagement has been assigned the role of final testing of the proposed marriage. If we assume that divorce is still regarded by most Americans as a tragedy, as the writer does, then engagement is the last opportunity a couple has to test their relationship and make sure, or reasonably sure, that their marriage will stand the test of time—and in modern America, with its average life span of about seventy years, most marriages have to stand up for about fifty years, since the average couple marries near the age of twenty. When one thinks of all the ups and downs a couple may have and very likely *will* have in fifty years, it becomes evident that the testing function of engagement has to be performed adequately if American marriages are to be successful.

Essentially, then, engagement functions as a final screening device, located at the end of the courtship cycle, to determine which couples are capable of living a lifetime together.

Let us see if we can analyze systematically all the things a successful engagement should accomplish in the American courtship system. It is not assumed that *all* engagements perform these functions, for a great many engagements are useless, or almost so. Hence our description will refer to the engagement that actually accomplishes what it is supposed to accomplish.

1. *A deeper and wider exploration of each other.*

We all know that dating can be extremely superficial. You go to a movie, have something to eat and drink (if the boy has any money left), talk about nothing at all, neck a while, then neck a little more, and then go home. As one college girl said to me: "I get so tired of the same old chit-chat—he likes Frankie Laine and I don't; or he thinks Marilyn Monroe is beautiful and I don't; he tells me about his professors and then I tell him about mine. *But it doesn't mean anything. We don't get any place talking like that.* I don't know him and he doesn't know me."

One girl told us recently that she had been dating a fellow for about six months, about twice a week, and that they were still on the chit-chat level. She felt that they hadn't gotten to know each other at all. It was very frustrating, she said.

Obviously, not many couples are still at this stage at the time of engagement, although the writer has interviewed numerous unhappily married couples who were still at this stage *when they got married.* These were couples who either had not had an engagement or had had an unsuccessful one, for one of the functions of engagement is to assure that the couple will know each other thoroughly *before* marriage.

Actually, this is a very difficult function to achieve, for a number of reasons. Most humans are complex and not at all easy to understand. Even the simplest person is amazingly difficult to understand on a deep level, as any psychiatrist will tell you.

In addition to this, most of us *resist* revealing our most intimate selves, even to persons close to us. In a beautiful book, *Gift From the Sea*,[2] Anne Morrow Lindbergh has stated that she doubts whether *any* person ever really knows another person, even in marriage. We are inclined to agree with her, but at least a good engagement should help us to know the other person better.

Psychiatry tells us that some facets of our personality—some of the deepest ones—are often unknown to ourselves, so that we could not tell our engagement partner about them even if we were willing.[3] And this complicates the situation immensely.

Perhaps another reason why it is so hard to know another person well is that our urban impersonal society does not encourage the revelation of our inner person. We pretend to know people well by calling them by their first names and referring to them as "old friends" if we have had two dates with them. Our whole courtship experience, up to the point of engagement, tends to produce essentially superficial or segmental relationships with our dating partners.

This concept of segmental relationship, developed by the social psychologists, is useful in analyzing courtship and marriage. It refers to the fact that in modern society we seldom, if ever, know the *whole* person; instead, our knowledge or experience is limited to a segment or a specialized aspect of the person. This partial or incomplete view of the person results from the fact that we see him only in certain *roles*. My students, for example, usually see me only in my occupational role as a professor, but they seldom see me in some of the other crucial roles: husband, father, son, neighbor, citizen, etc. Thus the average student has a very limited or segmental view of me, much more so than most of them realize.

And I, of course, see most of my class members in only one role, that of student, and my knowledge of them is usually segmental and superficial.

Now, for most purposes in modern society, a segmental understanding of others is all we need: if I know that Mr. *X* is a

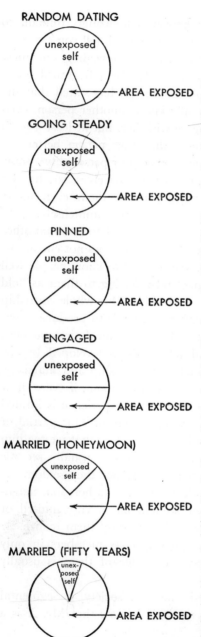

RANDOM DATING

GOING STEADY

PINNED

ENGAGED

MARRIED (HONEYMOON)

MARRIED (FIFTY YEARS)

Figure 5. Schematic Sketch of Personality Exposure at Various Stages of Courtship and Marriage

good plumber, and that his rates are not any more exorbitant than most plumbers, that is all I have to know if I need a plumber. Whether he is good to his mother, or a good sex partner for his wife, does not concern me.

When we *marry* a person, however, this type of segmental knowledge turns out to be entirely inadequate, for the simple reason that *in marriage we live with the whole person.*

This can be stated another way: in courtship, even in most going steady relationships, we expose a very small portion of our total self to our dating partner, whereas in marriage a very large proportion (but not all) of our self is revealed to our husband or wife. Thus, in a sense, one of the functions of engagement is to desegmentalize the relationship, to get the interaction down to bedrock, one might say. And at that level we begin to explore what the other person *really is*—his loves and hatreds, hopes and dreams, fears, family relationships, religious faith, attitudes toward money, ideas about rearing children, and all the rest of it.

In a sense, this function of broader and deeper exploration during engagement has as its ultimate purpose the reduction of the element of *surprise* after marriage, the elimination of the phrase so well known to marriage counselors: "But I didn't know he (or she) was like that."

This matter of exposure of the self can be diagramed as in Fig. 5.

These charts, of course, are just crude guesses as to the amounts of the self revealed, and the speed of exposure or exploration varies tremendously from one couple to another, which is why some couples can get by with a shorter engagement than others. It would be very helpful if we had a test for courtship couples that would show how far or how little this exploration process had progressed at any given point in the dating process. To our knowledge, such a test does not exist at present, although the Minnesota Multiphasic Personality Test has possibilities for this purpose.[4]

2. *A knowledge of each other's family.*

This is implied in the previous function but deserves separate treatment because of its importance. As was pointed out in Chapter III, it seems clear that we marry the other person's family, whether we know it or not, or whether we like it or not.[5] At the simplest level, this is true because we marry a person whose personality is largely a product of his family's influence, one way or another. For this reason alone it is essential for engaged couples to acquire considerable insight into each other's family and the similarities and differences between their families. One can be sure that they will acquire this knowledge *after* marriage, for it seems to be inevitable then, but it would be better if it could be gained before marriage as part of the testing period.

Judging by our marriage counseling experience, this function is not always accomplished during courtship and engagement, at least not by those who eventually consult a marriage counselor.

Most engaged couples *can* acquire this insight by several means: long intimate discussions of their families, visits to each other's homes, vacation trips with their families, and so forth. Attendance at a family reunion is often a revealing way to get to know your future in-laws.

3. *Engagement defines and makes specific the relationship between the couple.*

In most dating relationships, we are seldom, if ever, exactly sure where we stand. Does he love me? Do I love him? Should we get pinned? Is this the time to become engaged? All sorts of questions are forever popping up to make us wonder just where the courtship is going, if any place.

One of the beauties of engagement is the ending of all this uncertainty: we are going to get married. He has given me a ring: see it? We are not sure of the wedding date as yet but sometime in June. It will be in the paper Friday morning.

In the early American courtship system, and in the traditional European system from which ours developed, there was a custom of making the male suitor "declare his intentions"—that is, state whether or not he was "serious" or considering marriage with the girl. A man was usually given a few months to "pop the question," but if he failed to take any decisive action, the question was "popped" at him by the girl's mother or father. Our point in referring to this quaint custom is simply this: that in modern courtship, we need somehow to define now and then at what point a couple stand in their courtship, and engagement does this beautifully. If the girl declines, then the relationship is clarified. If she accepts, that clarifies the situation too.

The problem arises, however, when the affair goes on and on and on *and the man doesn't propose.* Since our customs insist that the woman shouldn't propose, what should she do? Our own belief is that she should be very blunt and ask the man to define the relationship: in other words, declare his intentions. Otherwise, the girl is helpless. She gives two or three years of her courtship period to a man, completely removes herself from circulation, and possibly ends with only a frustrated love affair.

Once, while we were leading a discussion on courtship at a

sorority house, a girl asked us this question: "What do you do when a fellow seems to like you very much, keeps coming to see you month after month, and *nothing happens?*" She went on to say that she was very fond of this chap but that their relationship seemed to be stymied or frozen at a certain level.

Our reply was the one given above: that the girl must "take the bull by the horns" and *force* a definition of the relationship. "But," she replied, "supposing he gets panicky, decides I am chasing him, and quits?" We said that she had to take that chance. After all, they were both Seniors and had been going steady for about a year, and, furthermore, that her very question indicated that she was concerned and confused by the situation. Why not share her concern with the man? If he quits, well and good. From her point of view, it would be better to quit now than a year or two from now.

Actually, as Waller has shown,[6] American courtship has some relationship to bargaining: the couple are selling their personal characteristics in the competitive courtship market, and in any such transaction the purchaser (suitor) has to face a time limit. He or she cannot wait forever to make up his or her mind. It is well to remember that in the traditional courtship system the male relatives or a professional matchmaker did all the bargaining for the young couple, whereas today the girl and boy have to handle these problems themselves. This may be considered an improvement, but it is rough on timid courtship partners.

4. Engagement makes public the plans of the couple.

It is true that this is not always the case because there are secret engagements, but in the vast majority of cases the engagement is announced to families, relatives, friends, and often the entire community through the newspaper.

Let us ask a legitimate question: What is the use of all this publicity? After all, modern marriage is basically an intimate relationship between two persons, so why should everybody know about it? Furthermore, with the increasing trend toward trial engagements, wouldn't everybody be better off if it were kept a secret until time for the wedding? In other words, does the announcement serve any purpose except that of carrying on a tradition?

The writer believes that the public announcement does serve a useful purpose in that it has a sort of sobering effect on the couple. A secret engagement is more apt to be taken lightly, it seems to us, and this is not what the couple need as they move closer to marriage. It requires courage and at least some facing of reality publicly to declare that Helen X and John Y are going to be married. Up to this point, during all their years of going with different persons, they have never been required to define accurately their courtship status, either for their family or the community. Therefore, it seems, a public declaration of intention to marry is a good thing. For once, the families, relatives, and friends "know what the score is," and we see no harm in that, and possibly some good.

Furthermore, it is a gross error in sociological analysis to regard marriage as a purely private matter. As Murdock makes very clear in his valuable study of the family, *Social Structure,*[7] marriage is *always* a matter of public concern in *all* societies. You and I cannot marry without a license from our government, and we cannot dissolve a marriage by mutual consent; this requires a court hearing and a judge's approval.

For any number of reasons, the public is concerned about marriages, and it seems to us that such a grave step deserves some public announcement.

In summary, it seems that the engagement stage in the American courtship system performs a number of extremely vital functions. Let us now turn to the extensive research on engagement and summarize the findings.

Research Findings on Engagement

Since the 1930's, four major studies of marital adjustment have been published,[8] all of which contain valuable data on the role of engagement as a factor in producing adjustment or maladjustment in marriage. One of these studies, *Engagement and Mar-*

riage by Burgess and Wallin, published in 1953,[9] is the most useful for our purposes at this point and will be drawn upon primarily in this discussion. In the later chapters on marital adjustment, the studies by Terman, Burgess and Cottrell, and Locke will be used extensively.

The Burgess-Wallin Research on Engagement

The most intensive study ever made of any phase of the American courtship system, in our opinion, is *Engagement and Marriage* by Burgess and Wallin. In this project, the research team began to study 1,000 engaged couples back in the years 1937–39, with the idea of following the couples through several years of marriage, in an attempt to discover to what degree marital adjustment could be predicted *during the engagement period*. In other words the design of the research involved two studies of the couples: one *before* marriage and another one some time *after* marriage.

As it turned out, 666 of the 1,000 engaged couples were actually restudied during 1940–43, after they had been married three to five years.

In order to keep the group homogeneous, and thus eliminate certain variables that would complicate the study, the sample was limited to couples one of whom must have had at least one year of college. Thus this study, like most of the research on marriage, is based on urban and suburban cases and does not provide any data on *rural* engagement patterns. In addition, it is limited to the middle range of income levels and tells us nothing about engagement practices among the very rich or the very poor.

The methodology of the study utilized an elaborate questionnaire, based on previous research, supplemented by interviews with some of the couples. Actually, about 200 of the 1,000 engaged couples were interviewed before marriage, and about 100 of the 666 studied after marriage were interviewed. *All* the couples received the basic questionnaire.

Before summarizing the findings a few more words might be

added about the limitations of the study. For one thing, the sample is deficient in the number of Catholic couples, as the authors recognize.[10] Also, the couples studied seem to represent extremely mature or long-lived courtships, for the couples had known each other an average of 45 months and had been engaged for 13 months. It is important to keep these facts in mind in interpreting some of the findings.

This study is so elaborate that over 700 pages are required to present its material. In the space available to us, we can only summarize what seem to be the basic findings. It is recommended that the interested student examine the volume and read the sections of most interest to him.

We will summarize in numerical order the conclusions we believe to be of most interest.

1. *Marital adjustment can be predicted at the time of engagement for some couples.*

Actually, all the elaborate studies of marital adjustment during the past twenty years have been aiming at a test or a battery of tests that would predict marital adjustment during the courtship period. Many persons, including some of our students, laugh at such attempts to apply scientific methodology to "love," as they put it, and yet who can tell what will eventually be accomplished in this area? We can remember when most persons were indignant at the idea of requiring a blood test before marriage, but this has come to be commonplace. Lewis Terman, one of the pioneers in the area of intelligence testing, has pointed out that people used to laugh at the idea that intelligence could be measured by a pencil and paper test; yet today such tests are universal in the better school systems, in our colleges, in industry, and in the armed forces. Terman believes that the same development will take place in marital prediction in the next twenty years. As a matter of fact, most placement tests used by high schools and colleges are only about 50 per cent accurate, according to Terman, and he already has a marriage prediction test as good as that.[11]

All the major studies in this area support the finding of Burgess and Wallin that marital adjustment can be predicted with reasonable accuracy for perhaps half of our engaged couples: those scoring in the top or bottom 25 per cent.

Naturally, none of our placement or prediction tests is infallible, and they must always be used by persons with sufficient training and judgment. Essentially, they all are based on a theory of probability: that given the test scores on a certain courtship couple, *the chances are* such and such that it will be a good marriage, or an average one, or a poor one. As Locke points out,[12] the statistical theory is very similar to that used by the life insurance companies in constructing life expectancy rates; the insurance companies do not know *who* will die in any given year, but they can predict very accurately what *groups* will have the highest or the lowest mortality rate during any given year or decade.

And that is exactly what the marital prediction tests are designed to do. This can be illustrated as follows: suppose Couple *X* come to a marriage counseling center and take a marital prediction test. Let us suppose also that they score very high, say in the upper 10 per cent, on the test. What can the counselor tell them? Two things: (1) That the chances of their marriage being a success are very good, that the odds in favor of their marriage are perhaps 10 to 1. But, you say, they still cannot be *sure*, it is still possible that their marriage might fail. This is granted. There is no such thing as absolute certainty in human society. A good friend of ours was recently killed in an airline crash, yet the insurance companies report that commercial air travel is amazingly safe. A student of ours with an IQ of 160 flunked out of college, although *all* the placement tests predicted that he would make a brilliant record. Let us not apply impossible standards to marital prediction tests. If you want absolute certainty, get a crystal ball, or consult a fortune teller, but don't go to a professional marriage counselor.

In addition to telling the young couple into what *risk group* their marriage would fall, the test administrator could give them some idea as to what areas of marital adjustment would *probably* be most difficult for them, because these can be identified by analyzing the test profiles.

Now let us suppose that Couple Y come to the center for a test and that their prediction score falls in the bottom 10 per cent. Can the counselor tell them that they *must* not marry because their marriage will fail? No, of course not. He can only tell them that the *odds* are against them, that perhaps the chances of their marriage's failing are 10 to 1, and he could also indicate the areas of conflict revealed by the test. He might suggest that they extend their courtship a year or so to give them time for deeper testing of the relationship, and then they would have to decide whether or not they wished to go ahead with the marriage.

Actually, this is not too far from the approach used in medicine. We consult a physician and he suggests surgery to correct some condition, on the grounds that an operation is *usually* the most effective treatment for this condition. And he is usually right, but not *always*.

In summary, *all* the studies to date support the theoretical proposition that marital adjustment can be predicted for some during the engagement period, as Burgess and Wallin report. The tests will undoubtedly be refined as more cases are tested, but they are already useful.[13]

2. The best single predictive item is success in engagement.

By "success" in engagement Burgess and Wallin mean the ability of a couple to go through a year or more of formal engagement without serious conflict.

This finding adds up to this: that probably the best insurance policy against divorce in our society is a thorough engagement. If this is true, then couples who decide to skip or bypass this stage of courtship do so at their own risk. Theoretically, engagement *should* be almost indispensable because of the functions it performs, as we saw earlier in this chapter. The Burgess and Wallin research tends to show that this is correct.

3. *Marital adjustment is actually well along in successful engagements before marriage takes place.*

To the writer, this is one of the most interesting findings of this vast research project. Interestingly enough, it supports a similar conclusion reached by Locke in 1951 in his *Predicting Adjustment in Marriage.*[14]

Most young couples, it seems, have a feeling that marital adjustment begins when you marry, and indeed this sounds logical enough, but it is in direct contradiction to the above finding.

The basic meaning of this point is actually this: that a year or so spent in engagement is not wasted time, as some couples seem to feel, because marital adjustment is actually being worked at during this period. This finding also means that engagement in the United States has become more like a trial marriage than has been realized.

It should be made clear, however, that engagements do not *automatically* establish marital adjustment; they have to be functional or realistic to accomplish this purpose. This means that during the engagement period the couple have to explore differences and potential conflicts, that they have to face issues instead of avoiding them.

Sometimes an engaged couple will announce to us: "We haven't had a single argument all year." We are always suspicious of such an engagement and wonder if it is serving its purpose.

4. *For every marriage in their sample there were about two engagements.*

This means that engagement has become much more tentative than it used to be, that it is essentially a trial or testing relationship. It also means, of course, that broken engagements are becoming common.

We can already hear the cry of anguish of the conservatives when they hear about all this. "Isn't it too bad," they will say, "that so many young people are breaking their engagements these days.

It didn't use to be that way." Burgess and Wallin, however, believe that the trend toward more tentative engagements is basically constructive, that it provides several additional months for testing the relationship beyond the former rigid or absolute commitment type of engagement.[15] The writer supports this position.

5. Sex relations before marriage were reported by not quite half of the couples.

This finding supports the earlier data published by Terman in 1938 in his massive study, *Psychological Factors in Marital Adjustment.*[16]

Whether you or I approve of this or not, it seems to be part of the attempt by engaged couples to test the basic adjustments required in a good marriage. Since a separate chapter is devoted to *Sex and Courtship,* our discussion of this finding will be found there.

6. Dating is real courtship.

They reject Waller's theory that most dating is an end in itself and represents a dalliance relationship. Their position, in which we concur, is that *all* dating is essentially courtship or preparation for marriage and was regarded as such by their couples.

7. The romantic complex is not as powerful in modern courtship as some writers believe.

The majority of the couples in this study did not *idealize* each other. They could look at each other realistically, facing the good as well as the bad. This was especially true of the better-adjusted couples in the sample. It is interesting to note that two thirds of the couples having successful engagements reported conflicts and disagreements during the engagement period.[17]

There was some evidence in this study that idealization of the engagement partner is found primarily among persons with inadequate personalities. In other words, the pattern is to "blow up" or enlarge the partner's virtues when we ourselves feel inadequate and need something to bolster our self-conception.

8. *The American courtship system is essentially sound if young people will use it properly.*

In other words, this study, the most elaborate ever made of courtship in the United States, does *not* condemn the courtship system, as so many persons do, but gives it a vote of confidence.

Note, however, that the system is sound only if used *properly*; and what does that mean? Basically, it means that young people *have to participate* in the system if they are to derive any benefits from it. At the moment, as we discuss elsewhere, perhaps a third or even more of our young people are nonparticipants in the courtship system at any given time.

And in addition to participating in the system, it is essential that couples *not skip stages* of the system if they are to gain its maximum benefits. In particular, they must not skip the engagement stage, according to the Burgess-Wallin research.[18]

Although the writer has no systematic quantitative data to cite, he has a theory that a large proportion of the unhappily married and divorced couples in our society bypassed some step in the courtship process, either random dating, going steady, or engagement. At least this seems to be true of a great percentage of the marriage counseling cases studied by the writer during the past ten years. It could be, of course, that a large percentage of the well-adjusted couples *also* skipped stages in the courtship process; the writer has no information on this, but it would make an interesting research project.

9. *Assuming cultural similarity, personality needs are dominant forces determining choice of engagement partner.*

This means that within homogeneous racial, religious, ethnic, and economic groups personality factors determine who chooses whom. Actually this doesn't tell us much, but additional research by Winch has revealed some of the dynamics of the rate selection process.[19] His theory, called the "theory of complementary needs," holds that the tendency for like to marry like (called *homogamy*), accepted by most researchers in the field, is true *only* of *cultural* selection but does not hold for psychological selection. In other words, it is true, as literally hundreds of studies have shown, that most of us marry *within* our own racial, religious, ethnic, economic, and geographic social world, largely because those are about the only persons we meet, but that it is *not* true that we marry within our own psychological world, so to speak. Winch argues, for example, that a shy person will very likely be attracted to an aggressive person and vice versa. A strong personality often seems to gravitate toward a weak or less capable type of individual, and so forth.

If Winch's theory is correct, and he has some convincing data in support of it, then the *how* of what Burgess and Wallin report in this conclusion will be illuminated. One of the virtues of Winch's theory, it seems to us, is that it helps us understand some of the courtships and marriages that seem so odd—the type that bring forth the exclamation, "What on earth did he ever see in *her*!" Winch's theory will explain most of these cases.

10. *That men and women approach marriage with different expectations.*

For example: only 21 per cent of the engaged men thought their wives would have to work after marriage, whereas 30 per cent of the women *expected* to work after marriage.[20]

In response to another question, 72 per cent of the men expected to help with the housework after marriage, but only 48 per cent of the women expected their husbands to assist with housework.[21]

Differences of this sort lead the writer to conclude that the male and female subcultures in our society, discussed in Part III, may be changing at different rates of speed, so that the two sexes may enter marriage with different sets of expectations. If this view is correct, then there seem to be some adjustment problems after marriage revolving around these differences. On the other hand, one might expect that most of these differences would be resolved before marriage.

11. *Women can predict marital adjustment more accurately than can men.*

To us, this is one of the fascinating findings of this study. As an illustration of this point, note the following: of the marriages in this study that ended in divorce, 70 per cent of the husbands had been very confident that the marriage would be a success, whereas only 48 per cent of the wives had been very confident of success. On almost every score, the women were more accurate, or more realistic, in appraising their marital risk than the men.[22]

Furthermore, the girl's family could predict the success or failure of the marriage better than the boy's family, but even this is not all: the girl's best friend could predict the outcome more accurately than the boy's best friend.[23]

As a man, this puzzles us, to say the least. How should one interpret a finding of this sort? Must we fall back on the old bromide of women's intuition? It is relatively easy to understand why the girl's family would have better insight into the future marriage, because they have a much better chance to observe the couple than do the boy's parents. The other findings, however, are not so easily disposed of. It may actually be true, as our folklore insists, that girls think more about marriage, that they spend more time analyzing it. This line of reasoning contends that marriage is a more central goal for women in our culture than it is for men, and that this leads women to spend more time at it, etc.

Whatever the explanation may be—and the writer must admit that his masculine intuition fails him at this point—this finding seems to indicate that men need more guidance or help in approaching marriage than women do. This may come as a shock to the men, but the Burgess and Wallin research certainly points in that direction.

12. *Parents and friends can help predict marital success or failure.*

There seems to be a tendency in our society for young people to assume that parents are always wrong, that their judgment is of little value in such matters as courtship and marriage. The Burgess-Wallin research does not support this view.[24] They find that the predictions of parents, especially those of the girl, are well worth listening to. The same thing is true of the predictions of the girl's close friends.

These findings suggest just one thing: that young couples are foolish to ignore the advice of their families and close friends in evaluating the marital prospects of any given courtship. This does not mean that one must cease dating a person because of adverse comments from family and friends, but it does mean that these comments should be seriously considered. We realize that this may not be fashionable these days, but the Burgess-Wallin research strongly supports such old-fashioned practices.

In summary, we believe it can be said that the Burgess-Wallin study represents the most elaborate research to date on engagement and its relationship to marriage. For this reason alone, their findings deserve serious consideration by all persons attempting to understand courtship and marriage in our society.

Problems of Engagement

As we have seen, no social system or subsystem works perfectly, and this is also true of the American engagement complex. Up to this point we have stressed its positive features, but the time has come to look at its negative aspects. Some of these are obvious, while others are not as easy to see. Let us begin with the obvious ones and perhaps the others will emerge as our analysis proceeds.

1. Our engagement system produces sexual problems.

It seems to be obvious that a considerable percentage of our engaged couples are unable to refrain from sexual intercourse until marriage. Both Terman and Burgess-Wallin found that roughly half of their engaged couples had been having complete sexual relations (not petting) by the time they were married. These were urban samples, of course, also white-collar and predominantly

Protestant. But if we accept Kinsey's basic finding that lower-income groups begin sexual relations *earlier* than middle-or upper-class groups, then it follows that the 50 per cent figure of Terman and Burgess-Wallin would be *low* for the general population. If we took a sample of young couples, for example, who did not go beyond the eighth grade, Kinsey's data would indicate that perhaps 90 per cent of them would have had sexual relations before marriage.[25]

In other words, it seems clear, at least to the researchers, that our system of engagement is incompatible with chastity at the point of marriage. Why is this so?

For one thing, the unofficial sexual code of young people, the one they have evolved and seem to adhere to, has no prohibition on premarital intercourse, but has a severe taboo on casual or promiscuous sexual affairs. In other words, their taboo is based on *with whom* rather than *when*. The basic requirement is that one must be in love, not necessarily married. This emerged clearly in some unpublished research done by the writer at a large university in 1946.[26] To state it bluntly, this sexual code is *relative* rather than *absolute*.

If our analysis is correct, then it becomes obvious that premarital sexual relations would be a distinct possibility, if not probability, for every engaged couple. Even the so-called "nice girl" may have no sexual defense when she loves a man, and by definition all engaged couples are in love. As we stated in an earlier chapter, the sexual defenses of the modern girl are essentially designed to resist the stranger or the casual date, and they work very well indeed under these circumstances, but they are not too much help when she falls in love.

To some extent, this has always been true in Western society. In a study of married couples in urban Sweden, for example, Karlsson reports that over 90 per cent of his sample admitted premarital relationships with each other.[27] Terman found that a lower percentage of his older couples had had premarital relations, but Kinsey believes that the basic revolution in our sexual code took

place during and after World War I. Still, there is some scattered
evidence to support the notion that sexual relations before marriage
for engaged couples have been rather commonplace in Western
society for some time, with the possible exception of groups maintaining strict chaperonage systems.[28]

We still have to face the question, does this high incidence
of premarital intercourse constitute a problem? And if so, *whose*
problem? Our own belief, based on considerable counseling experience with young couples, is that it is *not* a major problem for them,
for the simple reason that they do not adhere to the traditional code,
hence they are not in conflict. Their real problem is centered about
pregnancy and/or the fear that their love might fail.

It is interesting to note that in the Burgess-Wallin study
most of the couples who had had premarital relations said they did
not regret it, and that they would recommend the practice to other
engaged couples.[29] At the same time, the couples who had not had
premarital relations said *they* had no regrets and would recommend
their course of action. There seems to be a complete deadlock here.

Interestingly enough, neither Terman nor Burgess-Wallin
found any very significant correlation between premarital intercourse during engagement (with each other, of course) and subsequent marital adjustment, although there was a slight advantage
in favor of the couples observing the traditional code.[30] Both
studies, however, emphasize the fact that the difference is not statistically significant.

Does this modern sexual code create problems for parents?
Our impression is that parents are primarily concerned about pregnancy and promiscuity and do not concern themselves very much
about the sexual practices of engaged couples. For one thing, if we
believe Terman and Kinsey, the parents of today grew up themselves under the new code, even though they do not like to admit
it, and so it cannot be too shocking to them.

Actually, modern engagement is becoming a sort of trial
marriage. And if young couples wish to make their engagements
realistic, many may wish to test their sexual compatibility too. It is

still debatable, however, whether sexual compatibility can be adequately tested outside of marriage, but we will discuss this question elsewhere.

It is obvious, of course, that modern engagement lends itself readily to the unscrupulous for sexual exploitation, but one doubts that most men would wish to go that far to attain conquests. It seems to us that this problem would be much more common at the going steady and pinning stages.

2. *The problem of couples skipping engagement.*

The writer must admit that he has no systematic data as to the percentage of couples who marry without having had an engagement. One suspects that the figure would be low for the medium and upper range income groups, including all those who graduate from high school, whether or not they attend college. At the extremely low-income levels, the one called "lower lower" in the Warner social stratification system of analysis,[31] we believe the percentage who do not have a formal engagement to be rather high.

It appears that age and previous marital status affect the proportion who skip the engagement stage, judging by case studies made by the writer of second and third marriages by divorced and/or widowed persons. In the typical middle-aged courtship pattern revealed by these case studies, there is a very brief random dating stage, usually not more than a month in length, during which the couple have about one date a week; this is followed by an intensive going steady period of perhaps six months, during which things become serious very rapidly, and this leads directly into marriage. There appears to be no engagement as a rule, and nothing at all corresponding to the pinning complex of younger age groups. The writer estimates that a very high proportion of these previously married couples, perhaps 85 per cent, consummate the sexual relationship before marriage, a factor that may have something to do with their decision to skip the engagement stage.

If we accept Kinsey's data on the higher incidence of premarital sexual relationships at the lower income levels, this may also be a factor associated with what the writer believes to be a tendency to bypass engagement on the part of lower-lower-class couples.

As a matter of fact, it seems to us that there are striking similarities between the middle-aged courtship pattern described above and that of the high school age couples at the lower-lower-class level.

If the writer were asked to *guess* (and that would be the correct word) at the proportion of married couples who did *not* have an engagement period, he would estimate about 50 per cent. This estimate or "informed guess" is based on the known fact that about one fourth of our population are close to the lower-lower-class level at any given time, plus the fact that about four fifths of our divorced persons remarry. When we add the second and third marriages of widowed persons, who seldom have engagements, it seems possible that 50 per cent is not too high as an estimate of the proportion of our married couples who move directly from going steady into marriage.

Whatever the figure might be, what accounts for this tendency to skip engagement? And what are the consequences? It has already been suggested that the sexual habits of low-income and previously married couples may be a factor in this pattern, plus the probability of a relatively high incidence of pregnant marriages at the low income levels.

It also seems that some type of social maturation level is involved. The middle-aged couples, for example, consider themselves ready for marriage, and they seem to regard an engagement as a waste of time. It also seems to them that engagement is much more appropriate (customary) for the younger age groups. Just as the previously married person usually shuns an elaborate church wedding, so does he also tend to avoid an engagement.

This same thing is true, to a certain extent, of the low-income couples, even those of high school age, judging by the studies of Allison Davis and others.[32] These youngsters mature socially very fast: they leave school at the eighth grade or soon after and enter the adult economic world; they marry early, and they become parents at an early age also. To these couples an engagement is a luxury, a waste of time, perhaps an imitation of what they regard as "rich people's" customs. As Bossard and Boll have pointed out in their excellent study, *Ritual in Family Living*,[33] the subculture of low-income families lacks the rich family traditions so prominent at higher income levels. The lack of formal engagements may be part of this general poverty of family tradition.

We must now turn to the question, what are the consequences of this tendency to bypass the engagement stage? It seems clear, on the basis of the studies cited earlier in this chapter, that engagement performs basic functions in our courtship system, and if this is true, then there should be consequences for those who take short cuts to marriage.

The evidence on the consequences may not be conclusive, but the work of Hollingshead and others on marital stability and social class membership indicates that low-income marriages *are* relatively unstable.[34] The causes, however, are not very clear, and we do not know with certainty whether the engagement pattern has anything to do with it.

There is also some evidence tending to show that second and subsequent marriages by the widowed and the divorced show relatively high instability rates.[35] This group also tends to bypass formal engagement.

All this, of course, represents only what the lawyers call circumstantial evidence and does not by any means prove that the lack of engagement has any relationship to the relatively high rates of marital instability among the two groups discussed. The writer, however, is inclined to believe that this may prove to be a tenable theory as the research continues.

On a rational level, if we assume that couples in love are capable of rational thought, it might be that more couples would be willing to go through an engagement period if they had a better understanding of its functions and value. If they knew, for example, that time spent in engagement is not actually lost, as marital adjustment proceeds during this period, and if they knew that an adequate engagement is probably the best divorce insurance available in our society, then perhaps they would be more willing to forego an immediate marriage. It may be that an adequate community program in education for marriage could increase the use of the engagement period. If so, there is some reason to believe that the results would be worthwhile.

3. *The problem of nonfunctional engagements.*

This problem refers to engagements that are useless and do not accomplish the basic function of an engagement, an adequate testing of the compatability of the couple. It is an open question as to what percentage of American engagements fall into this category. In the Burgess-Wallin study of 1,000 engaged couples, 150 of the engagements were subsequently broken.[36] If we assume that these relationships *should* have been broken—in other words, that these would not have produced adequate marriages—then it seems that for these 1,000 couples the engagement period was actually one of intensive testing and re-examination.

It is interesting to note that of the 850 couples whose engagements resulted in marriage, only 33 had been divorced or separated by the end of the 3- to 5-year follow-up period.[37] This seems to indicate that engagement for this group was overwhelmingly functional, that it actually accomplished its basic purpose. Unfortunately, their sample does not represent a cross section of the population, so we do not know how effective engagement is for other groups.

It seems clear, however, judging from case studies, that some couples can move through an engagement of six months or longer and remain on a very superficial level of interaction. Judging by the writer's marriage counseling cases, these couples are apt to have one or more of the following characteristics:

1. They are past the usual age of marriage, especially the women, and do not wish to test the relationship, because of their intense desire to marry. This mechanism is usually unconscious, in our opinion.

2. They are separated geographically during the engagement period and carry on their courtship primarily by mail. Military service is very often the cause of the separation, but educational and occupational demands are frequently involved also. The writer has no data on the proportion of engaged couples faced with this problem, but the extensive mobility so characteristic of our society indicates that it may be large. A thorough discussion of the problems facing couples courting via Uncle Sam's mails will be found in the chapter on "Courtship and Military Service."

3. Excessive preoccupation with necking and petting, if not actual sexual intercourse, prevents their exploring the other basic areas of their relationship. In other words, their courtship becomes fixed at the sexual level and tests only that area of compatibility. Most of these couples will, of course, deny that this state of affairs prevailed in their courtship, but there is often good evidence to support the hypothesis.

4. One or both of the engagement partners is immature emotionally. We grant that the concept of immaturity has become a sort of catch-all theory for explaining a host of human problems, but once in a while it seems to be the only way of explaining what happens to people. In any event, something similar to emotional immaturity seems to prevent some couples from having an adequate or functional engagement.

Conclusion

In this chapter an attempt has been made to analyze systematically the functioning of engagement in the American courtship system. The analysis has revealed this stage to be a crucial step in the dating process, one that serves a vital screening function to prevent hasty or ill-advised marriages. Although adequate data are not available, it seems likely that a significant proportion of American couples bypass engagement, and it has been suggested that perhaps this is related to higher rates of marital instability for these groups.

This completes our analysis of the basic steps or stages in the courtship system. Beginning with group dating at the junior high school level, we have traced the pattern of movement through random dating, going steady, pinning, and engagement.

We are now ready for the analysis of some segmental aspects of the courtship process, and that will conclude this Part II of the book.

References

1. See especially the monumental work of Ernest W. Burgess and Paul Wallin, *Engagement and Marriage* (Philadelphia, J. B. Lippincott Co., 1953).

2. Anne Morrow Lindbergh, *Gift From the Sea* (New York, Pantheon Press, 1955).

3. For a classic statement of this point, see Sigmund Freud's *Autobiography* (New York, W. W. Norton & Co., Inc., 1935).

4. This statement is based on a lecture given by Dr. Rex Stewart at the 1950 University of Chicago Workshop on Family Research conducted by Evelyn Duvall and Reuben Hill. Dr. Stewart was describing his experiments with the Minnesota Multiphasic Personality Test in marriage counseling cases and seemed to think the test could also be adapted for courtship counseling.

5. For a discussion of this point, see Harvey J. Locke's study, *Predicting Adjustment in Marriage* (New York, Henry Holt & Co., Inc., 1951), pp. 358–395. See also Evelyn M. Duvall, *In-Laws, Pro and Con* (New York, Association Press, 1954).

6. See his classic discussion in Willard Waller, *The Family* (New York, The Cordon Company, 1938), chap. 10.

7. George Peter Murdock, *Social Structure* (New York, The Macmillan Company, 1949).

8. We refer to the following: Lewis M. Terman, *Psychological Factors in Marital Happiness* (New York, McGraw-Hill Book Co., 1938); Ernest W. Burgess and Leonard S. Cottrell, Jr., *Predicting Success or Failure in Marriage* (New York, Prentice-Hall, Inc., 1939); Harvey J. Locke, *op. cit.*, and the Burgess-Wallin study cited above.

9. *Op. cit.*

10. See their discussion of the sample, *op. cit.*, pp. 54–60.

11. See Terman, *op. cit.*, p. 6 for a discussion of this point.

12. See Locke, *op. cit.*, pp. 45–46 for an excellent discussion of this point. See also Burgess-Wallin, *op. cit.*, pp. 756–760 for a summary of the present state of marital prediction research.

13. For a criticism of such tests, see Albert Ellis, "The Value of Marriage Prediction Tests," *American Sociological Review*, 13 (1948), 710–718. The writer's position is simply this: that most of the criticisms cited by Ellis also apply to most of the other paper-and-pencil tests used so widely in our society. The main point is that persons using such tools must realize their limitations.

14. See Locke, *op. cit.*, p. 358. Burgess and Wallin discuss this point in chap. 5, *op. cit.*

15. See their discussion in chap. 9, "Broken Engagements."

16. See Terman, *op. cit.*, chap. 12, for his evidence on this point.

17. See Burgess-Wallin, *op. cit.*, p. 271.

18. *Ibid.*, chap. 13.

19. A more complete statement of this theory may be found in Robert F. Winch, *The Modern Family* (New York, Henry Holt & Co., Inc., 1952), pp. 404–433. Additional material may be found in the discussion by Thomas and Virginia Ktsanes, "The Theory of Complementary Needs in Mate-Selection," in Robert F. Winch and Robert McGinnis, *Selected Studies in Marriage and the Family* (New York, Henry Holt & Co., Inc., 1953), pp. 435–453.

20. Burgess-Wallin, *op. cit.*, p. 407.

21. *Ibid.*, p. 408.

22. See p. 565 of the Burgess-Wallin study.

23. *Ibid.*, pp. 565–566.

24. See pp. 560–576, *op. cit.*, for a discussion of this point.

25. For an analysis of this data, see Alfred C. Kinsey, Wardell B. Pomeroy, and Clyde E. Martin, *Sexual Behavior in the Human Male* (Philadephia, W. B. Saunders Co., 1948), pp. 347–351.

26. This was a survey of Junior and Senior women enrolled in a course in The Family. When asked whether or not they thought premarital coitus could ever be justified, 87 per cent replied in the affirmative—if the couple were "in love."

27. See Georg Karlsson, *Adaptability and Communication in Marriage* (Uppsala, Almqvist & Wiksells Boktryckeri Aktiebolag, 1951), p. 194.

28. See, for example, the discussion of this matter in Stuart A. Queen and John B. Adams, *The Family in Various Cultures* (Philadelphia, J. B. Lippincott Co., 1952), pp. 253–255.

29. See Burgess-Wallin, *op. cit.*, chap. 12.

30. Burgess-Wallin summarize these findings on pp. 367–371, *op. cit.*

31. For a brief and readable description of this system, see W. Lloyd Warner, *American Life* (Chicago, University of Chicago Press, 1953).

32. See Allison Davis and Robert J. Havighurst, *Father of the Man* (Boston, Houghton Mifflin Co., 1947).

33. James H. S. Bossard and Eleanor S. Boll, *Ritual in Family Living* (Philadelphia, University of Pennsylvania Press, 1950).
34. See William J. Goode's study, *After Divorce* (Glencoe, The Free Press, 1956), chap. 4, for a review and analysis of these data. See also Thomas P. Monahan, "Divorce by Occupational Level," *Marriage and Family Living,* 17 (1955), 322–324.
35. *Ibid.*
36. *Op. cit.*, chap. 9.
37. *Ibid.*, p. 52.

Suggested Readings

1. Ernest W. Burgess and Paul Wallin, *Engagement and Marriage* (Philadelphia, J. B. Lippincott Co., 1952). The following chapters are especially relevant: chap. 8, "Disagreements and Stresses in Engagement"; chap. 9, "Broken Engagements"; and chap. 10, "Measuring Success in Engagement."

2. Reuben Hill and Willard Waller, *The Family* (New York, The Dryden Press, 1951), chap. 12, "The Engagement: A Bridge to Marriage." An excellent analysis.

3. Thomas and Virginia Ktsanes, "The Theory of Complementary Needs in Mate-Selection," in Robert F. Winch and Robert McGinnis, *Selected Studies in Marriage and the Family* (New York, Henry Holt & Co., Inc., 1953), pp. 435–453. This presentation makes excellent discussion material.

4. Manford Hinshaw Kuhn, "The Engagement: Thinking about Marriage," in *Family, Marriage, and Parenthood*, edited by Howard Becker and Reuben Hill (Boston, D. C. Heath & Co., 1955), pp. 276–304.

CHAPTER IX

SEX AND COURTSHIP

Introduction

It has bcome fashionable to talk about sex in our society but this freedom does not carry with it any guarantee that the discussion will be either intelligent or constructive, and often it seems to be just the reverse.

To be honest, it is not easy to conduct a rational discussion of sexual behavior. If modern psychiatry has taught us anything about sexual behavior, it is this: that only a fraction of what people think or do in this area of life can be classified as rational behavior. The entire segment of human behavior related to the sex needs of men and women is complicated by conflicts and platitudes. For example, our culture supposedly contains a sexual ideal of chastity until marriage, yet for centuries this has been waived for males, and in recent decades a considerable proportion of our females have also been bypassing this moral standard. *But the code has not been changed*—it just is not observed very much any more. This is typical of the conflicts and confusions in this segment of modern life.

We give our youngsters very little, if any, sex education in the home or the school, including most colleges, yet we expect them to be informed and intelligent in facing sexual problems.

Our movies, television programs, and mass magazines are full of questionable sex themes, yet these are held up as educational media. It can truly be said that the average young American, for better or worse, has learned more about sexual behavior at drive-in movies than he has from his family, his church, his school, or his college.

It might be useful to make more specific some of the reasons why a worthwhile analysis of sexual behavior is so difficult in our society.

1. The research data are inadequate.

Even though Kinsey and others have punctured the Iron Curtain that formerly prevented research on sexual behavior, it is still true that we know relatively little about this phase of life. If one cites Freud, for example, the listener or the reader may not accept Freudian sexual theory. Others will reject any data taken from Kinsey's monumental research. Thus we fall back on fragmental personal knowledge, which may be more misleading than anything else. In this way most discussions of sex become "bull sessions" rather than systematic or scientific analyses.

2. Parents and other moral guardians are ultra-conservative in their sexual values.

For some reason, even parents who are liberal about most issues can be extremely stuffy about sexual problems. In over fifteen years of college teaching and counseling, the writer has found less than ten students who felt free to discuss *fully* their sexual dilemmas with their parents; yet hundreds of these same students felt free to confide anything else to their father or mother or both.

In a brilliant paper, Kingsley Davis has suggested that this sexual conservatism of parents may result because the parents have passed the peak of their sexual desire and have reached the point where they can afford to be philosophical about such matters.[1] Their adolescent youngsters, however, are just at the point when their sexual drives are most urgent, and this means that the two generations are separated by a wide and deep physiological gulf that prevents effective communication or communion on this problem.

To this physiological difference we add a social role differential: parents *as parents* have deep responsibility in our society for the welfare of their children, and this in itself pushes the parents toward conservative values, those that have stood the test of time, as they so often put it. The young person, however, does not have this burden of responsibility and is more willing to explore or seek new values and norms. Thus it seems to be rare, even in *good* families, for parents and their children of dating age to attain any semblance of understanding on such matters as necking, petting, premarital sexual relations, and related issues.

3. *Rapid social change is involved in all this.*

Deep down beneath all this, as Kingsley Davis points out in the paper cited above, is the unceasing and rapid evolution (or revolution) taking place in our civilization. America prides itself on being a progressive and dynamic society, but our citizens are not always aware that a price has to be paid for living in a constant state of flux. And part of this price is the fact that what one generation took for granted becomes a dubious assumption for the next. This, it seems, underlies the often heard lament of parents: "I just *can't* understand young people these days."

4. *Social class mobility is involved also.*

American parents struggle and save (if not slave) to give their children a better start in life: better medical care, better food, better clothes, more education, etc. Often this means that the youngster ends in a social class position somewhat higher than that of the parents. Since the Kinsey research shows that sexual patterns vary from one social class to another,[2] this vertical social class mobility (as the sociologists call it) means that the children will almost inevitably end with sexual values different from those of the parents. This may be unpleasant for both generations but true nevertheless.

5. Our cultural attitudes toward sex are schizoid or contradictory.

This was referred to briefly earlier in the discussion but a few illustrations may clarify the point. When a Hollywood actress becomes involved in scandal, her box-office appeal *increases* instead of declining. As a matter of fact, a movie's interest to the American public is enhanced if it has been banned in some community. As Wolfenstein and Leites point out in *Movies: A Psychological Study,*[3] it is difficult to make a Hollywood heroine interesting to an American audience unless she is made to appear to be a "bad girl" in the early part of the film. But since our formal moral code requires film characters to be "good" examples for young people, Hollywood has devised the "bad girl—good girl" type, in which the girl *seems* to be immoral but really is not. Thus the audience gets what it wants while the formal moral code is upheld.

During World War II an interesting reflection of our conflicting attitudes toward sex was seen in the attempts of the armed forces to satisfy the sexual values of different groups in our society: the medical profession, for example, wanted the men to be issued prophylactic devices, hoping to reduce the amount of venereal disease. Church groups, on the other hand, wanted the services to give lectures to the men, urging them to practice sexual abstinence. Being unable to reconcile these two points of view, but not wishing to offend anybody, the military adopted *both* of the above programs: the stern lectures were given, also the free (or almost free) prophylactics.[4]

To summarize this discussion, we have merely been trying to show that sex is not the easiest topic to discuss in our society, and we have tried to point out some of the reasons why this is the case.

We are now ready to plunge into the subject and see what facts and principles, if any, we can isolate that might help us think clearly about this important aspect of courtship and marriage.

Our Point of View

It is easy for middle-aged individuals to urge adolescent young people to sublimate their sex drive, to drain off their sexual energy in nonsexual activities, but the fact remains that sexual needs are among the basic needs of humans and not easily ignored or pushed aside. If sex were not such a deep and pervasive human need, it is likely that man would not have survived the various hazards he has encountered during the past several hundred thousand years. All this should be obvious, but one gets the impression at times that the sublimation advocates seem to regard sex as a relatively minor human impulse. An understanding of the role of sex in modern courtship can hardly be achieved if one proceeds on the above premise. As the comedians might say, *Sex is here to stay,* and we might as well face it. The correct approach, it seems to us, is not to *deny* the nature and the strength of the sexual impulse but to *understand* it.

It might be worthwhile to point out that Kinsey has concluded that the possibility of sublimation has been vastly overestimated, at least for the human male.[5] He found very little evidence that the men in his sample were able to resolve their sexual tensions by engaging in physical exercise or other substitute activities. Regardless of what one thinks of Kinsey's work, it must be recognized that he and his staff have studied sexual patterns in modern society more systematically than any other professional or scientific group.

If one chooses to reject Kinsey's work, the findings of modern psychiatry, dating back to Freud, support the notion that the sexual drive is one of the most pervasive and complex facets of human behavior, and one not to be lightly dismissed.

A survey of 1,600 high school students by Maureen Daly, using a nation-wide cross-section sample, reported sexual conflicts to be the most common problem facing these young people.[6] They also reported that this area was the one in which their parents and teachers had been *least* helpful. Thus the picture emerges of youth in conflict, with their elders either denying the existence of the problem or being unable to help.

In this discussion, our approach is to grant the urgency of the sexual drive in young people, to recognize the common conflicts surrounding its expression, but to *deny* that adults or outsiders are unable to help. The rest of the chapter will be an attempt to develop a point of view or a way of thinking about sexual behavior as it relates to courtship.

A Definition of Sexual Behavior

It is a mistake, we believe, to use a physical definition of sexual behavior in analyzing the role of sex in courtship. As a matter of fact, this has been one of the major criticisms of the Kinsey research.[7]

At the level of high school and college dating or courtship (we use the terms interchangeably), most sexual behavior is not sexual at all in the Kinsey sense, being confined largely to kissing, touching, and body contact not involving actual sexual intercourse. The conflicts, at least during random dating, center about such questions as *when* necking may be permitted, *how far* it should be allowed to go, and *how often*. Do I stall him off for the first date? And if so, will he come back for another? But if I give in too easily and neck too much too soon, will he talk? And will he get the wrong impression of me?

Later on, as she gets better acquainted with a particular boy, the girl will encounter a similar series of questions related to petting. When? (or with whom?) How soon? And how far?

Later still, when she gets to the stage of pinning or engagement, she will have to decide whether or not to permit premarital sex relations, and this too will be a knotty problem.

Strictly speaking, at least in the Kinsey sense, most of the above problems are not sexual at all, except that of the pinned or engaged couple. Yet these are the kinds of dilemmas young people refer to when they report sexual problems, and this is what we mean in this chapter in the title, "Sex and Courtship."

It is possible that most adults do not use the term "sex" in this diffuse sense, for married people tend to think of necking and petting as mere preliminaries to actual intercourse, a means to an end; but for vast numbers of young people, the necking and petting become *ends in themselves*. It would be helpful at times if parents kept this point in mind.

Why Do They "Neck"?

This question may seem redundant or unnecessary to young people, and perhaps it is, but it seems to us that parents and other adults require an answer nevertheless.

The answer, in all frankness, is simply this: that necking has become *customary* for young Americans, a basic part of the subculture of youth. Whether this has *always* been true of courtship, we do not know, but it may well have been, at least to some extent. In any event, once behavior of this nature has become embedded in the group patterns of youth, it is no longer necessary to ask *why* members of the group conform; at that point, the main problem is to explain why a few members of the group *do not* conform. In other words, the deviant girl or boy today is the one who *does not* neck, and they are the ones we have to explain.

To use an analogy, it could be pointed out that most American women today wear lipstick, not necessarily because they wish to or like to, but because it is *expected* of them. And so the women who do not use lipstick become different or unusual and their behavior requires explanation.

In the same way, a girl in modern society may neck whether she personally enjoys it or not. She wishes to be a member of the dating group, and this is one of the requirements for membership. It is certainly well known that many young people smoke or drink for this reason, so why should it be so difficult to see that they engage in mild sexual contact for the same reason? We are not referring, of course, to sexual promiscuity, any more than we are referring to alcoholism in the above reference to drinking.

We can already hear the reactions to our point of view, the

deans of women, the mothers, and the ministers who exclaim: "It isn't necessary for a girl to neck to be popular. Lots of studies have shown that." Well, we wonder. Let us take a good look at this point of view as it has a crucial bearing on this discussion.

In the first place, surveys of this sort operate at the *verbal* level of behavior with questions of this sort: "Do you believe that girls have to neck to be popular?" Girls, of course, reply in the negative, for an affirmative reply would reflect on the power of their other charms. Furthermore, a negative reply is in line with conservative attitudes and tends to support the traditional values of our society. It would take an unusual girl to answer "yes" to this type of question.

Likewise, it seems to us, boys are inclined to answer in the negative, for to do otherwise seems to imply that they cannot rise above sexual desire in choosing feminine companionship.

What do these studies or opinion surveys prove, if anything? In our opinion, they simply show that young men and women will give conservative verbal replies to questions of this nature, but we do not believe that they prove that popular girls do not neck. It seems to us that the evidence points to the opposite conclusion: that popular girls neck, but not with everybody.

Our position is based on the fact that the popularity of girls is not determined by girls but by boys (or young men), and there is ample evidence that young males prefer necking to almost any other form of recreation.

It is not implied that a girl, to be popular, has to engage in petting. The main requirement is that she has to have "sex appeal" and must permit enough contact to stimulate the boy and allow him to have a "good time," as the saying goes.

We think it should be repeated that the necking and petting patterns in our society are not based primarily on the desires of the girls, although they may set the absolute limit in most cases. It is the male whose sexual needs are most urgent during his teens and twenties,[8] and it is also the male who is most aggressive sexually in our society. It can be granted, however, that *some* girls may succeed in achieving popularity without necking, or with a minimum of necking, but these must be regarded as unusual cases, in our opinion. In general, we would argue, they are either very beautiful or very talented girls, who have so many other attractions that they can afford to minimize necking and/or petting. This does not mean, however, that *most* girls can follow the same policy.

Perhaps an analogy might help at this point. Young men seem to agree that an automobile is a tremendous asset in modern dating, but few of them would contend that it is impossible for a boy to get dates without a car; the point is that it is a lot easier to be popular with a car than without one. Likewise, it is a lot easier for a girl to be popular if she necks than it is if she does not.

The writer is well aware that many intelligent and well-informed persons disagree with this point of view, but this is the way it looks to us and we feel that an author should be honest, even at the cost of being in a minority.[9]

The Role of Sex in American Courtship

It is generally agreed by married couples and the students of marriage that sexual attraction and satisfaction play a basic role in marital adjustment. If this is the case, then what is the role of sexual factors in relationships leading up to marriage? The following analysis will attempt to answer that question.

It has already been suggested that sexual attraction and stimulation determine to a considerable extent which girls will be sought after by young men in our society. But once this attraction and stimulation have done their work, what is the continuing role of sexual factors in American courtship? In the writer's opinion, sex serves to gloss over differences between the couple, to reconcile incompatible traits, to sustain the relationship when otherwise it would collapse. To put it bluntly, most of our young couples "neck their way out" of problems that arise in courtship. If this is the case, it means that sex can be a very confusing force in courtship, and the writer believes this to be the case. As a matter of fact, this may be one of the chief explanations as to how so many couples in our society can be "terribly in love" before marriage and unhappy after.

It seems to us that sex is confusing during courtship for various reasons. Many girls, and especially "nice" girls, have never been completely aroused sexually until they meet a certain boy, and when they do meet him and find themselves stimulated sexually, then it has to be "love"; otherwise, they are "bad" girls: easily aroused by almost any man. Thus the well-behaved girl is especially prone to confuse sexual passion with "love," using this term to denote the type of personal compatibility necessary for happy marriage in our society.

Boys or young men, we believe, are equally confused by sex in courtship, but for different reasons. The young man has most likely been aroused sexually before, but usually by a girl below him in social status, a girl he would not normally consider marrying. This has been clearly demonstrated by Winston Ehrmann in a study at the University of Florida, in which the young men report that they have gone much farther in necking and petting with girls below them in social class structure.[10] And so when the young man finds a girl of his own or higher social class level who interests him sexually, he is apt to conclude that this *must* be love—"all this and sex too," as the men put it.

In the final analysis, it seems to us, sexual attraction is enough to hold most courtships together. The problem is created by the fact that sex alone does not seem adequate to hold *marriages* together. But that unfortunately is not learned until much later.

If our point of view is valid, then it follows that sexual factors become dangerous or misleading when they *dominate* the premarital relationship. Why? Because they prevent the adequate testing of other areas crucial for marital happiness. If a couple, for example, concentrate on necking and petting, they may very well determine that they are sexually well mated. But if we accept Terman's conclusion that sexual compatibility accounts at best for only about 20 per cent of marital adjustment, the couple still have 80 per cent of their marital relationship to test. From this point of view, it is not the necking and petting in themselves that are destructive: it is the fact that they have prevented adequate exploration of other important areas of interaction.

Some Research Findings

In the past three decades, impressive research has been published on sexual patterns in our society. The balance of this chapter will be devoted to a review of the findings relevant to courtship. Those related to marriage will be discussed in Part III of the text.

The Kinsey Research

In the writer's opinion, Kinsey and his associates have conducted the most elaborate research on sexual behavior in the United States, granting that their work is by no means complete.[11] Whether one admires the Kinsey research or not, it seems to us that its basic findings must be known and understood, even if they are not accepted. Some of the basic conclusions of this group are as follows:

1. *Males and females have basic sexual differences.*

In modern American there has been a long-range trend toward minimizing differences between men and women, at least in their social roles. Women now help to earn the family living, go fishing with their husbands, drive the car, pay the monthly bills, wear trousers, and in general, do almost everything that men do.

Men, for their part, wash clothes, prepare dinner, wax floors, give the baby its bottle, do the weekly shopping, and perform many other tasks formerly regarded as women's work. All this, it seems to us, may have served to produce a feeling that the two sexes are not really very different. The Kinsey research does not support such a belief insofar as sexual behavior is concerned. In Volume II, *Sexual Behavior in the Human Female,* deep differences in sexual patterns are reported for the two sexes.[12]

In the first place, Kinsey reports males to be much more active sexually in the teens than are females. This means that the very beginning of dating finds the boys much more interested and concerned with sexual play than are the girls. It is the beginning of the "battle between the sexes," reported fully in the comic strips and television programs. It also means that girls in their early years of dating are almost certain to meet sexual demands (necking and petting) earlier than they had expected. It may also mean, although we are not sure of this, that the sexual patterns of these early years will be determined more by the male desire than by the female lack of desire, because men are more aggressive sexually than are women in our culture.

According to Kinsey, it is not until the twenties that the sexual patterns of women begin to approach those of men.[13]

If Kinsey is correct in his analysis, then it seems almost inevitable that the early years of dating would be characterized by sexual "struggles" between girls and their boy friends. The writer believes this to be true, judging by his counseling experience, but the final opinion will be left to the reader.

Kinsey reports that men are more easily aroused sexually, that they respond much more quickly to visual stimuli, such as nude photographs; that they are more responsive to auditory stimuli, such as "off-color" stories; and that they are much more preoccupied with sex than are girls.[14] In other words, Kinsey finds that *most* men (but not all) are more highly sexed than are their girl friends or their wives.

If Kinsey should prove to be right, his findings raise some deep questions about the ideal of sexual equality for modern couples, for the simple reason that the sexual needs of men and women may not be equal.

Before marriage, the male in our society, according to Kinsey, equalizes this differential by two devices: (1) he resorts to self-satisfaction (autosexual or masturbatory behavior), or (2) he seeks out girls who are more highly sexed than his regular date.[15] Since both of these escape mechanisms are usually hidden from "nice" girls, it follows that most girls in our society may never know the true extent of the sexual needs of their boy friends. This may also be true of wives in our society.

Another of the interesting findings of Kinsey is this: that sexual patterns are highly correlated with social class levels, as measured by years of education and occupation of father.[16] This means that men dating below their social class level have a greater chance of sexual satisfaction than if they date on their own social level, and this may explain why there is a tendency for men in our society to marry a notch or so below their own socioeconomic level. It *certainly* means that cross-class dating in our society very often has sexual exploitation as one of its characteristics.

Another interesting Kinsey finding indicates that the basic revolution in American sexual norms took place following World War I rather than after World War II, and this implies that young people today may not be as different from their parents as one might think.[17]

In the last analysis, however, it seems to us that Kinsey's most relevant finding is his utter rejection of the idea that men and women in our society are equal in their sexual needs.[18] The full implications of this for courtship analysis have never been perceived, in our opinion.

It may also be worthwhile to note Kinsey's conclusion that individual variation in sexual desire in *both* sexes is greater than most persons think;[19] and this means that the sexual rapprochement in courtship as well as marriage can be very difficult.

For the reader who doubts the validity of these findings, we suggest that he read the relevant chapters in the Kinsey volumes cited in this chapter.

The Burgess-Wallin Research

In their study of 1,000 engaged couples published in 1953, Burgess and Wallin investigated in considerable detail certain facets of sex and courtship.[20] Perhaps their most interesting discovery is that about half of their engaged couples had sexual relations with each other before marriage. It is true that their sample was exclusively metropolitan and largely Protestant, hence not representative for the United States, but even after granting these limitations, it seems clear that chastity at marriage is no longer possible for a significant proportion of our engaged couples. As a matter of fact, the Burgess-Wallin figure may be too low, since theirs was essentially a middle-class or white-collar sample, and Kinsey has shown that low-income groups begin their heterosexual relationships *earlier* than do middle-income groups.

In studying the two groups of engaged couples, those that had premarital intercourse and those that did not, Burgess and Wallin were unable to reach any clear-cut conclusions about the *results* of such behavior. The chaste couples, for example, did score slightly higher in total marital adjustment, but their sexual adjustment score was slightly lower than that for the unchaste couples. *But in neither case were the differences great enough to be statistically significant.* In other words, one could not predict marital adjustment or maladjustment by using this item.

Even more interesting from the writer's point of view is the ability of both groups of engaged couples to rationalize or defend their behavior. Thus the conventional couples are sure they did the right thing, that their marriage is better because they waited, that they would pursue the same policy if they had it to do again, etc. And the unconventional couples are equally sure that their marriages are better because they did not wait, etc.[21] This seems to indicate a schizoid or conflict situation in our culture in regard to premarital intercourse for engaged couples. There appears to be no consensus and the individual must resolve the question as best he or she can. That this question may be of widespread interest and concern is indicated by the fact that a 1955 novel by Herman Wouk, *Marjorie Morningstar,* a Book-of-the-Month Club selection, devotes several hundred pages to the girl's conflict over whether or not she should have premarital intercourse with her lover.[22]

The Terman Research

In 1938 Lewis Terman and staff published a volume called *Psychological Factors in Marital Happiness,* a study based on 792 married couples living on the West Coast, most of them from California.[23] In general, Terman found a growing tendency for couples to have intercourse before marriage, the trend going back as far as 1890 in Terman's sample. His findings are similar to the later ones of Burgess-Wallin, except that the latter made no effort to discover long-term trends.

In all these research studies, there is general agreement that sexual norms have been changing for several decades in the United States, but the researchers do not always agree on details. Kinsey, for example, does not agree with Terman that the big revolution in sexual patterns began as early as the 1890's; Kinsey's data indicate that it followed World War I. Kinsey also believes that the increase in sexual activity at the college level has been mainly in necking and petting, not in actual intercourse.[24] It might be useful at this point to analyze petting practices to see what light, if any, they might reflect on the role of sex in American courtship.

The Petting Complex

It is probably traditional in our society, if not in others, to think of sexual behavior as actual intercourse between a man and a woman, but this is an extremely stereotyped conception of human sexual behavior and one that prevents an adequate understanding of the dynamics of sexual interaction in courtship and marriage. It is also disastrous to regard human sexual behavior as essentially physiological, for it always involves psychological and cultural factors as well.

Ford and Beach, in their excellent study, *Patterns of Sexual Behavior,*[25] make it clear that even at the subhuman level, the anthropoid apes use sexual urges for nonsexual purposes, such as the obtaining of food or the protection of a helpless associate. The

interested reader will find additional material illustrating these
points in Seward's extensive survey, *Sex and the Social Order*.[26]

In the case of young Americans, and especially those of
middle-class status, it seems clear that the bulk of their heterosexual
contacts are not sexual at all in the traditional sense, because they
do not involve actual sexual intercourse. At the superficial level,
they consist of necking, which can be translated very literally as
caresses or sexual contact "from the neck up." Necking also implies
that the main areas of sexual stimulation be kept covered by clothing, with the exception of the neck, lips, and ears, which are utilized
extensively as sexual objects in necking.

The term "petting," however, covers a different set of
behavior patterns. It includes literally every caress known to married
couples but does not include complete sexual intercourse.

A Case Study of Petting: In the following case study, based
on the writer's courtship counseling experience, petting can be seen
in its extreme form, or perhaps one should say in its fullest development.

The young man was twenty years of age, a Junior in college,
a nonveteran. His background was upper middle class, his father
being an executive in a medium-sized corporation. Both parents
were college graduates, church members, and apparently well
mated in their marriage. The boy himself had not done very well
in a private prep school and was not very well adjusted at the time
of our contact. His college grades were poor, although his aptitude
scores were about average. He had one sibling, a younger sister
with whom he did not get along very well.

The girl in this situation came from a similar background,
except that her parents were separated. Most of the time she lived
with her mother, but once a year or so she paid an extensive visit
to a wealthy aunt, who was divorced.

The young man described the girl as "very beautiful," and
his snapshots seemed to support this description. The girl was
attending one of the top women's colleges in the East, so it seems
safe to conclude that her high school record was excellent.

Her father was a highly successful physician. The mother had been in theatrical work before her marriage. Although the girl's parents were separated at the time of our contact, they were not divorced. The young man seemed to believe there was some chance of a reconciliation.

The writer did not have a chance to meet with the girl or her parents, but we did get to know the boy's parents superficially. As the result of many intensive counseling sessions with the boy, we came to know him well.

Here is a description of the petting pattern for this couple as described by the young man: they had started dating in the Junior year of prep school and had gone steady during their Senior year. They continued to date on a more or less steady basis during their first year of college, seeing each other often, since their schools were not too far from their suburban homes. At first they had engaged in mild necking, followed by heavier necking during the Senior year of prep school.

During the summer following their Freshman year at college, the petting pattern developed. Two or three nights a week all summer long, they would go to a secluded beach near their home community and engage in extremely intimate caresses. Except for the failure to have complete intercourse, the couple seemed to have exhausted the love-making possibilities utilized by most middle-class couples in our society.

These young people, it should be made clear, considered themselves "in love" and discussed at various times the possibility of marriage at some distant time in the future. The boy, in particular, seemed to be very much in love.

During their Sophomore year at college, the girl wrote to the young man, confessing that she had met "someone else" and wished to discontinue their relationship. Later on, during a college recess date with our informant, she confessed to having a new boy friend, apparently having spent several week ends with him at a metropolitan hotel. He turned out to be a football hero, somewhat older than the other young man, and apparently more aggressive.

This decision to end the relationship produced a severe adjustment crisis for our informant, and this was the point at which he came to us for help. In the process of trying to reconstruct what had happened, a great deal of information was obtained about the entire episode, only a fraction of which is reproduced here.

Analysis of the Case Study

Granting that the case presented represents an extreme example of petting, it still illustrates the basic characteristics of the petting complex as it has been elaborated during the past few decades in our society. These will be presented in numerical order for purposes of clarity.

1. *These were middle-class young people.*

There seems to be some evidence, at least in the Kinsey research, that petting is both more common and more elaborate among middle-class youth than it is among lower-income groups, the latter moving more directly to actual intercourse.[27] The data for upper-class groups is not very adequate but it seems likely that their pattern is similar to that of the white-collar and professional groups.

If we ask *why* petting is so characteristic of middle-class courtship, the research of Allison Davis and his associates indicates that middle-class children are trained to postpone the immediate satisfaction of needs so that their future progress and security will not be jeopardized.[28] A student of the writer's who was hoping to become a physician (his father was an accountant), wrote the following in a term paper: "I have never 'gone the limit' with a girl because I feel that I have too much at stake. My father and mother have worked hard to send me through school and are also willing to help me through medical school. So I don't want to get involved with any women until my education is completed." In another part of the paper, the young man indicates that his attitude is based largely on the fear that his girl friend might become pregnant and that this might force him to drop out of school. "So," he writes, "I stick to petting."

It may also be true, as some observers believe, that the middle class in our society is more moralistic than either the upper or lower class, and that this moral conservatism favors petting over actual intercourse.[29]

2. This girl was a "nice" girl.

Some persons, especially the older generation, might wish to dispute this point, but the fact remains that current sexual mores *do* permit a girl to pet and still be considered a "nice" girl, if she is not casual or promiscuous in choosing her petting partners.

Both the girl and the boy in this case came from families with good reputations, and neither of the youngsters had been considered sexual deviants by their parents, their friends, or their community.

3. This behavior did produce sexual satisfaction.

Here, again, some persons might wish to dispute the point, but the young man reported that *he* was satisfied, and there seemed to be some evidence that the girl found considerable satisfaction in the petting also. The fact that she later went on to complete sexual relations with another suitor might indicate that she was not completely satisfied, but there were other factors involved in the switch also: the new boy friend was a football hero, probably more handsome and more aggressive.

The fact that the boy usually reached orgasm and that the girl did occasionally is not too far from the pattern described for married couples by Terman,[30] and seems to indicate considerable satisfaction of sexual needs.

4. The girl remained chaste.

This may also be a dubious point, but she remained at least a "technical virgin." Her behavior was hardly within the spirit of the old moral law but it was within the letter of the law.

She could honestly say, for example, that she had never had sexual intercourse with a man; she probably still regarded herself as a virgin.

5. *The possibility of pregnancy was minimized.*

There seems to be every reason to believe that courtship couples today are as worried about premarital pregnancy as their ancestors were, and petting reduces this hazard close to the zero point. This is one of the main reasons why a girl will pet but refuse to have complete intercourse.

Actually, there has been no improvement of contraceptive devices as far as courtship couples are concerned. It is only the married couples who have benefited from modern research in this area. Hence the ability of petting to minimize the chances of pregnancy must be considered one of the main reasons for its popularity.

6. *Petting represents an ingenious compromise between moral demands and sexual needs.*

In a sense, petting permits young couples to "have their cake and eat it too." The girl satisfies the boy, her own sexual desires, and still stays within the letter of the moral law. She takes very little chance of becoming pregnant or of damaging her reputation in the community. And the same advantages apply to the boy as well. Thus, it seems, a basic conflict between the needs of the organism (especially the male) and the moral code of the group has been resolved. The resolution or compromise may not satisfy everybody, but compromises never do. The widespread diffusion of the petting complex in middle-class groups indicates, however, that the pattern has considerable merit, at least in the eyes of young people.[31]

7. *Petting usually involves a relatively deep emotional involvement.*

This was true of the young couple described in the case study: they believed themselves to be "in love." This appears to be essential for the girl; otherwise she becomes "promiscuous" and ceases to be a "nice girl," and this destroys one of the main values of petting, the retention of self-respect and group approval.

Thus, in its purest form, petting is incompatible with casual relationships.

8. *Parents know very little, if anything, about what petting actually involves.*

In this case, for example, the boy's mother was "shocked" to learn that her son had touched the nude breasts of a girl he had been dating more or less steadily for three years. Incidents of this sort seem to indicate that parents lack any real knowledge of the details of petting; a more likely theory, however, is that they block or repress such knowledge, or refuse to believe that "my son would do anything like that." This, of course, produces some odd emotions in the young couple as they wonder what their parents would think if they knew what *really* happened.

Conclusion

In concluding this discussion of the role of sex in courtship, it seems to us essential to re-emphasize the fact that girls do not necessarily determine sexual norms during courtship, in our culture,[32] any more than wives do in marriage. It is a fact that the human male has persistent sexual needs, that he is aggressive in seeking release from sexual tension, and that he tends to gravitate toward females who will help him solve his sexual problem. It may very well be true, for example, that most girls would prefer *not* to pet (or even neck) until marriage, just as many wives might prefer not to have sexual relations more than once or twice a year, if then. But Terman shows that wives as a group *do* try to help meet their husbands' sexual needs, and in similar fashion, there seems to be evidence that girls who "care" for their boy friends try to co-operate as best they can in meeting their sexual needs, even though this co-operation may not include actual intercourse.

For those adults who find it difficult to understand modern necking and petting patterns, it might be helpful to remember that it is a lot easier to be philosophical about sex at fifty than it is at twenty; also, that the parents of today were not exactly prudes in the 1920's or the 1930's, judging by the novels of that era or the work of Kinsey.

It might also help to remember that a significant proportion of human sexual behavior is at best nonrational—at least the psychiatrists believe so—and for this reason one cannot understand the role of sex in courtship by reference to logic and rationality alone. It seems to the writer that most married couples *know* this. All that remains is to get them and their children to remember this when considering problems related to necking and petting.

It might also be helpful if dating couples would remember that while sex may be enough to build a courtship on, it does not seem to suffice for marriage.

References

1. See Kingsley Davis, "The Sociology of Parent-Youth Conflict," *American Sociological Review*, 4 (1940), 523–535.

2. For a review of these data, see Alfred C. Kinsey, Wardell B. Pomeroy, and Clyde E. Martin, *Sexual Behavior in the Human Male* (Philadelphia, W. B. Saunders Co., 1948), chap. 10. For reasons not very clear as yet, the Kinsey group did not find as much social class variation in female behavior. See their second volume, *Sexual Behavior in the Human Female* (Philadelphia, W. B. Saunders Co., 1953), pp. 31–34. Hereafter these will be cited as Vol. I or Vol. II.

3. Martha Wolfenstein and Nathan Leites, *Movies: A Psychological Study* (Glencoe, The Free Press, 1950).

4. This discussion is based on the author's three years' experience in the armed forces during World War II.

5. See Kinsey, Vol. I, pp. 205–213.

6. Maureen Daly, *Profile of Youth* (Philadelphia, J. B. Lippincott Co., 1951).

7. See Jerome Himelhoch and Sylvia Fleis Fava, *Sexual Behavior in American Society: An Appraisal of the First Two Kinsey Reports* (New York, W. W. Norton & Co., Inc., 1955).

8. Kinsey, Vol. I, p. 219.

9. Since writing this, the author has explored this question more systematically with a mixed group of Senior college men and women who agree

that the analysis given here is essentially correct, judging by their experience in the current courtship system.

10. See Winston W. Ehrmann, "Influence of Comparative Social Class upon Premarital Heterosexual Behavior," *Marriage and Family Living,* 17 (1955), 48–53.

11. Our position on the Kinsey research is simply this: it offers the best data we have at the present time on many aspects of sexual behavior. It seems to us that many critics of Kinsey's work fail to see that the other studies available are even less adequate, especially in regard to their statistical group and their total coverage. For an elaboration of this point, see William G. Cochran, Frederick Mosteller, and John W. Tukey, "Statistical Problems of the Kinsey Report," *Journal of the American Statistical Association,* 48, December, 1953. For a critique of Kinsey, see *Family, Marriage, and Parenthood,* edited by Howard Becker and Reuben Hill (Boston, D. C. Heath & Co., 1955), Appendix I, pp. 807–822.

12. These comparative data are found at the end of most chapters in the volume on the female. See, for example, pp. 173–175 for a comparison of male and female patterns of masturbation.

13. See Kinsey, Vol. II, pp. 352–354.

14. This material is covered in Kinsey, Vol. II, Part III.

15. See Kinsey, Vol. I, Part III.

16. See Kinsey, Vol. I, chap. 10. Social class differences were not as pronounced in the female patterns reported in Vol. II of the Kinsey research.

17. See Kinsey, Vol. I, chap. 11.

18. See Kinsey, Vol. II, Part III, especially chap. 16.

19. Kinsey, Vol. II, pp. 537–543.

20. Ernest W. Burgess and Paul Wallin, *Engagement and Marriage* (Philadelphia, J. B. Lippincott Co., 1953). See especially chaps. 11 and 12.

21. Burgess and Wallin, *op. cit.,* pp. 371–379.

22. Herman Wouk, *Marjorie Morningstar* (New York, Doubleday & Co., 1956).

23. Lewis M. Terman, *Psychological Factors in Marital Happiness* (New York, McGraw-Hill Book Co., 1938). See especially chap. 12.

24. Kinsey, Vol. I, chap. 11.

25. See Clellan S. Ford and Frank A. Beach, *Patterns of Sexual Behavior* (New York, Harper & Bros., 1951).

26. Georgene H. Seward, *Sex and the Social Order* (New York, McGraw-Hill Book Co., 1946).

27. Kinsey, Vol. I, chap. 10.

28. See Allison Davis, "Child Rearing in the Class Structure of American Society," *The Family in a Democratic Society: Anniversary Papers of*

the Community Service Society of New York (New York, Columbia University Press, 1949), pp. 56–59.

29. This is the point of view presented in Robert F. Winch, *The Modern Family* (New York, Henry Holt & Co., Inc., 1952).

30. *Op. cit.*, chaps. 10, 11, and 12.

31. See Kinsey's analysis of the petting complex, Vol. I, chap. 16.

32. Some cultural anthropologists, such as Margaret Mead, believe that male and female sexual patterns are deeply affected by cultural conditioning. We do not necessarily deny the role of culture in determining such patterns: our analysis in this book is simply based on the patterns *existing* in our particular culture at this time. See Mead's *Male and Female* (New York, William Morrow & Co., Inc., 1949); also Ford and Beach, *op. cit.*

Suggested Readings

1. One of the best general books for the student when studying sexual patterns in human society is that of Georgene H. Seward, *Sex and the Social Order* (New York, McGraw-Hill Book Co., 1946). Chap. 12, "Adolescent Sexual Development," and chap. 13, "Adult Relationships between the Sexes," are especially relevant. The entire volume is excellent for book reports.

2. Clellan S. Ford and Frank A. Beach, *Patterns of Sexual Behavior* (New York, Harper & Bros., 1951) is excellent for the better or more mature student.

3. Donald Porter Geddes' *An Analysis of the Kinsey Reports on Sexual Behavior in the Human Male and Female* (New York, E. P. Dutton & Co., Inc., 1954) is a very useful collection of readings about the Kinsey group's work. This is available in a 50¢ paper edition as well as in the regular trade edition.

4. Ernest W. Burgess and Paul Wallin, *Engagement and Marriage* (Philadelphia, J. B. Lippincott Co., 1953). Chap. 11, "Sex and Engagement," and chap. 12, "Assessing Premarital Intercourse," are excellent.

5. August B. Hollingshead, *Elmtown's Youth* (New York, John Wiley & Sons, 1949), chap. 16, "Sex and Marriage." Most students find this very worthwhile reading.

6. Ruth Shonle Cavan, *The American Family* (New York, Thomas Y. Crowell Co., 1953), chap. 14, "Sexual Behavior." Cavan summarizes a vast amount of research data in this discussion.

CHAPTER X

COURTSHIP AND MILITARY SERVICE

Introduction

It has always been obvious that wars have a tremendous impact on love affairs, and some of our most famous novels, such as Ernest Hemingway's *Farewell to Arms*,[1] have this as one of their basic themes. What may not be as obvious, however, is the fact that this intrusion of the armed forces upon courtship is no longer limited to periods of war, but has become a constant factor that must be faced by almost all our young couples either before their marriage or soon after. All this, of course, is the result of the so-called "peacetime draft" by which all physically and mentally fit young men become subject to military service. The tremendous impact on courtship and marriage of this new draft legislation is only now beginning to be comprehended.

We first realized the great interest in this topic on the part of college students when we gave a talk on courtship to a large sorority gathering at a state university. For some reason, we had assumed that most of the questions raised for discussion after the talk would center about necking and petting, but this proved not to be the case. Instead, almost all the problems raised were related to the draft and military service.

Later, at a college marriage conference, we observed that one of the largest crowds turned out for a discussion of the topic, "Courtship and Military Service." The animated discussion at this session convinced us that a separate chapter should be devoted to this problem in this text.

Figure 6: Marriages per 1,000 Population, United States, 1939–1950.*

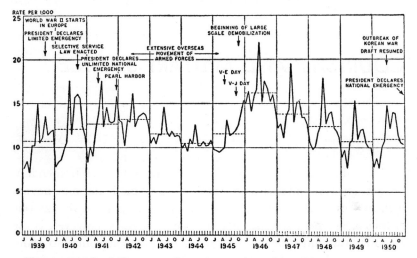

Here we see clearly how war affects the marriage plans of lovers.

* Source: Louis I. Dublin, *The Facts of Life from Birth to Death* (New York, The Macmillan Company, 1951), p. 39.

In a recent survey of a random sample of Senior women in a Midwest liberal arts college, it was discovered that military service, either actual or expected, had been a complicating factor in over 90 per cent of the serious love affairs experienced by this group. The student interviewers reported that this topic created as much interest, or more, than any other on the schedule.[2]

Some of the questions related to this topic are: Should I marry him before he goes in the service, or wait until he comes out? And if we do decide to go ahead and get married, should I become a camp follower or stay at home and wait for him? If we decide to wait until he has "served his time"—this sounds like the moll waiting for her man to get his parole—is it safe to get married as soon as he comes out? Or should we wait a while to make sure that we still feel the same way about each other? Do you think he will change much while he is in the service? Should I date while he is away?

These are, indeed, rather knotty questions. And yet, they are all very legitimate questions that thousands of young couples are wrestling with every day in our society.

In the old days, long, long ago, there used to be short periods of war, followed by long periods of peace, and it was only when the country was actually at war that a man could be drafted. As late as the early 1930's, it would have been unthinkable to tell a young couple in the United States that they could not be married because Draft Board 18 needed the young man to meet its June quota. There *were* no draft boards at that time. Only the men who had volunteered to join reserve units could be called into the armed forces.

Now, this former condition of war and peace seems old-fashioned and quaint, having been replaced by a state of permanent preparedness under which we are neither at war nor are we at peace. And so young lovers all over the land have to make their plans with one eye on selective service.

In this chapter we propose to state the basic problems created by almost universal military service and to analyze them as systematically as possible. We do not pretend to have any research data on these matters and will therefore base most of the discussion on case studies and notes made at various conferences where this problem has been debated.

Some Basic Questions

1. *Should we marry before he goes in or wait until he comes out?*

It seems to the writer that this question can hardly be answered until the basic one is answered: *Should we marry at all?* The main danger in marrying a man in the armed forces is not that he is in the Army or Navy or some other military outfit; the danger results from the inadequate courtship associated with so many service romances.

For this reason, we suggest that *when* you marry a service man is not the basic question, and that the main question is this: *Should we two persons get married?* And when that question has been adequately answered, then the time has come to settle on the date of the wedding.

Actually, this problem is not too different from that which faces thousands of engaged couples every day: *When* should we get married? Should we wait until graduation? Until he gets his next raise? Until my mother has had her operation? These and even more frustrating problems are always facing people in love.

We suggest this approach to analysis of the problem. Let us suppose that a girl named Ruth thinks she is in love with a young man named Bill, who is a Senior in college and expects to be called into service when he graduates in June. Should they get married then or wait until he has served his time? Isn't it obvious that we have to start back at the beginning and ask a whole series of basic questions? How long have they known each other? How long have they gone together? Have they had an engagement? Does it seem to have been adequate? Do they know each other's families very well? If so, what do the families think of the marriage plans? What reasons are there to think that this will be a good marriage? Are they skipping some courtship stage in order to marry before he goes in the service?

In all these questions, we are simply trying to discover whether or not the courtship has been adequate; and this is the same question which has to be faced by all couples considering marriage.

Here is another way to put it: suppose Bill were *not* going into the service, would Ruth be ready to marry him now? If not, then why should it make any difference whether or not he is going into the armed forces?

There may be some confusion here between peacetime military service and that involving actual combat. In the latter case, there is always a distinct possibility that the young man will not return, and so the couple grab a few days of honeymoon before he goes overseas. This was the pattern during World Wars I and II, and any one who has ever been in love can understand why some of these young lovers cut their courtships a little short.

Fortunately, however, most of our men in the service at this time are not facing such grim prospects. Therefore, to a large extent, the factors that produced hasty war marriages are not present today.

If the courtship has been adequate, then we see no reason why the couple should not marry before he enters service if they wish to. After all, no one can predict international developments in modern society, and it seems dubious for young couples to plan their lives in terms of what selective service or the armed forces will do. If they have adequately tested their compatibility for marriage—and this includes consulting their parents—then we believe they should marry when they feel ready. It is foolish to wait for peace or normality. After the catastrophic economic crash of 1929, many engaged couples postponed their wedding plans for a year, waiting for prosperity to return. A year later, however, economic conditions were even worse, and they continued to decline until 1932, by which time the engaged couples had been waiting for three years, and most of them decided to go ahead and get married. Actually, they would have had to wait *eleven* years for prosperity to return, since the economy did not recover fully until 1940. In view of the dynamic nature of modern society, it seems to us that today's conditions, whatever they may be, have to be accepted as normal and plans made on that basis. If we wait for things to return to normal, we may wait a long time.

2. *Will he change very much in the service?*

One might ask just the reverse of this question: will *I* change very much while he is away? Or will we *both* change very much during the separation?

Actually, the consensus of psychologists and psychiatrists is that basic personality patterns are remarkably constant in human beings and that most of the changes are superficial. This indicates that one need not worry too much about this problem.

Even if he *does* change while in the service, it need not be assumed that the change will be negative in nature. In the case of young men going into the armed forces, there is considerable reason to believe that most of the personality change will be for the better —in other words, that he will mature or "grow up." This sort of change should not pose any problems unless the courtship was superficial or of the "puppy love" type, in which case the relationship would probably not survive the reunion.

One of the advantages of not marrying too young is that personality patterns should be more stable in the twenties than in the teen-age period.

It should be recognized that personality change after marriage is a hazard that must be faced by *all* married couples, not just those facing military service.

In general, it seems to us that this hazard, although real, is not very great for couples past their teens who have had an adequate courtship.

3. *My parents are opposed to marriage while he is in the service. What can I do about it?*

Well, for one thing, you could try to *understand* the reasons for their opposition. It may well be, for example, that they do not approve of this particular person and are simply using the military service angle as a useful tool. It might also be that they do not feel that the courtship has been long or deep enough. And, of course, they could be right on one of or all these grounds for opposing an immediate marriage.

On the other hand, these parents may be confused about modern peacetime military service and may be regarding this as an old-fashioned war marriage, simply because the man is in uniform. It may help to remember that this is the first generation of young people to face a peacetime draft in our society, so that parents may need help in understanding how these marriages differ from those of World Wars I and II.

Case Study: In this case, the girl was a Senior in college and her boy friend was in military service, stationed in Europe. The girl's family was prominent in their community, members of the upper-class social set. Her mother, in particular, was a Brahmin and upheld the conservative customs of her illustrious ancestors. The couple had hoped to be married before the young man went overseas but the Air Force ruined these plans by flying him out of the country with short notice.

At this point the girl was resigned to waiting until his discharge when it was suggested to her that perhaps her family might permit her to fly to Europe after graduation and be married there. It was pointed out that her family had offered her a trip to Europe as a graduation present and that this might be worked in as part of the honeymoon.

When this plan was first suggested to the girl's family, the father approved of it at once, but the mother was less than enthusiastic. She was worried about chaperones, public opinion, and a host of other details. Finally, her approval was obtained when the chaplain of the air base in Germany wrote a fine letter, offering to marry the couple and to help with plans for the wedding. The mother did insist that an aunt make the trip with the girl since it would not be possible for the parents to go.

As it finally worked out, the young couple were married in a very old church in Germany one week after her graduation from college. The Air Force granted a two-week furlough and the couple spent their honeymoon in the Bavarian Alps. Furthermore, all these plans finally carried the complete approval of both families.

This case may seem almost too good to be true but it represents an actual couple well known to the writer. It is very important, however, to note a few facts about this case:

A. This was *not* a hasty courtship or a sudden decision to marry. This couple had started dating in high school and had continued through four years of college. Futhermore, they had been engaged for the past year. Thus their families had known for some time that the couple would be married; it was only a matter of *where* and *when.*

B. The girl *completed* her college work before marrying, and this had been one of her family's requests when she became engaged. Thus she had a good bargaining point when the time came to request permission to marry outside the country.

C. Both families fully approved of the marriage, so that they had no reason to use "military service" as a cover-up to hide their disapproval of the prospective son-in-law or daughter-in-law.

D. Finally, this case shows that many complicated situations involving military service, and some that seem impossible, can be solved when approached in the right way. In this case, for example, the girl was sure that her mother would never approve the plan— "You don't know my mother," she said. And yet the mother finally did give her complete support and even paid for the honeymoon as a wedding gift. As the old saying goes, "Where there is a will, there is a way," and this is especially true when people are in love.

4. *If we decide to marry when he goes in, should I become a camp follower?*

Well, the alternative is to stay at home and live apart, which is not much fun for a young married couple.

It is true that living conditions are far from ideal in or near military installations: rents are usually very high, the housing, even though expensive, is usually inadequate, and in general there are numerous problems facing married couples in the service.

On the other hand, they are living together, and most couples seem to feel that this basic goal is worth the hardships involved. During World War II the writer served as a personnel officer in the Naval Air Corps and saw a great many young married couples struggling with the problems under discussion here. In fact, housing and transportation were much more acute then than now. Most of these couples, it seemed to us, preferred living together, with all its difficulties, to the wife staying at home. It was often true, however, that the wife chose to go home, at least temporarily, when she was expecting a baby or had one already.

It should be remembered that living apart for long periods involves sacrifices that may in the long run be more damaging than those of "camp following."

It usually is possible for the wife without children to obtain work in military communities and this often counterbalances the high cost of living typical of such places.

In general, it seems to us that the odds are in favor of going with your husband, whenever this is at all possible.

Case Illustration: A girl known to us married a young man in the Air Force not long ago. When he was assigned to Alaska, her family and friends urged her to stay home, where she had a good job, and wait for him. She decided against this course of action and went to Alaska. They found a place to live, she obtained a job, and they had an interesting experience together. They also had a baby while there without any particular problems presenting themselves. They are now stationed in the United States and have just had their second child. They are glad they did as they did and "wouldn't have missed Alaska for anything."

In all these cases one can see the same pattern: the parents find it hard to understand that young couples today may find it necessary to live at almost any spot on the globe, much more so than was true of the past generation. If this is approached in the right spirit, it can be a "great adventure" for the newlyweds, an experience they will remember all their lives. Parents, however, usually do not see it that way and will often urge the wife to "stay home with us." This is a basic difference between the two generations that cannot always be reconciled easily.

5. *Supposing I don't go with him, how can we keep in close touch with each other?*

This problem presents itself when the couple postpone their marriage until the man's discharge, or when the wife decides to live at home until the discharge. In either case, a very real problem of communication is inherent in the situation.

Fortunately, this problem has been studied by Reuben Hill and the results are published in the monograph, *Families under Stress.*[3] This was a study of married couples in Iowa in which the husband had been drafted during World War II. Hill found that successfully married couples *did* maintain close and intimate interaction in spite of months and years of physical separation. How did they manage this rather remarkable achievement?

A. By frequent, almost daily, letters containing a mass of detail about what they were doing and thinking. Instead of writing "I love you I love you I love you," they wrote vivid descriptions of their daily lives, their problems, and their hopes for the future.

B. They exchanged frequent snapshots of each other, their families, and friends.

On special occasions, such as birthdays and wedding anniversaries, they sent telegrams or called each other via long distance telephone.

On the other hand, the couples who did not maintain good communication wrote infrequently, and their letters were brief and perfunctory: "I am well. Hope you are too. Love, Joe." They exchanged fewer pictures, tended to forget birthdays and anniversaries, and scarcely ever sent telegrams or called by long distance.

C. The better-adjusted couples exchanged frequent gifts, both between themselves and the members' of their families. The less well-adjusted couples did not.

Hill's study reveals that it *is* possible for married couples to maintain close interaction in spite of long and distant separation. In the case of unmarried couples, the same achievement should be possible, providing they are willing to work at it.

It does seem to the writer, however, that *all* correspondence tends to romanticize male-female relationships, and this can be a special hazard for the unmarried couples. When a man is stationed in Korea or Japan, *almost any* girl back home can seem pretty wonderful. If he has had a few pleasant dates with her before leaving the country, it is not hard to begin signing his letters "with lots of love," and pretty soon the mails are almost literally on fire with what seems to be the greatest romance since *Romeo and Juliet.* And yet, their relationship may have been casual, and may still be, if they only knew it.

From the girl's point of view, men in uniform *are* attractive, and it seems unpatriotic not to be "nice" to a poor boy in Alaska or some other far-off place. So she writes nice "gushy" letters, says "I love you" on almost every page, and he soon begins to believe her. As a matter of fact, she soon begins to *believe herself.* Then she tells her friends (but not her family) that she is engaged, etc., etc.

In these air mail love affairs in which the courtship has been brief and superficial, it is important that the relationship be adequately tested after the man returns to the United States. In other words, this is the type of situation in which an immediate marriage upon discharge might be disastrous.

6. *Should I date while he is away?*

If you are married, we think not. You do not have to stay at home every night, or cross the street every time a man tries to say "Hello," but it seems to us risky for a married woman or man to "date," using this term in its usual sense.

It seems to us that there are three distinct hazards in married persons dating:

1. The married partner may misinterpret the relationship, even assuming it to be harmless. After all, jealousy is a rather common emotion in human beings, and especially so in newlyweds who may not as yet be completely sure of each other. And jealousy may occur even after the husband or wife has given verbal approval of the dating.

2. Friends, relatives, neighbors, and the general public are most likely to disapprove of a married person dating, and they will most certainly think the worst of the relationship. It is very difficult for most Americans to believe that a married person can go out with some member of the opposite sex and not violate the marriage vows.

This may be silly or old-fashioned, but it seems to be a fact, nevertheless.

This was brought to our attention when we heard gossip about a college girl whose husband was in the armed forces and had asked his fraternity brothers to escort his wife to various campus events during his absence. The writer believes that there was every indication that these "dates" were entirely innocent and carried the full approval of the husband. Yet gossip *did* develop and damaged the wife's campus reputation. It seems to us that this incident on a so-called "enlightened" college campus indicates how deeply the American people distrust such dating.

3. This hazard is undoubtedly the most serious: namely, that the relationship will *not* remain innocent, even though it began that way. It is not unheard of for couples to fall in love as the result of such dating, but it is probably much more common for them to develop sexual affairs if the dating continues very long. The following case illustrates this type of situation.

A certain man had to leave the country for a year on a professional mission and was not permitted to bring his wife. When he left, he requested a very good friend, a bachelor, to "take his wife out to dinner occasionally." The friend did, and at first the relationship was innocent enough, although it did create some gossip. Within a few months, however, a sexual relationship developed that almost wrecked the marriage. Eventually, when the husband returned, the bachelor friend left the community and the wife was able to salvage her marriage. We would like to point out that both the wife and the bachelor in this case had enjoyed good reputations in this community up to this time and were *not* "promiscuous" persons.

It is not implied, of course, that platonic friendships are impossible for married persons who date, but public opinion seems to hold that they are atypical.

But what about dating while the boy friend is away if you are not married yet? This can be a difficult question, especially for the engaged couple.

It seems to the writer that such couples are probably better off if they agree in advance that each shall have the right to date, at least on a random basis. We suggest this policy for two reasons:

1. The courtship of such couples has often been telescoped or shortened by the man's entry into military service and has frequently been inadequate. Dating in these cases, we believe, will provide additional testing of the relationship.

The problem, of course, develops when the dating ceases to be random and becomes a going steady relationship, thus producing gossip and conflict. It still seems to us, however, that this crisis in itself will be helpful in determining the strength of the engagement.

2. Our second reason is that the chances of the man not dating while in the service are not very high, and it would seem ethical to admit this and grant the girl the privilege of dating also.

It may be that our discussion of this question may offend some of our readers; if this is the case, we can only say that our analysis is based on considerable observation during World War II, and we doubt that American behavior has changed much since then.

Case Study of Selective Service and Courtship: In this case, the young man graduated a year ahead of his girl friend and found his employment prospects seriously interfered with by the fact that he was subject to the draft. Many companies told him: "Come back and see us when you get out." He finally decided to take a temporary job for the year or so before he went into the service.

A year later, his fiancée graduated and they were ready to get married. His selective service board had indicated that he might be called in August—"but we're not sure." There was also a possibility that he might be rejected for military service because of an old high school football injury.

To complicate matters still further, the bride-to-be held a teaching certificate and wanted to teach in the fall, but all her prospective schools wanted assurance that she would stay for at least one full academic year; but how could she promise that when she wanted to be with her husband *if* he was drafted and *if* he was accepted?

And to top it all off, the girl's parents objected to her

marrying a "soldier" and wanted her to wait until "all this military business is settled."

In discussing the situation with us, the girl remarked: "How on earth can you plan when everything is up in the air?" A very good question, we would say.

Summary

In this chapter we have tried to face the fact that universal military service has become a standard feature of modern society and that any honest discussion of courtship and marriage has to face this fact. It is futile, in our opinion, to consider this state of affairs as "temporary" or "abnormal"; the generation of boys and girls now entering the courtship system were born about 1940 and have lived all their lives under the shadows of war or threats of war. As a matter of fact, most of their parents fell in love and got married with one eye on the local selective service board. Let us, then, not delude ourselves that peace is just around the corner. It may well be, but it seems very likely to be an armed peace, one that will not alter appreciably the draft situation.

If our analysis is correct, then it follows that profound repercussions will be felt, or *are* being felt, by our courtship and marriage system. And in this chapter we have been trying to see what some of these repercussions are. The research to date is not very helpful in this area and we have had to piece together some of the patterns through the use of case study material. How typical or modal our cases are cannot be determined until quantitative studies penetrate this area.

In our teaching and counseling, it has seemed to us that the biggest obstacle to clear thinking about courtship problems related to military service is the *newness* of the "peacetime draft," as they call it, plus the feeling (or hope) that the situation is only temporary. Thus it is hard for parents to see these matters clearly, and this in turn makes it more difficult for young people to grope their way through these dilemmas with any great degree of success.

In the last analysis, the courtship and marriage problems

related to military service are almost always soluble, but only for those couples and those families with enough courage and imagination to look at them honestly and creatively. Given these attributes, we subscribe to the old adage that "love conquers all."

References

1. Ernest Hemingway, *Farewell to Arms* (New York, Chas. Scribner's Sons, 1929).

2. This was a 1956 study conducted by two of the writer's students: Janet Layman and Barbara Van Epps. They drew a random sample of Senior women using lists supplied by the college registrar's office. The total sample included about one third of the graduating Senior women. The basic aim of the study, as yet unpublished, was to analyze the courtship patterns of the group as they looked back over their four years of campus dating. A loosely structured interview method was used to obtain the data.

3. Reuben Hill, *Families Under Stress* (New York, Harper & Bros., 1949).

Suggested Readings

1. Although not concerned with courtship problems as such, the monograph *Families Under Stress* by Reuben Hill (New York, Harper & Bros., 1949) is closely related to the issues discussed in this chapter. The basic difference, of course, is that the couples studied by Hill were already married, but the problem they faced was the same: military service on the part of the man.

2. Chap. 19, "Adjustment to External Crises," in Ruth Shonle Cavan's text, *The American Family* (New York, Thomas Y. Crowell Co., 1953) contains an excellent summary of the literature related to military service and marital adjustment.

3. Willard Waller's study, *The Veteran Comes Back* (New York, The Dryden Press, 1944) contains some material that can be helpful to persons wishing to know what some veterans of military service face when they return to civilian life. Women, in particular, might find this helpful.

4. James H. S. Bossard, "War and the Family," in *Family, Marriage, and Parenthood*, edited by Howard Becker and Reuben Hill (Boston, D. C. Heath & Co., 1955 edition).

5. Ernest W. Burgess and Harvey J. Locke, *The Family* (New York, American Book Co., 1953), chap. 21, "War and the Family."

PART III

MARRIAGE IN
MODERN SOCIETY

CHAPTER XI

MARITAL ADJUSTMENT

Introduction

In Part II of the text a great deal of space was devoted to the analysis of dating and/or courtship: the process by which individuals come to get married. Our justification for spending so much time on courtship was simply that prevention is better than cure—in other words, that more attention needs to be focused on what happens *before* marriage rather than concentrated on what happens *after* marriage. Now that we have traced, almost step by step, the path leading to marriage, we are ready to follow the newlyweds into their new home and see what happens to them.

In this part of the discussion, we will be selecting certain factors, such as money, which seem to be related to marital adjustment, and examining them in some detail. It may seem at times that we are ignoring the interrelatedness of all these factors, but this is not actually the case. It is impossible to look at all the basic elements of marriage simultaneously, except in certain types of statistical research, and this fact necessitates isolating each variable temporarily for detailed analysis. Eventually, however, we shall try to piece the puzzle together again, to look at marital adjustment as a total process.

THE SATURDAY EVENING POST

After our examination of marital adjustment and the factors involved in it, we will be ready to move on to parenthood, child-rearing, and the new community roles of the young parents. And that will bring us to the end of our journey.

The Concept of Marital Adjustment

It might be helpful at the outset if we could specify what is meant by "marital adjustment." Certainly, we are not referring to the perfect marriage, whatever that might be. On the contrary our concept of marital adjustment is one of *degree*: that some marriages are better (or worse) than others, but that all marriages could be better (or worse). If we assume that marriages can be scored from zero to 100 per cent, one might design a chart that would look something like this:

DEGREE OF MARITAL ADJUSTMENT

| 0%————25%————50%————75%————100% |
| Poor   Fair   Good   Very Good |

On purely theoretical grounds, one would expect to find relatively few, if any, marriages at the extreme ends of the scale or continuum. Interestingly enough, Locke found that even his divorced couples usually had some affection and/or mutual interests left, that even *their* marriages could hardly be scored at the zero point.[1] In the Terman study of marital adjustment, he found some very high scores but no marriages that could be rated as perfect.[2] For these reasons, it seems clear that marital adjustment is always a matter of *degree*.

Furthermore, it seems to be true that marital adjustment is always relative to a time factor—to *when* the evaluation is made. Any given couple, for example, may score high or low at one phase of their life and differently at another stage. This means that marital adjustment, just as personal adjustment, is a continuous process, that it is not fixed at marriage once and for all. Some marriages may get better and better, others may get worse and worse, while others might fluctuate but in no continuous direction. Some might even fluctuate widely while others might vary only slightly from some fairly stable norm.

Viewed in this way, marital adjustment can be conceptualized as a *capacity for adjustment* or adaptation, as ability to *solve* problems rather than as *absence* of problems. The latter view, it seems to us, is held by many, especially the unmarried, and represents an extremely superficial view of marriage. As a matter of fact, the main characteristic of well-adjusted married couples is not that they do not have problems but that they can work together at a solution of their problems.[3] The maladjusted couples, on the other hand, often do not seem to have insuperable difficulties, but somehow they cannot move toward a solution. Their time seems to be spent largely battling each other, leaving little time or energy for an attack on their mutual problems.[4]

In a recent critique of family research, Foote and Cottrell have suggested that the entire concept of marital adjustment be discarded.[5] Their main criticism seems to be that the term "adjustment" is too static, and that it leads to a false view of modern marriage—the adjusted couple who seem to live in a perpetual state of placid bliss. They feel that we need a new and more dynamic concept to describe the successful marriage, one that emphasizes change and the ability of married couples and their families to face the future and conquer it. As they put it: ". . . interpersonal competence is neither a trait nor a state. Competence denotes capabilities to meet and deal with a changing world, to formulate ends and implement them." [6]

The writer believes that there is much merit in the Foote and Cottrell critique, but it is too early as yet to see what impact this new theoretical approach will have on marriage and family research.

In addition to degree and time, marital adjustment seems to vary according to what *aspect* of marriage we are examining. A couple may have excellent religious rapport, for example, but a poor sexual relationship. Another couple might argue vehemently about money but get along well sexually, and so on. This means that *total* adjustment in marriage is actually a *composite* or an average of numerous subscores, each of which represents some basic facet of the relationship. This is actually the approach used in the several studies of marital adjustment published to date.[7]

This, then, gives us five basic characteristics of marital adjustment in our society:

1. It is always a matter of degree.

2. It varies from one time to another in the life cycle of any given marriage.

3. It varies from one aspect of the marriage to another.

4. It represents a sum total, or an average, of several adjustments, each of which relates to some important phase of the marriage.

5. Marital adjustment is best thought of as a *capacity for solving problems* rather than as a fixed amount of something or other.

The Problem of Defining a "Good" Marriage

Social scientists tend to be allergic to words such as "good" or "bad," and yet it is hard to avoid them completely in a discussion of marriage. One solution to the problem is to substitute other words: in place of "good," for example, we put "successful," and for "bad" we substitute "unsuccessful." This may be an improvement in that the terms substituted are somewhat more objective in tone, but have we really solved our problem? We think not, for we are still faced with the big question: What is a "successful" (or "good") marriage?

In functional analysis, we attempt to solve the problem by going back one step and asking a previous question: What is a marriage supposed to do in our society? In other words, what functions is it expected to accomplish? Once these are specified, it becomes possible to measure to what extent any given marriage succeeds (or fails) in achieving its basic goals.

This may sound fairly simple, but in actuality it is not. The reason is that the "experts" do not agree on what the basic functions of marriage are in our society. The marital prediction group, for example,[8] the individuals who have done the most empirical research on the system, have taken couple satisfaction as the basic test of marital success or failure. Essentially, they have based their criteria on the romantic complex, the idea that personal compatibility between a man and woman is the ultimate test of any marriage in our society. And one must admit that this approach seems to be very plausible indeed.

There is another group of scholars, however, who reject the

above criteria and seek to evaluate marriages in a broader context. These include Hill,[9] Kolb,[10] Foote and Cottrell,[11] Davis,[12] and Murdock.[13] This group has argued that we need something better than "happiness" or "adjustment" in attempting to define "successful" marriage.

The writer must confess that as a sociologist he believes "couple satisfaction" to be too narrow a base for the evaluation of an institution as basic as marriage. We agree with Linton [14] that marriages, in *any* society, perform a variety of functions, such as the production and rearing of children, and that these are too important to be ignored in establishing criteria for evaluating marriages.

One of the reasons why it is difficult to agree on the criteria of successful marriage is that the functions of the family itself have been changing in our society.[15] The home is no longer a miniature factory, as it was in colonial America; the school and other social agencies have taken over many of the family's traditional jobs. This, undoubtedly, has emphasized the psychological or personality functions of the family, and this is reflected in the use of couple satisfaction by the marital prediction research groups.

The writer sides with those who reject that type of criterion and will attempt at this point to suggest an alternate set of standards by which modern marriages can be judged.

Alternate Values for Evaluating Marriages

If couple satisfaction or couple happiness is to be rejected as an inadequate base for evaluating any given marriage in modern society, it becomes necessary to specify an alternate set of values as a measuring stick. The following are suggested as possibilities:

1. *The potentials for growth or maturation in each partner are at least partially achieved.*

It seems clear that most of us are only partially grown when we marry, and this is increasingly so as the age of marriage declines, as it has in recent decades.[16] From this point of view, the first five or ten years of marriage become crucial in determining whether or not we will develop into the man or woman we are capable of becoming. Duval [17] and Elder [18] have shown that the definition of the "good" parent in our society more and more includes this developmental [19] ingredient: that the best parents are those who can help their children attain the physical, emotional, intellectual, social, and moral growth of which they are capable. Should this not also be a test for the good husband or wife?

All of us have observed marriages in which this has not been the case. In one known to the writer, the wife had a deep need to be emotionally dependent upon other persons. Her husband, with whom she was very happy, encouraged her in this dependency. Many years later, when the husband died unexpectedly, she had an extremely difficult time adjusting to the deprivation. It was at this point that she and her close friends were able to see a serious flaw in what had otherwise been a very fine marriage. It is not suggested that this was a poor marriage, for it was not; but the fact remains that it would have been a better relationship if the husband could have helped the wife outgrow her dependency need instead of having encourged it.

In another marriage studied by the writer, the husband has strong egocentric or selfish tendencies. His first wife tried to help him overcome this trait, but after her death he married a woman who did not oppose his egocentrism. This man is well satisfied with his second marriage—it is very comforting, to say the least—but his close associates feel that he has deteriorated.

It should be made clear that by "growth" in this discussion we do not mean economic advancement or a rise in social status. On the contrary, we are referring to emotional maturation, the expansion of intellectual horizons, the development of moral stature, etc.

It is readily granted that this criterion is not easily measured. But it seems to be true that marriages in our society cannot be adequately evaluated without reference to this type of standard.

2. *There is a mutually satisfying relationship between the married couple and their parental families.*

In a child-centered society, such as ours, parents are apt to suffer a major deprivation if the marriage of their children destroys or seriously damages the parent-child relationship. Given an urban, impersonal, mobile society such as we have, it becomes crucial to maintain at least a few deep and permanent interpersonal relationships. For this reason, we believe that one criterion of a successful marriage in our society must include the extent to which it solidifies parent-child and married couple–parental relationships. If it does not satisfy this requirement, it is to that extent an unsuccessful marriage.

We realize it is not popular to talk about parents' rights in our culture, but considering the central role played by children in the lives of modern parents, it seems only fair that they derive some satisfaction from the marriages of their children. Otherwise, the twenty years of effort they put into the child may have been in vain.

3. *In a good marriage there is love for children and a desire to rear a family.*

This is an absolute necessity from society's point of view, and it is also one of the reasons for the existence of marriage in human society. Most of the marital adjustment studies to date have found "desire for children" to be positively associated with marital adjustment.[20]

It is not meant that all couples actually have to produce children, for this is not always physically possible, but they should love children and look forward to the possibility of having a family.

In a sense, this criterion is related to the first on growth or development. Having children is a normal part of becoming an adult and one expects that a successful marriage would enable the partners to achieve this goal.

4. *In our society, a successful marriage has to be adaptable.*

This means that the patterns of family organization must be flexible, that crucial roles can be reassigned to various members of the group if necessary.

In various studies of American families in crisis during the past twenty years,[21] it has been shown that our dynamic and rapidly changing society places a premium on adaptability, not only for personal survival, but also for group survival.

In a recent study of the two-income marriage by Dyer,[22] it was discovered that the most successful were those in which the husband and wife were able to share and help each other with the various tasks related to family living. Foote and Cottrell emphasize this characteristic in their monograph.[23]

In one marriage known to the writer, the husband can cook, change diapers, do the wash, and even iron a shirt if necessary. His wife, on her part, can paint the house, run the power mower, sand floors, and support the family if she has to (as she did for several months at one time when her husband was unemployed). These couples are resilient: they can adapt their way of living to almost any crisis. They seem to have the secret of survival in modern society.

5. *The husband and wife, and their children, look toward the home for their deepest satisfactions.*

In good times or bad, the home and the family it houses stand ready to aid and support all members of the group. The family members "face in" for their deepest needs. In our kind of society, this type of security is crucial. In poor marriages, one gets the impression that one or both partners find it necessary to look elsewhere for their basic need—sex, love, companionship, or whatever it may be. This also seems to be true of children living in disorganized or poorly organized families—most juvenile delinquents, for example.

It is recognized that the five basic criteria advanced above are only tentative, and that another text might present an entirely different list.[24] It is suggested that the reader apply these values to the marriages he knows and see whether or not they are helpful. Perhaps class discussion will reveal how adequate or inadequate the criteria are.

We are now ready to ask another big question: What factors are associated with marital adjustment? The rest of this chapter will be devoted to the answering of this question.

Factors Associated with Marital Adjustment

Although it is recognized that marital adjustment may be affected by a multitude of factors, there must be some variables more crucial than others. Therefore, this discussion will not attempt to enumerate or analyze *all* the influences operating on any given husband-wife relationship but will focus on those that seem to be basic in their impact.

Fortunately, this is an area in which a great deal of research has been published, so that one does not need to "fly by the seat of the pants," the pilot's description of what he has to do when his instruments are not giving him adequate information.

Judging by the research in courtship and marriage to date, the following factors appear to be the most crucial for marital adjustment:

1. Personality factors	6. Attitudes toward money
2. Family background	7. Religion and basic values
3. Social class background	8. Children
4. Sexual factors	9. Male and female subculture
5. In-law relationship	

It may well be, of course, that other factors, as yet undetected by observers, are equally basic. It is well known, for example, that *sheer determination* to make a success of marriage is an extremely important variable in marital adjustment. This is hard to measure and is not adequately reflected in our current marital adjustment tests. It seems obvious, however, that some couples enter marriage with many advantages and still fail, whereas other couples begin their marriages with "two strikes against them" and still succeed. Every athletic coach knows that determination to win is a basic factor in competitive athletics, just as colleges know that two students with similar placement test scores may make very different academic records. There is every reason to believe that the same principle operates in marital adjustment.

In the above list of nine sets of factors crucial to marital adjustment, it should be pointed out that the third one, social class background, does not appear in most discussions of courtship and marriage and some readers may be surprised to find it here. Our justification for stressing it is simply this: in the last decade of social science research in the United States, the evidence has become overwhelming that almost everything we do, from voting to kissing our wives, is affected by the subculture of our socioeconomic level. For this reason, plus the fact that the average student is relatively unaware of such influence, we have felt justified in giving some detailed analysis to social class background and its relationship to marital interaction.

It may also be true that some readers will be puzzled to find the sixth, attitudes toward money, in our list, since most of the marital adjustment studies do not stress this factor. The reason is simply that we believe very profoundly that most of the marriage studies to date have failed to discover the role of money in modern marital adjustment.[25] In the two chapters devoted to this topic, we have attempted a critique of these studies and have analyzed in some detail what seems to us to be the very profound role played by money and attitudes toward money in American marriage.

In the same vein our ninth set of factors, male and female subculture, also represents a belief of the writer that the research to date has failed to isolate the profound effect of male and female social backgrounds on marital expectations and the role these play in marital adjustment. We hope to demonstrate the relevance of this material in the two chapters devoted to the topic.

It can readily be seen that the basic plan of Part III of the book is to devote specific chapters to each of the variables believed to be most crucial for marital adjustment. This will get us into parenthood and child-rearing as well, since these are intimately related to marital interaction. Then, before concluding our discussion, it seems essential that we try to give the student some perspective on marital failure in modern society, how to view his own parents if they are unhappily married or divorced, and what to do if he should feel at a later date that his own marriage was failing.

The book will close with an analysis of the young married couple in the community: their relationship to their neighborhood, community, and the larger society.

References

1. See Harvey J. Locke, *Predicting Adjustment in Marriage* (New York, Henry Holt & Co., Inc., 1951), pp. 55–57.

2. Lewis M. Terman *et al.*, *Psychological Factors in Marital Happiness* (New York, McGraw-Hill Book Co., 1938), p. 63.

3. Locke, *op. cit.*, chap. 4.

4. For an excellent analysis of constructive argument, see Reuben Hill and Willard Waller, *The Family* (New York, Dryden Press, 1951), pp. 309–312.

5. See Nelson N. Foote and Leonard S. Cottrell, Jr., *Identity and Interpersonal Competence* (Chicago, University of Chicago Press, 1955).

6. *Op. cit.*, p. 49.

7. For a general review and discussion of these studies, see Ernest W. Burgess and Paul Wallin, *Engagement and Marriage* (Philadelphia, J. B. Lippincott Co., 1953), chap. 2.

8. This statement refers to the studies reviewed in the Burgess-Wallin reference above.

9. See Hill's rather severe critique of the marital prediction studies in Hill and Waller, *op. cit.*, pp. 353–361.

10. William L. Kolb, "Sociologically Established Family Norms and Democratic Values," *Social Forces*, 26 (1948), 451–456.

11. *Op. cit.*, chap. 2.

12. Kingsley Davis, *Human Society* (New York, The Macmillan Company, 1949), chap. 15.

13. George Peter Murdock, *Social Structure* (New York, The Macmillan Company, 1949).

14. Ralph Linton, *The Study of Man* (New York, Appleton-Century-Crofts, Inc., 1936), chap. 11.

15. The classic discussion of this is to be found in William F. Ogburn, "The Changing Functions of the Family," *Journal of Home Economics*, 25 (1933), 660–664.

16. For a review of this data, see W. F. Ogburn and M. F. Nimkoff, *Technology and the Changing Family* (Boston, Houghton Mifflin Co., 1955), chap. 4.

17. Evelyn M. Duvall, "Conceptions of Parenthood," *American Journal of Sociology*, 52 (November, 1946), 193–203.

18. Rachel Ann Elder, "Traditional and Developmental Conceptions of Fatherhood," *Marriage and Family Living* (August, 1949), 98–104.

19. For a discussion of the concept of "development," see Robert J. Havighurst, *Human Development and Education* (New York, Longmans, Green & Co., 1953), chap. 1.

20. For a review of this material, see Burgess and Wallin, *op. cit.*, chap. 21.

21. For a review of these studies, see Reuben Hill, *Families Under Stress* (New York, Harper & Bros., 1949), chap. 2.

22. Everett D. Dyer, "A Study of Role and Authority Patterns and Expectations in a Group of Urban Middle-Class Two-Income Families," unpublished Ph.D. dissertation (Madison, University of Wisconsin Library, 1955).

23. *Op. cit.*

24. See Hill's discussion, for example, in Hill and Waller, *op. cit.*, pp. 361–370.

25. See William J. Goode, *After Divorce* (Glencoe, The Free Press, 1956) for data supporting our point of view on this question.

Suggested Readings

1. Nelson N. Foote and Leonard S. Cottrell, Jr., *Identity and Interpersonal Competence* (Chicago, University of Chicago Press, 1955), chap. 2, "Interpersonal Competence." This discussion tackles the general proposition of evaluating marital relationships in our society.

2. Reuben Hill and Willard Waller, *The Family* (New York, The Dryden Press, 1951), chap. 17, "Marital Success." This is one of the more penetrating discussions of the problem of defining successful marriage.

3. Ernest W. Burgess and Paul Wallin, *Engagement and Marriage* (Philadelphia, J. B. Lippincott Co., 1953), chap. 2, "The Study of Marriage," pp. 33–44. This gives a relatively complete review of the attempts to define, measure, and predict marital adjustment or success.

4. Albert Ellis, "The Value of Marriage Prediction Tests," *American Sociological Review*, 13 (1948), 710–718. Reprinted in abridged form in Robert F. Winch and Robert McGinnis, *Selected Studies in Marriage and the Family* (New York, Henry Holt & Co., Inc., 1953), pp. 493–506. Ellis presents the critical view of the marital prediction studies.

5. Lewis M. Terman and Paul Wallin, "The Validity of Marriage Prediction and Marital Adjustment Tests," *American Sociological Review*, 14 (1949), 497–504. Also reprinted in adapted form in Winch and McGinnis, *op. cit.*, pp. 507–518.

CHAPTER XII

PERSONALITY FACTORS IN MARITAL ADJUSTMENT

Introduction

It should be obvious, even to the least discerning person, that an individual's personality or temperament would have a deep effect on his (or her) marriage. After all, it does not take elaborate research or a battery of IBM calculating machines to determine that "pleasant" persons might be easier to live with than "grouchy" persons; or that well-adjusted men and women make better marital partners than do maladjusted ones. All this seems obvious enough. At the same time, however, there is still a lot we do not know about *how* personality factors affect marital adjustment. Isn't it true, for example, that some couples who look as though they could not adjust to each other actually do get along together very well? Isn't it also true that some couples who seem well mated do not seem to be very happy living together? Is it also not true that most of us have known a person we considered well adjusted who does not seem to be able to make the transition to marital happiness?

241

In all the above situations it may well be that personality factors are not the basic problem, that in-laws or something else may be the main problem. The function of this chapter is to explore *how* personality affects marital interaction, and how it is related to other factors involved in marital success. We would like to know if there are personality types not suited for marriage, or if any type is especially well suited for this way of life. Is the extremely brilliant person, for example, or the artist, a poor marriage risk? Are introverts harder to live with than extroverts? Can anybody live happily with a neurotic? [1]

As you can see, these are not simple questions. But they are all relevant questions that we need to think about in analyzing modern marriage. It may very well be that we will not be able to answer some of these questions, but at least we can state them clearly, demonstrate their relevance to marriage, and examine such evidence as we can find. Even if we succeed only in discovering what is *not* known about personality factors in marriage, our work may be worthwhile.

The Terman Research

In 1938 Lewis M. Terman and associates at Stanford University published an elaborate study of 792 married couples, *Psychological Factors in Marital Happiness,*[2] the main purpose of which was to investigate the role of personality (or temperament) factors in marital adjustment. In general, the study concluded that individual temperament *is* one of several major determinants of marital satisfaction. As a matter of fact, what Terman really discovered was that well-adjusted persons are well adjusted: in other words, that persons who could be described as well adjusted *before* marriage could usually be described in the same terminology *after* marriage. His main point seems to be that one's personal adjustment precedes marriage and tends to persist at roughly the same level after marriage.[3]

If we think about it, Terman has a valuable point for us:

that there is nothing miraculous about the marriage ceremony that makes a new person out of us, that our basic personality patterns are not that flexible. This seems reasonable enough. Actually, if this were not the case, one might hesitate to marry for fear that the other person might change into something (or somebody) entirely different, once the minister had pronounced the magic words.

It seems that almost everything psychology and psychiatry tell us about adults tends to support Terman. Most of us are fairly stable and predictable in our basic personality patterns.

Does this mean that individuals do not change at all after the age of marriage? It does not. It does mean, however, that the changes may be *much less* than is often assumed. It also means that it is a questionable move to marry someone on the theory that "he'll change after we're married." He probably will, at least to some extent, but does it follow that the changes will be in the *desired direction?* Or will he change *enough?* These seem to be crucial questions. Americans have a tendency to regard all change as progress or improvement, but the social scientist knows this is not true. It could very well be that as many marriages are damaged by personality changes after marriage as are improved. As a matter of fact, one of the common complaints of the unhappily married person is that the partner has changed.

In Terman's study he found that the happiness of parents had a significant relationship to the marital adjustment of the child.[4] Essentially, this seems to mean that the intense parent-child relationship in our society tends to produce adjustment patterns that are relatively continuous from one generation to another. If one accepts Terman's work, it appears that marital adjustment and personality adjustment tend to run in families, as the geneticists used to say. The other marital adjustment studies tend to support Terman in this finding.[5]

Does this mean that we all have to marry into happy families? Terman would certainly recommend it, but the plain fact is that we cannot always do it. For one thing, there are not enough of these so-called "happy" families to meet the demand, and further-more, we often find ourselves in love with persons not fortunate enough to be reared in a nest of bliss and contentment. As a matter of cold fact, at least a third of the courtship partners available in most American communities have probably come from somewhat disorganized families. Does Terman's work mean that one should avoid marrying one of these individuals? Does it mean that you or I should not marry if we come from an unhappy family situation? No, it does not mean that. If it did, a lot of us could never look forward to marriage. We know that some persons actually have *better* marriages for having grown up in homes characterized by conflict. Such a person has seen what a poor marriage can do to parents and children and is determined not to let this happen to his own marriage.

The picture is not always this rosy, however. Some persons are actually damaged by their family environment and emerge from it not well suited for marriage.

Basically, all that Terman has found is this: that a well-adjusted family experience is an asset in looking forward to mar-riage, and this seems reasonable enough. Conversely, he has found that an unhappy, disorganized family experience is a liability in looking forward to marriage, but not usually an impossible liability; not usually one that cannot be overcome.

But, you say, what should I do if I come from one of these poor family environments? The main thing to do, it seems to us, is to acknowledge the fact, and then to try to understand yourself and the needs that resulted from the unfavorable family relation-ships. The next step is to find a person who can meet your particular needs, and whose needs you can meet.

It probably boils down to this: that those of us not lucky enough to grow up in happy families are probably somewhat more complex personalities, with perhaps more acute emotional needs. If this is so, it follows that we have to approach marriage with more insight and more caution than the persons from more favorable family backgrounds.

It may be, of course, that some persons have had such traumatic family experiences that marriage may be a questionable goal for them. Such persons should have psychiatric consultation before attempting a relationship as complex as modern marriage. In some cases, a later marriage seems to be the solution to such problems.

It is important not to assume that *all* persons from well-organized families are well adjusted, or that *all* persons from poorly organized families are maladjusted. Terman is talking about statistical *probabilities*, not certainties. The writer recalls a student who came up after a lecture on Terman's study and said: "According to Terman I should be maladjusted, because my mother has been married four times, but I don't think I'm maladjusted at all." We came to know this student very well and agreed wholeheartedly that he was an exception to Terman's conclusions. However, this student had actually lived most of his life with his maternal grandparents, with whom he had a deep and satisfying relationship, and this was probably the explanation as to how he had escaped being damaged by his neurotic mother.

Can the Maladjusted Person Solve His Problems Through Marrying the "Right" Person?

Students often suggest that marriage can "solve" personality problems if the maladjusted individual marries "the right person." On purely theoretical grounds, this should be possible, providing that the two individuals are properly matched. We are inclined to believe, however, that students tend to exaggerate the *probability* of this type of ideal mate selection. Let us assume, for the purposes of discussion, that *all* of us could make an adjustment to marriage given the right partner (a very dubious assumption, in our opinion). The next question is: What are the chances that the maladjusted individual will be able to select the type of person most helpful to him? It seems to us that the chances are not very good for two reasons: (1) the supply of the special type of individual needed to accomplish this therapy is probably not very large, thus reducing the chances of finding one; and (2) the tolerance range for this type of marital partner is lower than average, which would make it more difficult to find a compatible person to marry. This is essentially what is meant when it is said that courtship is more complex for neurotic or maladjusted persons; it is harder for them to find satisfactory courtship and marriage partners because their requirements are more specialized.

This picture is further complicated by the fact that marital failure is often more damaging for the maladjusted person; other persons close to him have failed him before, usually members of his family, and he cannot afford marital failure as well. The more acute his problem, the less he can stand failure in his marriage.[6]

For all these reasons, we tend to be skeptical of marriage for therapeutic reasons. It seems to us that a person needing therapy would do better to go to a therapist rather than buy a marriage license. It is easy to assume that just the right combination of persons will solve the problem, but aren't the chances just as great that the *wrong* combination will make matters even worse?

If one reflects long enough on Terman's findings, some interesting questions about the utility of divorce and remarriage present themselves. *If* most of our unhappy married partners were unhappy before marriage, as Terman believes, will a change of marriage partners really help them? Or will the next marriage be as unhappy as the first if not more so?

The answer seems to be that for most of them the switch will not do much good. A new husband or a new wife may alleviate the condition but hardly remove it.[7] However, for those who were relatively well adjusted before marriage, a change of partner may be what is needed. In the former case, the problem is essentially *within the self,* whereas in the latter situations the basic problem is in the *relationship* between the two persons. As we shall see in a later chapter on "Marital Failure," this is not always clear to persons involved in an unhappy marriage.

At the same time, all of us have seen miracle marriages in which two persons have overcome what seemed to be hopeless odds. The following case describes such a marriage.

A man known very well to the writer failed in his first marriage. In fact, the relationship was so poor that the wife tried to commit suicide before a divorce was agreed upon.

After the divorce, the friends of this man urged him not to remarry. He was an extremely difficult person to work with, often getting into violent arguments with colleagues, and very few of his associates believed he was capable of sustaining a relationship as close and as pervasive as modern marriage. In other words, they did not believe he could ever find a woman who could live with him successfully.

At the same time, this man was extremely brilliant, accomplished in many different areas of interest, and could be an excellent companion when in a good humor (which was not often).

Amazingly enough, this man met a woman during World War II, married her, and has apparently achieved a successful marriage. They have had one child, have lived together now for almost ten years, and actually seem to be compatible.

The question is: how is this possible? Has the man changed his personality? He does not seem different to his colleagues. What is the answer? Well, this seems to be one of those rare cases of the perfect match. The wife is not upset by her husband's outbursts and feels that they are not directed at her. She is an extremely mature and secure person, one not easily threatened. She feels that she loves her husband and that he loves her. She also admires his learning and his other accomplishments. So far as the close friends can tell, this appears to be a stable and satisfying relationship for both partners.

Cases like this should make us hesitate to say that such and such a person could never be happily married. On the other hand, one should not underestimate the problem faced by such persons in finding a compatible partner.

Winch's Theory of Complementary Needs in Mate Selection

For many years social scientists have been attempting to identify the process by which mate selection in our society takes place. Specifically, we wish to describe the dynamics of *marital choice*, the force or the attraction that pulls the individual toward one particular person and away from others. Until recently, the major theory advanced has been that of *homogamy*, a theory that holds that persons in our society tend to marry persons like themselves. Protestants, for example, marry Protestants more often than they marry non-Protestants; middle-class individuals tend to marry middle-class individuals, etc. These patterns of marriage within our own social group have been confirmed by literally hundreds of studies.[8]

Along with homogamy, another theory has advanced the principle of *propinquity*, which holds that we tend to marry persons spatially in proximity to us, persons who live in our neighborhood, or with whom we went to high school or college, or individuals we work with, etc. In a sense, all that propinquity means is that you cannot marry somebody you have never met—at least not in our courtship system—and your chances of meeting individuals who live and work near you are statistically much greater than your chances of meeting those who reside elsewhere.[9]

Actually, neither the theory of homogamy nor the principle of propinquity really explains *how* particular individuals gravitate toward each other. These two theories simply define a "field of contact and eligibility" but do not reveal the dynamics of individual choice *within* the field. This is what Winch has tried to do with his theory of "complementary needs" in courtship and marital interaction.[10]

Winch states his theory as follows: "While recognizing that mate-selection has been found to be homogamous with respect to numerous social characteristics (religion, socioeconomic status, etc.), the writer has hypothesized that with respect to individual motivation (or at the psychic level) mate-selection tends to be complementary rather than homogamous." [11] To test this hypothesis Winch subjected to intensive study twenty-five husbands and their wives. Using a projective test (the TAT) and two interviews with each spouse, Winch and his staff identified a total of 388 interspousal correlations. He concludes that the bulk of the evidence supports the hypothesis that mates tend to <u>select each other on the basis of complementary needs.</u>

In another study by Ktsanes, an associate of Winch, the findings also support the theory of complementary needs.[12] Ktsanes concludes: "The findings of this study, based upon a sample of recently married, college-age, middle-class couples, indicate that for the population sample the tendency for an individual to select a spouse unlike himself in total emotional make-up far exceeds the tendency for him to select a spouse like himself in that respect." [13]

If these findings are corroborated by other studies,[14] it will mean that the dynamics of individual choice within the field of contact and eligibility will have been explained. Essentially, it will also mean that the folk observation that opposites attract may have something in it after all.

In the opinion of the writer, the implications of the Winch theory for marital adjustment are profound. The theory may explain why marital adjustment is such a complicated process. For example, let us suppose that a mild, unaggressive man chooses (consciously or unconsciously) a dominant female, presumably because he needs such a spouse to complement his need pattern; in other words, he needs a strong wife to lean on. This may explain why he marries Girl *A* instead of Girl *B*, who happens to be meek and mild like himself. But now let us suppose that this man also resents persons who dominate him, and especially dominant women. If this were the situation, the stage would certainly be set for a difficult marital adjustment.

But the possibilities for trouble are not ended. Let us suppose that the wife in this case needs to be dominant in her marriage but at the same time cannot respect a man who submits to her: here again we could expect trouble.

Lest the student dismiss this case as purely theoretical, we will state that it is taken directly from the writer's marriage counseling experience. The husband was essentially a weak person who had married an aggressive, superefficient wife. Both of them had obviously gravitated to the other to meet certain emotional needs in line with Winch's theory. In fact, the marital choice could not be explained on the basis of any other theory. But within ten years this man and woman hated each other, the man resenting bitterly his wife's domination and the woman despising her husband's weakness. Perhaps this is the key for understanding some of the marriages which "look good" but do not work out too well.

It could be that the basic requirement here is *acceptance of the self*.[15] If a man does not accept his need for a strong wife, if he is still struggling against his "weakness," will he focus this struggle on his wife after marriage? And will this prevent a good marital adjustment?

The picture is further complicated by the fact that the marital partners are usually unconscious of these needs and hence do not really know how or why they picked each other. Thus one gets a picture of mate-selection which resembles the game of blind man's buff played by children.

If Winch is correct, then the question is raised as to how rational marital choice can be. It almost seems as though everyone would need to be psychoanalyzed to determine his or her need patterns before marriage. Actually, however, the picture is not that dark, or that expensive. Most persons seem to have some insight into their basic needs and can choose accordingly. The fact that at least half of our marriages are successful supports this point of view.

For the rest of the population, it would probably be very helpful if a relatively simple needs pattern test could be devised for the use of high school and college teachers, ministers, etc. This seems not unlikely in the near future.

From the point of view of the unmarried reader, the main implication of the Winch theory is this: you have to have insight into the deepest needs of both yourself and the other person if marital choice is to reflect any rationality. The fact that you are both Protestants and both like Dixieland jazz music is not enough.

A Case Illustration: We believe that the following case study may serve to illustrate the basic mechanism involved in the theory of complementary needs in marital interaction. The persons involved are an elderly couple known to the writer for a number of years.

In this marriage, the wife was obviously the dominant personality and was recognized as such by the seven children, the neighbors, and the family friends. The mother made the basic decisions involving the children, managed the money, and fought the family's battles in the community. The children, as well as the husband, referred to her affectionately as "The Boss." A large woman, she often reminded one of a busy old hen protecting her flock of chicks and the rooster too.

The husband, a large man physically, was beloved by all and taken advantage of by many. He was the sort of man who could never say "No" when imposed upon by his legion of friends. In fact, everyone in the small town was his friend, for he had no enemies. He was a big lovable "shaggy dog" type of man, the sort of father whom the children adore, but not very practical.

The following typical incident illustrates the way in which these two persons complemented each other. We had been invited to their home for a chicken dinner and upon arrival learned that "The Boss" had had to kill the chicken, as the husband was too fond of the flock to chop any of their heads off. He had, however, caught the hen for his wife, sharpened the hatchet for her, and gave moral support during the cleaning process, but the wife had to do the actual killing. This did not bother her, however, as she had come to expect that sort of role distribution in their marriage.

Was this a good marriage? Well, they reared seven children and celebrated their golden wedding anniversary before death came in their late eighties. It was considered an excellent marriage by the children and all who knew them.

It is true that "The Boss" would become irritated once in a while at the husband for his impracticality, but deep down she enjoyed mothering him and meeting his dependency needs. And he knew that without such a wife he would be almost helpless in facing the world.

The one criticism of this marriage we might make, using the criterion advanced in the chapter on "Marital Adjustment," is that the husband never outgrew his dependency needs; nor did the wife ever gain much insight into her need to mother everybody. But basically it was a good marriage. Our criticism merely shows that it was not a *perfect* marriage.

Winch would argue, of course, that this man and woman were pulled toward each other by their mutual need patterns. We find it hard to dispute that interpretation.

What Is Love?

Sooner or later in this book we will have to tackle the question, *What is love?* We avoided it during the discussion of courtship, largely because we felt that the topic could best be handled in relationship to our analysis of marriage. Now it seems that it can no longer be postponed (or evaded) and the issue must be faced. *What is love?*

Well, for one thing, there are certainly different kinds of love. A man may love to fish, or play poker, but this is hardly the same as the love he feels for his wife. He may even love his automobile, or the music of George Gershwin, but this has little to do with the kind of love we are discussing.

A man usually loves his mother, his sister, and maybe even his mother-in-law, but this again is something different from love in marriage.

A person may love to eat, or love a good horse race, and this too is something else.

The fact is that Americans overwork the verb "love" and use it to describe their feeling for almost anything or anybody ("I just love the traffic cop on that corner. He is *so* polite").

Christianity as a religion places tremendous stress on love: love of God, love of Christ, and love for our fellow human beings. "Love thy neighbor as thyself," we are told.

Democracy as a political philosophy tends to reflect this emphasis upon love—love of one's country, love of freedom, etc.

And then in our families we place great stress on everybody loving everybody else: Dad should love Mother, she should love him, they should both love all their children, who in turn should love each other, etc.

In spite of all the varied and somewhat loose usage of the word "love," however, it still has a certain core of meaning. Essentially, it refers to somebody (or something) we cherish very much; somebody whom we enjoy as an end in himself or herself and not as a means of achieving some other end; it refers to somebody we can accept wholly (or very nearly so) as he is, without the need to remake him.

We think the marriage vow puts it very well: "To love and to cherish, through sickness and health, until death do us part." This is love in a Christian, romantic culture.

It is obvious that marriage love includes the sexual relationship, whereas love for other humans is essentially platonic or nonsexual, at least in overt manifestation.

It seems equally obvious that we would all do well to use the word "love" more discriminately, but this is expecting too much in a culture such as ours.

Undoubtedly, many a courtship relationship that passes for love is actually infatuation—that is, temporary feeling that lacks depth and maturity. Many married couples who appear to be "in love" are not in love at all: they merely play the part for the benefit of their children and their friends.[16]

One might raise the question, Are individuals actually in love when they marry, or is real love achieved only after years of living and sharing together? That is a very neat and very debatable question. Ralph Linton, the anthropologist, has argued that most human societies do not expect young couples to be in love at marriage, believing that this will develop as they live together.[17] To some extent, this represents the notion held by parents in the early American colonial period: that any "nice young couple" could "learn to love each other in time."

But these societies had courtship systems different from ours, and to some extent their couples hardly knew each other at the point of marriage.

For these reasons, we say that most young couples in America probably are "in love" when they marry, but not in the same way they will be on the day of their golden wedding anniversary. In a good marriage, the relationship should broaden and deepen with the years.

Perhaps a more relevant question is this one: How many of us are actually capable of the type of love expected of happily married couples in our society? The writer confesses that he is unable to answer this question, but it is certain that not everybody has this capacity. Psychiatric literature makes frequent reference to the inability to love other persons.[18] It is essential to know our capacity for love in approaching marriage in our society.

Need Patterns or Personality Types

For several decades, psychologists and psychiatrists have attempted to classify individuals according to psychological or personality types: the extrovert-introvert sort of classification. Although all these efforts leave much to be desired, they tend to persist because of the deep need for them. In the systematic (scientific) analysis, it is not enough to conclude that "it depends on the individual," or that "everyone is different." We know this to be true, but if the social scientist is to be helpful, he has to go beyond this point and discover ways of classifying people into categories that will predict most (not all) of their behavior.

For these reasons, it seems necessary in this chapter to attempt to sketch some system of need patterns or personality types that the reader can attempt to apply to himself and his potential (or actual) marital partner.

For our purposes, the work of Winch is probably the most useful.[19] Basing his system on earlier work by Murray, Winch has derived a classification system that includes thirteen specific needs and three general traits. We have used the Winch list intact but have taken the liberty of modifying the description of the needs and traits in an effort to make them more meaningful to the average reader. The list is as follows:

Needs

Abasement—The need to devalue oneself in relation to the marital partner. A need for blame, criticism, or punishment. Has some similarity to the Freudian concept of masochism (the need to be punished in the sexual relationship).

Achievement—The need to work very hard, to create something. This type of person would feel very frustrated if he were not accomplishing something in his work or marriage. This would not bother other persons at all as long as they were "getting by." In the armed forces this type is called "eager."

Approach—A deep need to associate with other persons, to be with people. Has some relationship to the older classification "extrovert." The opposite need is to *withdraw* from people.

Autonomy—This is a relatively new concept referring to independence or freedom from domination. A person with this need pattern could not tolerate a dominant spouse; neither could he stand the clinging type of courtship or marital partner.

Deference—The need to pay homage to the love partner. Has some relationship to *Abasement*. The opposite might be the need to humiliate the partner or to feel superior to the partner.

Dominance—The need to influence and/or control the partner. Also implies an unwillingness to allow the partner to grow up and achieve independence, maturity, or autonomy.

Hostility—The need to injure, hurt, or destroy the partner, usually (but not always) by the use of verbal or other symbolic weapons. In divorce courts this is called "mental cruelty." It involves the absence of warmth and acceptance of the marital partner.

Nurturance—The need to mother the partner, to take care of him or her. It implies that the partner is weak or sick and cannot take care of himself. Such a husband or wife would be frustrated if the partner grew up and no longer needed to be mothered. A husband with this need pattern would tend to think of his wife as his "little girl."

Recognition—A deep need for constant admiration, praise, and recognition from the marital partner and others as well. May be related to what most persons have in mind when they think of someone with an "inferiority complex." A spouse with a need pattern of this sort might complain that the partner "doesn't appreciate me." These individuals can never get enough praise or acknowledgment of their efforts.

Sex—The need to develop and maintain an erotic relationship and to engage in sexual relations. As with the other needs in this list, all normal persons exhibit this need to some extent, but the extent and the expression of the need vary greatly from one person to another. The opposite of this need is represented by the frigid partner who could not respond to sexual overtures and would be perfectly happy if sex were eliminated from human society.

Status Aspiration—A deep admiration for persons of higher social class position and a wish to move up in the social class system.

Status Striving—The person who actually *struggles* to move up in the social class system. Very similar to the preceding need, but places more emphasis upon the *effort* to rise socially. The social climber is a rough illustration of this type. The opposite is a person who "had no ambition," who was "satisfied not to get anywhere." In a study by Carson McGuire it was found that marital partners often differ in their desires and efforts for upward mobility.[20]

Succorance—The need to be mothered by the partner and/or other persons. The opposite of *Nurturance* in this list. A husband or wife with a dominant need of this sort feels frustrated or unhappy if treated as an autonomous equal by the partner. A girl with this need might visualize her husband as the "protecting father," while the man would think of his wife as "mother." In his interesting book, *The American People,* the British anthropologist Geoffrey Gorer maintains that most American men have this conception of their wives—that the wife is really a composite wife-mother.[21]

General Traits

Winch uses three of these in his analysis:

Anxiety—A constant state of apprehension, a fear that something terrible may happen, a deep lack of security. The opposite is the optimistic, cheerful type of person.

Emotionality—The tendency to react to almost any situation with a great show of feeling, as contrasted with the type who always says, "Let's look at this calmly."

Vicariousness—Pleasure from knowing that another person is deriving satisfaction from a situation. An illustration might be the mother who denies herself enjoyment and seems to require only that the children are getting what they need.

Discussion of These Needs and Traits

It is important to recognize that *all* of us have these needs to some extent, but the importance of specific needs (or combination of needs) varies enormously from person to person. Most of us cannot be adequately described by reference to only one or two of these needs but must be visualized as representing a certain *pattern* or combination of needs. Our marital partner, then, would have to represent a need pattern that would complement (fit in with) our need pattern. If the patterns were too much in conflict, one or both partners would feel frustrated and unsatisfied in the relationship.

Essentially, a "need" in this system of analysis emerges as something the courtship or marriage partner cannot live happily *without*; in other words, the need has to be met if the individual is to be well adjusted. As the little boy said in trying to define salt: "It's what makes the food taste funny when you don't put it on."

Likewise, a need is what ruins the marriage when it (the need) is not satisfied.

In case the reader has a tendency to scoff at need patterns or personality types, we suggest that you try describing yourself or some person known well to you *without using* concepts or classifications of a sort similar to those in this discussion. This was illustrated for us the other day in a courtship conference by a girl who described her boy friend as "very independent" (this would be "autonomy" in Winch's list). Later on she described herself as a girl who likes to "mother" her friends (this would be "nurturance" in the Winch list). Another student recently described his girl friend as "very apprehensive" (this would be "anxiety" in the Winch system of analysis).

We all use categories of some sort in analyzing people because *we have to*. Notice the use of these concepts or types by yourself or your associates:

1. Inferiority complex
2. Very aggressive
3. Extremely independent
4. An introvert

5. Very hostile person
6. Immature
7. Very dependent

Obviously, we all have these traits to some degree (assuming we are normal), but in some persons we notice them to be more prominent. Now, having gone this far, it is only necessary to hypothesize that these needs are clustered into *patterns* and we have developed, as did Winch, a theory of marital adjustment. In good marriages, the partners are able to meet at least some minimum of the basic needs of each other. In poor marriages this is not possible, for the basic reason that the needs are in conflict.

Actually, this is only part of the story, as there are other nonpsychological factors also basic to marital adjustment. So far in our analysis of the factors related to marital adjustment, we have been assuming that the couple came from compatible (or homogamous) social environments and that the main adjustment in cases of this sort would be psychological and/or emotional. In later chapters the role of nonpsychological factors will be analyzed.

The Role of the Courtship and Marriage Counselor

If the theory of complementary needs in mate selection is accepted, there are at least two complications, both of which present problems: (1) Can mate selection ever be conscious or rational if some of our basic needs are unconscious? And (2) what can the courtship or marriage counselor accomplish, assuming that basic need patterns are not easily altered?

In regard to the first complication, it seems to be perfectly clear, at least to the marriage counselor, that a great deal of mate selection in our society is not rational, that parents and friends are often helpless to prevent what seem to be destined to be hopeless marriages. This undoubtedly represents a significant proportion of the couples whose marriages fail. These couples either have no insight into their basic needs or are unable to act upon what insight they have. The other possibility is that they are willing to gamble that "things will work out all right."

But to balance the ledger, a great many couples—probably the majority—*do* choose persons whose basic needs are compatible with their own. If these needs are to a large extent unconscious, as most Freudians argue, then how do these couples manage to choose so well? Is it insight? Are they just "plain lucky"? Is it possible that some of this group possess a sort of skill at just sensing the sort of person with whom they would be compatible? Athletic coaches claim that some gifted athletes seem to sense what is going to happen in a tight game a moment or so before the actual event. Do some young people have a sixth sense that enables them to choose a marital partner with a high degree of success?

In the writer's opinion, the research to date is of no help in answering questions of this sort. We do know, of course, that an adequate courtship helps couples to test the compatibility of their basic needs, but it is amazing how some couples have been able to choose well on the basis of very brief courtships. We recognize that these couples probably represent unusual cases, but they still arouse curiosity as to how they could happen at all.

For example: a man known to us met his wife on a train, dated her for two weeks, was married, and has been blissfully happy ever since. He and his wife seem to be ideal mates.

In another case, a college professor whom we know well met his wife while on furlough during the war and married her after three weeks of hectic courtship. They too are happily married and seem to be ideal mates for each other.

Are couples like this just statistical freaks, the "one in a million" cases? Or could they represent psychological types who do not need a year to test their compatibility? The writer confesses his inability to answer this question, but it seems to him that there are too many of these successful quickie courtships to dismiss them as freaks. It would be helpful if somebody would do a systematic analysis of such cases and attempt to discover their essential features.

In the second question raised above, we were concerned as to what, if anything, the courtship or marriage counselor could accomplish if these basic need patterns cannot be readily altered. It seems that the counselor's basic role in this area is to help the person or the couple gain more insight into the basic need patterns involved in the courtship or marriage. This, in our opinion, is not the sole function of the courtship or marriage counselor, for not all the factors in marital adjustment are psychological. But assuming the problem in a given case to be one of psychic nature, the counselor's role seems to be that described above. We personally do not believe that most counselors have either the time or the skill to alter the basic need patterns of the partners, which means that whatever adjustment might result would have to operate within the basic need patterns present at the time counseling was initiated. This sets serious limitations on the potentialities of marriage counseling, which is the main reason why this book emphasizes courtship insight rather than marital hindsight.

Conclusion

In this chapter we have been taking a good look at the role of personality factors in marital adjustment. It is not hard to convince the average American that this is an important ingredient in a good marriage, for "psychology" and "personality" are magic words in our culture. And, of course, it is true that personality *is* a basic variable in determining success or failure in marriage, as we have seen in this chapter. Our emphasis on the work of Winch and his theory of complementary needs in mate selection was an effort to reveal *how* personality factors affect marriage.

The main danger at this point is that the reader will conclude that psychological characteristics (plus sex) *determine* marital adjustment. This, however, is not the case, as even Terman, a psychologist himself, concluded.[22]

Therefore, the rest of the chapters in Part III will focus on nonpsychological elements basic to successful marriage.

References

1. The term "neurotic" has been used so loosely that it has become almost an epithet to use for persons we do not like or approve of. For a definition of the term, see Karen Horney, *The Neurotic Personality of Our Time* (New York, W. W. Norton & Co., Inc., 1937). Essentially, the term refers to persons who have some psychic disability but who are not disabled enough to be considered psychotic.

2. Lewis M. Terman *et al.*, *Psychological Factors in Marital Happiness* (New York, McGraw-Hill Book Co., 1938).

3. See *op. cit.*, chap. 7.

4. *Op. cit.*, chap. 9.

5. For a review of the various findings on this point, see Ernest W. Burgess and Paul Wallin, *Engagement and Marriage* (Philadelphia, J. B. Lippincott Co., 1953), pp. 512–519.

6. For a graphic case study of this sort, see Lucy Freeman's interesting account in *Fight Against Fears* (New York, Crown Publishers, 1951). This tells the story of marital failure and its impact on a neurotic personality.

7. Goode's study seems to support the notion that second and subsequent marriages are less stable than first ones. See his review of the data in William J. Goode, *After Divorce* (Glencoe, The Free Press, 1956), chap. 22.

8. Over one hundred of such studies are analyzed in Ernest W. Burgess and Paul Wallin, "Homogamy in Social Characteristics," *American Journal of Sociology*, 49 (1943), 109–124.

9. For a review of these studies, see Marvin R. Koller, "Residential

262 Modern Courtship and Marriage

and Occupational Propinquity," *American Sociological Review*, 13 (1948), 613-616.

10. See Robert F. Winch, "The Theory of Complementary Needs in Mate-Selection," *American Sociological Review*, 20 (1955), 552–555; see also an earlier article by Robert F. Winch and Thomas Ktsanes, "The Theory of Complementary Needs in Mate-Selection: An Analytic and Descriptive Study," *American Sociological Review*, 19 (1954), 241–249.

11. See the 1955 article, p. 552.

12. Thomas Ktsanes, "Mate Selection on the Basis of Personality Type," *American Sociological Review*, 20 (1955), 547–551.

13. *Op. cit.*, p. 551.

14. An earlier but less well designed study by Strauss reached somewhat similar conclusions. See Anselm Strauss, "Personality Needs and Marital Choice," *Social Forces*, 25 (1947), 332–335.

15. This seems to be the point of view of some clinical psychologists. See Allan Fromme, *The Psychologist Looks at Sex and Marriage* (New York, Prentice-Hall, Inc., 1950), p. 21.

16. For an excellent case study of such a marriage, see the novel by John O'Hara, *Ten North Frederick* (New York, Random House, 1955).

17. Ralph Linton, *The Study of Man* (New York, Appleton-Century-Crofts, Inc., 1936), chap. 11.

18. See, for example, the references in Horney, *op. cit.*

19. See Robert F. Winch, *The Modern Family* (New York, Henry Holt & Co., Inc., 1952), pp. 408–409. The work upon which this list is based, as Winch states, is H. A. Murray *et al., Explorations in Personality* (New York, Oxford University Press, 1938).

20. Carson McGuire, "Conforming, Mobile, and Divergent Families," *Marriage and Family Living*, 14 (1952), 109–115.

21. Geoffrey Gorer, *The American People* (W. W. Norton & Co., Inc., 1948).

22. See Terman, *op. cit.*, chap. 14.

Suggested Readings

1. Lucy Freeman, *Fight Against Fears* (New York, Crown Publishers, 1951). This vivid account of how personality factors helped destroy one marriage is excellent for book reports.

2. Karen Horney, *The Neurotic Personality of Our Time* (New York, W. W. Norton & Co., Inc., 1937). This is a classic that most students find very helpful in attempting to understand "neurotic" individuals.

3. Lewis M. Terman *et al., Psychological Factors in Marital Happiness* (New York, McGraw-Hill Book Co., 1938), chap. 7, "The Personalities of Happily Married and of Unhappily Married Persons." The student may wish to disagree with some of the statements in this discussion.

4. Geoffrey Gorer, *The American People* (New York, W. W. Norton & Co., Inc., 1948), chap. 2, "Mother-Land."

5. Allan Fromme, *The Psychologist Looks at Sex and Marriage* (New York, Prentice-Hall, Inc., 1950). This is a very readable presentation of the psychological approach to marital adjustment.

6. Thomas and Virginia Ktsanes, "The Theory of Complementary Needs in Mate-Selection," in Robert F. Winch and Robert McGinnis, *Selected Studies in Marriage and the Family* (New York, Henry Holt & Co., Inc., 1953), pp. 435–453. This is a very complete summary of the work done to date on this research project by Winch and his associates.

CHAPTER XIII

FAMILY BACKGROUND PATTERNS AND MARITAL ADJUSTMENT

Introduction

If we assume that the average American is to a large extent the product of his family, as most authorities do, then it follows that family background should be one of the basic variables determining marital adjustment. Our problem in this chapter is to discover exactly *how* family background affects marital adjustment.

The writer believes that the parental family's impact on marital adjustment results from two sources: (1) the child's emotional life patterns are formed in the home, setting up certain psychic needs that will be basic in married life; and (2) the family transmits to the child a *subculture* (or combination of subcultures) that play a dynamic role in determining marital expectations: how to keep house, attitudes toward money, etc. Let us attempt first to analyze the child's emotional development in the home and its relationship to subsequent marriage, after which we will examine the transmission of subcultures and their relationship to marital adjustment.

The Parental Family and Emotional Needs

In the preceding chapter, it was suggested that we all have somewhat different need patterns, and that these determine the kind of marital partner we will require for a satisfying marriage. Our problem here is to discover where these need patterns come from and how they are developed.

At the present time, the evidence seems to be overwhelming that our families are the most crucial agents in shaping these emotional needs.[1] Why? Because the family gets us first; because its relationships are deep and pervasive; and because the child is most impressionable during the preschool years, the very time that his family has him almost exclusively.[2]

The child's mother, for example, plays a crucial role in personality formation in our culture.[3] She feeds, bathes, changes, punishes, rewards, plays with, ignores: literally millions of meaningful interactions take place between most small children and their mothers in our society. Winch has found that even as late as college, the American young person feels closer to his mother than any other human being.[4]

At present about one out of five children in our society have no father in the home at any given time, because of divorce, death, and other factors,[5] and this accentuates even more the mother's crucial role.

The fact that the father in urban society works away from the home, as contrasted with the earlier farm father, also emphasizes the mother's impact on the child. It is true, of course, that the shorter work week may be making it possible for the American father to be more of an influence on his children, but the move to the suburb, with its long commuting distances, has offset this to some extent.

It may come to pass, as more and more mothers work outside the home, that fathers will play a more equal role in personality formation, but this is not the case at the moment. Middle-class mothers, in particular, do not usually accept outside employment when their children are in the formative years, normally waiting until their children are in high school or college before going back into the labor market.[6]

Fathers, however, do have deep impact on their children in various ways. Indirectly, they affect the mother's handling of the children by establishing an "emotional climate" for the mother to work in. If they love the mother, satisfy her needs, and support her efforts with the children, her job is much easier and she performs it better. On the other hand, if the husband-wife relationship is poor, or if they disagree on child-rearing methods, the mother's efficiency level will be lowered. She may even take out (displace) on the children hostility aroused by the husband.

On a direct level, the father often bathes the child, changes it, feeds it, plays with it, and puts it to bed. As a rule, however, the father does these things very much less often than the mother.

The father determines to a considerable extent the general feeling of security in the home, largely because of his crucial role as breadwinner.

In the writer's opinion, the father's *indirect* influence on the preschool child (such as his relationship with the mother) is apt to outweigh his direct influence.

The child's brothers and sisters (siblings) are also extremely influential in the relatively small American family of modern times.[7] The ordinal position (first, second, third child, etc.) is important.[8] The first child is apt to be the "guinea pig," the one the parents "learned on," while the last child, as "the baby," seems to be treated somewhat differently. We need to know more about the impact of ordinal position on the child, but there seems little doubt that it is basic.

From all these intimate experiences, day by day, month by month, and year by year, our families shape our emotional lives. Playmates and schoolmates have some effect too, but these seem to operate more on the surface.

Out of all these experiences emerges a personality, and it is this personality that goes into the marriage. The future marital partner also is going through a similar process. When these two personalities marry, therefore, there is actually a merger of the products of two family settings. This is why the research to date has reported that family background is one of the basic factors affecting marital adjustment.[9] Terman, for example, believes it to be as crucial as sex,[10] a finding that surprised many persons when it was first reported in the 1930's.

Precisely, what sorts of personality traits emerge from our family experiences? Our ability to love, which is crucial in modern marriage. A psychologist, Fromme, puts it this way: "The capacity to love is primarily determined in our childhood. . . . Our own childhood reactions to our parents, the first adults we ever knew, will in large measure determine our affections later on. It is in the early years of our lives that our personal reservoir of love is built up." [11]

Our sense of security or insecurity; our fears and doubts; our likes and dislikes; our dependence or independence; our attitudes toward sex; our feelings about money; our religious values— all these basic characteristics, and a host of others, are rooted in our family experience. In a very real sense, the American family is the crucible in which the basic personality is forged.

Family Subcultures and Their Transmission

We are now ready for the second part of our analysis: the way in which families transmit subcultures and how these affect marital interaction after the child marries.[12]

Since the concept of *subculture* is used extensively in this and subsequent chapters, let us pause briefly to review its meaning and usage.

It is a truism that America is a heterogeneous, complex society, a melting pot for peoples from all over the world. This means that there are literally endless varieties of *subcultures* existing side by side in the culture that we call "American." It may be true that there is an "American way of life," but it is equally true that there are a great many varieties of that way of life.[13]

Each distinct group in our society, according to sociological theory, has its own *subculture* consisting of relatively distinct values, attitudes, and related behavior patterns. Orthodox Jews, for example, not only believe in certain food practices but also have some rather specific ideas about husband-wife relationships.[14] The Italians in our society, even today, are not exactly like the Swedes.[15] It is this almost endless variety of patterns that produces much of the complexity of American life.

From our point of view, the child is not born into "American society": he is born into a specific family, a specific community, etc., and emerges into the larger society only after years of exposure to the subcultures of his local groups. This is also true of his future wife, so that when they eventually meet and marry, it is not enough to say that "two Americans are getting married," even though this is usually the case. What we need is to specify the subculture out of which each came if we are to understand the adjustment problems they will face in marriage. Two youngsters from the same high school in many communities could come from extremely diverse social worlds. The boy, for example, could be Catholic, while the girl was Protestant. He could be of Polish stock as contrasted with her French origins. The boy could be of lower social class, whereas the girl's family could be middle class. It is true that we *usually* marry within our own social world, but in a society as mobile as ours, cross-cultural marriages occur frequently enough to merit some attention.[16]

It might help if the major subcultures in our society could be specified. We suggest the following:

1. Occupational subcultures
2. Male-female subcultures
3. Regional subcultures
4. Social class subcultures
5. Religious subcultures

6. Age-group subcultures
7. Urban-rural subcultures
8. Ethnic subcultures
9. Racial subcultures

Some persons may wish to modify this list. There is considerable disagreement, for example, concerning the power of ethnic (nationality) backgrounds to influence behavior in third-generation young people (those whose grandparents were immigrants).[17] It is also doubtful that racial groups *as such* possess distinct subcultures in modern America.[18] Our list is meant to be suggestive and not definitive.

Since separate chapters are devoted to social class, male-female, and religious subcultures, these need not be considered here.

For the most part, the individual's exposure to subcultures is determined by family membership, which means that on a cultural level the family determines, at least indirectly, the child's preparation for marriage.

This matter of family background is further complicated by the fact that any given family may represent almost any unique combination of these subcultures, and this means that any particular boy or girl can be a rather complex mixture of subcultural traits. To be specific a young man may be from New England, but also a Catholic whose family came from Ireland; furthermore, his family could be upper middle class, Republicans, vegetarians, etc. Now let us suppose that this boy goes into the Army Air Corps and serves some time at Dallas, Texas, where he meets a girl and falls in love. Her family are Southerners (*Texans,* really), Baptists, Democrats, meat-lovers, etc. They may also be upper-class people, a group with an extensive subculture of its own. Thus we see that these two young people, both native-born "Americans," have not grown up in exactly the same social world. And if they should marry they will have to merge these two social worlds in their marriage, at least to a considerable extent.

We do not mean to imply that this will be an impossible task, but it will certainly be more complex and more exciting than if the boy had married within his own social world and the girl had held out for a son of Texas.

How Subcultures Are Transmitted

The process by which our family background affects marital interaction is simply this: as the child grows up, he is intimately exposed, day after day and year after year, to the norms and values of his parents and their social world; gradually these behavior patterns become *internalized* in the child, and at this point they become *him*.[19] By the time he is married these ways of thinking, feeling, and living are imbedded so deeply that he is normally unconscious that he has them and lacks any clear understanding of where they came from.

This is not always the case, of course. Some of us revolt against the family background and try to be as different from it as possible. *But even in these cases,* family experiences are operating as a basic factor in determining marital adjustment.

In the rest of this chapter, we will analyze certain family subcultures that may affect marital interaction and adjustment as the child emancipates himself from his family of origin and seeks to establish his family of creation, the one he makes for himself.

Patterns of Power Distribution

Theoretically, there are five very different power distribution patterns in modern marriage. (1) *Patriarchal* (or patricentric) in which the husband-father is the dominant figure; (2) *matriarchal* (or matricentric) with the wife-mother tending to be the central figure; (3) *equalitarian* (or democratic) in which the married partners tend to share responsibility and power; (4) *family council,* in which the parents *and* the children share major decisions; and (5) *child-dominant* homes in which one or more of the children actually control the family.

From studies by Godfrey and Dyer,[20] it appears that middle-class families tend to be equalitarian in their power distribution patterns, whereas lower-income groups tend to reflect traditional patriarchal patterns when a male head is the chief breadwinner. Rural families also lean toward patriarchal patterns. Relatively little is known about upper-class power patterns, except that the *elderly* upper-class person (often a grandparent) who still controls family wealth may exercise considerable power. It is also known that lower-lower-class families show a tendency to be matricentric because the group is often supported by the mother and/or the maternal grandparents.

Now, when you and I marry, we have certain expectations about the balance of power we expect to find in our marriage. It is not implied that these expectations will necessarily reflect the patterns of our own family, but it seems reasonable to assume that our basic models for such patterns tend to be based on those we have seen at close range.[21] Probably the dynamic factor here is the degree of admiration or rejection we feel for our parent models.

It is possible that persons coming from diverse power distribution family patterns might have some difficulty reconciling their expectations in this area of marital interaction.

Patterns of Expressing Affection

Analysis of term papers written for the author's marriage course reveals wide family differences in the display or expression of affection.[22] One student, for example, writes: "I can hardly ever remember seeing my father and mother kiss each other but I'm sure they love each other. They did kiss us children, however." Compare this student's family training with this one: "My father always kissed my mother when he came down for breakfast, when he left for work, and when he returned home in the evening. He always kissed us children when he left for work and before we went to bed. He also kissed mother 'goodnight' when they went to bed. Then if any member of the family went on a trip, we all kissed them when they left and again when they got back."

Differences in Family Ritual Patterns

Bossard and Boll have analyzed this sort of difference between families in a very interesting book, *Ritual in Family Living*,[23] and report great variation in all sorts of family rituals: holiday celebrations, birthday observances, gift-giving, family meals, vacation practices, etc. They believe that to some extent these tend to vary according to social class membership, but even within the same socioeconomic level there is considerable variation.

Recently, the author interviewed a married couple who illustrated Bossard's thesis clearly. Among other complaints, the wife resented her husband's "hiding behind a magazine or book" every evening. "At our house," she said, "my father and mother would often spend all evening *just talking* to each other." When we discussed this matter with the husband, he admitted that he usually spent the evening reading but he defended himself by saying: "Our whole family did a lot of reading. I can remember lots of nights when all of us would sit near the fireplace, each with his own book or magazine. My father had a library full of books. But my wife's family reads only the daily newspaper. There are very few books or magazines in her house." We were especially interested in this family difference because both the husband and the wife in this case came from very similar social class backgrounds.

We do not mean to imply that this reading difference was the major factor in this couple's marital conflict, but it does seem that such family differences have to be regarded as contributing factors in marital adjustment.

In another marriage counseling case, the wife complained that her husband wasn't affectionate. Investigation revealed that this woman came from a kissing family and the husband from a nonkissing family. Actually, the husband did seem to love the wife but he seldom demonstrated it by kissing and/or embracing her. He described her family as "gushy" and his as "just the opposite." In this case, counseling was relatively easy because the husband *had* the affection and was willing to learn how to express it.

Even telephone habits vary considerably from one family to another. In one marriage known to the writer, the husband often jokes that his only complaint about his wife is the "long distance telephone bill every month." It seems that in his family long distance calls are only resorted to in the event of death or serious illness, whereas his wife's family uses the telephone as a means of maintaining family solidarity. As the husband puts it, "They don't write letters; they telephone." Both the husband and the wife in this marriage are from approximately the same social class. This is essentially a very good marriage, so that the telephone problem is more of a joke with them than anything else. But in a poor marriage, differences of this sort can be utilized to attack the other person and complicate the adjustment process.

Housekeeping standards vary considerably in modern society, often within the same social class. In groups not having full-time maids, and this means most Americans, it is not unusual to have a husband complain that "My wife is not the housekeeper my mother was." In one case referred to the author for counseling, the husband came from a family in which the mother scrubbed and polished all week long, whereas the wife's family felt that cleaning was a "necessary evil, not to be overdone," as she put it. She felt that her husband had a neatness complex, and he in turn regarded her as a sloppy housekeeper. There were deeper problems, of course, but many of their fights had been precipitated by his comments about her housekeeping.

In some families gift-giving is a highly developed ritual, whereas in others only Christmas calls for a present to anybody.[24] Some fathers never return from a trip without presents for everybody, while others regard this as a needless expense.

Some families make a great day out of each member's birthday; they stage big family get-togethers at Easter, or Thanksgiving, while other families pay relatively little attention to such days.

Families as Models

A girl's idea of what a husband or a father should be is often based on her own father.[25] Mothers may influence sons in a similar way. A boy's version of girls may reflect his relationship with his sister, and vice versa.

Attitudes toward smoking, drinking, card-playing, etc., seem to be closely related to family norms. Patterns of attending church seem to be highly correlated with family experience.[26] Ideas about sex are often internalized from family conditioning.

One could extend this list indefinitely, but the point should be clear by now. We do not mean to imply that minor differences in family background will pose insoluble problems for most married couples. But it might be helpful to expect such differences, to understand their origin, and to be prepared to reconcile them. In poor marriages, these differences often seem to be focal points for the expression of hostility.

Ethnic Subcultures and Marital Adjustment

Historically, the United States has embraced ethnic (nationality) groups from various parts of the world, mostly from Europe, all of whom possessed more or less distinct cultural patterns.[27] This mixture of peoples has certainly enriched life in our society, but it has complicated the process of courtship and marital adjustment. The writer, for example, once had a very beautiful girl in class who came from a devout Greek Orthodox Catholic family. In spite of her beauty and charm, this girl dated very little on the campus, largely because her parents were afraid she would "fall in love" and marry outside her religion. Except for her religion, however, it was difficult to detect any other survivals of Greek culture in this girl.

In a study by Kennedy of couples marrying in New Haven, Connecticut, it was shown rather conclusively that religion is about the only factor in ethnic subcultures still affecting marital choice in the descendants of immigrants.[28] To be specific, one could not predict that a girl of French ancestry would marry a boy of French extraction, but one could predict that she would normally marry a Catholic. In this sense, ethnic subcultures in the United States do influence choice of mate. Beyond this point, however, ethnic subcultures are not regarded by social scientists to be very important in marital adjustment.

The reason for this is simply that we live in a society in which the mass media, the public school system, and the peer group tend to eliminate ethnic differences. Once a child is reared in the United States, he becomes an "American," which means that ethnic subculture seldom survives the second generation (those born in this country).

For the most part, it appears that social class subculture has replaced ethnic subculture as a predictive factor in marital adjustment.[29]

It may be, of course, that this point of view can be pushed too far. For example, would anybody argue that the American Indian's subculture is nonexistent today? No, but this is a very extreme case, for it involves racial factors as well as ethnic subculture. Furthermore, a great many Indian children have grown up on reservations, have not attended public schools, and in general have not participated fully in American life.

There are some religious minority groups in the United States, however, who have preserved their subcultures relatively intact—such groups as the Amish of Pennsylvania and Ohio, the Hutterites of the Dakotas, and the Mormons of Utah—and in these cases the subcultures have to be taken into account in analyzing marital adjustment. These are not ethnic groups in the traditional use of the term, however, and do not alter the main thesis that ethnic subcultures seem to have relatively little effect on marital adjustment in the second or third generation. It is granted that the religious component in ethnic subcultures *does* tend to survive and *does* affect marital adjustment. This matter receives extensive analysis in a separate chapter.

Racial Subcultures and Marital Adjustment

Social scientists are not convinced that there is a distinctive subculture of the American Negro.[30] Most of the behavior patterns considered as "Negro customs" can be accounted for by reference to social class subculture (the lower-lower class in Warner's terminology), or by reference to regional subculture (the South). Perhaps a few illustrations will clarify this point.

The Negro's religious behavior, with its rhythmic hymns

and its emotionalized worship, has been regarded as characteristic of the Negro. We now know, however, that the same type of religious worship is also characteristic of "holy roller" churches attended by low-income whites.[31] In other words, this is lower-lower class subculture and is not correlated with race. As a matter of fact, the book, *Black Metropolis,* by Drake and Cayton, demonstrates conclusively that middle- and upper-class Negroes in Chicago worship as sedately as one could imagine.[32]

To cite another illustration, it has been customary to think of the Negro family as matricentric (mother-centered) because historically the Negro family has had a female head; the mother, for example, has often had to rear the family largely by herself. But Hollingshead has shown that death and desertion produce very much the same pattern among low-income white families as well, so that this too is essentially social class subculture and not racial.[33] There undoubtedly is *some* Negro subculture but it seems to be less dominant than that of income level.

If this line of analysis is essentially correct, then it follows that interracial marriages are much more likely to succeed if the partners came from similar socioeconomic levels. It is possible that some interracial marriages fail *not* because of race but because of deep socioeconomic class differences. If a white woman, for example, marries a Negro man, she will normally come from a lower background than her husband, and this in itself may be a major factor in complicating their marital adjustment.[34] Attitudes of their families and friends will be determined, to some extent, by such class factors also. But even if we ignore the attitudes of their associates, their personal compatibility will reflect to some degree their social class subculture.

When one turns from the Negro to the American Indian, it seems obvious that this racial group has preserved strong subcultures which would affect interracial marriages with this group.[35] Even here, however, it would be found that Indians of the higher income levels tend to be more assimilated into "American" culture than low-income Indians.

When we consider Chinese, Japanese, or other Asiatic racial groups living in the United States, it seems that the subcultures of these groups seldom survive the second generation. In other words, their behavior patterns and values are not *racial* but ethnic or cultural, so that the second or third generation Chinese or Japanese person will be the same as the second or third generation Italian— that is, he will be an "American." For all practical purposes, then, the customs of his ancestors can be ignored in predicting marital adjustment. The success or failure of any marriage of a Japanese-American with a person of another racial-ethnic background is determined by the same set of factors involved in any other marriage, with this addition: that feelings and attitudes about racial intermarriage by their associates might complicate the picture. There is also a possibility that religious differences might be involved, and if so, this has to be taken into account.

In general, it appears that racial groups in the United States will not have any more success in maintaining their traditional subcultures than ethnic groups have had, and this means that this factor as such will not be a major problem in interracial marriages in the United States. This does not mean, however, that interracial marriages will not continue to be more complicated than marriages within a race, but the major problem will be created by the attitudes toward such marriages rather than by distinct racial subcultures as such.

Rural-Urban Subcultures in Marital Adjustment

Most of the marital adjustment studies, especially those of Terman, Burgess-Cottrell, and Burgess-Wallin, used urban samples, so they tell us very little about the possible effects of rural-urban subcultures on marital interaction.[36] Burgess-Cottrell did find that persons reared in the country tended to have somewhat higher marital adjustment scores, but their study has no adequate treatment of this variable.[37]

In the Locke study, however, part of the sample was drawn

from the rural population in the county studied, but Locke was unable to find any significant relationship of rural-urban background to marital adjustment.[38]

It may be that our society has become so standardized that rural-urban subcultures have been obliterated, but the writer is by no means convinced that this is the case. Politicians, for example, seem convinced that there is a rural voter who is a different species from the urban voter, and if this is true, it seems logical to expect other rural-urban differences in behavior and values as well. As a matter of fact, the study of family patterns in Illinois by Godfrey *did* reveal significant rural-urban differences in such areas as male dominance and child-rearing philosophy.[39]

It seems likely that none of the studies to date has focused on rural-urban subcultures intensively enough to detect their role in marital interaction. Fully to illuminate the interplay of such factors, it would be essential to compare marriages involving rural-rural, rural-urban, and urban-urban backgrounds. To our knowledge this has never been done.

It may be, of course, that what most of us think of as rural behavior is largely the pattern of rural low-income groups, farm tenants and farm laborers. At the middle- or upper-income levels, the rural-urban differences may diminish or disappear entirely.

It seems to the writer that there might be significant adjustment problems in a marriage in which *both* rural-urban and social class differentials were involved. But of itself, it seems unlikely today that rural subculture is sufficiently different to create major difficulties in American marriages.

Summary

In this chapter we have been looking at the influence of the parental family on the child's subsequent marital adjustment. We have seen that our parents and siblings are considered to be crucial agents in the shaping of our basic personality patterns. A brief description of *how* this takes place was presented.

But in addition to the above type of influence, the parental family also transmits a subculture or combination of subcultures to the child, and these also play a dynamic role in subsequent marital interaction. When one remembers the almost endless combination of these subcultures possible in the United States, it becomes clear that every American can actually be said to have a *unique* social background, just as he has a unique personality. And this seems to be true in spite of the standardization of behavior in our society.

If this analysis is correct, it means that marital adjustment involves the merging or reconciling of two unique subcultural backgrounds, just as it involves the integration of two unique personalities. One gets the impression that undergraduates can see clearly the psychological uniqueness of their courtship partners but that they fail to see subcultural uniqueness, or to appreciate its relevance for marital interaction.

The writer is willing to grant that the major marital adjustment studies to date have failed to identify or specify the role of subcultural factors in marital interaction, but most of the studies *do* specify family background as being basic in marital adjustment; and since our family membership usually determines our exposure to subcultures, this finding supports the basic thesis of this chapter.

Undoubtedly, from the point of view of current research, the major subcultural influence in our society is that of socioeconomic position or social class, and this is the subject of our next chapter.

References

1. One of the better analyses of this is to be found in James S. Plant, *Personality and the Cultural Pattern* (New York, Commonwealth Fund, 1937). See also Theodore M. Newcomb, *Social Psychology* (New York, The Dryden Press, 1950), pp. 513–520. Meyer F. Nimkoff's text, *Marriage and the Family* (Boston, Houghton Mifflin Co., 1947) has an excellent discussion in chap. 11.

2. This has been analyzed in detail by James H. S. Bossard in his classic study, *The Sociology of Child Development* (New York, Harper & Bros., 1948). See Part II, "The Child and His Family Setting."

3. Geoffrey Gorer has emphasized the role of the American mother

in his analysis of personality patterns in our society. See his *The American People* (New York, W. W. Norton & Co., Inc., 1948), chap. 2. See also Margaret Mead, *And Keep Your Powder Dry* (New York, William Morrow & Co., Inc., 1942), chap. 6.

4. Robert F. Winch, "The Oedipus Hypothesis," *American Sociological Review*, 16 (1951), 784–793.

5. See Nimkoff, *op. cit.*, pp. 611–612, for an analysis of these data.

6. For an analysis of these data, see *The American Family, a Factual Background* (Washington, D.C., U.S. Government Printing Office, 1949), p. 64.

7. See Bossard, *op. cit.*, chap. 5, for an analysis of the interaction between siblings.

8. Bossard, *op. cit.*, pp. 108–117, reviews the material on this point.

9. For a review of this work, see Ernest W. Burgess and Paul Wallin, *Engagement and Marriage* (Philadelphia, J. B. Lippincott Co., 1953), pp. 512–519.

10. See Lewis M. Terman *et al.*, *Psychological Factors in Marital Happiness* (New York, McGraw-Hill Book Co., 1938), chap. 14.

11. Allan Fromme, *The Psychologist Looks at Sex and Marriage* (New York, Prentice-Hall, Inc., 1950), pp. 17–18.

12. In our use of the concept "subculture," we are indebted to the valuable analysis of Albert K. Cohen in his monograph, *Delinquent Boys* (Glencoe, The Free Press, 1955).

13. Some of these variations on "the American theme" are to be found in the penetrating study by Robin M. Williams, Jr., *American Society* (New York, Alfred A. Knopf, Inc., 1951).

14. There are very few published data on the American Jewish family. Our reference here is to the patriarchal nature of the traditional Orthodox Jewish family as described in term papers written by students from this subcultural group.

15. The classic description is "Ethnic Family Patterns: The Italian Family in the United States," by Paul J. Campisi, *American Journal of Sociology*, 53 (1948), 443–449.

16. See, for example, the study of Catholic and non-Catholic marriage rates by John L. Thomas: "The Factor of Religion in the Selection of Marriage Mates," *American Sociological Review*, 16 (1951), 487–492.

17. The most complete discussion of this topic is to be found in Milton L. Barron's monograph, *People Who Intermarry* (Syracuse, Syracuse University Press, 1946).

18. The reference here is primarily to the American Negro, not the American Indian.

19. See Cohen, *op. cit.*, for a detailed analysis of this process.

20. Eleanor P. Godfrey, "A Construction of Family Types and Their Initial Empirical Validation," unpublished Ph.D. dissertation (Cambridge, Radcliffe College, 1951); also Everett D. Dyer, "A Study of Role and Authority Patterns and Expectations in a Group of Urban Middle-Class Two-Income Families," unpublished Ph.D. dissertation (Madison, University of Wisconsin, 1955).

21. Anselm Strauss has attempted to measure the influence of parents on marital choice. His basic conclusion is that parents *do* influence marital choice but not in any very simple way. See his study, "The Influence of Parent-Images upon Marital Choice," *American Sociological Review*, 11 (1946), 554–559.

22. Bossard and Boll have an excellent analysis of family differences in expressing affection. See James H. S. Bossard and Eleanor S. Boll, *Ritual in Family Living* (Philadelphia, University of Pennsylvania Press, 1950), pp. 64–68.

23. *Op. cit.*

24. Bossard and Boll, *op. cit.*, have a very thorough analysis of gift-giving as a ritual in family life.

25. In the study by Strauss cited above it was discovered that parental models do not influence the son or daughter in any simple one-to-one way. The process is complex and siblings may be very differently influenced by the same parents. There are also negative as well as positive influences.

26. This statement is based on an analysis of over two hundred student autobiographies written for the writer's marriage courses.

27. Oscar Handlin has a graphic description of some of these cultural variations among American immigrants. See his study, *The Uprooted* (Boston, Little, Brown & Co., Inc., 1952).

28. Ruby Jo Reeves Kennedy, "Single or Triple Melting-Pot? Inter-marriage Trends in New Haven, 1870–1940," *American Journal of Sociology*, 49 (1944), 331–339.

29. The writer bases this statement on the fact that relatively few studies of the traditional ethnic groups have appeared in the past decade, whereas there has been a mass of research published on social class and its value as predictive material. For a brief summary of this social class literature, see W. Lloyd Warner, *American Life* (Chicago, University of Chicago Press, 1953).

30. The most extensive treatment of this question may be found in the classic by Gunnar Myrdal, *An American Dilemma* (New York, Harper & Bros., 1944).

31. See the study by John B. Holt, "Holiness Religion: Culture Shock and Social Reorganization," *American Sociological Review*, 5 (1940), 740–747.

32. St. Clair Drake and Horace R. Cayton, *Black Metropolis* (New York, Harcourt, Brace & Co., 1945).

33. See August B. Hollingshead, "Class Differences in Family Stability," *The Annals* of the American Academy of Political and Social Science, 272 (1950), 39–46.

34. See Drake and Cayton, *op. cit.*, for a description of this process.

35. See John Collier's study, *Indians of the Americas* (New York, W. W. Norton & Co., Inc., 1947), for a description of some of the subcultural remnants of the American Indian.

36. For a review of these studies and their samples, see Burgess and Wallin, *op. cit.*, chap. 2.

37. Ernest Burgess and Leonard S. Cottrell, Jr., *Predicting Success or Failure in Marriage* (New York, Prentice-Hall, Inc., 1939), pp. 85–86.

38. Harvey J. Locke, *Predicting Adjustment in Marriage* (New York, Henry Holt & Co., Inc., 1951), p. 338.

39. *Op. cit.*

Suggested Readings

1. Albert K. Cohen, *Delinquent Boys* (Glencoe, The Free Press, 1955), chap. 3, "A General Theory of Subcultures." The better student will find this very worthwhile.

2. James H. S. Bossard and Eleanor S. Boll, *Ritual in Family Living* (Philadelphia, University of Pennsylvania Press, 1950). This makes an excellent book report, or specific chapters can be assigned. We think it one of the best for giving the student the "feel" of how families differ in very subtle and almost endless ways.

3. E. Franklin Frazier, *The Negro Family in the United States* (New York, The Dryden Press, 1951). This revised edition has some excellent chapters on the "new" Negro family; see chap. 20, for example, "The Brown Middle Class."

4. Ruth Shonle Cavan's text, *The American Family* (New York, Thomas Y. Crowell Co., 1953) has an excellent summary of data on the family patterns of different ethnic groups in our society. See chap. 8, "Ethnic Families."

5. L. J. Carr and J. E. Stermer, "Life in the Trailers," in Marvin B. Sussman's *Sourcebook in Marriage and the Family* (Boston, Houghton Mifflin Co., 1955), pp. 154–160. This selection is abridged from the study *Willow Run* (New York, Harper & Bros., 1952) by Carr and Stermer. The article reveals the tremendous variety of family situations in a society such as ours.

CHAPTER XIV

SOCIAL CLASS AND OCCUPATIONAL FACTORS IN MARITAL ADJUSTMENT

Introduction

In recent years, American anthropologists and sociologists have demonstrated rather conclusively that one of the most pervasive influences on the individual in our society is his socioeconomic or *social class* background. Warner of the University of Chicago,[1] Hollingshead of Yale,[2] and Kinsey of the University of Indiana[3] have published studies that reveal in considerable detail how social class influences what we eat, how we eat it, how we dress, the decoration of our homes, whom we vote for, etc. In his first volume on the American male, Kinsey concluded that how a man makes love to his wife can best be predicted by knowing his socioeconomic status.[4]

In the Warner system of analysis, there are at least six social class subdivisions, each with a relatively distinct "way of life" or subculture. Warner labels these six levels as follows: lower-lower,

283

upper-lower, lower-middle, upper-middle, lower-upper, and upper-upper.[5] In the average college, most students (and their professors too) range from upper-lower to upper-middle in family background. In state universities one usually finds a wider range than in the privately endowed colleges and universities.

Although Warner uses a six-class system of analysis, it is not to be assumed that all communities will be stratified into six socioeconomic levels. A metropolitan area such as New York City might have a great many more than six, while many smaller communities may well have less than six.

The interested student would do well to read Warner's little book, *American Life,* in which he describes the methodology and summarizes the major findings of this research.[6]

If one reads these social stratification studies, the impression is gained that some of the older subcultures, such as those of ethnic or nationality groups, are tending to disappear, and that this is gradually making the social class subcultures more dominant. Thus a lower-class Italian-American today would have more in common with a Puerto Rican of his own social class level than he would with an upper-class Italian-American.

The social scientists seem to believe that rural subculture is tending to decline in importance, so that today one could not predict a person's behavior very accurately just by knowing that he was a farmer. It would be necessary to know whether he was a farm *owner,* a farm *tenant,* a farm *laborer,* or a *migratory* farm worker.[7]

It even seems to be true that racial membership has less predictive value than it once had. Today, it is not enough to know that a person is a Negro; in fact, this may be irrelevant for many purposes. We have to know whether he is an upper-class Negro, a middle-class Negro, etc.[8]

If the social scientists are correct in their emphasis upon social class as a determinant of behavior, it means that marriages *between* social classes are more complex than marriages *within* social classes. This was demonstrated, at least in part, by Roth and Peck in a restudy of the 526 marriages analyzed by Burgess and

Cottrell.[9] When these cases were restudied using a social class variable (which the original 1939 study did not use), it was found that there were statistically significant differences between the marital adjustment scores of couples belonging to similar social class levels and those who did not. The findings of Roth and Peck support the theory that social class is a significant variable in determining marital adjustment.

This sort of material is very hard for most Americans to accept because we like to think that "there are no social classes in America." It may help the reader if we point out that we are not talking about a *caste* system in which social status is defined once and for all at birth. We are talking about an *open class* system in which social status is *flexible,* but *not absent.*

Actually, we all recognize that the Rockefellers live differently from the people across the tracks, and if this is so, then it follows that there must also be less obvious differences between families not at the extreme ends of the socioeconomic scale. And this is essentially what Warner and the others are claiming.

Another reason why social class factors tend to be minimized by most persons is that these influences are mostly unconscious. Since we are not aware of them, we tend to deny their existence. Just as Freud discovered that a great deal of human behavior is buried so deeply that persons do not know "why" they do certain things, in the same way most of us are unaware of our social class background.

This point is well demonstrated by the fact that most Americans consider themselves "middle class" in spite of the fact that at least half of our population is either above or below the middle-class level.[10]

Parents in particular are reluctant to mention social class differences in opposing a courtship they do not fully approve. To refer to such matters when discussing a daughter's boy friend is to be a "snob," if not unAmerican. For this reason parents disguise their social class objections by questioning the personal compatibility of the couple. Comments like this are common: "Do you really

think he is the type for you?" "Don't you think he is rather rude?"
"Isn't he apt to be unstable?" And so on *ad infinitum*.

Actually, there is no real reason why social class differences
should not be discussed by parents, just as psychological differences
are discussed. And such discussions need not be snobbish. This
type of question, for example, seems quite legitimate: "Do you
both realize the difference between the way his family lives and the
way we live? Will this be a problem if you marry? Have you discussed it? Will they accept you as their equal? And will you be
comfortable as a member of that group?"

Notice that these questions avoid the issue of superiority and
inferiority and focus on *differences*. Also, the *right* of the individual
to marry across economic lines is not questioned, although the
complexity of such a marriage is pointed out.

It may be a fine thing in a democratic society to minimize
economic factors in the choice of marital partners, but this does
not mean that we should ignore them. If the social scientists are
correct in their findings, interclass marriages should be regarded as
cross-cultural marriages, comparable to the mixed marriages of
different religious groups. Obviously, the differences are not very
great when the social class levels are close, as is true in most marriages, but they could be deep and diffuse where the economic
backgrounds are widely dissimilar.

We feel that a word of caution is necessary: if you are
considering marriage with a person of different social class background, be sure to explore the subtle differences very carefully
before marriage. These can be elusive before marriage and annoying
after marriage. Perhaps the best way to expose them is by extensive
visiting with the other family and its friends. We do not mean to
imply that marriage should be avoided when social class differences
are deep, only that the differences should be clearly seen and their
implications for marital adjustment appreciated *before* marriage.
After marriage may be too late.

Case Illustration of Social Class Factors: We were once
consulted by a man who was dissatisfied with his marriage, although

he was not willing to seek a separation or divorce. There seemed to be no serious conflicts in the marital relationship, yet neither of the couple felt that the marriage was what it should be.

As the picture of the marriage emerged, it developed that the husband came from a prominent family in the East, a family proud of its name, with a distinguished lineage stretching back to the *Mayflower* and beyond. The man had attended a famous Eastern preparatory school and had gone on to Harvard. He had also studied in Europe. Their family name often appeared in the society page of the most conservative paper in that metropolis. In the Warner system of social class analysis, this family would have been classified as "upper upper."

The wife, in contrast, came from a moderately prosperous middle-class family in the Midwest. She had attended public high school and had graduated from the state university. Their courtship began when they met while spending a vacation at a mountain resort in the West. Most of their courting was done in her home community. By the Warner system, her family was probably "upper-middle class," her father owning a succesful retail business.

After their marriage, the young couple settled in the man's home community in the East. Trouble began soon after when the wife asked the husband to move "out West." She did not feel comfortable in the East and felt that Easterners were cold and unfriendly. Although she admitted that her in-laws had all been very nice to her, she did not feel comfortable with them. Ten years after moving to the husband's community, she reported that she still felt like an outsider. As she put it: "Anybody who came here after 1800 is regarded as a *newcomer.*"

The husband was distressed and hurt by all this. At times he felt as if his wife were ungrateful for all the things his family had done for her, such as getting her elected to the exclusive women's clubs, etc. He reported to us that he would have sought a divorce except for the presence of three small children.

Our analysis of this marriage was that it was essentially a cross-cultural or mixed marriage that had not worked out. The couple had failed to appreciate social class differences and had believed that personal compatibility would overcome the deep differences in their social worlds. And indeed their personal compatibility *did* prevent the relationship from becoming a "horrible" marriage, but at the same time the social class differences were great enough to prevent the union from being a really good marriage.

One might ask how such a marriage ever took place. It seemed to us that the wife never felt the full impact of the husband's upper-class world until after the marriage, when they settled in his home community. This was possible because almost all the courtship had taken place in her Midwest city on her social class level.

The marriage was also made possible, it seemed, by the fact that the young man was in part in revolt against his social background, so that both he and the girl did not take it too seriously. But after the marriage, when his work required that they settle in his home community, his revolt seemed to be superficial. Thus the girl found herself married to a Brahmin, something she had never counted on. And the husband found that, after all, these were his parents, his brothers and sisters, and their way of life was essentially his way of life. If his family relationships had been basically negative, then he might have emerged as a deviant, settling in a different part of the country and striving to be as different from his people as possible. But this was not the case. He *did* love his family and, with a few reservations, he did admire their way of living.

However, the marriage might have still worked out if the wife had admired "upper-class Easterners" and had been willing to imitate them and assimilate their subculture. They were willing to help and accept her, but she declined to join them. And so she never really belonged to their world and the marriage never became what it should have.

In the Roth and Peck study, it was discovered that interclass marriages can be successful if one of the partners is *mobile* and willing to assimilate the subculture of the partner.[11] This was not so in this case. The wife probably thought that the husband was mobile and would give up his social class norms, and very likely the husband believed that his wife would be glad to "improve" her social position, but this proved not to be the case.

One might argue that *regional* subcultures were involved in this case, and it is true that the wife was deeply motivated to live in the West or the Midwest and that she had a negative attitude toward "Easterners." It seems to us, however, that the basic sub-cultural differences in this marriage were socioeconomic in nature and not regional.

Some persons may also feel that the wife and/or the husband in this marriage was "neurotic." This word is so poorly defined that one can apply it to almost anybody who does not fit in in our society. But does it explain anything? In this case, the wife once consulted a psychiatrist, who did not seem to feel that she needed psychiatric treatment. Neither the husband nor the wife has ever exhibited signs of personal maladjustment. It seems to be only in the marital relationships that difficulty is encountered.

At our last contact this couple was still married and it seems unlikely now that they will ever separate or divorce. But they are still disappointed in their marriage and feel that it has not worked out as they had hoped. It remains our belief that social class factors are deeply imbedded in their problems.

Unfortunately, none of the marital prediction studies published to date has employed the concept of social class in its study design.[12] The monumental work of Burgess-Wallin on engagement and subsequent marriage, for example, has no reference to social class in its index, and the various chapters have no systematic analysis of social class as a factor in courtship and marriage.[13]

If one wonders why these studies have not employed a social class variable, since so much current research in the social and behavioral sciences does, the answer seems to be related to the following: (1) the long cycle of marital prediction research dates back to the 1930's, an era preceding the findings of the social class research group. Except for the earlier work, *Middletown,* by the

Lynds,[14] which did employ social class as a conceptual tool, the other major studies on social stratification did not begin to appear until the 1940's.[15] By that time, Terman and Burgess-Cottrell had already completed their research,[16] while that of Locke and Burgess-Wallin was already in process.[17] This time factor, plus the usual lag before new findings are reflected in research, meant that none of these major studies of marital adjustment in modern America really employed social class as a variable and hence did not subject its influence to systematic analysis. (2) With the exception of Locke,[18] all these studies have employed essentially homogeneous middle-class samples, thus eliminating for the most part socioeconomic differences. And (3) all these studies have tended to assume that psychological factors were more basic than socioeconomic factors.[19] Thus, as Goode has pointed out,[20] these studies have failed to reveal the impact of socioeconomic influences in modern marriage. Except for the Roth and Peck study,[21] the area remains practically untouched.

At the same time, a series of studies by Goode, Kephart, Hollingshead, Monahan, and Schroeder have demonstrated rather convincingly very deep differences in marital stability rates between different social class groups in the United States.[22] In view of these findings, unchallenged as yet, the writer believes that social class and occupation (the two are closely related but not synonymous) must be given serious attention in any analysis of marital interaction in our society.

It should be pointed out that some of the more recent family textbooks, such as those by Winch[23] and Cavan,[24] have devoted considerable space to social class membership and its relationship to marital success or failure.

Occupation and Marital Adjustment

Perhaps the most important single factor in determining social class membership is the occupation of the chief breadwinner, usually the husband.[25] The writer is of the belief that occupation *in itself,* even apart from social class, has a deep effect on both family life and marital adjustment. The rest of this chapter will be devoted to an attempt to support this hypothesis.

In a sense, every occupation is really a "way of life." This is obvious in the case of ministers or theatrical people, but it is true to some extent of all occupations. Farming, for example, is certainly more than a way of earning a living; it is also a *way* of living. Being a college professor, or a school teacher, or a physician—all these professions have profound effects on family living.

In a term paper written for the writer, one student describes how her father's dry-cleaning business affected their family life. "On big holidays," she writes, "such as Easter or Christmas, we were never able to celebrate the way other families did because we would be swamped with clothes to clean and deliver. I spent one Christmas Eve on the delivery truck until eleven o'clock. Our whole family was affected by the business."

Another student writes: "My father is a minister—and you know what that means. We lived in small towns for the most part and it was like living in a fish bowl. We always had to set a good example for the other children. It's not very easy being a minister's son."

In some families, the father's work requires him to travel extensively, and this often means that the mother rears the children more or less alone.

One of our students lived most of his youth in a trailer. He writes: "Most people I know are prejudiced against rearing children in trailers but it worked very well for our family. My father's work required him to travel all over the United States, so he decided to buy a big trailer and take the family with him. Usually, we would be in each community about three or four months. I guess I have attended 15 or 20 different schools. It was an exciting life—like being on a perpetual vacation trip. We all seem to be well adjusted and I think the experience was good for us."

In an interesting book, *The Railroader,* Cottrell has demonstrated how deeply the railroader's occupation affects his family and their participation in community affairs.[26] A similar analysis, we feel, would demonstrate that most occupations and professions have profound effects on both marital interaction and family living.

The effects of occupation can be seen in two ways: (1) occupation of parent, and (2) occupation of spouse. Let us analyze them separately.

Effects of Parent's Occupation

In a marriage well known to the writer, the wife's father was a Protestant minister whereas the husband's father was a traveling salesman. When it came to such matters as drinking, smoking, or telling stories, there was a vast difference in their conceptions of proper behavior. The wife, for example, could never remember an off-color story being told in her home, whereas these had been a daily staple in the husband's home. The wife's father had never participated in male society—hunting, fishing, drinking, etc.—whereas the husband's father was active in such things.

As a result of all this, the wife had a conception of men and male behavior at odds with that of the husband. She resented his "going out with the men," for example. She also regarded some of his language as crude. But to him, all this seemed perfectly natural—"After all, my father did it," he would say, "and my mother didn't object." Although this deep difference in family background did not destroy this marriage, it certainly complicated it a great deal. This is obviously an extreme case, but less obvious differences can be detected in many marital situations if one looks closely.

Since the father's occupation is crucial to the entire family, it is difficult to see why it would not affect, in some way, almost every facet of family life. The problems are: *How?* In what ways? And to what extent? We will ignore, for the present, the double impact of occupation when the mother is employed.

To begin with, the family's standard of living is affected:

what kind of a house, what sort of neighborhood, how much education, etc. This in turn sets up expectations for later marriage.

The level of security in the home and its general emotional climate are very apt to be related to the father's occupation: How steady is his income? How much strain does he work under? How does the future look? These are all closely tied to the shop or the office.[27]

In his interesting study, *Parent and Child,* Bossard points out that the family effects of occupation have not been systematically analyzed by sociologists and other students of the family as yet.[28] He comments: "This lack of systematic development is not in keeping with its undoubted importance in the life of the individual and society." [29]

Bossard was able to find many studies of occupations by social scientists, but none directly related to family life or child-rearing.[30]

In 212 student papers describing their family life, the writer discovered that 38 per cent of the group felt that their father's occupation had had deep significance for their parents' marriage and their general life as a family.[31] One girl wrote: *"What* family life? My father was married to his job. My mother and I hardly ever saw him—except when he was too tired to work any longer. To this day, my father seems almost a stranger to me."

Although such cases are undoubtedly not typical, one wonders what adequate research would reveal about the ability of the job to reach into the home and influence its residents.

In the next part of this discussion, we will try to pin down this analysis by looking at the immediate effect of the *husband's* occupation (not the parent's) on marital adjustment.

Effects of Spouse's Occupation

Although the writer knows of no systematic studies of the effects of occupation on marital interaction, it seems obvious that such factors as the kind of job a man has, the kind of business he is in, or the nature of his profession—almost inevitably affect his participation in marriage. The dynamics of this seem to be as follows.

1. The satisfaction or lack of satisfaction of the spouse's basic psychological needs on the job would be felt almost inevitably in the marital relationship. This is partly what is meant when some writers describe the modern home as a "psychological dressing station"—when our work is unsatisfactory, we come home for psychological first aid. This means that the marital relationship then has to be good enough to carry the additional load. In cases of extreme occupational frustration, the marital relationship may become overloaded and be unable to compensate for lack of satisfaction in the work situation. Where both the husband and the wife are employed outside the home, both occupations tend to affect the marital relationship.

In situations where the job imposes great strain, even when it is essentially satisfying, the spouse normally has less "reserve" to give his wife, or their children, and this would usually have a negative effect on the marriage.

Stated positively, one could phrase a generalization of this sort: the greater the satisfactions from the occupational role of the breadwinner, the less strain on the marriage. Thus a moderately satisfying marriage might survive if the husband had an occupational role that was pleasant, satisfying, and not too demanding, whereas such a marriage might fail if the occupational role were too frustrating or too demanding.

2. Even when the occupation is rewarding and satisfying, severe strains can be imposed on marriage by the "long arm of the job," as it is often called. This can be seen in the medical profession, a field that often makes excessive demands on the husband-father's time and energy. The physician's first duty is to his sick patient, but this is hard to explain to his wife and children. Family dinners, family celebrations, trips, all may be seriously interfered with at times by emergency calls. The same is true of many positions in business and industry. Mr. Harlow Curtice, for example, President

of General Motors, is reported in *Fortune* to have complete living quarters near his office, so that he has to return home only *on week ends.*[32] He also has to travel several months a year as part of his job. To whom does Mr. Curtice owe first allegiance, his family or General Motors?

Lest the reader dismiss this case as being completely atypical, as it is, it may be well to remember that a great many small business owners, physicians, and less famous executives than Mr. Curtice also work a very long week. And in addition, it is not uncommon for lower middle-class and blue-collar workers in our society to hold down *two* jobs, both made possible by the "shorter" work week of the modern era.[33]

One of the best studies of the effects of occupation on marriage is to be found in Leo Rosten's classic, *Hollywood.*[34] Here it is shown that movie actors and actresses find it almost impossible to have a stable and satisfying marriage because of the very nature of their profession. Their careers have to come first if they are to survive in the highly competitive industry, and this means that their marriages have to come second or even third. Rosten develops the thesis that Hollywood people are not necessarily maladjusted or neurotic but that they are caught in an inhuman and abnormal occupation. He grants, of course, that the theatrical profession probably attracts an undue proportion of high-strung, complex personalities, but he doubts that this explains the Hollywood movie colony's divorce rate.

Perhaps the most ambitious attempt to isolate the effects of occupation on marital adjustment was made by Lang, who had friends and acquaintances rate 17,533 marriages covering sixty different occupational groups.[35] His findings suggest that occupation is related to marital adjustment but fail to show *how*.

As analyzed by Burgess and Cottrell, Lang's data point toward two general conclusions: (1) that "transient" occupations show a higher proportion of less satisfactory marriages; and (2) that low-income occupations show an undue proportion of unhappy marriages.[36]

Suggestive as Lang's findings are, his study fails to isolate certain occupational factors that are essential if we are to understand the relationship of occupation to marital adjustment. These factors are as follows:

1. What relationship exists, if any, between *job satisfaction* and marital adjustment?

2. What relationship exists, if any, between *job pressure* (or responsibility) and marital adjustment?

3. What relationship exists, if any, between *occupational mobility* (or advancement) and marital adjustment?

In some studies, such as that by Aberle and Naegele, the analysis has focused more on *social class* than on occupation itself.[37]

Upon analysis, it can be shown that almost any job or occupational role includes a "way of life" or a subculture. This is obvious in the case of farmers and motion-picture stars, but it may be equally true, if less obvious, of other occupational groups.

In the following section, the writer presents a series of case studies, in all of which occupation seems to have been a major factor in marital adjustment. We do not mean to imply that any given occupation in itself will *prevent* marital adjustment: all we mean is that some occupations present hazards to marriages not found in other professions.

Case Studies of Occupation and Marital Adjustment

The Meat Salesman: In this marriage, the husband reports that he has found that his gross sales are directly related to the personal relationship between himself and the meat buyers for the large markets in his territory. He also finds that this personal relationship with his customers can best be developed by spending time with the meat buyers—more specifically, visiting with them after closing hours, going hunting with them, and taking them to see professional baseball or football games—all of which normally includes drinking a great deal of beer. As the husband puts it: "The meat business is highly competitive. Furthermore, prices, quality, and service are about the same among the major competitors. Therefore, the main factor determining sales is the personal relationship between the meat buyer and the meat salesman. And since most butchers are great beer drinkers, this means that the amount of beer consumed is directly proportional to the amount of meat sold." He feels that he has proved this in his sales this past year: "I am selling more meat than any other meat salesman in the territory—and drinking more beer with more butchers."

He goes on to point out that, since most butchers cannot drink during working hours, most of this salesman-buyer companionship *has* to take place in the evening, on holidays, or on week ends, "time that should belong to my family."

The major problem in this case was that the wife resented all this and had threatened to leave the husband unless he modified his habits. She had an aversion to butchers, for one thing, and she bitterly resented her husband's not coming home at five for supper.

Although there was some sexual difficulty in this marriage, the basic problem seemed to be a conflict between the husband's occupational role and his family roles (both as husband and as father). He was certainly not an alcoholic, as his wife described him to us, and he seemed to have genuine warmth and affection for both his wife and children (who adored him). He was highly successful in his job and well regarded by his business associates. There was no evidence of personal maladjustment in either the husband or wife, although the wife seemed less emancipated from her family than one might wish.

The writer submits that in their case the "long arm of the job" was damaging the marriage. It is true, of course, that the meat industry would be the first to deny that meat sales depend upon this type of informal social relationship between the salesman and the local buyer, but this would not necessarily disprove the point.

The writer has been informed by a steel salesman that in his field the portrait of the selling process as described above by the meat salesman is "100 per cent accurate." In steel, according to this man, price and quality are uniform, which means that sales depend upon the personal relationship between the salesman and the purchasing agent. "My main job is to entertain and become close friends with purchasing agents. The steel sells itself." He adds that this usually involves a lot of drinking, but not always; "Once in a while you find a purchasing agent who doesn't drink, but not often."

In another situation involving a salesman of crackers and biscuits to retail grocery stores, the meat salesman's description of the selling process was confirmed. In this case, however, the wife did not object and there was no negative effect on the husband-wife relationship. There was an obvious effect, though, on the amount of time the husband could spend with his family.

We do not wish to push the point too far, but it seems clear that in occupations such as those above there may exist a definite conflict between occupational roles and family roles.

The Newspaperman: In this situation the husband's work for a large newspaper syndicate involves a great deal of travel. In some election years, for example, this man is away from home most of the time for six months or so. But that is only part of the problem, for even when he *is* home, most of his work comes during the late afternoon or evening, since he works for morning newspapers instead of evening papers (a paper published in the morning tends to feature late afternoon and evening news). Furthermore, the work often requires that most of the week end be devoted to some big news break. During periods of international crisis, such as the Korean War, the husband often sleeps on a cot in his office where he can be close to the news teletype report and other sources of information.

Even this is not all, for this job involves other hazards as well. This man is exposed to a wide variety of women, some of whom are not only attractive but brilliant as well—magazine writers, photographers, public relations workers, etc. There is some evidence that he has not always been able to resist all his opportunities for extramarital relationships.

This man is highly successful in his work and ranks high

in his profession, but his marriage has failed. His wife put it this way to the writer: "I could not compete with his job, which is his first love. The children and I always had to come second—or third. Some weeks and months we hardly saw him at all. I finally couldn't take it any more and got a divorce." She went on to say that in her opinion "a man with a job like that shouldn't be married—at least they shouldn't have any children." She feels that her husband's job was the main reason for the failure of their marriage.

It is undoubtedly true that *some* men with similar work patterns do achieve stable and satisfying marriages, as Rosten points out in his study of Hollywood, but could it not be that *they* are the exceptions rather than the norm? It seems, at least on theoretical grounds, that any marriage that could survive strains of this sort would have to be above average in compatibility. In the case just described we would rate the marriage as "average." There were several years of relative satisfaction before the children came, and during this period the wife spent a great deal of her time either working or downtown with her husband. But after the children were born and the husband began to move up in his profession, two separate worlds seemed to develop—the wife and the children out at their suburban home, and the husband downtown at his office. Gradually, these two worlds became farther and farther apart until they were no longer compatible.

We would not argue that other factors were not involved in this marital failure, but we do believe that in this case there were really two love affairs and two marriages on the part of the husband: he was in love with his work and his wife too (at least in the beginning), and he was married to his job as much as he was to his wife. In fact, he was more attached to his job for it always came first.

The Athletic Coach: In this marriage there has been a long history of dissatisfaction on the part of the wife. She feels that her husband neglects her, that his job is more important than his family, that she lives the life of a "widow," etc. On several occasions she has separated from the husband but she always comes back.

The husband does not deny most of his wife's charges. His coaching responsibilities are very heavy and he devotes most of his time and energy to his job. He is highly successful in a very competitive field and feels that one can succeed in this type of work only by working the way he does. He puts it this way: "All the successful men in my field have the same family problems that I have. They all put their job first—and when they stop doing that, they will be looking for a new job. Our wives and our children simply have to get used to our work, just as a doctor's wife has to. The only other solution is to get another wife—and lots of them have tried that, too."

This man is under tremendous strain several months of the year. Can anyone doubt that a job of this kind subjects a marriage to severe strain?

In the writer's case studies, which obviously do not represent a random sample, it seems clear that the man who is most successful in his job puts his work *first,* which means that his family and marital roles are subordinated to his occupational roles. In his interesting study of mobile young business executives, Henry discovered that these men gave their first loyalty to their employers and were prepared to cut themselves off from any human ties that might hamper their economic advancement.[38] If this is true, then it seems obvious that such men require a certain kind of wife, one who could adjust to being subordinated to the demands of her husband's job.

Recent articles in popular magazines suggest that business firms today seem to think they are hiring the wife as well as the husband.[39]

It may well be that the job in our society breaks up as many marriages as the "other woman." A recent best-seller, *Man in the Gray Flannel Suit,*[40] has attempted to portray this conflict between wife and dictaphone in vivid scenes. The immediate reception of the book by the public suggests that the problem may be a fairly common one.

It seems to the writer that girls in particular should ask themselves *before marriage* whether they are willing to pay the price if they marry an extremely ambitious man. In the three case studies presented earlier, none of the wives seemed willing to pay the price. They all wanted to come first, to have the job subordinated to them and their children. Somewhere, and somehow, it seems, it has to be recognized that marital choice represents a *choice of values,* and that "you can't have your cake and eat it too" in marriage any more than you can in other areas of life. This does not seem to be very clear to many Americans.

Summary and Conclusion

In this chapter the main thesis has been that social class background and occupational factors are intimately related to marital adjustment. We have supported Warner and associates in their belief that social classes in our society possess distinctive subcultures and that marriages between social classes should be regarded as cross-cultural or mixed marriages. We also agree with Roth and Peck that *mobility* within and between social class levels may well be the decisive factor in determining whether or not a cross-cultural marriage will be successful.[41] This seems to include three factors: (1) the *desire* to move, (2) the *ability* to assimilate rapidly the subculture of the new class, and (3) the ability to *emancipate* oneself from the ties and the subculture of the class from which the person is moving.

Unfortunately, most of this is unconscious or unknown to most of us. The psychologists and psychiatrists have been successful in showing the importance of personality factors in marital adjustment, but the social scientists have failed, at least for the most part, in showing the relevance of cultural factors for marital adjustment. It is hoped that this chapter has made some contribution toward this understanding.

References

1. See W. Lloyd Warner, *American Life* (Chicago, University of Chicago Press, 1953) for a readable summary of Warner's work. This little volume also contains reading lists of the other major studies of social stratification in the United States.

2. Although he has published several studies related to social stratification, the best-known work by August B. Hollingshead is *Elmtown's Youth* (New York, John Wiley & Sons, 1949).

3. Alfred C. Kinsey, Wardell B. Pomeroy, and Clyde E. Martin, *Sexual Behavior in the Human Male* (Philadelphia, W. B. Saunders Co., 1948), and *Sexual Behavior in the Human Female* by the same authors (also published by Saunders, 1953).

4. See the 1948 volume, chap. 10.

5. These are described and analyzed in Warner, *op. cit.*, chap. 3. See also W. Lloyd Warner and Paul S. Lunt, *The Social Life of a Modern Community* (New Haven, Yale University Press, 1941).

6. Warner, *op. cit.* The interested student might also wish to look at *Social Stratification in the United States* by John F. Cuber and William F. Kenkel (New York, Appleton-Century-Crofts, Inc., 1954).

7. See Charles P. Loomis and J. Allan Beegle, *Rural Social Systems* (New York, Prentice-Hall, Inc., 1950), Part III.

8. See E. Franklin Frazier, *The Negro Family in the United States* (New York, Dryden Press, 1951), Part V. See also St. Clair Drake and Horace R. Cayton, *Black Metropolis* (New York, Harcourt, Brace & Co., 1945).

9. Julius Roth and R. F. Peck, "Social Class and Social Mobility Factors Related to Marital Adjustment," *American Sociological Review*, 16 (1951), 478–487.

10. See Warner, *op. cit.*, p. 58.

11. *Op. cit.*

12. We refer to the following: Lewis M. Terman *et al.*, *Psychological Factors in Marital Happiness* (New York, McGraw-Hill Book Co., 1938), Ernest W. Burgess and Leonard S. Cottrell, Jr., *Predicting Success or Failure in Marriage* (New York, Prentice-Hall, Inc., 1939), Harvey J. Locke, *Predicting Adjustment in Marriage* (New York, Henry Holt & Co., Inc., 1951), and Ernest W. Burgess and Paul Wallin, *Engagement and Marriage* (Philadelphia, J. B. Lippincott Co., 1953).

13. *Op. cit.* They do consider "background factors" but do not relate these to the systematic analysis of social class. Because his sample includes a wider socioeconomic range, Locke has more information about different social class groups in his study. He does not, however, have anything approaching a systematic analysis of social class and its relationship to marital interaction.

14. Robert S. Lynd and Helen Lynd, *Middletown* (New York, Harcourt, Brace & Co., 1929).

15. This statement is confirmed by a review of the publication dates of the various stratification studies cited by Warner, *op. cit.*

16. Terman published his material in 1938, while the Burgess-Cottrell study appeared a year later, in 1939.

17. Both of these projects were under way by the early 1940's.

18. Locke's sample did include blue-collar workers and some rural couples. See his description of his groups, *op. cit.*, chap. 2.

19. See, for example, the discussion by Burgess-Wallin, *op. cit.*, p. 515.

20. William J. Goode, "Economic Factors and Marital Stability," *American Sociological Review*, 16 (1951), 802–812.

21. *Op. cit.*

22. All these studies are summarized and analyzed in William J. Goode, *After Divorce* (Glencoe, The Free Press, 1956), chap. 4, "Socioeconomic Factors and Divorce."

23. Robert F. Winch, *The Modern Family* (New York, Henry Holt & Co., Inc., 1952).

24. Ruth Shonle Cavan, *The American Family* (New York, Thomas Y. Crowell Co., 1953).

25. Warner makes it clear that occupation is not the *only* factor determining social status. See his *American Life* cited above.

26. W. Fred Cottrell, *The Railroader* (Stanford University, Stanford University Press, 1940).

27. There is some reference to this in a study by David F. Aberle and Kaspar D. Naegele: "Middle-Class Fathers' Occupational Role and Attitudes Toward Children," *American Journal of Orthopsychiatry*, 22 (1952), 366–378.

28. See James H. S. Bossard, *Parent and Child* (Philadelphia, University of Pennsylvania Press, 1953), pp. 202–204.

29. *Ibid.*

30. *Op. cit.*, p. 204.

31. These papers were written for the author's marriage course and were based on a rather detailed outline supplied by the instructor, which meant that the information recorded was relatively uniform and could be tabulated.

32. See the article by Robert Sheehan, "Harlow Curtice Earns His $750,000," in *Fortune*, February, 1956.

33. A survey of bartenders by one of the writer's students discovered that over half of these men held down two jobs. This, of course, is not unheard of among school teachers, or even college professors.

34. Leo C. Rosten, *Hollywood* (New York, Harcourt, Brace & Co., 1941).

35. R. O. Lang, *The Rating of Happiness in Marriage*, unpublished

M.A. thesis (Chicago, University of Chicago, 1932), as summarized in Burgess and Cottrell, *op. cit.*, pp. 139–143.

36. *Ibid.*

37. *Op. cit.*

38. William E. Henry, "The Business Executive: A Study in the Psychodynamics of a Social Role," *American Journal of Sociology*, 54 (1949), 286–291.

39. See "Your Wife Is Your Business Partner," by Lester and Irene David in *This Week Magazine* for April 15, 1956; also "The Wife Problem," by William H. Whyte, Jr., in *Life* for January 7, 1952; see also "Goddess of Success" in the section on Management, *Time*, March 26, 1956.

40. Sloan Wilson, *Man in the Gray Flannel Suit* (New York, Simon and Schuster, Inc., 1955).

41. *Op. cit.*

Suggested Readings

1. W. Fred Cottrell, *The Railroader* (Stanford University, Stanford University Press, 1940). This has become a classic in the sociology of occupation. It shows the close relationship existing between the railroader's job and his family life.

2. Sloan Wilson, *Man in the Gray Flannel Suit* (New York, Simon and Schuster, Inc., 1955). This best-seller describes very neatly the problems of a modern husband-father who had to choose between his wife and children and the demands of his employer.

3. Leo C. Rosten, *Hollywood* (New York, Harcourt, Brace & Co., 1941). This classic portrays in very readable fashion the often insoluble conflict between making films and making a success of marriage.

4. William H. Whyte, Jr., "The Wife Problem," *Life* for January 7, 1952. This is reprinted in adapted form in *Selected Studies in Marriage and the Family*, edited by Robert F. Winch and Robert McGinnis (New York, Henry Holt & Co., Inc., 1953), pp. 278–295.

5. William E. Henry, "The Business Executive: A Study in the Psychodynamics of a Social Role," *American Journal of Sociology*, 54 (1949), 286–291. Reprinted in adapted form in Winch and McGinnis, cited above, pp. 269–278. This is not hard for undergraduates to read, in spite of its title.

CHAPTER XV

IN-LAWS: FRIENDS OR ENEMIES?

Introduction

In our society there are endless jokes about in-laws, and mothers-in-law in particular. Indeed, it almost seems that some radio and television comedians would be deprived of their livelihood if mothers-in-law did not exist. It seems odd that so many of these so-called "jokes" focus on the mother-in-law, and one of the tasks of this chapter will be to explain this riddle.

It appears very likely that most of the thinking (if that is the word) about in-law relationships in our society is at the level of *folklore,* and we shall want to take a good long look at this heritage.

We will also have to look into the sociology of in-laws, the reasons why in-laws are inevitable, and the specific in-law patterns to be found in our particular culture.

And, finally, we will want to examine the research data on in-law relationships in our society, although this is not very impressive to date. Let us begin by analyzing the sociological reasons why we have in-laws.

305

The Sociology of In-Laws

Essentially, in-laws are made inevitable in *all* human societies by the universal incest taboo prohibiting marriage within the
nuclear or immediate family—that is, between brother and sister,
or between parent and child.[1] It is true that a few societies have
permitted at least ceremonial marriage between brothers and
sisters of the royal family, but these rare exceptions do not alter
the basic universality of the prohibition on incestuous marriage.
How *widely* this prohibition is extended, however, differs considerably from one culture area of the world to another, so we know
there is nothing innate or instinctive about the incest taboo. As a
matter of fact, there has never been a completely satisfactory theory
advanced to account for the world-wide distribution of incest pro-
hibitions.[2] One can report their existence, but to *explain* them is
quite another matter.

But whatever the explanation may be, the practical results
of the taboo are to insure that in-laws will be universal, for the
simple reason that we are forced to marry out of our own kinship
group and into another, and the members of this other group automatically become in-laws (related by law but not by blood). As
Murdock and Parsons have pointed out,[3] a new marriage unit in
our society is always formed by uniting two persons of opposite sex
from two unrelated nuclear family groups. Thus we see that every
marriage joins in matrimony not only two individuals but two
kinship groups.

From a theoretical point of view, this combining of two
families to form every new marriage unit has a decided advantage:
it provides a bigger and broader group of people to help the young
couple in the event of illness or other misfortune. And in a study
of middle-class families, Sussman found that both sets of in-laws *do*
help out the newlyweds, especially so in times of economic crisis.[4]
Duvall also found this in her study, *In-Laws: Pro and Con.*[5]

Unfortunately, however, there is a negative side to this
picture also: by having two sets of in-laws there are *twice* as many

relatives to intervene or interfere when the young couple experience domestic crises, and this intervention is not always constructive. In other words, two sets of relatives can be twice as helpful or twice as difficult, depending upon the situation.

In the United States this picture is complicated by two basic characteristics of our society, its mobility and its heterogeneity. Because of the tremendous mobility in modern America, it often (if not usually) turns out that the two kinship groups are total strangers to each other, perhaps meeting for the first time at the wedding. They may be from different regions of the country, or from different social class levels. Also, because of the "melting pot" nature of our society, the two groups may have diverse ethnic, religious, or racial backgrounds. It is true, of course, that we usually marry within our own social set, just as we usually marry someone from our part of the country, but this by no means eliminates the situations described above. World War II in particular produced a great many marriages between diverse family groups. In rural-village societies, in contrast with our urban-industrial society, marriages are almost always within a local homogeneous group of families. Even here, however, there may be some conflict between in-laws since the parents may belong to different cliques within the local community.[6]

As a matter of fact, anthropologists seem to take the position that in-law relationships have been the source of difficulty in a great many societies of the world. Linton, Fortune, and Hart, for example, have argued along these lines.[7]

Very often in-law relationships are related to systems of residence—that is, where the newlyweds will reside after their marriage. In traditional Chinese society, for example, a bride moved to her husband's ancestral village, this being referred to as patrilocal residence. Under such a system, the bride would usually be at a disadvantage, since she would be living among strangers, whereas her husband would be surrounded by his family, his relatives, and his male friends.

In a matrilocal residence system, such as that of the Hopi

Indians of the American Southwest, the groom came to live in the bride's village, so that he was at a disadvantage under this system.[8]

In R. F. Fortune's study, *The Sorcerers of Dobu,* he describes a bilocal system of residence in which the newlyweds alternate between the villages of the bride and groom, spending six months of the year in each.[9] Fortune claims that this system seems to produce an unusual amount of in-law trouble, more so than the systems that settle the residence issue once and for all.

It is interesting to note that Americans have invented what amounts to a new residence system, often described as "neolocal residence," a system under which newlyweds are encouraged to live by themselves, not only in a separate house from either set of parents, but also in a new community. Margaret Mead points out that very few societies, if any, have ever felt that young married couples should live in such isolation from their families.[10] This appears to be a reflection of the basic American values of independence, freedom, and individualism.

Viewed in this perspective, it appears that Americans are ambivalent about in-laws: since they are inevitable, one must accept them, but let's live as far away from them as possible. They must not be permitted to *dominate* us—that seems to be the great worry—but it's all right for them to *help* us at times, as Sussman's study reveals.[11]

When one adds this schizoid attitude toward in-laws to the fact that the two groups are often strangers of diverse backgrounds, it can be seen that the in-law problem in American society is indeed complex.

The Folklore About In-Laws

No matter what aspect of social life one examines, whether it be courtship or weather prediction, a certain amount of folk belief or folklore seems to be inevitable. The in-law area is no exception, as we shall attempt to show in the next few pages.

The most striking folk beliefs about in-laws in our society appear to be the following:

1. *That in-laws are unimportant.*

This belief holds that "one does not marry the family, just the individual." It rests upon a false assumption that a person can be extracted from his family, much as one extracts a square root.

This little bit of folklore is contrary to what almost every married person knows: that for better or worse, *we join another family when we marry.* Courtship couples very often fail to see this, or *refuse* to see it, even though they are forced to recognize it after they have been married for a few years.

Briefly, there are two basic reasons why this folk belief is fallacious: (1) the person we marry has been shaped and molded by his family, hence we are marrying a product of his family; and (2) relationships in the small American nuclear family are deep and intense, so that they normally endure all through life, influencing the new marriage in endless ways.

Folklore that ignores basic facts of this nature can be dangerous and harmful.

2. *That one can "move away" from in-laws.*

It is true, of course, that the United States is a big place and that a married couple can get pretty far from their relatives, but this separation refers to *physical* distance and not *social* or interpersonal distance. A girl may live in California and her parents in Maine, but she will still be upset if her mother is ill and has to have a major operation. She may, as a matter of fact, be *more* upset living that far off because she can't run across the street and talk to her mother, or her father, or the family doctor. In this sense, geographical separation may often complicate in-law relationships rather than simplify them. And if the mother should become seriously ill, the problem of going back home can be knotty, especially so when there are small children.

3. *That in-laws are usually "difficult."*

Americans tend to have a negative complex about in-laws, just as we do about "cops" (policemen). We are allergic for fear they will try to "push us around," or "tell us what to do." We tend to regard them as potential enemies instead of potential friends. Yet as Duvall points out in her study of in-laws in America,[12] the facts are that in-laws are often the best friends our newlyweds have, and this is even true of that "horrible person, the mother-in-law.

Actually, the belief that in-laws are usually a problem to newlyweds is largely a myth, and one that we could well do without.

If this book can serve to help young couples think more realistically and more constructively about in-law relationships, it will have served a useful purpose.

The Mother-in-Law Complex in Our Society

It seems clear that Americans have a complex about mothers-in-law. If folk humor can be taken as a criterion, there is ample evidence that the mother-in-law runs a close second to the step-mother in being the most difficult person to get along with in our society. We do not have to rely exclusively on analysis of mother-in-law jokes to establish the existence of this complex, for Duvall has produced sufficient evidence.[13] Granting, then, that American culture contains a mother-in-law complex, how does one explain it?

The answer, it seems, is to be found in an analysis of child-rearing in our society. As Gorer points out in his interesting book, *The American People,*[14] and as Margaret Mead reveals in her study of America, *And Keep Your Powder Dry,*[15] the American mother devotes and dedicates her life to her children, not so much in the sense of scrubbing and cleaning for them, but rather in the sense of molding their personalities and preparing them to face the world. In a society in which women are theoretically free *not* to become mothers, to pursue all sorts of fascinating careers, the women who *do* become mothers need very much to feel that their work (rearing children) is tremendously important, which it is, and that they have done and are doing a fine job. As the result of all this, mothers end with a deep and pervasive investment in each child, and consequently they are not inclined to permit the new marriage partner to destroy or damage their life's product.

On a very rough basis, one could draw an analogy here between the mother hen and her protection of her young chicks; nobody ever heard of the rooster being worried or concerned over the dangers threatening the brood. (If chickens could talk, they probably would report a mother-in-law complex also.)

In the case of the American father, it is true that he loves his children and devotes what time he can to them, but this usually turns out to be only a fraction of the time they spend with their mother—and this is especially true of the formative preschool years.

As the result of all this, it is the mother who usually attempts to influence courtship, who tries hard to help the newly married couple whether they wish help or not. And so it is the mother-in-law and not the father-in-law who is feared and resented and made the butt of the in-law jokes.

Notice how different this line of analysis is from the traditional idea that "women are just naturally more difficult," etc., etc.

Actually, in matrilineal and matrilocal societies, such as the famous Trobrianders studied by Malinowski,[16] there tends to be a maternal uncle complex, for in such cultures the mother's brothers have to provide the food and discipline for their sisters' children. It seems clear that in-law complexes can be traced to family structure.

If this is the case, one might ask whether the mother-in-law complex in our society might not decline in severity as more mothers have jobs outside the home and as child-rearing becomes more of a joint enterprise? The answer, according to Duvall's research, is that this actually seems to be the trend, and that mothers-in-law, especially since World War II, have started to come into their own as human beings interested in helping their married children when needed.[17] Theoretically, there is every reason to expect a change in this direction as fathers participate more in infant care (such as bottle feeding), home management, and child-rearing in general. With the shorter work week for men, and the broad tendency for male and female roles to be blended in modern America, it seems that the mother-in-law complex should be on its way out. We for one would say, "good riddance."

It is interesting to note, as Duvall points out,[18] that one might expect to find a grandmother complex in our society, for the simple reason that grandmothers are nobody but the mothers-in-law in disguise. By some magical means, however, the birth of the first child to the young married couple transforms that old ogre, the mother-in-law, into a kind and loving grandmother, beloved by all of us (or at least *most* of us). This magical transformation is certainly one of the unexplained miracles of reproduction in our society.

The answer to this riddle may be something like this: by the time children are born, the young couple have worked out an adjustment with their mothers-in-law, their fears and hostilities have been resolved, and it becomes possible to convert the ogre figure into the "doting grandmother" figure. Furthermore, by this time the marital adjustments have been fairly well ironed out, or the marriage dissolved, so that it becomes less and less necessary (or possible) for the mothers-in-law to "interfere" with the new marriage. It may also be true that parenthood speeds up the emotional maturation process so that the young couple are more capable of viewing the mothers-in-law more objectively. Judging by Sussman's study, one gets the impression too that the young couple have come to depend on "the folks" for economic aid occasionally, and this may help produce a more kindly view of the two sets of parents.[19]

In the last analysis, it seems that the newlyweds in our society have a fear of not being allowed to achieve independence, even after their marriage, and so they erect a sort of barrier or defense mechanism to protect themselves from parental domination, and from mother-in-law interference in particular. But once they have been married for a while and have achieved autonomy, then it becomes possible for them to restructure their conception of their in-laws, and at this point the "kindly grandparent" or "doting aunt" stereotypes become possible.

The Research on In-Laws

The most extensive study of in-law relationships in our society is that by Duvall and reported in her book, *In-Laws: Pro and Con*.[20] In this study, published in 1954, Duvall analyzed over 5,000 letters about mothers-in-law submitted to a national radio program. In addition, the general area of in-law relationships was explored by Duvall with seventeen discussion groups in various parts of the country. Although this study covers only part of the ground, the writer believes it to be the best analysis available at the present time. The student approaching marriage would do well to read this report in its entirety.

Briefly, these are the major findings of this study.

1. There is a deep negative attitude toward mothers-in-law in our society which tends to prejudice young married couples against their mothers-in-law. Duvall believes this stereotype needs to be revised if we are to approach in-law relationships in a constructive way.[21]

2. There is a definite trend toward rejection of the mother-in-law stereotype, especially among young urban couples. The folk belief tends to remain strong among older couples and couples living in small communities.[22]

3. Among couples reporting in-law difficulties, the mother-in-law is by far the most frequently reported as the cause of the difficulty. For example, of 992 couples who complained about their in-laws, 49.5 per cent singled out the mother-in-law as the most difficult.[23]

4. Contrary to a widely held belief that sons-in-law have more trouble with in-laws than do their wives, Duvall found that 9 out of 10 complaints came from the *daughter-in-law*. This seems to indicate that in-law problems in our society are chiefly "women's troubles." [24]

5. The previous finding is reinforced by the fact that the sister-in-law is next to the mother-in-law in frequency of complaint. Out of 1,337 complaints about in-laws, for example, 36.8 per cent

listed the mother-in-law first with the sister-in-law running a close second with 20.3 per cent.[25]

The female dominance pattern can be seen clearly by the fact that father-in-law was reported most difficult by only 5.0 per cent and brother-in-law by only 5.4 per cent.[26]

6. This study reports that *over half* of the sample had *no* mother-in-law complaints and that a significant proportion of the couples report deep feelings of respect and gratitude toward their in-laws.[27]

7. Duvall believes there is an encouraging trend, especially among the younger couples, to regard their in-laws as allies rather than as agents of interference and frustration.[28]

Other Research on In-Laws: In a study reported by Landis and Landis, couples married for 20 years reported in-law relationships to have been high in their ranking of marital adjustment problems. The wives, for example, put in-law relationships second and the husbands third in a ranking of six areas of marital adjustment.[29]

In another questionnaire study by the same authors, 544 couples in the early years of marriage listed in-law relationships *first* in their list of difficult areas. This same study reported a highly significant relationship between in-law adjustment and marital adjustment.[30]

In his careful study of urban married couples in Sweden, Karlsson came up with an unusual finding: that there was *no* association between residence with in-laws and marital adjustment.[31] He comments: "Residence with in-laws is usually regarded as a strain on the marriage, but this finding suggests that at least in some cases it may also be an advantage to have in-laws living in the home." [32]

In a careful review of the research on in-law relationships, Komarovsky found that wives in our society appear on the average to be less emancipated from their parents, especially the mother, and that this tends to create in-law problems after marriage.[33] She seems to believe that this problem is rooted in the differential training received by boys and girls in our society; parents are more concerned about their daughters and hold them closer to the home than they do their sons.[34] Thus, at the point of marriage, the daughters are not as emancipated as the sons, and this is reflected in subsequent in-law problems.

This finding is supported by a study by Wallin in which he reported that (*a*) wives were more often "homesick" for parents than were their husbands, and (*b*) that wives visited their parents more often than did husbands.[35]

Along the same line, Stryker found wives to be significantly more dependent on their mothers than their husbands were, and this was a factor in creating later mother-in-law problems for the husband.[36]

Winch, in a survey of college men and women, found that both sexes felt closer to the mother, as a rule, than the father.[37]

All these studies point to the same pattern: that in-law problems are closely related to the training received by women in our society, and that "mom" is apt to be in the center of any fight with the married children.

Some Reasons Why In-Law Problems Might Be Expected in Our Society

In any human society there are certain elements of social structure that make it almost certain that particular problems will be found. As we have already seen, the mother's dominant role in child-rearing has produced a mother-in-law problem rather than a father-in-law problem in our society, and we have also seen that in some matrilineal societies a maternal uncle problem is more or less inevitable.

In this part of the discussion an attempt will be made to push the analysis deeper and look at some features of American society that predispose our families to certain kinds of in-law problems. It is recognized that many families do not develop these problems, and this means that they are not *inevitable*, but on the other hand these factors *will* produce in-law tensions almost certainly in a certain proportion of our married couples (one fifth of them, according to Landis). Now, what are these factors?

1. *The emancipation problem in American families.*

Reuben Hill, one of the foremost students of the American family, has pointed out that perhaps the biggest problem for American parents is to let the child go.[38] This is one of the prices we pay for being a child-centered society: they mean so much to us that we hate to see them grow up. It may very well be that American parents satisfy too many of their emotional needs through their children and thus are not prepared to give them up when the time comes. If this is true, it means that some young couples will have to struggle through emancipation problems *after* marriage, instead of having this accomplished *before* marriage.

We do not know of any easy way to measure emancipation from parents, but this much can definitely be said: if you or your proposed marriage partner has failed to achieve normal emancipation (whatever that is) by the time of your marriage, you are almost certain to have an in-law problem after your marriage takes place.

2. *Marriage in our society takes a child "away" from the parents.*

It is possible for parents in modern America to adopt two diametrically opposed attitudes toward the marriage of one of their children: (1) we are losing our daughter (or son), and (2) we are gaining a son-in-law (or daughter-in-law). If parents have both of these attitudes, as seems likely, then they are *ambivalent* about their children marrying.

In societies having patrilocal or matrilocal residence for newlyweds, one family may lose a child at marriage while the other one gains one. With our system of neolocal residence, however, it may be that *both* families lose a child, or at least feel that they do.[39]

If this analysis is correct, it means that in-law trouble will be produced in a certain proportion of cases by parents attempting to get the married son or daughter to move back home.

3. *In our family system parents are displaced by the new married partner and later by the children.*

In the traditional Chinese family system, parents could look forward to their old age with the knowledge that their sons would live near them and take care of them, knowing that no daughter-in-law would displace them in their son's affections and responsibilities. In the American system, one cannot be sure of this. Once a son marries in our society, his primary obligation becomes the care of his wife and children. If this takes all his money, or his time, then his parents are deprived of his aid and support. If there is a conflict between his wife and his parents, he is expected to support his wife; otherwise he is not emancipated from his family.

With a few minor differences, the same pattern holds true for the married daughter. If she works, most of (or all) her income will be needed by her husband and children. She undoubtedly continues to aid her parents in various noneconomic ways, but in the event of conflict between the husband and the parents, she is expected to support the husband.[40]

To young persons, this probably sounds reasonable enough, but it is a fact that a great many societies of the world have viewed it differently, and it also is a fact that this system often hurts parents deeply in our society. Actually, on purely logical grounds, the parents usually have a great deal more emotional and economic investment in the son or daughter than the spouse has; and this is especially so in the case of couples wed only a few years, which is the period when in-law problems usually develop if they are going to arise at all.

It seems to the writer that parents must often feel a sort of resentment when they are superseded or displaced by the young husband or wife. And if they feel this resentment, then they may feel justified in interfering when they see their son or daughter being hurt in the new marriage.

It is recognized that not all parents feel this way about their young in-laws, and we are even willing to grant that *most* parents probably do not feel this way, but we are trying to account for in-law *problems* in our society, which means that we are looking at the cases that do not fit into the system very well.

4. *The very close mother-child relationship.*

From our previous analysis of the mother-in-law complex, it seems clear that the extremely close and all-pervading relationship between American mothers and their children lends itself very well to the production of in-law problems. Winch and Stryker have shown that this is not just a mother-son syndrome, as the Freudians believe, but includes also an extremely close mother-daughter relationship.[41] In other words, both male and female children in our society feel closer to the mother than to the father, and this provides the setting for the majority of our in-law problems.

5. *The emphasis on the child in our society.*

For the past few decades ours has been a child-centered society, one in which the child has been more or less the center of the parents' lives. Under these circumstances, it is hard to see how parents can let the child go, for it means almost a complete restructuring of the parents' emotional and social patterns of living. American married couples now have about one third of their lives left after the last child has married.[42] This has produced what has been described as "the empty nest." For the mother in particular, this can be a critical period, for unless she develops new interests, the tendency will be for her to concern herself too much with the affairs of the newlyweds. The economic role of the father seems to help him avoid some of the stresses of this period.

In concluding this section of the chapter, an attempt has been made to point out certain features of our societal structure that seem to provide the setting for our in-law problems. It is not meant that these make in-law difficulties inevitable; but it does mean that they make them decidedly *possible*.

Case Studies in In-Law Relationships

In thinking about any aspect of courtship and marriage in our society, it is essential that we cut through the folk beliefs, the superstitions, the clichés, and view the patterns realistically. The case studies to follow were selected with this purpose in mind.

Case A: In this situation, a young couple were married just after World War II when the housing shortage was acute. Two apartments were finally available, one of which belonged to the wife's parents and was located on the second floor of their residence, while the other was across town and was twice as expensive. For days, according to the husband, he debated whether to move in the same building with his in-laws or to locate in the other section of the city. Actually, he liked his wife's parents and had always gotten along well with them, but he was worried about having them as his landlord, or as close neighbors. His friends cautioned him about "living with his in-laws" and predicted dire consequences if he moved into their apartment. But on the other hand, it was a nicer apartment at a lower rental. His wife left the decision up to him.

Finally, after several days of "sweating," as he put it, he decided to risk it and took the apartment above his in-laws. When we interviewed him several years later, he was able to laugh about the whole episode. "We never had a moment's trouble," he said. "Her parents didn't try to interfere with our marriage and we got along fine. In fact, we stayed there three years and saved enough in rent to accumulate a down payment for the house we live in now. I often laugh when I realize how jumpy I was about moving in there."

In this case, we see how negative stereotypes make it difficult for young couples to think clearly about in-law relationships.

Case B: This is a family situation in which two sons built homes across the street from their parents, much against the advice of their friends. There was also some apprehension on the part of the wives, even though they got along well with each other and with their husbands' parents.

As it turned out, in-law problems did *not* develop and there was no reason whatever to regret the action. The two sisters-in-law became very close to each other, their husbands enjoyed being near each other, the children loved to run across the street to visit the grandparents, and in general the family came to be a very strong and closely knit unit. When we discussed the matter with them some ten years after the sons located across the street, there was a unanimous belief that the advantages of the arrangement far outweighed the disadvantages. And yet the sons almost gave up the desirable building sites offered free by their father for fear of "running into in-law trouble." Here again one sees the fears created by the negative stereotype of in-laws in our society.

Case C: In this case the wife complains constantly that her husband is dominated by his mother and that the mother interferes in their married life. It seems clear that the wife's respect for her husband has been damaged by what she calls "his being afraid of his mother."

Interestingly enough, the husband admits all this. "It is true," he says, "that I cannot stand up to my mother, but it is also true that *no man* that I know can stand up to her. My father couldn't and neither can my two brothers. In fact, she dominates almost everybody with whom she has any contact. I believe that I am less dominated by her now than I was ten years ago, but I still cannot oppose her on certain issues."

In this case, the wife's mother also tends to be domineering but the daughter seems to be able to resist better than the husband. But the husband dislikes his mother-in-law and feels that she has been a negative influence in their marriage (which is not very good).

In this case, the married couple seem to suffer from aggres-sive, power-seeking mothers, with the fathers being relatively mild "nice" persons. This case presents almost the classic picture of the mother-in-law complex: the mother who will not allow her son to grow up, who wishes to run the lives of the young couple, who constantly creates tensions and conflict.

We think it interesting to note that this couple attempted to solve their in-law problem by moving to the West but found that distance alone did not provide a solution. As the wife said: "My husband can be as upset by a letter or telephone call from his mother as by a visit. Moving to the West Coast didn't solve anything—and we missed our friends back home." So they eventually moved back to the Midwest, but not in the same town as their families. The in-law problems in this case seem to continue regardless of where the couple live.

It might be pointed out that both husband and wife in this situation come from upper-class families, and it may be that family units are tighter at the upper-class level. In this case, the married couple still receive financial aid from both families, even though they have been married several years and are now in their early thirties.

Case D: In this situation, there is a daughter-in-law problem. The son's wife appears to be mentally ill and is jealous of her husband's close relationship with his parents and his sister (the only other child in his family). The wife has opposed her husband's visiting his parents or helping them in any way. She has also been hostile toward the husband's sister and has tried to damage that relationship.

This case illustrates how family problems *radiate* through the entire group, so that mental illness in a daughter-in-law reaches out to hurt not only the husband, but his parents, also his sister and her husband. We believe this case illustrates once again the basic principle that we marry the whole family and not just the individual.

Some Suggestions for Getting Along with In-Laws

While it is recognized that not all in-law problems can be avoided, it should be possible to reduce their frequency and also to minimize their impact.[43] The suggestions to follow are not to be thought of as representing a panacea or cure-all for in-law difficulties, but we do believe that they can be of aid to young couples approaching marriage.

1. *Get to know them before marriage.*

We know that marital adjustment begins *before* marriage, and this certainly includes adjustment to in-laws. Make every effort to become close friends with your in-laws before you get married. Go to visit them and stay until your welcome wears out. Spend part of your vacations with them if possible. Try to see them in different situations to deepen your understanding of them. And try to help them understand *you.*

2. *Don't try to separate your spouse from his or her family.*

Remember that the parents have devoted a large part of their lives to rearing this person you are now in love with. Recognize that they are still deeply concerned about the welfare of their son or daughter, that they will be tremendously concerned that things go well in the new marriage. Write to them, telephone them on special occasions. Think of them as though they were your parents too, which they are in a very real sense.

3. *Don't enter marriage prejudiced against in-laws.*

Don't be a "sucker" for nightclub jokes or cartoons reflecting cultural stereotypes. You wouldn't want them to think of you as a stereotype, so why think of them that way?

4. *Approach marriage with a positive attitude toward your in-laws.*

This assumes that you know and like them. If you do not know them, you can at least decide that you will *try* to like them when you do get acquainted, that you will go at least halfway in trying to understand and love them.

If you do know them and feel sure that you will not be able to like them, perhaps you should reconsider marriage to this person. Does he (or she) know how you feel about this family? Do you know *why* you feel that way? How much of the problem stems from *your* personality and background? And most important of all, is it possible that you reject part of your courtship partner when you reject his family? This would normally be the case unless he had revolted against his family and had rejected them himself.

5. Don't assume that you can escape in-laws.

As we have already seen, moving away does not always work, nor does it seem likely that many of us can actually get away from our families, even if we wanted to. The main reason why this is so is that our families *are us*: their values and behavior patterns have become internalized in us, so that to escape our families means that we have to escape ourselves.

6. Remember that you will very likely need some sort of help from your in-laws sooner or later.

This may sound gruesome, or impossible, but Sussman's study, cited earlier in this chapter, indicates that it is common, at least for middle-class parents, to help their married children. When one remembers all the illnesses, divorces, wars, depressions, and other crises facing married couples over a period of several decades, it seems reasonable to assume that all of us might need assistance at some time or another.

7. Remember that in-laws are not always wrong.

If they have suggestions about your marriage, your house, or your cooking, maybe they are right and you *could* improve your married life by at least considering their ideas. After all, the parents are older, have lived a long time, and sometimes they *do* have a wisdom unknown to newlyweds. Why not benefit from their mistakes instead of "learning the hard way" through your own mistakes?

Conclusion

The reader may feel that we have sided with the in-laws in this chapter, and perhaps this is true. If so, our purpose has been to counterbalance the negative stereotypes about in-laws revealed clearly in the Duvall study. Actually, it might help to think of this as a type of *prejudice,* similar to racial or religious prejudice, a behavior pattern that condemns all members of a group regardless of individual merit. If you and I are opposed to racial and/or religious prejudice, then it seems reasonable that we should be against in-law prejudice as well. Actually, all we are suggesting is the observance of an old Anglo-Saxon legal custom: that in-laws be considered innocent until proved guilty. If we can extend this right to criminals, it should not be asking too much to extend it also to the parents, the brothers and sisters, of the person we are about to marry.

References

1. Our discussion in this chapter has been influenced by our association with Prof. C. W. M. Hart, anthropologist at the University of Wisconsin. See the discussion by George Peter Murdock, *Social Structure* (New York, The Macmillan Company, 1949), chap. 10.

2. Murdock rejects all the traditional theories, but believes that the Freudians have come closest to explaining the taboo. See the chapter cited above for a full discussion.

3. Murdock, *op. cit.,* and Talcott Parsons, "The Social Structure of the Family," in *The Family: Its Function and Destiny* (New York, Harper & Bros., 1949), edited by Ruth Nanda Anshen, pp. 173–201.

4. Marvin B. Sussman, "The Help Pattern in the Middle-Class Family," *American Sociological Review,* 18 (1953), 22–28.

5. Evelyn Millis Duvall, *In-Laws: Pro and Con* (New York, Association Press, 1954).

6. This point is emphasized by Loomis and Beegle in their classic analysis of the rural family in the community. See *Rural Social Systems* by Charles P. Loomis and J. Allan Beegle (New York, Prentice-Hall, Inc., 1950), chap. 5.

7. Ralph Linton, *The Study of Man* (New York, Appleton-Century-

Crofts, Inc., 1936), R. F. Fortune, *Sorcerers of Dobu* (New York, E. P. Dutton & Co., Inc., 1932), and C. W. M. Hart in unpublished lecture on "In-Laws" given in Sociology 60 at the University of Wisconsin, 1952–53.

8. These problems are analyzed in a report, "Matrilineal Descent Systems," published in the *Items* of the Social Science Research Council, 9 (1955), 5–8.

9. *Op. cit.*

10. See Margaret Mead, *Male and Female* (New York, William Morrow & Co., Inc., 1949), chap. 16.

11. *Op. cit.*

12. *Op. cit.*

13. *Ibid.*

14. Geoffrey Gorer, *The American People* (New York, W. W. Norton & Co., Inc., 1948).

15. Margaret Mead, *And Keep Your Powder Dry* (New York, William Morrow & Co., Inc., 1942).

16. B. Malinowski, *The Sexual Life of Savages in Northwestern Melanesia* (New York, Liveright Publishing Corp., 1929).

17. *Op. cit.*, chap. 3.

18. See chap. 8.

19. *Op. cit.*

20. *Op. cit.*

21. See chap. 2, "Mother-in-Law Jokes."

22. Chap. 3.

23. See chap. 10. These figures are on p. 187.

24. *Ibid.*

25. See table on p. 188.

26. *Ibid.*

27. The exact figure was 51 per cent. See page 89 and the other material in chap. 6.

28. Chaps. 3 and 6 in particular report encouraging trends.

29. Judson and Mary Landis, *Building a Successful Marriage* (New York, Prentice-Hall, Inc., 2d ed., 1953), pp. 302–303.

30. *Op. cit.*, pp. 303–304.

31. Georg Karlsson, *Adaptability and Communication in Marriage* (Uppsala, Almqvist and Wiksells Boktryckeri Aktiebolag, 1951).

32. *Op. cit.*, p. 106.

33. Mirra Komarovsky, "Continuities in Family Research: A Case Study," *American Journal of Sociology*, 62 (1956), 42–47.

34. See her earlier paper, "Functional Analysis of Sex Roles," *American Sociological Review*, 15 (1950), 508–516.

35. Paul Wallin, "Sex Differences in Attitudes to In-Laws: A Test of a Theory," *American Journal of Sociology*, 59 (1954), 466–469.

36. Sheldon Stryker, "The Adjustment of Married Offspring to Their Parents," *American Sociological Review*, 20 (1955), 149–154.

37. Robert Winch, "The Oedipus Hypothesis," *American Sociological Review*, 16 (1951), 784–793.

38. See Reuben Hill and Willard Waller, *The Family* (New York, The Dryden Press, 1951), chap. 20.

39. There is an excellent discussion of this point in the excerpt, "Chinese and American Marriage Practices," by Francis L. K. Hsu in Marvin B. Sussman's *Sourcebook in Marriage and the Family* (Boston, Houghton Mifflin Co., 1955), pp. 8–12. See also the fuller discussion in Hsu's book, *Americans and Chinese* (New York, Henry Schuman Inc., 1953).

40. See the study by Robert M. Dinkel, "Attitudes of Children Toward Supporting Aged Parents," *American Sociological Review*, 9 (1944), 71–83.

41. See the studies cited above by these authors.

42. Paul C. Glick, "The Life Cycle of the Family," *Marriage and Family Living*, 17 (1955), 3–9.

43. Duvall, *op. cit.*, has a very complete discussion of ways to avoid in-law problems.

Suggested Readings

1. Evelyn Millis Duvall, *In-Laws: Pro and Con* (New York, Association Press, 1954). This should be required reading for engaged couples. Makes an excellent book report.

2. Talcott Parsons, "The Social Structure of the Family," chap. 10 in *The Family: Its Function and Destiny* (New York, Harper & Bros., 1949), edited by Ruth Nanda Anshen. This discussion has become a classic. The better student will find it very worthwhile.

3. Marvin B. Sussman, "The Help Pattern in the Middle-Class Family," *American Sociological Review*, 18 (1953), 22–28. Reprinted in Sussman's *Sourcebook in Marriage and the Family* (Boston, Houghton Mifflin Co., 1955), pp. 304–310.

4. Francis L. K. Hsu, "Chinese and American Marriage Practices," in Sussman, *op. cit.*, pp. 8–12. Originally appeared in Hsu's study, *Americans and Chinese* (New York, Henry Schuman Inc., 1953).

5. Judson and Mary Landis, *Building a Successful Marriage* (New York, Prentice-Hall, Inc., 1953), chap. 14, "In-Law and Marriage Adjustment."

CHAPTER XVI

RELIGION AND MARRIAGE

Introduction

The American family is confronted with a much more complex religious situation than is the case in a great many human societies. Our culture contains over 200 Protestant denominations, a very large Roman Catholic group, all shades of the Jewish faith, a rapidly growing Christian Science movement, small Greek Catholic elements, plus endless emergent sects of all kinds. In addition, about one third of our population has no formal church affiliation at all.[1] Thus our society contains within itself a kaleidoscopic range of religious faith and nonfaith ranging from the most conservative orthodox Jew through a host of moderate faiths on into the limbo of nature worshipers, ending with the militant atheists (the Communists, for example).

Furthermore, the situation is even more complicated by the fact that *within* any given religious group there are wide variations in the degrees of strength with which the faith is felt and adhered to.

This picture is not typical of Western societies. While serving in England during World War II, the writer was impressed by the relatively homogeneous religious composition of the English people. They seemed to be apathetic toward organized religion, but at the same time their courtship and marital adjustment problems were simplified by their religious consensus.

This, of course, is not true in the United States, especially in our urban centers. And when one recalls that more and more Americans are living in urban communities (if we include their suburbs), it seems clear that young people today in our society are exposed to a variety of religious faiths as they move through the courtship years.

For those of us committed to cultural pluralism, it is good that America has a diversity of religious faiths. We would not wish to have a state church, as many European countries have. At the same time, however, we must not delude ourselves that this diversity does not create problems in courtship and marriage.

What Is a "Mixed" Marriage?

Technically, any marriage between our major religious faiths, Protestant, Catholic, and Jewish, is regarded as a "mixed" marriage. Actually, marriages can be "mixed" on any number of factors—age, social class, educational background, personality type, etc., but the term usually refers to a religious mixture.

It seems obvious that the marriage of Protestants, Catholics, and Jews does not exhaust the possibilities of mixing the various religious subgroups in our society; in fact, it scarcely scratches the surface. Protestants themselves are an extremely diverse group. A High Episcopalian, for example, is much closer to the Roman Catholics on the issue of divorce than he is to his fellow Protestants; when it comes to birth control, however, he is closer to the Protestants. What does a Presbyterian or a Congregationalist have in common with a Holiness sect on the issues of smoking or drinking? Yet they are both Protestants.

Things may seem simple for the Roman Catholics, but this is largely an illusion. The fact is that considerable social distance separates a really devout Catholic from a less devout member of that faith. At the moment, for example, we know a married couple, both Catholic, who are having severe conflict over the issue of birth control, even though the church's position on this is clear. The wife in this marriage is more devout, and more literal, in her Catholicism. The husband is rather liberal in his version of Catholicism. Theoretically, this is not a mixed religious marriage, but in actuality it is. A Protestant married to a Jew, for example, would have a better chance of agreeing about birth control than these two Catholics have.

If we shift our attention to American Jews, it is only too obvious that this minority group in our society has no unified religious subculture at the present time. Split into three main congregations, Conservative, Reformed, and Orthodox, Jews in the United States are by no means sure of religious agreement merely by virtue of marrying within the Jewish faith. As one of our Orthodox students remarked after attending a Reformed service: "My father wouldn't consider that a religious service at all. It was more like a meeting of the Brooklyn Rotary Club."

If our analysis of American religious subgroups and their subcultures is valid, it follows that young persons considering marriage will need to explore beneath *formal* church affiliation to determine religious compatibility. In superficial courtships, this will seldom be accomplished.

This point is emphasized by Pike in his book on interfaith marriages.[2] In an interesting chapter called "We're Both Protestants," he makes this statement: "The word 'Protestant' not only covers the churches which reflect Reformation theology; it also means 'miscellaneous'—and is used for such diverse possibilities as Mormons, Christian Scientists, Ethical Culturists, and outright secularists affiliated with nothing. There are important ways in which a high-church Presbyterian is nearer in basic belief to a Roman Catholic than to a Unitarian. Actually high-church Episcopalians—and, interestingly enough, many Baptists—do not regard themselves as Protestants at all."[3]

It is essential to keep this relativity of faith in mind as we proceed with our analysis.

Religions as Subcultures

In this book we have utilized rather extensively the concept of *subculture,* the way of life of a subgroup in the total population. We have noted that ethnic groups, racial groups, social class groups, age groups, occupational groups, and sex groups (male and female) tend to have more or less distinct subcultures. It is our belief that the role of religion in modern marriage can also be analyzed more clearly if we employ the subculture concept. This section of the chapter will be used to illustrate this approach.

Catholic Subculture in the United States

Let us begin by analyzing Catholic subculture in our society. Fortunately, Father Thomas of St. Louis University has published an excellent study of this, entitled *The American Catholic Family.*[4] Using this source we can delineate the main features of Catholic subculture, as follows:

1. *Catholics are a minority group in our society.*

Historically, America has been predominantly a Protestant culture, and this was especially so before World War I. The early colonial leaders were basically of Anglo-Saxon stock—in other words, Protestants. Father Thomas, in fact, organizes his study of the American Catholic family around the minority group concept.[5]

If Catholics *are* a minority group, as they surely are, it follows that a great deal of prejudice and misinformation would be found in the majority group (Protestants) about Catholics. This means, in turn, that a non-Catholic in love with a Catholic would normally have two problems: (*a*) understanding his *own* ideas and feelings about Catholics and their religion; and (*b*) dealing with the attitudes and ideas of *his family* and *his friends* about Catholics. Both of these operations can be fairly difficult.

2. Historically, Catholics have been "lower-class" people in America.

This is not intended as a reflection on American Catholics. It is simply true that the Protestants, as a group, got here first and got a head start. Warner demonstrates this very explicitly in his study of *Yankee City* (Newburyport, Massachusetts).[6] Here, the early shipping business, and later the shoe factories, were almost all owned by the pioneer Anglo-Saxon Protestant families. When the waves of Catholic immigrants came later (1880–1920), they went to work on the docks and in the factories as laborers.

This picture, of course, has been changing radically in the last few decades,[7] but the *attitudes* toward Catholics tend to persist; they are still thought of as being from the "wrong side" of town.

We would like to suggest that often parents are as concerned about *social class* differences as they are about *religious* differences; but since it is snobbish to talk about a person's social class background, parents often concentrate on religion in opposing a courtship.

It may well be that some of the adjustment problems in Protestant-Catholic marriages result from social class differences rather than those associated with religion as such.

3. The Catholic position on birth control is not popular in our society.

It seems reasonable to believe that most middle-class Americans, including significant numbers of Catholics, believe in planned parenthood.[8] In its flat opposition to modern contraceptives, the Catholic church has created grave problems for Protestant-Catholic marriages. This is also a source of difficulty between unmixed Catholic couples when one spouse is more devout than the other.

This basic difference between Catholic doctrine and that of

Protestants and Jews must be carefully analyzed if mixed marriage with a Catholic is contemplated.[9]

4. *The Catholic position on divorce is extreme.*

It is true that most Protestant and Jewish groups *deplore* divorce and remarriage, but the Catholics *prohibit* it. In view of the long-range trend toward more frequent divorce in the United States, Catholics find themselves in a very unpopular position.[10]

Perhaps enough has been said to illustrate what is meant when it is said that there is a Catholic subculture in our society. For the student who doubts the survival of the elements described above, we suggest some reading in the books cited by Thomas and Pike.

Now, when a Catholic marries a non-Catholic, the problems *unique* to this marriage are going to revolve about the merging or the adjustment of the two religious subcultures and the attitudes related to them.

Protestant Subculture

1. *The diversity of denominations.*

There are over 200 Protestant groups at present in the United States, although a majority of the membership is concentrated in a few large denominations.

2. *There are some basic differences between these denominations.*

These can be seen most clearly if we look at certain "moral issues" in our society: divorce, the use of alcoholic beverages, war versus pacifism, literal vs. liberal interpretation of the Bible, etc. It is possible to be a Protestant and disagree with other Protestants on a great many moral issues.[11]

3. *Protestants are the majority group in our society.*

This means that, consciously or unconsciously, they tend to feel superior to Catholics and Jews. They are very often prejudiced against these groups. This is a major problem to any person attempting to unite a Protestant family with a non-Protestant family. And the arguments about the issues are not apt to be noted for their rational content.

4. *Protestants are relatively decentralized in their church organization.*

This has been part of their anti-Catholic feeling. They are extremely proud that they have no Pope.

5. *Most Protestant groups are relatively liberal in their position on birth control and divorce.*

This sets them off sharply from Roman Catholics. A great many conflicts between the two groups are related to these issues. It is interesting to note, however, that Catholics are more liberal than Protestants on such issues as moderate drinking and gambling, also smoking.

6. *Protestant clergy are permitted to marry.*

This was one of the issues in the Protestant Reformation, of course. Catholics are often criticized by Protestants because the Catholic clergy are not allowed to marry. Note that Jews and Protestants are in agreement on this issue.

Although this by no means covers Protestant subculture, perhaps some of its major features have been described.

Jewish Subculture

1. *Jewish people are an extremely small minority group in our society.*

This makes it almost inevitable that most Americans will be uninformed or *misinformed* about the Jewish faith and its related subculture.

2. *Jews are the victims of extreme prejudice in our society.*

It is probably true that the vast majority of Americans are anti-Semitic. This means that not many families could view very rationally a Protestant-Jewish or Catholic-Jewish courtship and/or marriage. Furthermore, it probably means that the participants themselves may have mixed feelings about the other group. Thus a man might fall in love with a particular Jewish girl and regard her as "wonderful," at the same time not caring for "most Jews." This sort of split attitude can be exceedingly dangerous in modern marriage.

3. *Jews have a number of unique beliefs.*

These include the following: (*a*) the belief that the Jews were originally the "chosen people" of God; (*b*) they do not recognize Jesus Christ as the Son of God; hence they are not Christians; (*c*) the husband-father is a powerful figure in the traditional Jewish family; (*d*) they are forbidden to eat pork or pork products; (*e*) their Sabbath falls on Saturday; (*f*) all male babies are required to be circumcised; (*g*) scholarly achievement is valued very highly —more so than commercial or business success; and (*h*) Jewish families are closely knit and do not usually approve of their children marrying non-Jews. In fact, among Orthodox Jews a son or daughter was traditionally considered as dead if he or she married outside the faith.[12]

In summarizing this brief description of the Protestant, Catholic, and Jewish subcultures, it is recognized that not all the important points have been covered. Perhaps the class itself can fill in the gaps. Our main purpose has been to show that there *are* some basic differences between the three major religious groups in America that are relevant in an analysis of marital adjustment.

It is obvious that a more complete description would have to include the Unitarians, the Christian Scientists, some of the conservative Lutheran groups, the numerous Pentecostal denominations, etc. Space prohibits our doing this.[13]

In closing this discussion, it is essential to remind ourselves that all the above groups also have a great deal in common as Americans. It is undoubtedly true that they agree on a great many more points about life and marriage than they disagree about. It is this common core of values and practices, of course, that makes interfaith marriage possible in our society.

Interfaith Marriages in the United States

Our first problem is to discover *how often* the three major faiths, Catholic, Protestant, and Jewish, intermarry in the United States, after which we will attempt to find out *what factors* determine the intermarriage rate; and, finally, we will ask the big question: *How successful* are interfaith marriages?

Now for the first question: *How often do Americans marry outside their faith?* The answer to this question depends partially on what study you select. One survey of 885 marriages in rural Minnesota, for example, reported 92.9 per cent of the Protestants married to Protestants.[14] This might be taken to indicate a very low interfaith marriage rate in the United States. A New Haven, Connecticut, study by Hollingshead, however, reported only 74.4 per cent of the Protestants to be married to Protestants.[15] In the same study, 93.8 per cent of the Catholics and 97.1 per cent of the Jews were married to persons of their own faith.

One of the most surprising results of this 1948 study was this: "A striking point that emerged from our data is that the effects of religion on marital choice have not changed between the parental and present generation." [16] This seems to be contrary to what one might have expected.

In a later study by Thomas, an outstanding Catholic sociologist, Hollingshead's data on Catholics were seriously challenged.[17] Thomas' research on Catholic parish records showed that the interfaith marriage rate of Catholics is at least 30 per cent, and probably higher; furthermore, he found "a gradual but more or less constant increase from 1910 to the present." [18] It seems impossible to reject Thomas' position that the New Haven Catholic interfaith marriage rate is not at all typical of the United States.

It seems clear, however, that both Catholics and Protestants intermarry more than do Jews in our society.[19]

Fortunately, the state of Iowa in 1953 began including the question of religious denomination on its new statistical forms for the reporting of marriages and divorces to the state office. This is beginning to yield some worthwhile information not hitherto available (other states do not collect this information).

In 1955 Chancellor and Monahan published some interesting preliminary findings based on the new Iowa forms. The major conclusions are as follows: [20]

1. Forty-two per cent of all marriages involving a Catholic in 1953 (the year studied) were *mixed*. This was 12 per cent greater than the figures available from Catholic church records. Note that this Catholic intermarriage rate supports Thomas' assertion that Hollingshead's data for New Haven are atypical.

2. Protestants in Iowa in 1953 overwhelmingly married *within* their own faith—92 per cent of the husbands and 91 per cent of the wives. This, again, indicates that the New Haven pattern for Protestants is not typical.

3. There are significant differences between first marriages and subsequent marriages. For example: in first marriages, only 22 out of 100 Catholics marry outside their faith, whereas in subsequent marriages (when either party has been married before), the rate goes up to 42 out of 100. This seems to indicate that people become less choosy in their religious preferences as they move into remarriages.

In summarizing this part of our discussion, it seems clear that Americans *usually* marry within their faith, but that both Protestants and Catholics have shown a strong tendency to marry across religious lines in recent decades. This seems to be less true of the small Jewish minority.

Now let us ask our second question: *What factors determine the interfaith marriage rate?* Thomas suggests the following:[21]

1. The proportion of Catholics (or any other religious minority) to the total population. Thus, the rate of Catholic interfaith marriage in Raleigh, North Carolina, where Catholics comprise only 2 per cent of the population, is 76 per cent, but in El Paso, Texas, where Catholics are a majority group, the interfaith marriage rate is not over 10 per cent.

The basic mechanisms here seem to be *opportunity* to find marriage partners within your own group, plus *exposure* to courtship partners of another religious faith.

2. The presence or absence of cohesive ethnic groups in the community. In such cities as El Paso, Texas, the Spanish or Mexican subculture is an additional factor preventing marriage of Catholics with non-Catholics. Hence the interfaith marriage rate is considerably lower than one might expect.

This, apparently, accounts for the relatively low interfaith marriage rate of Jews in our society; they have a subculture that is more than just a religion.

3. The socioeconomic or social level of the religious minority. For Catholics, Thomas found that the interfaith marriage rate in an urban community ranged from 8.5 per cent in the lower income areas to 19.3 per cent in the higher socioeconomic groups of the suburbs.

Judging from the work of Thomas, it seems that the chances of any given person marrying outside his religion depend upon his *exposure* to eligible mates from another group, plus his *willingness* to intermarry; and this latter seems to be partially the result of his economic and educational level.

We are now ready for our third question about interfaith marriages: *How successful are they?*

In the Iowa study cited above by Chancellor and Monahan, some interesting data on divorce are to be found. They found that Catholics married to non-Catholics had roughly twice as many divorces as did Catholics married to Catholics. When Catholics married within their own group and it was a first marriage for both parties, Catholics had 7 per cent of all divorces, even though they comprised 18 per cent of the first marriages in Iowa for the year. In other words, the unmixed first Catholic marriages were only half (or less) as prone to end in divorce as marriages in general.

This study supports the theory that interfaith marriages are less stable than unmixed marriages. It does not show that interdenominational unions are under any particular stress.

A recent study of divorce by Goode, using a random sample of divorced women in Detroit, found interfaith marriages to be less stable than nonmixed marriages, but the author does not seem to think that religious differences were a *major* cause of divorce in his sample; in other words, the mixture of religious backgrounds seemed to be a *contributing* factor.[22]

In opposition to this finding is that of Locke, who compared 200 divorced couples with 200 happily married couples, using a relatively representative sample drawn from a single county in Indiana.[23] He did not find religious differences to be a significant factor in his divorced group; in fact, he found such differences *just as often* in his successfully married group. This study leads one to be rather skeptical of the argument, not too rare, that "religion doesn't mix in marriage."

In 1949 Judson Landis published some interesting facts about interfaith marriages, using his students and their parents at Michigan State College as his sample.[24] Among other things, Landis discovered that about 50 per cent of the students in his marriage course would be willing to marry *outside* their faith if they met the right person, and, interestingly enough, there was little difference between Protestants and Catholics in this respect. As Landis points out, this rather liberal attitude of college students toward interfaith marriage does not seem to be shared by parents or religious leaders. About one third of the students willing to marry outside their faith also expressed a willingness to change to the faith of the partner. Catholics, on this point, were less willing than Protestants to become converts.

The most relevant part of this study for our present purposes, however, was the attempt to discover the effects of religious differences on marital stability. Using a sample of 4,108 marriages, all of which represented the parents of college students, Landis arrived at this conclusion: "Approximately 5 per cent of the Catholic and Jewish marriages had ended in divorce or separation, 8 per cent of the Protestant marriages, 15 per cent of the mixed Catholic-Protestant, and 18 per cent of the marriages in which there was no religious faith." [25]

Although this study indicates that marriage outside one's faith is more hazardous than marriage within the fold, the fact remains that even the interfaith marriages in this sample were remarkably stable: 85 per cent of the Catholic-Protestant unions, for example, apparently survived.

It is most interesting to note that in this study, marriage to a person of *no* faith was more hazardous than marriage to a person of *another* faith. But the number of cases in this subgroup was very small (39).

In a breakdown of the data, Landis discovered that the divorce rate was highest when a Catholic man married a Protestant woman; 21 per cent of these mixtures ended in divorce, but only 7 per cent if the husband was Protestant and the wife Catholic. This seems to indicate that it may be difficult for the mother to rear her children in a faith not her own.

Landis believes the presence of children to be the central factor related to conflict in interfaith marriages. As he puts it: "A study of childless mixed marriages might show entirely different results than are revealed in this study. In fact, the results of our study among couples with children would lead us to believe that if there are not children, the Catholic-Protestant marriage has few elements which would make marital adjustment difficult." [26]

The student should recognize that there are at least two major methodological weaknesses in this study. (1) The data were obtained *from students* and not from the married couples themselves. This may not seem very important, but our own experience has been that college students can be very inaccurate in giving information about their families unless they are given time to consult their parents. Landis does not state whether or not this was the case in this study. (2) Even granting the accuracy of the students' reporting, it is possible that factors *other than religious differences* might explain the higher instability of the mixed marriages. Let us explore this possibility briefly. To begin with, it is well known that Protestants and Catholics as a group have occupied somewhat different social class positions in our society.[27] This is still true today, but it was even more characteristic in the 1920's and 1930's when the parents of these college students were getting married. Therefore, it is possible, if not probable, that a greater proportion of the mixed Protestant-Catholic marriages involved a *social class difference.* If so, this in itself could account for a higher divorce rate, for we now know that interclass marriages are more complex, hence less stable, than intraclass marriages. Here we see one of the major flaws of this study: the failure to hold other significant factors constant.

Furthermore, it may be that to marry across religious lines in the 1920's and the 1930's required a certain amount of courage; that only the less conventional men and women were willing to do this in those days. If this were true, it would mean that the mixed Protestant-Catholic group would contain a higher proportion of *unconventional* people; and we know that conventionality (being conservative) seems to be highly correlated with marital success.[28] Here, again, is another uncontrolled variable.

It is also true that these marriages cut across two major cultural crises in our society, the economic crisis of the 1930's and World War II, and one would like to know more about the possible differential impact of these crises on these various groups of marriages. For example, the Protestant-Protestant marriages may have felt the depression less than the Catholic-Protestant, especially those in which the man was Catholic, as Catholics were more apt to have been wage earners in the 1930's. Note that this group had next to the highest divorce rate.

We do not mean to detract from Landis' study. It has been a

valuable contribution and represents an attempt to get *facts* about an important problem. It is only suggested that the data can be interpreted so that variables other than religious differences may be involved.

This rapid survey of some relevant research on interfaith marriages seems to indicate, with some exceptions, that mixed religious marriages are less stable than marriages within one's faith. Exactly *why* this is the case, however, is not very clear as yet. In subsequent sections of this chapter we will attempt to show *under what circumstances* religious differences are likely to create marital adjustment problems.

Some Research on the Function of Religion in Marital Adjustment

Most of the major studies of marital adjustment in the United States (plus one in Sweden) have attempted to assess the part played by religion in marital success or failure. In this section of the chapter we will review their findings.

One of the main problems facing the researcher in approaching this problem is the definition of "religious faith." In our society, an individual's religious convictions are a highly personal matter. State universities in many states, for example, are prohibited from even asking students to indicate their church affiliation. Furthermore, about one third of our population has no formal church membership, yet the majority of these persons are probably "religious." Public opinion polls find that very few Americans are actually nonbelievers; their status is more accurately described as "nonmembers" of any particular church.

In general, the research teams have resolved this problem, at least to some extent, by asking for church affiliation (if any), by identifying religious background (parental religion), and by getting some indication of degree of devoutness (Kinsey used this).

It seems obvious that the above fails to uncover the real dynamics of religious faith and the basic role it may (or may not) play in marital interaction. These, it seems to the writer, can only be analyzed by means of the intensive case study, and later in this chapter we will present a specific case for this purpose.

With this preface, let us look at the findings of the marital adjustment studies.

1. *The work of Terman.*

At various times in this book we have referred to Terman's 1938 study of 792 middle-class married couples in California.[29]

In a study of "complaints" made by these couples, "religious beliefs" ranked 27th in the wives' complaints and 28th in the husbands' list.[30] This indicates that for these couples religion was not a major problem.

In his general evaluation of the role of religious background in marital adjustment, Terman concluded that it was a relatively insignificant factor. His data showed some tendency for persons with a moderate type of religious background to score slightly higher than persons with very strict or no religious training. It is evident that Terman does not believe religion to be very important in determining marital adjustment.[31]

It may be observed, however, that Terman's study did not focus on the religious variable to any great extent; furthermore, his married couples appear to be an unusually well-adjusted group, so that one would not expect to find very many couples with serious religious conflicts in this study; hence the variable appears to be unimportant.

Terman *did* find a happy family background to be very significantly related to marital adjustment, which might be interpreted to mean that religious agreement (absence of conflict) is important in preparing youngsters for marriage.

2. *The work of Burgess-Cottrell.*

In this 1939 study of 526 middle-class married couples, the authors make this statement: "Apparently, according to the testimony of our group of married persons, and popular opinion notwithstanding, disagreements over religion . . . play only a relatively small part in marital unhappiness." [32] Since their sample was about 75 per cent Protestant, it appears that religious conflict per se would not appear often in this study either.

Burgess and Cottrell did conclude, however, that agreement on religious matters had a positive correlation with marital adjustment in their sample. It was not one of their major items, though, being considered only half as important as demonstration of affection or agreement on friends. [33]

Actually, in this particular study, there is a great deal of *indirect* evidence that religious behavior does affect marital adjustment. This can be seen in two highly significant items in their predictive scale: matters of conventionality and philosophy of life. Both of these items seem to reflect religious values. These authors find, for example, that being married in a church and attending church are positively associated with marital adjustment. This is essentially what they mean when they say that conventionality is correlated positively with marital adjustment. In general, this study seems to support the theory that religious faith and its related practices are factors in a good marriage.

3. *Locke's study.*

In 1951 Locke published a comparison of 200 divorced couples with 200 happily married couples. [34] His data are especially interesting in that his sample was more representative of the general population than the previous studies.

In general, Locke found his successfully married couples to be more religious than his divorced couples. He tends to interpret this in two ways: (1) it is a sign of conventional behavior, thus indicating adjustment with the social environment; and (2) religious activities, when shared, give the couple a basic interest in common. [35]

It is interesting to note that Locke did not find *differences of religion* to be a problem in either his adjusted or his divorced couples. This tends to support the theory that religion functions to *support* marriage but is not usually a factor in the *destruction* of marriage. It may also be that our courtship system screens out those couples who would have religious conflict if they married. In other words, men and women who feel *that strongly* about religion do not marry persons who do not share (or at least tolerate) their religious convictions.

4. *Karlsson's Swedish study.*

In 1951 Karlsson published in Sweden a study of 205 Swedish urban couples, using the same questions (with minor changes) that Locke used in the United States.[36]

Karlsson was somewhat surprised to find that religious interest and activity either had *no* association with marital adjustment (the husbands in his sample), or else it had a *negative* effect (wives in his sample). He interprets this to mean (*a*) that Swedish urban couples are not very religious, and (*b*) that Swedish urban wives turn to the church when their marriages are failing.[37]

5. *The Burgess-Wallin study.*

The latest and perhaps the most elaborate study available for this analysis is that of Burgess-Wallin, published in 1953[38]

The basic finding of this study is that religion itself is not a predictive factor in marital adjustment. As they admit, "These findings do not mean necessarily that these premarital factors are not significant for marital success. They may only document the point that relevant data were not obtained in the interview." [39]

It is also significant that the 1,000 couples in this sample were predominantly of the same religion, thus minimizing religious differences.

6. *The Landis research.*

In a survey of 409 couples who had been married an average of 20 years, Judson Landis discovered that 74 per cent of his couples reported satisfaction from the beginning in their religious adjustment.[40] Interestingly enough, 10 per cent of his couples indicated that they had never attained a satisfactory religious adjustment. This is even more significant in view of the fact that these couples had been happily married for 20 years. This certainly indicates that religious differences *can* be tolerated, just as Terman found that sexual differences can be tolerated.

Discussion of Research on Religion and Marriage

In spite of the quantity of data on religion and marital adjustment, one has serious doubts about its *quality*. Most of the material has been collected by the questionnaire technique, with very few interview data. The absence of intensive case studies is also striking. These, it seems to us, are essential for the analysis of the dynamics of religious interaction in marriage. It is also obvious that the vast bulk of these cases represent the well-adjusted couples of similar religious faith. Except for Locke's sample, the groups do not approach being representative of the general married population.

In the writer's opinion, the studies to date have not probed deeply or intensively enough to assess fully the function of religion in modern marriage.

What Determines When a Mixed Marriage Will Be Successful?

Although it must be admitted that we can cite no systematic studies in support of our position, the writer is convinced that religious differences often play a minor role in interfaith marriages that fail. This belief is based on several intensive case studies of such marriages made by the writer in the role of marriage counselor.

It is not very difficult to see why persons would hold religion responsible for such marital failures. The line of reasoning appears to be as follows:

1. *A* and *B* marry.
2. They are of *different* religious faiths.

3. Their marriage is not successful.

4. Since the religious faith is a *known* quantity, it is concluded that religious differences were *the cause* of the marital failure. It seems that the weakness of this type of reasoning would be apparent but such does not seem to be the case.

It should be obvious to any impartial observer that any number of factors other than religious conflict might be involved. This can readily be seen in the fact that a sizable proportion of American divorces are granted to spouses who belong to the *same* religion.[41]

Perhaps the following hypothetical case may make our point clearer. Let us assume that there are ten basic factors that determine marital success or failure. If we include religion as one of these basic variables, this means that even in marriages between persons of the *same* religion, *only* 10 per cent of the total determinants of marital success have been accounted for. In other words, 90 per cent of the factors still remain *undetermined*.

If we assume that *five* basic factors are crucial to marital success and include religion as one of these, it follows that 80 per cent of the variables remain unaccounted for in marriages of similar religious faith. The writer knows of no scientific study that weights the religious factor any greater than this, while most weight it less than this.

The above illustration indicates that interfaith marriages must not be analyzed as if they were completely different from all other marriages. Actually, a marriage in our society can be mixed on a variety of bases, as was seen earlier. For this reason, it is essential to identify *all* the basic differences in any given marriage and not just those related to religion.

Case Study of an Interfaith Marriage Which Failed

In this case, the writer has had a total of thirty-six interviews with the couple, either alone or together, over a period of five years. Although a systematic effort was made to identify all the conflicts in this marriage, religion itself did not emerge as a basic source of difficulty. The marriage failed, however, and the general opinion of both friends and relatives was that "mixed marriages don't work." In this analysis, we propose to show the factors that actually seemed to doom this marriage almost from the beginning. We will then leave it to the reader to decide what factors caused this marriage to fail.

1. *Family background.*

Ample evidence exists to show that both the man and tne woman came from families characterized by conflict and poor marital adjustment. In the wife's family, for example, the parents were separated on numerous occasions but, being Catholic, did not divorce. The mother and father fought openly before the children. The father was known to be sexually unfaithful to the mother.

The wife's only sister is now separated from her husband. Only the brother has been able to achieve a successful marriage in this family. If we add the marriages of the parents, the two daughters, and the son, we find that three out of four of the marriages in this family in the last two generations have been unsuccessful. Terman's research, which emphasized the importance of family background for marital adjustment, would lead one to consider this wife a poor marital risk to begin with.

The husband's background is about the same. His parents had bitter conflicts all through their marriage and also fought openly before the children. On at least one occasion the mother left the father. She also accused him of sexual affairs with other women. If divorce had been more common in those days, or if there had not been four children, it is likely that their marriage would have been terminated.

In the present generation, two sisters are considered to have good marriages, one brother is divorced, and the other son (our case) is in the process of getting a divorce. Thus, in the husband's family adding the marriages of the parents and the children, we find that three out of five of the marriages have been poor, or have been terminated.

The total score for the two families, then, is six poor or terminated marriages out of a total of nine. On the basis of such crude statistics alone, one might predict the marital prospects of *any* member of these two groups not to be too good, even assuming religious background to be similar. In a sense, both of these families show a *tendency toward marital failure,* regardless of *why.*

It is most interesting to note that of the six marital failures in these two families, only one (our case) involved a mixture of religions. This in itself should cause us to be critical of the theory that religion was the basic cause of marital failure in the case under analysis.

2. *Sexual compatibility.*

The husband in this case was vociferous in his sexual complaints against his wife. He consistently rated sex far above religious differences as a cause of their marital conflict. The wife admitted that she was not interested in sex.

3. *Social class background.*

The wife had been reared in what was essentially an upper-middle-class status, her father being manager of a local factory.

The husband was of lower-middle-class background, his father being employed as a nonprofessional government white-collar worker.

In the marriage itself, it is apparent that the wife often compared her husband unfavorably with her father as a breadwinner.

4. *Educational level.*

The wife completed high school, whereas the husband dropped out his first year and did not return. This was later cited by the wife in derogation of the husband when their children surpassed him in scholastic achievement.

We might mention the fact that high school drop-outs (the husband, in this case) probably have a relatively high rate of marital failure, compared to high school and college graduates.[42]

5. *Alcoholism.*

The major complaint of the wife in this case was related to the husband's excessive drinking (well documented). Granting that it is extremely difficult to explain alcoholism, there seemed to be no evidence that either the wife or the husband considered it to be related to their religious differences. Actually, there is a history of alcoholism in *both* of the parental families, and religious differences are not present in *any* of the other cases of alcoholism in either family.

6. *Child-rearing.*

There has been considerable conflict over child-rearing, but very little of it can be traced to religion itself. Before the marriage, it was agreed that the children would be baptized Catholic but would attend the public schools. This agreement has been held to and was not cited as a source of conflict by either the husband or the wife.

7. *Personality.*

Terman cites this as a basic factor in marital adjustment. In this case, the husband seems to be insecure and easily threatened, whereas the wife is tough and fights back vigorously. She seems to enjoy needling the husband. He appears to be much easier to hurt than the wife.

8. *Religious patterns.*

It is hard to imagine religious conflict between this couple for the simple reason that the husband *has no religion.* He is not sufficiently interested in religion to argue about it. He never voluntarily discussed religion in any of our interviews.

The wife, however, is very devout and would no doubt have been pleased if the husband had shared her religious faith; but she

makes no complaint about her husband's lack of interest in her
church, perhaps because she knew before their marriage that he
was not deeply religious. As long as he does not interfere with her
religion or that of the children, which he has not, she is satisfied.

In summary, the writer can see very little evidence that
religious differences have destroyed this marriage. It is true, of
course, that there has been a religious *void* in this marriage, but this
is a very different thing from religious *conflict*. It is our belief that
religion does not account for over 5 per cent of the problems in this
marriage. This belief, incidentally, is shared by the husband and
wife. To the general public, however, and to the two families concerned, this domestic tragedy is just further proof that "you should
marry within your own religion."

The writer does not cite this case to "prove" that religious
differences do not or cannot become the central conflict in problem
marriages. Our only point is that religion is *only one* of several
basic factors determining marital adjustment and that *all* these
must be analyzed in discussing the general problem of interfaith
marriages in our society.

Suggestions for Exploring Religious Compatibility

The evidence indicates that an increasing proportion of
young Americans will have to decide whether or not to marry
outside their religion. The surveys of Thomas and Landis, cited
earlier, lead one to suspect that at least one fourth of the Protestant
and Catholic young people in many of our urban communities have
to face this decision.

The writer does not pretend that he has the answer to this
knotty problem. Judging by the research and the analysis in this
chapter, however, it is possible to advance a few principles to be
kept in mind when considering an interfaith marriage.

1. Religion is only one factor determining marital adjustment. In most of the studies so far, it has not been demonstrated
that religion per se is even a *major* factor in marital adjustment

or marital failure. Terman, Locke, Burgess-Wallin, and Goode, the most elaborate studies, do not emphasize religion in their basic findings.

2. It is certainly possible to tolerate religious differences in marriage. Although the successful interfaith marriages have received less publicity than the unsuccessful, it is obvious to any student of marriage in our society that a vast number of couples have created successful marriages in spite of religious differences. In the Landis survey itself, cited earlier, 85 per cent of the Catholic-Protestant marriages did *not* end in separation or divorce. This does not prove, of course, that these marriages were successful, but at least they survived.

3. In considering an interfaith marriage, it is crucial to explore nonreligious areas of compatibility: sex, educational level, mutual friends, common interests, personality needs, social class backgrounds, etc. Most of our best studies have found these to be even more vital than religious similarity. Remember that even after religious compatibility has been determined, as much as 90 per cent of the factors important to a good marriage remain unaccounted for. It may be relatively easy for a marriage to support religious differences *if it does not also have to carry a variety of other basic differences.*

4. Landis' study seems to indicate that the most hazardous mixed marriage, as far as religion is concerned, may be between a devout person of *any* faith and a person with *no religion at all.* This is a point often overlooked.

5. It is essential to consider depth and intensity of faith in attempting to determine religious compatibility. Mere membership in some sect or denomination often tells us very little.

6. It is helpful to differentiate between religious *differences* and religious *conflicts.* A man we know, for example, is not very religious but he *admires* persons who are. For this reason, this man, a Protestant by background, is able to live happily with his devout Catholic wife, since he is glad that his wife has the religious faith that he wishes he had. This couple, in other words, have a

deep religious difference, but no religious *conflict*. Note, however, that if this man were prejudiced against the Catholic faith, as so many non-Catholics are, then the marriage would hardly be as harmonious. It is also obvious to the friends of this couple that in most other areas they are very compatible.   •

7. In considering an interfaith marriage, the writer believes it to be more important than ever to become well acquainted with each other's family and to have their support in your marriage. Otherwise, the chances of in-law trouble are going to be magnified. If you cannot accept the other person's family, or if they cannot accept you, it may be a good reason for reconsidering the marriage.

8. Finally, it is essential that the religion of the children be carefully considered *before* an interfaith marriage takes place. This seems to be the major finding of the Landis study analyzed earlier.

If young couples approach the question of interreligious marriages in the proper spirit, we do not doubt that they will find that religious differences are not an insurmountable barrier to happy and creative marriage in modern society.

References

1. Report of the National Council of Churches, August, 1956.
2. James A. Pike, *If You Marry Outside Your Faith* (New York, Harper & Bros., 1954).
3. See pp. 147–148.
4. John L. Thomas, *The American Catholic Family* (New York, Prentice-Hall, Inc., 1956).
5. See pp. 24–29.
6. W. Lloyd Warner and Paul S. Lunt, *The Social Life of a Modern Community* (New Haven, Yale University Press, 1941).
7. Pope shows that Catholics have been moving into the middle class rapidly during and since World War II. See Liston Pope, "Religion and the Class Structure," *Annals* of the American Academy of Political and Social Science, 256 (1948), 84–91.
8. Catholic families seem to limit reproduction less than do Protestants, but there is considerable evidence that middle- and upper-class Catholic couples do practice some sort of planned parenthood. See Thomas, *op cit.,*

pp. 141–144 for a review of fertility data. There is also an analysis of the birth control movement in the United States, pp. 317–321.

9. Pike, *op. cit.*, has an excellent discussion of this. See chap. 3.

10. Thomas, *op. cit..* pp. 321–323.

11. See Pike, *op. cit.*, chap. 9.

12. Lewis Browne, *How Odd of God* (New York, The Macmillan Company, 1934). See also Pike, *op. cit.*, chap. 8.

13. See Robin M. Williams, Jr., *American Society* (New York, Alfred A. Knopf Inc., 1951), chap. 9 for an excellent analysis of this material.

14. Charles P. Loomis and J. Allan Beegle, *Rural Social Systems* (New York, Prentice-Hall, Inc., 1950), p. 57.

15. August B. Hollingshead, "Cultural Factors in the Selection of Marriage Mates," *American Sociological Review*, 15 (1950), 619–627.

16. *Ibid.*

17. John L. Thomas, "The Factor of Religion in the Selection of Marriage Mates," *American Sociological Review*, 16 (1951), 487–492.

18. *Ibid.*

19. Milton L. Barron, *People Who Intermarry* (Syracuse, Syracuse University Press, 1946). Also Hollingshead, *op. cit.*

20. Loren E. Chancellor and Thomas P. Monahan, "Religious Preference and Interreligious Mixtures in Marriages and Divorces in Iowa," *American Journal of Sociology*, 61 (1955), 233–239.

21. See the 1951 study cited above.

22. William J. Goode, *After Divorce* (Glencoe, The Free Press, 1956).

23. Harvey J. Locke, *Predicting Adjustment in Marriage* (New York, Henry Holt & Co., Inc., 1951). See pp. 221 and 338.

24. Judson T. Landis, "Marriages of Mixed and Non-Mixed Religious Faith," *American Sociological Review*, 14 (1949), 401–406.

25. *Ibid.*

26. *Ibid.*

27. See Liston Pope, *op. cit.*

28. All the major studies of marital adjustment—Terman, Burgess-Cottrell, Locke, and Burgess-Wallin—have emphasized this finding.

29. Lewis M. Terman *et al.*, *Psychological Factors in Marital Happiness* (New York, McGraw-Hill Book Co., 1938).

30. See p. 105.

31. Page 236.

32. Ernest W. Burgess and Leonard S. Cottrell, Jr., *Predicting Success or Failure in Marriage* (New York, Prentice-Hall, Inc., 1939), p. 51.

33. See p. 64.

34. *Op. cit.*

35. See, for example, the statement on p. 360.
36. Georg Karlsson, *Adaptability and Communication in Marriage* (Uppsala, Almqvist and Wiksells Boktryckeri Aktiebolag, 1951).
37. *Op. cit.*, pp. 107–108.
38. Ernest W. Burgess and Paul Wallin, *Engagement and Marriage* (Philadelphia, J. B. Lippincott Co., 1953).
39. *Op. cit.*, p. 586.
40. Judson and Mary Landis, *Building a Successful Marriage* (New York, Prentice-Hall, Inc., 2d ed., 1953), p. 259.
41. See the study by Goode cited above, also that of Chancellor and Monahan cited earlier in the chapter.
42. This statement is based on an unpublished study made by the Guidance Department of the Madison, Wisconsin, public school system in 1950–52.

Suggested Readings

1. John L. Thomas, S.J., *The American Catholic Family* (New York, Prentice-Hall, Inc., 1956). In the writer's opinion, this is the best study yet published of the Catholic family and its stresses in American society. Students contemplating marriage into the Catholic faith should find it very worthwhile.
2. James A. Pike, *If You Marry Outside Your Faith* (New York, Harper & Bros., 1954). This little volume, although reflecting the point of view of the Protestant essentially, is an extremely readable and interesting discussion of the various problems to be faced in the interfaith marriage.
3. Judson and Mary Landis, *Building a Successful Marriage* (New York, Prentice-Hall, Inc., 2d ed., 1953), chap. 15, "Religious Attitudes and Family Life."
4. Ray E. Baber, "Religion and the Family," *Annals* of the American Academy of Political and Social Science, 256 (1948), pp. 92–100. Reprinted in Marvin B. Sussman, *Sourcebook in Marriage and the Family* (Boston, Houghton Mifflin Co., 1955), pp. 262–269.
5. W. Lloyd Warner, *American Life* (Chicago, University of Chicago Press, 1953), chap. 7, "American Ethnic and Sectarian Groups."
6. Robin M. Williams, Jr., *American Society* (New York, Alfred A. Knopf, Inc., 1951), chap. 9, "Religion in America."

CHAPTER XVII

SEXUAL ADJUSTMENT IN MARRIAGE

Introduction

Most Americans, married or unmarried, are willing to grant that sex is an important factor in marriage. In a culture as sex-conscious as ours, it would be difficult to believe otherwise. As we remarked earlier in the text, the main problem in discussing the role of sex in marriage with most Americans is to keep them from assuming that sex is *the only* factor determining marital happiness or unhappiness.

Sex is a topic about which it is hard to be objective. The unmarried person with his sexual frustrations is hardly in a good position properly to assess the importance of sex; to a starving man, food takes on value out of all proportion to its normal role in human life.

On the other hand, married persons are not much better in their assessment, for each of them tends to have a sexual bias: using a statistical sample of one case (their marriage), they are usually prepared to give any willing (or trapped) listener the low-down on sex in marriage. We recall a physician who once insisted

355

to us, at great length, that "women are *never* passionate." It did no good to cite Kinsey to the contrary, for this man was married to a sexually unresponsive woman.

We urge the student not to accept too literally the sex data offered by married couples or by persons who seem to have had considerable experience. The subject is too complex for hearsay evidence. The role of sex in marriage requires systematic analysis that takes into account all the biological, psychological, and cultural factors involved in sexual behavior. And then, in addition, it is necessary to adapt all this general knowledge to specific men and women as they attempt to work out a satisfying pattern of sexual love in marriage.

Folklore About Sex and Marriage

Since there is a great deal of sex folklore in our culture, it may help to begin with a discussion of this. We should then be in a better position to present more reliable information. The following list makes no claim to being exhaustive but is intended to reveal some of the major folk beliefs about sex in marriage. Later sections of the chapter will point out other sex fallacies.

1. *That the honeymoon period is a good test of sexual compatibility.*

Actually, the honeymoon for some couples represents perhaps the poorest level of sexual adjustment they will ever have. The first night in particular can be quite disappointing, and in some cases this disappointment may extend over a period of days, weeks, and even months.

The main reason for this failure to arrive at an immediate sexual adjustment is very simple: *sexual behavior on the human level is learned.* As a matter of fact, Ford and Beach in their excellent study, *Patterns of Sexual Behavior,* show conclusively that sexual behavior among the anthropoid apes and other subhuman mammals is also learned, especially on the part of the male.[1]

On the human level this means that time is required for most couples to learn how to interact sexually just as they have to learn how to interact in the other major areas of marriage.

The main difference with sex is that our culture does not encourage as much premarital learning in the sexual area as we do in the other areas of marriage, so that a great deal of the sexual learning has to be postponed until after marriage. Our necking and petting patterns, however, do permit considerable sexual learning, even for conventional couples, to precede marriage.

This sexual learning process in marriage is further complicated by the necessity of *unlearning* a great deal of our childhood and adolescent sexual conditioning. As Ruth Benedict has pointed out in a brilliant article, there is almost complete "discontinuity" in the average American's sexual training.[2] Little boys are first taught that they should treat all girls as sisters; then later the male peer group teaches a completely different code: that all women are objects for potential sexual exploitation. Then, after marriage, the man finds that neither his parents nor his male peer group has taught him the right code; he is now supposed to be the "great lover" type, and "sex" is supposed to be synonymous with "love," something he never knew before. He finds that his wife certainly doesn't want to be treated "like a sister," as his parents had taught him long ago; but neither does she want to be treated as a "sexual object," as his male peer group had taught him. So we see that the average American male, the member of the honeymoon pair who is supposed to know "all about sex," finds that a lot of his learning has to be unlearned, that there is a third code (sexual love) which his wife will have to teach him.

For the girl, the same process of unlearning has to precede, or be continuous with, her sexual learning in marriage. What has always been "terribly wrong" now becomes "terribly right," at least morally and legally. Instead of repulsing her boy friend, she is now expected to become (overnight) a passionate woman with hardly any sexual inhibitions at all. Acts that she has always considered perversions may now be expected by her husband, as Kinsey points out very clearly in his analysis of middle- and upper-class sexual norms in marriage.[3]

This is not being written in an attempt to discourage or frighten potential honeymooners. By all means expect to enjoy your honeymoon, but don't expect that you will achieve sexual adjustment just by virtue of the fact that you are staying at "Honeymooner's Haven," or because you occupy the bridal suite. It simply is not true that sexual relations on the human level consist of "doing what comes naturally." There undoubtedly is a biological base in human nature for sexual desire, but the attitudes and techniques necessary to satisfy the desire are learned.

2. *That married couples are well informed about sex.*

There is a tendency among Americans to feel that married couples *by virtue of being married* know a great deal about sex and its role in human life. This is not true. In the writer's sex education classes for parents, for example, it is amazing how inadequate they feel, after years of marriage and parenthood, to explain sex to their children. This is actually the reason why many parents do not give their children more sex education: they feel inadequate.

Perhaps the major lack in our sexual knowledge is an adequate sexual vocabulary, one that can be used in the living room and in mixed groups as well as behind the garage. For the most part, high schools and colleges do not teach this sort of vocabulary. Peer groups do not do so either. So most of us have a difficult time acquiring it.

Kinsey shows conclusively that men have very erroneous ideas about female sexual physiology and response, and there seems to be reason to believe that women lack adequate knowledge about male sexuality.[4]

Therefore, as we prepare for marriage, let us acknowledge our need to know more about this part of marriage. Physicians, clergymen, parents, professors, books—all these can be used to help us achieve a reasonable level of sexual understanding. The list of readings at the end of this and the next chapter has proved helpful to many students approaching marriage.

3. *That sexual relations before marriage qualify a person for sexual adjustment in marriage.*

American men in particular are apt to believe this. There seems to be considerable evidence that deep and significant differences exist between sex outside marriage and sex in marriage. For one thing, sex in marriage is supposed to include love for the partner, and this is often not a requirement outside marriage. For another thing, sexual satisfaction in marriage (at least at the middle-class level) is supposed to be mutual, and this is often not expected outside marriage. The promiscuous male, for example, who depersonalizes the sex act, has probably had very poor preparation for "sex as love" in marriage.[5]

This same sort of illusion may prevail in couples who have had premarital sex relations with each other; they too may assume that they have adequately explored this area of marriage. If so, they will have much to learn.

4. *That after marriage there is no sexual frustration.*

This myth visualizes marriage as a sort of sexual heaven, a place of refuge from the sexual starvation of singleness. We are sorry to report that this is not true. While marriage for most of us represents the best solution to our sexual needs, there are innumerable factors that interfere from time to time with sexual satisfaction: illness, pregnancy, military service, business travel, fatigue, etc. One can legitimately expect less sexual frustration after marriage than before in our culture but it is foolish to be unrealistic about the sexual limitations of marriage.

5. *That a change of marital partners will solve sexual problems.*

Persons who are dissatisfied with their sexual life often blame their marital partner, and this leads to the belief that the sexual problems would disappear if married to a different person. In some cases, of course, this would be true, but in many cases it would be

an illusion. In the Terman study of 792 married couples, for example, he made an elaborate attempt to determine whether the
inability of the wife to have a sexual climax could be related to the
husband's sexual technique.[6] His findings were essentially negative
and he concluded that most of these wives (about 30 per cent of the
sample) were *unable* to have an orgasm. If Terman is correct—
and his findings on this point are debatable—it means that many
of these wives would find that a new husband would not be able to
bring them to climax either.

In one case studied by the writer, the husband blamed his
wife for what he considered to be an unsatisfactory sex life. He
eventually left his wife and had an affair with another woman. After
about eight months of separation, the husband asked his wife to
resume their marriage. It seems that he found that his sexual frustrations were largely within himself, because they soon developed
in his new relationship. In this case we felt that the man was beginning to feel old (he was in his late forties) and had convinced
himself that a new woman would make a new man out of him.
We recognize that in some cases a change in marriage partners does
rejuvenate people, but in this case the miracle did not happen.
Why? Because the man's marriage was essentially a good marriage
and there was really nothing that another woman could do to
help him that his wife was not already doing. In other words, his
problems were *within himself* but he was blaming (projecting) them
on his wife.

In cases of severe marital discord, it is often true that a new
love partner will rekindle the spark of sexual love, but one should
not assume that this will always be the case.

**6. *That the sexual relationship in marriage
can be separated from other phases of
the marital relationship.***

Actually, it is very difficult to determine when a married
couple has a sexual problem, because conflicts in other areas of
interaction often radiate into the sexual area. And conversely, sexual

maladjustment often appears to be money trouble or something similar.

It probably is true that husbands can isolate or localize sex from the rest of the marriage more successfully than most wives, but in most married people the sexual relationship is improved if the rest of the marriage is improved, and vice versa. If a wife feels hostile toward her husband, for whatever reason, she usually finds it difficult to respond to him sexually, and yet their real difficulty may not be sexual at all. It could be over in-laws, or child-rearing, or money, or almost anything.

In one case known to the writer, a married student complained that his wife was frigid. Discussion revealed, however, that this couple had been strongly attracted to each other sexually before marriage; in fact, they had begun having sex relationships a few months after they met and had been forced to marry because of pregnancy.

Interviews with the wife revealed that she had always blamed her husband for the pregnancy and had resented being forced into marriage before she was ready. She admitted, however, that she had been "in love" with her husband and that they were planning to become engaged when they learned of the pregnancy.

The baby was six months old when we were first consulted and up to then the wife had been unable to resume sexual relations because of her frigidity. Our analysis was that the wife's resentment toward her husband over the pregnancy, plus her fear of becoming pregnant again, had produced a temporary block that prevented her responding. It was suggested to the husband that he would have to be patient and do everything possible to help his wife through this critical period. Basically, there was a great deal of love for the wife on the part of the husband, and as this was gradually made clear to her, she began to respond sexually. By the end of six months the frigidity had disappeared.

In concluding this discussion about sexual folklore and marriage, it might be well to point out that folk beliefs are bound to persist in the area of sex until we have more and better sex education in our society. In some cases the folklore may do no particular harm, but this is not always the case. It seems worthwhile, therefore, to replace folk beliefs with more systematic knowledge whenever possible.

Kinsey's Research and Sex Adjustment in Marriage

While granting that considerable controversy exists over the adequacy of the Kinsey research, the fact remains that this long-term project represents the most systematic analysis of sexual behavior in our society.[7] For this reason, we propose to review at this point a few of the more relevant findings of the Kinsey research. We will then review the data on sex to be found in the research of Terman, Burgess-Wallin, and Locke. In the writer's opinion, these four sources represent the best research published to date on male and female sexual behavior in our society and should provide us with the basic facts to complete our discussion of the role of sex in marital adjustment.

We believe the following Kinsey conclusions to be relevant to our discussion.

1. *The great individual variation in sexual activity.*

In both the male and the female volumes, Kinsey points out repeatedly that the range and variation in sexual behavior reported by his subjects was almost beyond belief.[8] Although he believes it possible to differentiate between male and female patterns *as statistical averages,* Kinsey cautions against assuming that any given man or woman will conform to such an average.

What relevance does this have for our discussion? Simply this: that we must not enter marriage with stereotyped notions of what male and female sexual behavior is. Your husband or my wife may vary a great deal from what we consider to be the norm for that sex. You and I must be prepared to *learn* what the sexual nature of our marital partner is, and they must be prepared to learn what ours is as well.

It seems to us that this finding has another implication also: that young couples *have* to be permitted some necking and petting to determine their sexual compatibility. This does not necessarily mean that complete sexual relations are required before marriage, but at least some sexual interaction seems necessary to rule out gross sexual incompatibility.

2. *The sexual subculture of the male in our society.*

In the writer's opinion, some of the most valuable work of the Kinsey group is to be found in their analysis of male and female sexual differences in our society.[9] We like to refer to these differences as subcultures, but we recognize that it has not yet been determined whether these differences are learned, innate, or both.

The essentials of the sexual subculture of the American male are as follows:

A. **He likes to talk about sex more than his wife does:** In technical terms, he is sexually more stimulated by auditory impulses (what he hears) than the average woman. Thus, he tells more "dirty" stories, uses more "dirty" (Anglo-Saxon) words, and in general talks about sex more than the *average* woman (note the word average).

This means that many wives consider their husbands crude and obsessed with sex. In some cases, this creates friction between married couples.

B. **The male likes to look at sex more than does the average female:** He is more excited by visual stimuli than is the average woman.

C. **The average American male is more highly sexed than his wife:** Whether this is true all over the world or just in certain cultures is not clear at the moment. Ford and Beach point out that in subhuman mammals the male has a more *persistent* sex drive the year around, but that the female *in season* or when fully aroused can outlast the average male; in fact, she is often capable of outlasting several males.[10]

At the human level, females do not usually have a seasonal

sexual cycle and are capable of sexual arousal at almost any time. The male, however, according to Kinsey, is *more easily* and *more often* aroused than is the *average* female. This is clearly demonstrated by the Kinsey data on autosexual (masturbatory) practices, which are reported far more frequently by American men than women.[11] Premarital sexual experience is also reported more frequently by men than women.[12]

In the data from Terman and also from Burgess-Wallin, to be reviewed shortly, it will be seen that Kinsey's conclusions on this point are confirmed by the other major studies.

D.   **The average American male attains the peak of his sexual desire before marriage:**   Kinsey bases this finding largely on autosexual practice rather than heterosexual activity. He does not reach the same conclusion for girls. Thus he reports a conflict pattern in which the boy has his most urgent sexual needs during his late teens, whereas the average American girl will not experience her full sexual arousal until in her twenties.[13]

If Kinsey is correct in this finding, it may explain why girls complain that boys are sexually too demanding in courtship. It may also shed light on the traditional male practice of having two girl friends, one "nice" and one "not so nice."

This finding might also indicate that many couples would be more compatible sexually in their twenties and thirties than when first married; the husband's desire begins to decline somewhat while the wife's tends to increase.

E.   **The average American male has a very erroneous notion of female sexual neurology:**   Space does not permit us to review these Kinsey findings at greater length, but husbands would do well to read these chapters in the second Kinsey volume on the female. It does seem, at least to this writer, that Kinsey is correct in his basic point, that men tend to have a male version of what women are like sexually. If this is so, then most men enter marriage with a false notion of the sexual nature of the other sex. Obviously, we are not referring to the traditional variety of sexual ignorance—where babies come from, etc.—but to more subtle kinds of *misinformation* rather than ignorance itself.

We believe that Kinsey's analysis of these data is basically sound and that it has relevance for sexual adjustment in marriage.

3. Female sexual subculture.

Most of the basic points have already been stated or implied in describing the sexual subculture of the male; hence we will simply review the main points briefly.

A. The average American woman is less highly sexed than the average American man: This can be demonstrated by reference to several types of data in the Kinsey studies: she resorts to autosexual (self) satisfaction less often than the male; she begins heterosexual relations at a later age; she engages in homosexual relations only about half as often as does the male; she has fewer extramarital relationships than the male; she is more difficult to arouse sexually; all these findings indicate a less active sex life than that of the male.[14]

One must always remember, however, that these generalizations represent statistical averages and do not mean that any specific wife would be less highly sexed than her husband. As a matter of fact, the individual with the most active sex life reported in the first two Kinsey volumes *was a woman.*

B. The average female is not as aroused sexually by visual or auditory stimuli as is the average male: [15] This produces frequent points of irritation between husbands and wives, who are often "disgusted" by the "vulgar" language and "off-color" stories of their husbands. Wives have a tendency to consider their husbands as crude or even "filthy." The men, in defense, often consider their wives to be prudish. Some men will also argue that women actually enjoy male sexual talk and only pretend to be offended.

In our marriage counseling practice we have had wives describe what seemed to us to be relatively normal male sexual behavior but which the wife regarded as abnormal or perverted.

C. Women have a feminine version of what men are like sexually: The average "nice" girl has never been fully exposed to the sexual subculture of the male until she is married. Until then she is apt to think that men are pretty much like women, "only more so."

For example, she will expect her husband to be gentle during the sex act, to use only "nice" words during sexual intercourse, to regard the act as making love rather than as "just sex," etc. Perhaps most husbands do come up to this level of behavior, but the Kinsey data suggest that a considerable proportion do not.

It seems clear that the average American middle-class girl is the victim of discontinuity in her sexual conditioning and that she is poorly prepared for her sexual role in marriage. There is another possibility, of course, and that is that the girl is properly prepared for sexual love in marriage but that the boy is not. In any event, the two sexes usually enter marriage with deep sexual differences, both innate and cultural in origin, and the adjustment of these two sexual natures in marriage is not always an easy accomplishment.

D. **The average woman tends to regard sex as "love," whereas the average male regards it as "sex":** Women do not usually think of sex in physical terms but tend to integrate it with their conception of love. A great many men, perhaps most of them in our society, are unable to integrate sex and love. Hence they are capable of a casual approach to sex that is apt to shock many women. Men are capable of depersonalizing sex and hence are apt to be more promiscuous than women in our culture. This is often a source of difficulty between married couples.[16]

In discussion of the deep sexual differences between men and women in our culture, the Kinsey research group makes this statement: "Sexual adjustments between husbands and wives could be worked out more often if males more often understood that the reactions of their wives represent characteristics which are typical of females in general, and if females more often understood that the sexual interests shown by their particular husbands represent qualities which are typical of most males." [17]

In summarizing this discussion of Kinsey's research, we recognize that we have cited only a few of his major findings and that another author might choose to select an entirely different set of findings. Part of the difficulty in adapting Kinsey's mass of material to our discussion stems from the fact that Kinsey is not studying courtship or marriage as such; he is simply recording male and female sex practices in our society.

It does seem to us, however, that his findings are highly relevant for our purposes, as we have attempted to show.

To those who reject completely the work of Kinsey, we ask this question: Are any of the other studies any better? In our opinion, they are not only not any better but less adequate for most purposes.[18]

The Terman Research

In various chapters we have used the findings of Terman's study of 792 married couples in California published in 1938.[19] A great many very frank questions about sexual behavior were asked by Terman, and in some ways it is still the most adequate quantitative study of the role of sexual factors in marriage in our society.

The following findings seem to be relevant to our discussion:

1. Sexual adjustment alone will not sustain the average marriage.

Terman found that sex is indeed a basic factor in marital adjustment but *only one of four or five basic* factors. He concluded that the "sexologists" had overestimated the role of sex in marriage.[20] The writer's marriage counseling experience has supported this Terman finding, in that numerous couples have reported that sexually they get along well but could not resolve other conflicts in their marriage.

Note that Terman does not say that sex is unimportant in marriage; he only cautions that we regard other factors, such as personality adjustment, as being *equally* important.

2. That "good" marriages can tolerate sexual inadequacies in the marital partners.

His main point here is that the sexual adjustment need not be completely satisfactory if the marriage is satisfying in other ways. A wife, for example, who found her husband to be deficient sexually, would not necessarily regard her marriage as a failure if he satisfied her in other ways—affectionately, economically, etc. Terman feels that the "sexologists" (one of his favorite terms) had failed to make this clear in their books.[21] The writer agrees with Terman in stressing this tolerance of sexual deprivation when the other areas of adjustment are satisfactory.

3. *That husbands desire sexual relations more often than their wives.*

This is made clear in the Terman study.[22] It should be remembered, however, that the Terman sample was predominantly urban and middle class. Upper- or lower-class studies might reveal some variation on this point, although the Kinsey data seem to make this unlikely. Rural patterns might be somewhat different also.

4. *About one third of the women in this study were usually unable to achieve sexual orgasm or climax.*

Of Terman's total sample of 792 wives, 63 had never achieved climax, while 191 achieved it only sometimes. In contrast to this group, 338 wives achieve climax usually and 168 always.[23] He found that failure to achieve climax had a significant association with marital adjustment.

Terman made an elaborate study attempting to determine the cause or causes of this failure to achieve climax. His findings are amazing: he was unable to find any association with early sex conditioning of the wife, type of birth control used, husband's sex technique, or any of the other factors one would expect to be involved. Finally, Terman was forced to postulate a physical (neurological) factor as being the most likely cause.[24]

It seems to us that Terman's work on orgasm inadequacy has a lesson for married couples: that one should not blame too readily the marriage partner for sexual inadequacies. It is likely that a great many of the wives in Terman's sample who did not achieve climax tended to blame their husbands for this inadequacy, yet Terman, after elaborate research, could not demonstrate that the husbands were responsible.

5. *Premarital sex relations with future spouse only do not significantly affect marital adjustment.*

A great deal of argumentation has revolved about whether or not engaged couples should have complete sexual relations. Terman's research did not show that this has any appreciable effect on marital adjustment one way or the other.[25] There may be valid moral reasons why engaged couples should, or should not, have premarital sex relations, but on purely scientific grounds it seems to be a matter of personal choice.

Terman did find, however, that persons who had had sexual intercourse with *more* than the future spouse, both men and women, tended to score lower in marital adjustment.

It seems to us that these are the most relevant findings from the Terman research. The interested student will find some of the chapters in this study well worth reading.

Relevant Data from Locke's Study

In 1951 Locke published a volume, *Predicting Adjustment in Marriage,* in which he compared the characteristics of 200 happily married couples with those of 200 divorced couples.[26] This study has a much more representative sample than earlier studies, not being limited to middle-class couples.

The following findings of the Locke study seem relevant to our discussion of the role of sex in marital adjustment.

1. *Premarital sex activity by husbands with other than future spouse has a negative correlation with good marital adjustment.*

Locke found that a significantly higher percentage of his divorced men reported premarital intercourse with other than future spouse than did his happily married men. His data on wives on this point were not significant.[27]

Premarital sex relations with future spouse alone did not have any significant association with marital adjustment.

Locke's data seem to indicate that male promiscuity may be more of a problem in preventing marital adjustment than has generally been realized. It has been traditional to think of a young man "sowing his wild oats" and then "settling down," but it may be that the transition from premarital promiscuity to marital monogamy is not as easy as some have thought.

2. *Relatively equal interest in sex by husband and wife is associated with marital adjustment.*

A significantly higher proportion of the divorced couples reported an unequal interest in sex as compared with the happily married couples.[28] This is, of course, what one would expect.

Stated in a different way, Locke found that his happily married couples "reported much greater sex satisfaction with the mate than did the divorced." [29]

3. *Sexual satisfaction in marriage tends to prevent desire for extramarital sex relationships.*

This means that sexual frustration tends to set up an additional hazard for the marriage: the dissatisfied person (or persons) will tend to seek sexual satisfaction outside of marriage.[30] It is known, of course, that some marital partners cannot be satisfied sexually because they have a compulsion or are using sex to attain nonsexual ends (recognition, affection, etc.).[31] But assuming a relatively normal married couple, Locke's data indicate that a good sexual relationship between the married couple does much to prevent extramarital affairs from developing.

4. *Sex in marriage is best understood as "intimate communication."*

In his final summary, when he attempts to pull together his basic findings in this unique study, Locke makes this statement: "Sexual intercourse, when coupled with affection, satisfaction, and enjoyment of the sex act, is one of the most subtle and potent forms of communication between the persons involved, and tends to weld them together." [32]

It seems to us that in this summary Locke has hit upon the key to sexual adjustment in marriage: it combines the relief of sexual need with the satisfaction of emotional needs, but it also functions to meet certain needs of the marriage itself, one of which is the need for intimate communication. Many husbands and wives are unable to communicate adequately—they cannot "talk things over," or they are unable to express adequately their love for each other—and for these couples a good sexual relationship becomes a "way of talking" or a "language of love."

A close physical presence is a tremendous aid in bringing us close to another human being mentally and emotionally; notice how a mother hugs her child as she expresses her love for it. This is one reason why young couples neck so much: it helps them believe they are fond of each other. As an experiment, to test this, try telling your boy friend "I love you," while sitting ten feet away. It will seem very awkward. Most of us can do this when talking over the telephone, or when making love by air mail, but this becomes something quite different when the partner is living in the same house or apartment. So the happily married couples in Locke's study communicate, at least in part, when they love each other sexually.

Unfortunately, Locke's finding has a negative side too: when a couple's marriage begins to fail, one of the very likely symptoms will be decline in their sexual relations, which means that one of their most vital means of communicating with each other will be less available at the very time they need it most. This shows the *gestalt* or interrelatedness of the total marital relationship.

The Burgess-Wallin Research

In their elaborate study of 1,000 engaged couples and their subsequent marriages, Burgess-Wallin obtained some interesting data on sex and marital adjustment.[33] Some of the most relevant for our purposes appear to be the following:

1. Premarital sexual relations with future spouse are not predictive of subsequent marital adjustment.

Although couples who refrained from premarital relationships had a slightly higher marital adjustment score later, the difference was too small to be statistically significant.[34]

On the other hand, the couples who did have complete sexual relations before marriage had a slightly better sexual adjustment after marriage, but again the difference was too small to be significant.

2. Sex alone will not sustain a marriage.

They agree with Terman that a successful marriage in our society needs more than sex to keep it alive.[35]

3. The husband's sexual satisfaction is more crucial for the marriage than is that of the wife.

In other words, the husband usually (not always) takes his sex more seriously—it is more important to him—and any sexual dissatisfaction on his part is more apt to lower his rating of the marriage.[36]

This finding is essentially in line with that of Terman and Kinsey.

4. Sexual problems do not necessarily destroy a marriage.

Burgess-Wallin report that ". . . a substantial proportion of men and women with low sex scores have high marital success scores. It might therefore be concluded that although good sexual adjustment increases the chances of high marital success, poor sexual adjustment by no means precludes it." [37]

5. That sexual problems are rather common in American middle-class marriages

They support both Terman and Kinsey in the conclusion that American men seem to have more interest in sex than do their wives.[38] Since this problem is analyzed in detail in the next chapter, no further comment will be made at this point.

Burgess-Wallin concluded that "a large proportion of middle-class marriages are confronted with a real problem of sexual adjustment. It is clear that many couples are failing to achieve the physical and psychological gratification inherent in a harmonious sexual relationship which is satisfying to husband and wife." [39]

Summary

In this first chapter on the role of sex in marital adjustment we have focused on folklore and research data. In the next chapter, an attempt will be made to bring the discussion down to a more practical level—to focus on the actual sexual problems of married couples, to look at specific cases, to explore a philosophy of sex in marriage, and, finally, to examine a few stereotypes critically.

References

1. Clellan S. Ford and Frank A. Beach, *Patterns of Sexual Behavior* (New York, Harper & Bros., 1951). See especially pp. 261–267. In the writer's opinion, this book is required for anyone wishing to view human sexual behavior in perspective.

2. Ruth Benedict, "Continuities and Discontinuities in Cultural Conditioning," *Psychiatry*, May (1939), 161–167. This classic analysis has been made available in *Sociological Analysis* edited by Logan Wilson and William L. Kolb (New York, Harcourt, Brace & Co., 1949), pp. 223–231.

3. Alfred C. Kinsey, Wardell B. Pomeroy, and Clyde E. Martin, *Sexual Behavior in the Human Male* (Philadelphia, W. B. Saunders Co., 1948), pp. 573–582. Hereafter this volume will be cited as "Kinsey, 1948."

4. See *Sexual Behavior in the Human Female* by the above authors (Philadelphia, W. B. Saunders Co., 1953), especially Part III. Hereafter this volume will be referred to as "Kinsey, 1953."

5. See the discussion by Ernest W. Burgess and Paul Wallin in their study, *Engagement and Marriage* (Philadelphia, J. B. Lippincott Co., 1953), chap. 20.

6. Lewis M. Terman *et al., Psychological Factors in Marital Happiness* (New York, McGraw-Hill Book Co., 1938), Appendix I.

7. In defense of our generous use of the Kinsey work, we would like to cite a recent statement by a sociologist who is himself engaged in sexual research: ". . . it is interesting to note that the findings of other investigators in studies of actual sexual behavior . . . generally confirm those of the Kinsey group." See Winston Ehrmann, "A Review of Family Research in 1955," *Marriage and Family Living*, 18 (1956), 168–176.

8. Kinsey, 1948, chap. 6; also the 1953 volume, chap. 13.

9. These findings are reported in almost every chapter of the 1953 volume on the female.

10. *Ibid.,* p. 81.

11. *Ibid.,* p. 173.

12. *Ibid.,* p. 330.

13. *Ibid.,* chap. 16.

14. Most of these findings are reviewed in chap. 16 of the 1953 volume on the female.

15. *Ibid.*

16. Kinsey discusses this point at length in chap. 16, *ibid.*

17. *Ibid.,* p. 666.

18. This was also the opinion of a committee of statisticians appointed to evaluate the quantitative methods used by the Kinsey group. See William G. Cochran, Frederick Mosteller, and John W. Tukey, "Statistical Problems of the Kinsey Report," *Journal of the American Statistical Association,* 48, December, 1953.

19. *Op. cit.*

20. See chap. 13 for this discussion.

21. Chaps. 11 and 12.

22. *Ibid.*

23. See pp. 375–376 for a discussion of this point; also Appendix I.

24. Appendix I contains the complete analysis of the data bearing on this point.

25. See pp. 319–335.

26. Harvey J. Locke, *Predicting Adjustment in Marriage* (New York, Henry Holt & Co., Inc., 1951).

27. See p. 133.

28. Chap. 7 contains this analysis.

29. *Op. cit.,* p. 144.

30. See pp. 148–149.
31. See Richard A. Koch, "Penicillin Is Not Enough," *Journal of Social Hygiene*, 36 (1950), 3–6, as reprinted in Landis and Landis, *Readings in Marriage and the Family* (New York, Prentice-Hall, Inc., 1952), pp. 427–429.
32. *Op. cit.*, p. 359.
33. *Op. cit.*
34. See their chap. 12 for a complete review of these data.
35. See pp. 679–680.
36. Page. 690.
37. Page 692.
38. Pages 695–696.
39. *Op. cit.*, p. 695.

Suggested Readings

1. Ernest W. Burgess and Paul Wallin, *Engagement and Marriage* (Philadelphia, J. B. Lippincott Co., 1953), chap. 20, "The Sex Factor in Marriage."

2. Ruth Benedict, "Continuities and Discontinuities in Cultural Conditioning," *Psychiatry*, May (1939), 161–167. This is available in Logan Wilson and William L. Kolb, *Sociological Analysis* (New York, Harcourt, Brace & Co., 1949), pp. 223–231.

3. Allan Fromme, *The Psychologist Looks at Sex and Marriage* (New York, Prentice-Hall, Inc., 1950), chap. 5, "Sex in Marriage." This is a good discussion of the question as to what is "right" or "wrong" in sexual relationships between husband and wife.

4. Judson and Mary Landis, *Readings in Marriage and the Family* (New York, Prentice-Hall, Inc., 1952), chap. 14. This contains several excellent discussions from diverse points of view.

5. Clellan S. Ford and Frank A. Beach, *Patterns of Sexual Behavior* (New York, Harper & Bros., 1951). An anthropologist and a psychologist combine their disciplines to give the reader wide perspective on human sexual behavior.

6. Georgene H. Seward, *Sex and the Social Order* (New York, McGraw-Hill Book Co., 1946). This little volume contains a mass of useful research information. Highly recommended.

CHAPTER XVIII

SEXUAL ADJUSTMENT IN MARRIAGE (CONTINUED)

Introduction

In the last chapter the folklore and research about sex in marriage were explored at some length. In this chapter we wish to focus the discussion more specifically on the married couple and some of the problems they may encounter as they work out their sex adjustment. To balance the discussion, we will close the chapter with a few positive principles to keep in mind as a "philosophy of sex" in approaching marriage.

Sex Problems of the American Wife

It may well be that some or all of the following points will not apply to the average woman reading this book, but it seems likely that some of them *will* apply. In any event, we will try to cover the sex problems of the so-called "average" American wife. In a later discussion, the so-called "abnormal" person will be ana-

376

lyzed. It should be clearly recognized, however, that there is no clear-cut line between the normal and the abnormal in discussing sexual behavior. What most people do or do not do is usually defined as "normal," but this varies widely according to age, social class, and other factors, which means that there are several different sexual codes existing simultaneously in our American society. Furthermore, because of the private and secret nature of sexual behavior, people are often unaware of the sexual practices in existence at any given time among any given group. This means that we really have two types of sexual norms: those being practiced and those people *think* are being practiced. In view of the complexity of this material, the writer has no illusions that other equally qualified writers on the subject would agree on the points to be presented below. The student should regard these observations as "informed opinions."

With this preface, we suggest that the following factors are apt to create sexual difficulties at some time or other for the *average* American wife.

1. Her early sexual conditioning.

She has been taught to be a "nice" girl, to repress her sexual desires, to think of sex as a "spiritual" or "love" relationship. In marriage, however, sex is not always "nice," not even between happily married couples. Nor is it always spiritual or psychological; it is often quite physical and even animalistic, to be honest about it.[1] Kinsey, for example, discovered that at least half of the college graduates in his sample used oral-genital contacts at some time in their sexual relations.[2]

Actually, there seems to be very little realistic preparation for either men or women regarding the exact nature of sex in marriage. The tendency is either to romanticize it (the spiritual approach), or to degrade it (the male peer group approach).

If most of these observations are correct, then it would seem quite possible for the average "nice" girl to suffer some shock as she attempts to adjust to sex in marriage. And when this happens, she is most likely to blame her husband—that is, to regard him as crude or abnormal. Actually, his desires or preferences may be fairly typical for his social group, and he could just as legitimately consider his wife a prude, even though she too is typical of her social group.

If one thinks a moment about the Hollywood actresses considered to have the most sex appeal for American men, it is obvious that they are not noted for their spiritual qualities. In his deepest dreams, the average American man, at least at the middle-class level, probably visualizes his future wife as a cross between the Grace Kelly type of woman and the Marilyn Monroe type.

In a study of American movie heroines, Wolfenstein and Leites have shown definitely that audiences prefer actresses who are a combination of "good girl" and "bad girl," good enough to be loyal and trustworthy but not so good as to be dull or unexciting.[3] This probably describes very well the sexual dilemma of the average American wife.

2. *Fear of pregnancy.*

Although Terman and Locke did not find this item to be associated with the sexual adjustment of wives,[4] the writer is not convinced that this is the case. During the depression of the 1930's, we had occasion to interview several hundred married women about their problems, and these wives often stated very explicity that their fear of pregnancy interfered with their enjoyment of the sex act. They also claimed that their frequent attempts to avoid sexual relations with their husbands were often based on fear of pregnancy rather than on dislike of sex itself.

In a survey of 1,444 Protestant, urban married couples in 1941–42, it was discovered that over one fourth of the sample had experienced unplanned pregnancies.[5] About 7 per cent of the couples had *two or more* pregnancies than they had planned for. This study makes one think that modern birth control methods still may not have banished fear of conception entirely, and if this is the case, this factor may inhibit sexual response on the part of the wife (or the husband, or both).

Newly wed couples in particular may be concerned about

an early pregnancy, especially those in which the wife is working to help her husband complete his professional training. This seems to be a sizable group today.

Furthermore, at least one fourth of American married couples have some affiliation with the Roman Catholic church, which prohibits birth control as such.

All in all, the writer believes there is reason to think that fear of pregnancy must be considered when analyzing the sexual response of the American wife.

3. *Difficulty in achieving sexual climax.*

It will be remembered that this problem was reported by about one third of the wives in the Terman study.[6] It should be clearly understood that these women *are not frigid*; they are able to respond sexually to their husbands but are usually unable to bring the act to a satisfactory conclusion. Terman found this inability to have a significant effect on marital adjustment.[7]

It may very well be that this failure of the woman to have a climax may affect the husband as much, if not more, than the wife, for the simple reason that it threatens the man's conception of himself as a virile man. In male subculture, there is a great deal of "kidding" or joking about the ability of men to satisfy their wives sexually. For the husbands of wives inadequate in orgasm response, this joking may take on a threatening tone: if *you* can't satisfy your wife, perhaps some other man could. Even in the absence of such joking, the husband may conceptualize himself as an inadequate sexual partner, even when his wife does not blame him for the situation. For this reason, it is important for both partners that an attempt be made to eliminate or reduce orgasm inadequacy in the wife when this problem exists. Very few wives, of course, report an orgasm always. In the Terman research, wives reporting a climax usually were considered adequate. The wives reporting never or sometimes were considered inadequate.[7]

Later in this chapter some suggestions for improving sexual adjustment will be presented.

4. *Fatigue and child-rearing.*

Up until the arrival of children, American wives are usually able to consider the various needs of their husband (including sex) *first.* With the arrival of children, however, this changes: the baby (or the child) now comes first and the husband second.

This may seem to some readers to be a false dichotomy, but one has to appreciate the nature of child-rearing before the point becomes clear. A young human infant requires care from 12 to 15 hours a day, seven days a week, 365 days a year, for several years. In the case of three or four small children, the present trend, the average mother has a full-time job as a mother—in fact, judged by the modern 40-hour week, she has the equivalent of *two* full-time jobs just in her child-rearing role alone.

But in addition to taking care of babies and young children, she also has a *house* to manage and a husband to be a wife-companion to, plus her various community obligations. It does not require much imagination to see that many of these women, especially during the preschool child-rearing years, are chronically tired and exhausted.[9]

Now what does this have to do with sexual adjustment in marriage? Simply this: good sexual relations require *energy*—a great deal of energy—and these young mothers often just do not have it. And when we remember that married couples, especially those with small children, can normally have sex relations only at night, when the mother is most exhausted, it can be seen that the setting for love-making is far from ideal.

Stated technically, the woman here is caught in a conflict between her role as a mother and that of wife, with her husband competing with the children for her time and energy. In a child-centered culture such as ours, is there any doubt as to who will come first?

The writer cannot cite empirical proof that this is a major factor in the sexual adjustment of couples in our society, but judging from our parent discussion groups, plus our marriage counseling experience, we believe this to be a very common situation among young parent couples.

Sexual Problems of the American Husband

1. *His sexual conditioning.*

A great many American men have received most of their sex education from the male peer group, and in general the content of this sex education can best be described as a "behind the barn" (or garage) variety. The terms used are apt to be crude and vulgar; the attitude and values are likely to be cheap and promiscuous; sex and love are not linked together but are regarded as separate entities.

As a consequence, the average American man is not any better prepared for marriage sexually than the wife, in spite of the fact that the man may know more than the wife. The trouble is that he knows the wrong things and has to unlearn much of his sexual training. Presumably, some of this relearning takes place during the latter stages of courtship—pinning and engagement—when necking and petting are at their peak.

As we see it, then, both the man and the woman are apt to approach marriage with the wrong kind of sex conditioning and both must be reconditioned if their sex life in marriage is to be harmonious. The function of necking and petting during engagement is to begin this process of reconditioning, in addition to testing the couple's ultimate sexual compatibility. The reconditioning process seems to continue on into marriage and may, in some cases, last for several years.

Perhaps the most crucial need in this retraining for the man is to forge a link *between sex and love*. The male peer group makes practically no contribution along this line. It is nice if you happen to be fond of a girl you sleep with, but this is by no means essential. The main requirement in this code is that the girl be attractive—that is, she must not be a "creep" or a "beast" (or whatever the current terms are). It is not immoral to have sex relations with a girl you do not love; the real offense is to lower your aesthetic standards too much, for this would indicate that you were hard up or unable to compete successfully for the pretty girls.

Fromme, a psychologist, puts it this way: "Sex can be completely divorced from any of the more tender sentiments. In many men, the desire for sexual conquest is part and parcel of their aggressive approach to life itself. The number of women they have seduced goes on an emotional scorecard. . . . When this is the case, sex obviously has little if anything to do with love. It is neither an outgrowth nor an expression of such sentiments." [10]

We think it fairly obvious that this is poor preparation for marriage. We also argue that this type of exposure is becoming even more common as military service becomes almost universal in our society. This belief is based on three years of observation while in the service during World War II.

2. *His exposure to other women.*

To some extent, this will depend upon the husband's occupation, but a great many married men in modern society are exposed almost daily to attractive women who may not be unwilling to have an affair with a married man if the right opportunity (man) presents itself (himself). The average American woman is no longer shocked if a married man "makes a pass" at her—in fact, she is apt to be flattered.[11]

As a man moves up in his business or profession, this exposure becomes even more dangerous; he travels more, he meets more attractive women, and he is considered a better catch for any woman on the loose.

This is obvious in the case of Hollywood producers, directors, and actors, but is it not also true of the business executive, the physician, and some other occupational groups?

If a man is handsome, successful, and interested, he will have numerous opportunities in our urban society for extramarital affairs. It will be up to him to resist such opportunities—but has his sexual training before marriage taught him any sexual resistance? Or did the peer group always say that a man was a fool to turn it down when it was offered?

Kinsey shows that perhaps one half of American husbands are unable to resist all these extramarital opportunities.[12] Locke also shows that male sexual promiscuity seemed to be a significant factor in the broken marriages in his Indiana sample.[13]

If we add to these two factors (male sexual conditioning and sexual opportunities) the fact that a great many husbands are sexually frustrated with their wives, we get a potentially dangerous situation. We will have more to say about this later.

3. *His preoccupation with sex.*

If Kinsey is right, the average American husband thinks about sex a great deal more than does his wife.[14] From the wife's point of view, the husband may seem to have an obsession about sex —as one woman said to us, "he gets the urge at the darndest times." This seems to annoy some wives, and in turn the husband often feels that his wife is cold and unresponsive.

It may help some couples if they would simply recognize this male-female difference in sexual interest and take what steps they can to minimize it.

4. *His rapid climax.*

A great many couples, especially in the early years of marriage, seem to have difficulty in timing their orgasms during sexual intercourse. As a rule, the husband attains his climax before his wife has reached that point. Then, unless the husband can use other techniques to complete the act for the wife, she is apt to be unsatisfied.

In the past, it has been thought that women required longer to reach a climax, but Kinsey has challenged this.[15] He claims that most women are capable of reaching an orgasm in slightly less than four minutes when relieving their own sexual tension through masturbation, and this compares with 2 to 4 minutes for the average male under similar circumstances. Kinsey believes that the average husband *appears* to reach a climax faster because he is more aroused when the love-making begins: that is, he can be aroused by merely *thinking about* sex relations whereas his wife requires actual physical contact to begin her movement toward orgasm. If this Kinsey finding is correct, as the writer believes it to be, then there are some important implications for sex technique in marriage. These will be covered later.

5. Interruptions of married sex life.

Modern society and modern business often force the separation of husbands and wives for considerable periods of time. During the last war, or any war, for that matter, this separation may go on for three or four years. On a lesser scale, many men are required by their occupation to spend weeks and even months away from their wives. In addition, illness and pregnancy often make it impossible for married couples to carry on normal sexual relationships. These separations, of course, impose hardship on wives also, but the data cited earlier in these chapters indicating a greater sexual need among men lead one to suspect that the husbands find these separations more frustrating than the wives.

This is undoubtedly one reason why the extramarital contacts reported by Kinsey are as high as they are.

Unfortunately, this is the type of problem that is very difficult to solve or even alleviate. In the case of military service it is sometimes possible for the wife without children to become a camp follower until her husband goes overseas, but in most cases one simply has to be mature and philosophical about it. This may not be easy, but then there is nothing in the marriage vow about any of the obligations of marriage being easy.

The Problem of Extramarital Sexual Affairs

Although it may not be a very pleasant subject for discussion, it seems necessary to say something about the problem of extramarital sexual affairs in modern marriage. Kinsey investigated this problem extensively and found that about one fourth of the wives in his sample had had at least one extramarital sexual relationship at some time during their marriage;[16] the comparable figure for husbands in Kinsey's sample was one half.[17] Even if we grant that these figures are subject to error, it still seems likely that here is a problem encountered sooner or later by a significant proportion of American married couples. As a matter of fact, Kinsey's error in this area, as he himself suggests, is probably in the direction of under-enumeration, because of the secretive nature of extramarital sexual behavior. In other words, the actual percentages may be even higher than Kinsey reports.

Once we agree to recognize this problem and to bring it out into the open for discussion, certain questions present themselves: Why do married people seek sexual satisfactions outside of marriage? Do such relationships solve any sexual problems? Do they usually ruin the marriages of the persons involved? Is it ever possible to forgive a husband or wife for having extramarital sexual relations? Recognizing that this topic is fraught with moral and emotional complexities, we will attempt to suggest some answers to these important questions.

In Kinsey's data on women, the incidence of extramarital intercourse is relatively low until about the age of thirty, and the highest percentages are found during the thirty to forty-five age span.[18] This seems to indicate that at least three different factors may be involved: (1) sexual boredom or monotony, creating a desire for variety; (2) a gradual disillusionment with their marriage partner as a sex mate, culminating in the decision that the only solution to the sexual problem is an extramarital affair; (3) an earlier decline of sexual interests in husbands than wives (as suggested by Kinsey).[19]

In the case of men, the fact that perhaps half of them have had extramarital sexual relations certainly seems to indicate rather widespread sexual frustration or maladjustment among American husbands. In the writer's opinion, the male peer group in our society definitely does not prepare the average young man for sexual monogamy. Kinsey's data seems to show that a great proportion of our men never actually make the transition from premarital promiscuity to postmarital fidelity.

Adultery is universally a ground for divorce in our society, and this might lead one to conclude that Americans have very little tolerance for persons who commit adultery. There is considerable evidence, however, that this may not be entirely true. In the Kinsey female study, for example, in 221 cases of wife adultery known to the husband, the husband created no difficulty in 42 per cent of the cases.[20] There was only minor difficulty in 16 per cent and serious difficulty in 42 per cent. If we combine the "minor difficulty" and the "no difficulty" categories, we find that 58 per cent of these husbands were apparently able to tolerate or forgive extramarital sexual intercourse by their wives. These figures are surprising and indicate more male tolerance than one might have expected.

Kinsey's data suggest that wives are even more tolerant of extramarital relations than their husbands.[21]

The average reader may find this material hard to accept, and it certainly is not a type of behavior to view lightly, but the writer has been impressed by the ability of both husbands and wives to forgive extramarital affairs in his marriage counseling practice. Perhaps a few case illustrations may help the student to see these situations more realistically.

A. In this case, a married man was publicly sued by a woman in the community on a paternity charge and agreed to settle out of court. The community expected his wife to divorce him, but she did not. It was her feeling that except for this weakness, he was a good husband and a good father. She also considered herself partly responsible because she did not care much for sexual relations. Several years later this woman, her husband, and their three children were living together in apparent harmony.

B. A woman telephoned her husband in another community where he was temporarily employed and his hotel reported that he was not available but that she could speak to "Mrs. ———." It then developed that he had registered with another woman as a married couple. When confronted with the evidence, the husband admitted the facts to be true. The wife's family urged her to sue for divorce but she decided not to. Now, several years later, they have an excellent marriage and are proud of their grown children.

C. A man discovered that his wife had had sexual relations with one of his best friends. Although badly shaken by the incident, he was willing to forgive if the wife agreed not to see this man again, which she did. They are still married.

D. A man known to the writer discovered that he was no longer able to have sexual relations with his wife, a very highly sexed woman. He suggested that she seek some "respectable" man to satisfy her sexual needs. When gossip later developed about the wife, the husband defended her behavior. They lived together in harmony until her death some years later. The community was never able to accept this woman's behavior very well but the husband did.[22]

In all the above cases, one fact stands out: in each case, the extramarital relationship was essentially limited to sex and did not involve a total love relationship. In each case, the offending partner could say, and *did* say, "Yes, I admit to having had sexual relations with this other person, *but I still love you.*" This apparently is one of the prerequisites for being forgiven—that one still loves the married partner rather than the illicit sex partner.

Another characteristic of all the above cases is this: that odd as it may seem, all of these were basically good marriages in the sense that there was deep affection between the partners and in the sense that there was good adjustment in the basic areas of marriage except that of sex.

In concluding this discussion, it seems clear that the majority of American wives are sexually faithful to their husbands. A significant minority, however, have at least one sexual slip sometime during their marriage. Their husbands, however, for whatever reason—biological drive or social training—are more apt to be involved with some other woman at some time during the marriage.

Although one can hardly condone extramarital sexual behavior, it does seem clear that some American couples have found it possible to create satisfying marriages even after one (or both) partners have admitted sexual contact with another person.

If this crisis should ever strike your marriage, try not to act hastily. Take a good look at the *total* person you are married to, and at your *total* marriage. The isolated act is seldom sufficient for judging a human being in any area of life, including marriage.

Is Sexual Equality Possible in Modern Marriage?

It seems clear that one of the dominant trends in American marriage is that of fuller companionship and equality, and this applies to sex as well as the other major areas of married life.

However, on the basis of the research findings cited in these two chapters, it seems legitimate to ask whether it is possible for most husbands and wives to achieve sexual equality. Kinsey, Terman, and Burgess-Wallin, the three major studies in this area, all report greater sexual desire on the part of the husband than of the wife.[23] Looked at realistically, what we have achieved in modern American marriage is sexual *inequality*, with the wife reporting greater satisfaction than the husband.

In earlier periods in American history, it was recognized that the man was usually more highly sexed than the woman, and this differential in sexual desire was handled in two ways: (1) The wife considered it her duty to satisfy her husband's sexual desire, whether she felt like it or not; it was one of the obligations she assumed in taking the marriage vow; and (2) there was a double standard of sexual morality that permitted, at least covertly, to the husband sexual outlets denied the wife—either prostitution or a mistress, usually a woman of lower economic status.

In modern marriage, however, a strong attempt has been made to abolish all three of the male's sexual prerogatives: the double standard, prostitution, and the extramarital affair. In the process of evolving a single standard of sexual morality, it has been assumed that the two sexes are relatively equal in sexual desire, that the average wife enjoys sexual relations as much and as often as her husband. One can admire the democratic and equalitarian goal involved, that of complete mutuality in married sex life, but does it fit the facts? In other words, how practical is the goal for the average American couple? To what extent are the two sexes *actually equal* in extent and nature of sexual desire?

The writer submits that the research to date does not support the theory that the two sexes are equal or highly compatible in sexual desire and interest. Murdock, for example, in his study *Social Structure,* surveyed 250 societies from five major culture areas of the world and found only 43 that were strictly monogamous, 2 that were polyandrous (plural husbands for the wife), and 193 that were polygynous (permitted plural wives).[24] While it is recognized that plural marriage may not be primarily concerned with sexual satisfaction, status being a basic factor in most polygynous systems, the fact remains that in vast areas of the world men have usually had sexual access to more than one woman. In Africa, Asia, the Middle East, early Western society, and even in modern Latin cultures, males have usually had plural marriage or extramarital sexual outlets. The concubine, the harem, the prostitute, and the "other woman" have a long history in human society. One does not find similar sexual outlets for women. Could it be that these differential sexual arrangements reflect a difference in sexual desire between the two sexes? Or do they reflect other considerations, such as power distribution, status considerations, or other nonsexual matters?

If we go back to prehuman types, such as the anthropoid apes, the evidence is inconclusive. Some studies indicate the male to be sexually dominant and inclined toward plural sex companions, while others report cases of female dominance in sexual relations.[25]

When we focus on studies of American men and women, however, the evidence tends to support the theory that men are more highly sexed than women. Kinsey reports earlier and more frequent autosexual, homosexual, and heterosexual activity on the part of the male; he also reports more extramarital activity on the part of husbands; Terman reports husbands consistently desiring sexual relations more often than their wives; Burgess-Wallin report that sexual frustration of the husband has more negative impact on his marital adjustment—that is, it *means more* to him.[26]

Let us ask this question: What evidence is there to support the contrary point of view, that American wives are more *highly* sexed than their husbands? Kinsey reports numerous cases of women more active sexually than most men, but these tend to be exceptions and not the norm.[27] Kinsey also indicates that the sexual interest of women may not *decline* as early as that of men, so that in the later decades of marriage wives might have greater sexual interest than their husbands.[28]

In the Ford and Beach study, *Patterns of Sexual Behavior,* it was clearly shown that a *fully aroused* human female is more than a match for the average male.[29] But this does not alter the fact that the average male is aroused *easier* and *oftener* than his mate.[30] And therein seems to be the problem.

The writer does not believe that there is any substantial body of data tending to show that the average American female is more highly sexed than the average male.

We should probably ask a third question: What evidence is there that the two sexes are relatively *equal* in sex drive? The writer knows of no systematic studies of marriage that support this hypothesis. It is undoubtedly true, however, that a great many couples have worked out a reasonably satisfactory sex adjustment, and one may legitimately ask the question as to how this is possible if the two sexes are different in their sexual interests.

The writer is of the opinion that most married couples with a satisfactory sexual relationship are distinguished by the following characteristics:

1. They have given up the idea of complete mutuality or complete sexual equality. The wife, in particular, has come to the conclusion that sex is something more important to her husband than herself. The husband recognizes this also.

2. The wife enjoys doing things which her husband enjoys —this is part of her love for him—hence she is willing to have sexual relationships whenever he desires (within reason).

3. The husband is sexually considerate of his wife. He keeps his demands within reason, he expresses affection and love during the sexual act, he is appreciative of her sexual favors.

4. Both the husband and wife are relatively normal in their sexual interests. When this is not true—if one is much more highly sexed than the other, for example—we doubt that the above pattern will work.

In contrast to the above description of a good sexual adjustment is the ideal of complete mutuality in sex. The man is supposed to woo his wife, or vice versa, and attempt to arouse her sexually, and if she is not interested, he should retreat and try another time. Neither has any responsibility for relieving the other's sexual tension unless there is a desire to have intercourse.

We submit that, in view of the research data presented earlier, this approach will not work for most American couples. It will eventually produce sexual frustration in the husband, which in turn will make him more difficult to live with. In our opinion, a girl approaching marriage with the idea of complete sexual mutuality will usually prove to be a poor sexual companion for her husband.

It may well be, of course, that the differences in sexual interests between American men and women today are not due to innate and inevitable characteristics of the two sexes, but may actually represent social training. Margaret Mead, for example, in her study, *Sex and Temperament in Three Primitive Societies,* suggests that most of what we believe to be innate masculine or feminine behavior is actually the result of social training.[31] This is not too hard to believe when one considers the vastly different behavior of American women today from that of their great-great-grandmothers. As a brief illustration, one may cite the nineteenth-century belief that men were *innately* superior to women in intelligence, a view considered preposterous today. Is it not possible that another fifty or seventy-five years may shatter our present conception of the sexual nature of women? The writer would not care to wager too much against this possibility.

As a matter of fact, this has already happened to some extent. We now know that some wives are more highly sexed than their husbands, that "nice" girls have sexual desire, that a fully aroused woman is harder to satisfy than the average man, etc. Kinsey's description of female sexual behavior today hardly fits the beliefs of 1900.

It is certainly true that girls are still receiving a type of sexual training that is quite different from that received by boys—not so much from parents as from the boy and girl peer groups. If this early conditioning could be equalized, or partly so, it seems likely that the goal of sexual mutuality in marriage would become much more practical. Until then, however, it seems to us that a more realistic approach, as described above, needs to be taken.

Some Suggestions for Improving Sexual Adjustment

On the basis of the material presented so far in these two chapters, the following suggestions seem likely to improve the sexual adjustment of the average married couple in our society.

1. *More extensive foreplay or preparation.*

A common complaint of wives is that the husband is in too much of a hurry when he makes love to his wife. This often means that the wife is not adequately prepared, either physically or psychologically, for sexual intercourse. She then submits to her husband but does not participate on an equal level.

On a physical plane, this foreplay includes kissing, embracing, touching of the various parts of the body, and close physical proximity in general. Kinsey suggests that the wife needs this physical stimulation even more than the husband.[32]

It must be remembered, however, that there is also a *psychological* preparation for sexual intercourse, something that some married couples seem to forget. This consists of expressions of love and a general renewal of the emotional bonds between the couple. In poor marriages, this is hard to achieve because the basic feeling is not there to be expressed, but in some good marriages, when deep affection *is* present, sexual relations are permitted to become mere physical interaction, and this makes the act incomplete.

Actually, in the ideal situation, the married couple approach sex about as they did in courtship, except that they can go further in expressing themselves: that is, they include a considerable amount of necking and petting as part of their total love-making pattern.

2. A better time for sexual relations.

Most married couples, especially those with small children, usually fall into a routine of having sexual relations when they go to bed at the end of the day. In some ways, this is the worst possible time because they are both too tired for the proper relationship. One or the other, usually the wife, is apt to say, "Let's hurry and get it over with. I'm tired." Many of these couples would find it much more satisfactory if they could find some other time, perhaps earlier in the evening after dinner (if there are no children), or right after the children go to bed.

If this is not possible, an occasional trip somewhere alone, without the children, will often do wonders to restore sexual interest. Some couples known to the writer take a honeymoon every year, and they seem to come back with renewed love for each other.

3. Adequate birth control measures.

If a married couple are worried about an unplanned pregnancy, it seems unlikely that they will participate in sexual relations with complete freedom. If their religious beliefs permit, they should consult a physician for the proper contraceptive measures. The readings at the end of this chapter include two books on birth control written for the general reader. Except for devout Catholics, birth control is essentially a medical problem and as such the method used should be prescribed by a physician.

As a matter of fact, some couples will find that their major problem is not to *avoid* conception but to *achieve* it.[33] A medical examination for the wife at the time of marriage may help to determine whether sterility is apt to be a problem, and at the same time contraceptive measures can be prescribed.

4. *A variety of techniques.*

There are almost innumerable techniques used by different married couples to achieve sexual satisfaction. The readings given at the end of this chapter provide detailed descriptions of the major variations.

5. *Reading and counseling.*

Let us admit freely that most of us at the point of marriage know relatively little about sex as it should be understood for full marital satisfaction. Once this attitude is reached, there are numerous books one can read to acquire a more adequate understanding.

In some cases, not too many, reading will not be enough and individual counseling may be required. Physicians, psychiatrists, ministers, psychologists, social workers, marriage counselors—all these specialists are potential sources of help for those needing individual assistance. In a society such as ours, all of us are apt to be within reach of someone who can help. The main thing is to recognize when we need help and to seek it before the total marriage has been damaged.

6. *Improving the marriage itself.*

Since sex can hardly ever be completely separated from the rest of the marriage, it follows that anything that improves the basic relationship between husband and wife should automatically improve their sexual adjustment.

This may seem obvious but it is not, at least not to the married couples who seek help with their sexual problems.

We believe that with reasonable effort most couples can work out a satisfactory sexual adjustment. In a few extreme cases, this may be impossible. We will briefly indicate in the next section what these cases may be and suggest an approach to them.

Cases Involving Sexual Deviation

Although we know from several surveys that sexual deviants comprise a very small proportion of the population, the fact remains that such persons *do* marry.[34] Hence, without meaning to exaggerate the frequency of such problems, it does seem worthwhile to identify some of these deviations and to suggest an approach to such problems.

In the case of men, these patterns usually assume one or more of the following forms:

1. *Impotency.*

The husband cannot perform the sex act with his wife.

2. *Lack of desire.*

The husband has a very low level of sexual drive or interest. His wife is more highly sexed and becomes frustrated. Sometimes she turns to other men.

3. *Promiscuity.*

The man is unable to control his sexual impulses and has numerous affairs with other women.

4. *Homosexuality.*

The man is essentially homosexual but may have some heterosexual interest as well. He may be *bisexual* with almost an equal interest in both sexes.

5. *Sexual abnormality.*

The man offends his wife with his sexual taste—she considers him abnormal or perverted. Usually, he wishes her to do things that she considers wrong. He may be cruel (sadistic) when making love to her.

If any of these problems turn up in your marriage or in a marriage known to you, it is strongly recommended that a *psychiatrist* be consulted. As a rule, these are not superficial problems but have deep roots in the total personality. In some communities there may be clinical psychologists or psychiatric social workers who could help. Most friends and relatives are useless, or worse, in analyzing such deviations. In our society, the psychiatrist is best prepared to help with these problems. And even they are not always successful in these situations.

When we turn to women, the main sexual deviations seem to be these:

1. *Frigidity or coldness.*

The wife may be completely unable to respond to her husband, or else he considers her response to be inadequate, the latter being much more common.

2. *Homosexuality.*

The wife may be more interested in women than in men, or she may be bisexual.

3. *Promiscuity.*

She is unable to control her sexual impulses (nymphomania).

4. *Perversion.*

She wishes to use techniques that offend her husband, practices he regards as abnormal.

In most of these cases, with the possible exception of coldness, it seems to us that a psychiatrist is needed. It may be that some couples can help themselves, or can be helped by a skilled third person, but a psychiatrist is usually best if one can be obtained. It is not always necessary that the psychiatrist conduct the treatment himself, but it helps to have him diagnose the problem and estimate its severity. He may even be able to outline a treatment program that the couple can pursue themselves.

In all these situations, the desire of the person to change is crucial; nobody can help if the person will not struggle to help himself. It is also essential that the rest of the marital relationship be essentially good. Otherwise, the partner will not be willing to co-operate in the treatment program.

In closing this brief discussion, let us repeat that these are abnormal situations not encountered in the vast majority of American marriages.

Conclusion

In concluding this discussion, it may help to state a few *positive* principles to keep in mind.

1. In Terman's study, one of the most elaborate to date on sex in marriage, he concluded that couples *can tolerate* sexual inadequacies if the rest of the marriage is reasonably good.

2. In a recent study of divorce in Detroit, Goode found that sex was only a minor problem in the 425 marital failures in his sample.[35]

3. In the Burgess-Wallin study, as we saw in the previous chapter, a significant proportion of the couples achieved good marital adjustment scores in spite of an inadequate sexual adjustment.

4. *Most* persons are reasonably normal sexually. We read and hear a lot about the homosexual and other sexual deviants but they probably do not comprise more than 1 to 3 per cent of the general population.

5. Modern courtship, with its necking and petting, probably gives most couples a reasonably accurate understanding of their sexual compatibility, even for those couples who do not engage in complete sexual relations before marriage.

6. And, finally, many sexual problems in marriage can be

solved with the help of psychiatrists, psychologists, social workers, or other skilled counselors.

References

1. See Clellan S. Ford and Frank A. Beach, *Patterns of Sexual Behavior* (New York, Harper & Bros., 1951) for a detailed comparison of human and subhuman sexual behavior.

2. Alfred C. Kinsey, Wardell B. Pomeroy, Clyde E. Martin, and Paul H. Gebhard, *Sexual Behavior in the Human Female* (Philadelphia, W. B. Saunders Co., 1953), p. 361. Hereafter this will be cited as "Kinsey, 1953."

3. See the very interesting analysis of movie heroines in Martha Wolfenstein and Nathan Leites, *Movies: A Psychological Study* (Glencoe, The Free Press, 1950).

4. Lewis M. Terman *et al.*, *Psychological Factors in Marital Happiness* (New York, McGraw-Hill Book Co., 1938), p. 373, and Harvey J. Locke, *Predicting Adjustment in Marriage* (New York, Henry Holt & Co., Inc., 1951), p. 348.

5. Robert B. Reed, "The Interrelationship of Marital Adjustment, Fertility Control, and Size of Family," *Milbank Memorial Fund Quarterly*, 20 (1947), 382–425.

6. *Op. cit.*, Appendix I.

7. See pp. 300–309.

8. *Ibid.*

9. This observation has been adequately substantiated since this was originally written by a series of articles in *The Ladies Home Journal* dealing with the problems of young wife-mothers. See "Plight of the Young Mother," February, 1956, and "My 15-Hour Day," April, 1956.

10. See Allan Fromme, *The Psychologist Looks at Sex and Marriage* (New York, Prentice-Hall, Inc., 1950), p. 83.

11. See the best-seller by Philip Wylie, *Generation of Vipers* (New York, Rinehart & Co., Inc., 1942).

12. Alfred C. Kinsey, Wardell B. Pomeroy, and Clyde E. Martin, *Sexual Behavior in the Human Male* (Philadelphia, W. B. Saunders Co., 1948), p. 585. Chap. 19 contains the complete analysis of these data. Hereafter this volume will be cited as "Kinsey, 1948." The actual percentage for high school and college graduate husbands in Kinsey's sample was about 40 per cent.

13. *Op. cit.*, chap. 7.

14. Kinsey, 1953, chap. 16.

15. See the 1953 volume, pp. 625–627.
16. 1953 volume, p. 416.
17. 1948 volume, p. 585.
18. Kinsey, 1953, pp. 416–417.
19. Same volume, p. 353.
20. This discussion is in the 1953 volume, p. 434.
21. *Ibid.*, p. 436.
22. Kinsey reports numerous situations of this sort. See the 1953 volume, pp. 434–435.
23. For the Kinsey data, see Part III of the 1953 volume; for the Terman findings, see *op. cit.*, chaps. 11 and 12; for the Burgess-Wallin findings, see chap. 20.
24. George Peter Murdock, *Social Structure* (New York, The Macmillan Company, 1949), chap. 2.
25. See Ford and Beach, *op. cit.*, also Georgene H. Seward, *Sex and the Social Order* (New York, McGraw-Hill Book Co., 1946).
26. These statements have been documented in previous citations in this and the preceding chapter.
27. See the 1953 volume, pp. 537–539. The Kinsey group actually found a wider range of sexual behavior in their female sample than in the male. See pp. 537–538.
28. *Ibid.*, p. 353.
29. New York, Harper & Bros., 1951.
30. Kinsey, 1953, chap. 16.
31. Margaret Mead, *Sex and Temperament in Three Primitive Societies* (New York, William Morrow & Co., Inc., 1935).
32. See the 1953 volume, pp. 626–627.
33. See Robert Reed, *op. cit.*
34. Kinsey has extensive discussion of this matter. See the 1948 volume, chap. 21.
35. William J. Goode, *After Divorce* (Glencoe, The Free Press, 1956).

Suggested Readings

1. Alfred C. Kinsey, Wardell B. Pomeroy, Clyde E. Martin, and Paul H. Gebhard, *Sexual Behavior in the Human Female* (Philadelphia, W. B. Saunders Co., 1953) chap. 16, "Psychologic Factors in Sexual Response." This chapter is a summary of the psychological differences between the two sexes as the Kinsey group sees them.
2. Allan Fromme, *The Psychologist Looks at Sex and Marriage* (New

York, Prentice-Hall, Inc., 1950). This is a very readable and relatively short summary of the sexual relationship as the consulting psychologist sees it. Excellent for book reports.

3. Norman E. Himes, *Your Marriage* (New York, Rinehart & Co., Inc., 1940), chap. 22, "Sex Life in Marriage," and chap. 23, "Sexual Adjustment and the Art of Love."

4. Margaret Mead, *Male and Female* (New York, William Morrow & Co., Inc., 1949), Part Four, "The Two Sexes in Contemporary America."

5. Amram Scheinfeld, *Women and Men* (New York, Harcourt, Brace & Co., 1943). There is a mine of information about the two sexes in this volume. Well written.

6. Hannah and Abraham Stone, *A Marriage Manual* (New York, Simon and Schuster Inc., 1952 ed.). This has become a classic and is excellent for engaged couples.

CHAPTER XIX

MARRIAGE AND MONEY

Introduction

In this chapter our purpose is to take just one variable, money, and subject it to intensive analysis, to turn it over in our hand, so to speak, and look at it exhaustively. Does money affect marriage? If so, how? Or why? Is it the *amount* of money a married couple has, or is it what they do with it? Or could it be that *what* they do with it does not matter as much as whether they *agree* on what to do with it?

In the next chapter, we will focus on some of the more practical aspects of family finances—budgeting, consumer credit, etc.

Do Economic Factors Affect Marital Adjustment?

Burgess and Cottrell, in their study of 526 married couples, concluded that there was no significant relationship between size of income and marital adjustment score, but they did find the type of occupation to be related to marital success.[1] It might be noted, however, that their sample consisted of a rather homogeneous middle-class group, so that their study was not designed to reveal the operation of income extremes. Furthermore, their data were gathered through a questionnaire technique, which would not uncover some of the diffuse effects of money on husbands and wives.

In support of Burgess and Cottrell, one could cite Terman's study of 792 married couples, in which he also concluded that there was no significant relationship between amount of money and marital adjustment.[2] Here, again, the sample was middle class and did not explore economic extremes.

It is interesting to note, however, that the complaint "insufficient income" was checked more often than any other item by both husbands and wives in a check list of domestic grievances used in Terman's study.[3] This seems to indicate that financial problems were often the *focus* in marital disagreements in this group, even if they were not the *cause* of such difficulties.

When the complaints were analyzed in terms of "seriousness" (Terman's phrase), the complaint "insufficient income" was ranked 14th for husbands and 15th for wives.[4] In general, Terman was not convinced that economic factors have very much to do with marital success.

In the Burgess and Wallin study of 1,000 engaged couples, 666 of whom were also studied after marriage, the following conclusion was reached: "The so-called economic factors in marital success can be almost entirely accounted for by other factors, such as personality, family background and social participation." [5]

What should one conclude from such studies? Given the materialistic values of our society, and the basic role played by money or the absence of money, does it seem credible that economic factors can be ignored in analyzing marital adjustment? We think not. It is the writer's contention that some of the research in this area has failed to reveal the dynamic role played by money in marriage, because the samples have been too selective—that is, both the Burgess-Cottrell and Terman samples were volunteer groups, unusually well adjusted in their marriages, and in rather stable income brackets. Let us look, therefore, at some of the later research which seems to indicate that income *does* affect marital adjustment.

In the first place, a restudy of the original Burgess-Cottrell cases by Roth and Peck indicates that persons from the same socioeconomic background score significantly higher in marital adjustment than do couples from diverse socioeconomic backgrounds.[6] Although this finding does not measure the direct effects of income on marital adjustment, it does support the hypothesis that economic *level* may be related to marital adjustment.

In a relatively recent study of 200 happily married and 200 divorced couples, published in 1951, Locke concludes that income is related to marital adjustment in several ways:[7]

1. Fluctuations in income.
2. Agreement or disagreement over the handling of money.
3. Level of economic "expectation."
4. Appreciation of the role of the husband, or wife, in providing the income.

Thus it can be seen that Locke did find economic factors to be significant in determining marital success or failure. We think it interesting that only Locke has more than one socioeconomic class in his sample, and that his study is also the only one to compare divorced and happily married couples.

In 1951 Goode published a careful review of the research on economic factors and marriage, concluding that economic factors seem to be significantly related to marital stability.[8] Goode's analysis does not help us understand *how* these economic factors operate in marriages, but his work does support the belief of persons like the writer that economic factors in our society must be related somehow to marital adjustment. This belief rests on the assumption that since money seems to permeate almost all facets of life in America, that it must also impinge on husband-wife interaction.

More recently, Goode has published a study of 425 divorced women and has concluded that economic stress appeared to be a major factor in these marital failures.[9] Although the precise ways in which money (or its absence) affects marriage may not be very clear as yet, Goode's study leaves little room for doubt that economic factors are crucial in marital adjustment.

As we saw in Chapter XIV, social scientists in recent decades have become convinced that social class membership is closely related to a wide range of behavior in our society. Now, if this research is valid—and there seems to be considerable evidence that it is—then it seems that this supports the idea that economic factors *do* play a dominant role in a wide range of behavior in our culture, including marital adjustment.

Perhaps a more specific illustration would help to clinch the point. In a 1953 study, "Social Stratification and Psychiatric Disorders," Hollingshead and Redlich found a very close association between socioeconomic position and mental illness in New Haven, Connecticut.[10] Their basic table is reproduced as Table 4.

TABLE 4

DISTRIBUTION OF NORMAL AND PSYCHIATRIC POPULATION BY SOCAL CLASS

	Normal Population		Psychiatric Population	
Social Class	Number	Per Cent	Number	Per Cent
I	358	3.1	19	1.0
II	926	8.1	131	6.7
III	2500	22.0	260	13.2
IV	5256	46.0	758	38.6
V	2037	17.8	723	36.8
Unknown	345	3.0	72	3.7
	11,422	100.0	1,963	100.0

In this table it will be seen that Class V, the lowest socioeconomic group, contributes over twice as many psychotics as would be expected in terms of their proportion of the population. In this same study, it was found that neuroses also seem to be correlated with socioeconomic status.

The point is this: if mental illness is related to economic factors, what reason is there to assume that economic factors are not also related to marital adjustment?

Let us return to the position of Burgess and Wallin: "The so-called economic factor in marital success can be almost entirely accounted for by other factors, such as personality, family background, and social participation." [11] All this means, it would seem, is that all these factors are *interrelated*, but it does not show that economic factors are the *dependent* variable while the others are *independent* variables.

On the same grounds, would it not be possible to argue that sexual behavior is not a basic factor in marital adjustment because it too can be "almost entirely accounted for by other factors, such as personality, family background, and social participation"?

As a matter of fact Burgess and Wallin themselves, in another chapter, state: "The economic circumstances of the young married couple often necessitate a major adjustment in the marriage." [12] In this discussion, they have reference to unemployment or fluctuation in income.

Summary to this point

We have been trying to answer a very significant question: Do economic factors affect marital adjustment? Our review of the earlier studies indicated that economic factors do not affect marital adjustment; at least they did not appear to be basic in the middle-class couples used in most of these studies. A look at some more recent research, however, led us to question the earlier studies and to re-examine the data. And this, in turn, resulted in our concluding that economic factors *very likely* do enter into marital adjustment, even if we do not know *how*.

In the next portion of the chapter, an attempt will be made to determine *in what ways* economic factors play a role in husband-wife interrelationships.

How Do Economc Factors Affect Marital Adjustment?

There seem to be at least four different ways in which economic factors can and do affect marital relationships. These will be analyzed systematically in this section of the chapter.

1. *Level of economic expectations.*

In a broad sense, the *amount* of income a couple has after marriage may not be a crucial factor, except possibly at the extreme ends of the income scale, but their *level of expectation* may be very important. In other words, it may not be how much they have but how much they *expected to have.* This is where social class background would begin to operate. Let us suppose that a girl whose father averages $25,000 a year marries a young man whose income never exceeds $6,000 a year. It may be difficult for such a wife to get used to living comfortably on about one fourth of what her family was accustomed to having. If the husband's income is only temporarily low, as during the first few years of marriage, there may not be any real adjustment, but the situation can be very different if the differential in income is permanent. It is not implied, of course, that such a situation would automatically make a good marriage impossible. The point is that such marriages would be more complicated and would require more maturity, more careful planning, and a thorough courtship in which the economic future is faced realistically. The study by Roth and Peck, cited earlier in the chapter, supports this line of reasoning in its analysis of interclass marriages versus intraclass marriages, with the latter scoring higher in marital adjustment.

These levels of economic expectation can operate in other ways also. If a young man has been unduly optimistic about his economic future, both he and his wife may be somewhat disappointed when the high economic brackets are not attained. If a girl has had a profession before marriage and has become used to a certain standard of living, such as buying expensive clothes, she may find it difficult to live on what her husband earns. In one situation known to the writer, a professional woman earning several thousand dollars a year married a high school teacher making about $4,500 a year. When the wife gave up her position to have a child, she experienced a rather difficult adjustment learning to live on a lower economic plane. As a bachelor girl, for example, she had loved beautiful, well-tailored clothes and had frequented expensive shops. She also liked to have her hair done at one of the more expensive beauty salons, and so forth. All this she had to give up as the children were born and her husband's income did not increase greatly. This woman succeeded in making the adjustment, and she does not regret marrying a high school teacher, but she also believes that such matters should be thoroughly discussed and faced before marriage.

In the chapter on *Wives Who Work*, it is pointed out that young couples who both work may have difficulty when the first baby arrives and the wife no longer has a weekly pay check. This, again, involves economic expectations and the realistic appraisal of the husband's future earning capacity.

2. *Attitudes toward money.*

Do you believe in buying things such as washing machines on the installment plan? Does your future husband or wife? You may be surprised, as we have been, to learn that some men and women, even today, reject the very thought of buying anything "on time." In a recent panel discussion on this topic with a group of other faculty members, the writer was the only panel member to defend installment purchases by the young married couple, and this in spite of the fact that the vast bulk of the cars and household appliances in our society are now sold on the installment plan.[13] The only exception this group was willing to make was in the buying of a home. If you take the pains to find out, we believe you will discover that attitudes of this sort are closely related to family background. Persons whose families "always paid cash" are apt to view consumer credit with alarm, if not fear. Social class and personality factors are also involved in such attitudes.

Here is an illustration of how attitudes of this sort operate in marriage. In a neighborhood observed by the writer, all the women except one acquired an automatic clothes washer several years ago. One of the husbands, however, was deeply (almost vehemently) opposed to installment purchases, so his wife had to wait a year or so until she acquired one of the new automatic washers. The same situation prevailed when the wave of television sets hit this neighborhood about two years later. Please note that we do not imply that this husband was wrong in his fiscal policy— our point is that it is essential for such couples to *agree* on financial policies of this sort if there is to be peace in the house. And this is even more true when it involves something the children are clamoring for, such as bicycles or a television set.

These attitudes toward money can be very complex. A woman once told us that her husband, who was otherwise a "nice guy," had never revealed to her his exact salary. This man (some wives would have other terms to describe him) kept his checkbook at the office, so that she could not check his deposits or the balance. In other respects he was a very reasonable and pleasant person to live with.

Another man known to us refuses to have a joint checking account with his wife, or to give her an account of her own. All their middle-class friends, however, seem to have joint checking accounts. This husband, too, is a good husband in most other ways. He simply does not believe that women should write checks, and this in spite of the fact that surveys reveal that American wives now handle the bulk of family purchases.

A woman counselee of ours, whose husband objected to her "excessive expenditures" (as he called them), stated that her philosophy about money was very simple: "Money exists to buy things with, to help people enjoy life. That was the way it was used in my family and that is the way I propose to use it. The problem is that my husband believes that money exists to *put in banks,* so the balance will grow. That's the way it was in his family and that's the way he would like to have it in our family."

Interestingly enough, there was a great deal of truth in what this woman said. She and her husband *did* have very different philosophies about money and its uses; furthermore, their families apparently had been the same way. In this case, there was no lack of money. The problem was what to do with it.

3. *Emotions and money.*

It is amazing, and rather puzzling, to find out that a large proportion of American married couples seem to have financial difficulties at some point in their marriage. One survey, for example, revealed that a majority of the couples interviewed felt that they could manage well *if they had about one fourth more income per month.*[14] When it is remembered that the average American family has perhaps the highest per capita income in the world, facts such as the preceding one seem hard to understand. Therefore, let us ask a question: *Why* do American couples have so many budgetary problems? Why can they not live within their incomes?

One of the answers, according to psychiatrists,[15] is that money arouses all sorts of feelings, or emotions, in most of us. In an excellent novel about Hollywood, *The Producer*,[16] Brooks points out that a person's salary in the film colony symbolizes how much the company thinks of a particular star or director. This, then, explains why an executive may threaten to resign if his salary is not increased from $1,750 a week to $2,000, even though he knows that most of the increase will go to the federal government for income tax. The man has simply learned that a rival of his is getting $2,000 a week, so the other executive has to have a raise to that amount to assure himself that his talents are appreciated by the firm. Income, as such, has nothing to do with the situation.

On a smaller scale, we are all like this. A girl, for example, whose figure does not permit her to eat candy, will welcome a box of chocolates from her boy friend on Valentine's Day, because this reassures her that he still thinks of her—perhaps that he loves her. Wives, of course, being women too, appreciate such a gift also, even though their figures may need the extra calories even less.

According to American folklore, "It is not the gift but the thought behind it," although this seems to us to have obvious limitations, either during courtship or after the wedding.

In all the above, there is an implication that *when we stop giving things we stop loving.* This may reflect the basic materialism in our civilization, but it still seems to be true.

To psychiatrists, money symbolizes power, or love, or rejection, or security. A man will accumulate money he does not need, and cannot spend, because it makes him feel strong and omnipotent.[17] If such a person loses his wealth, as in the 1929 stock market crash, he may commit suicide. Another man, such as the hobo on Skid Row, may despise wealth or material possessions, because to him they symbolize responsibility and curtailment of freedom.

Did you ever know a miser, the type of person who starves to death with thousands of dollars in the bank? Such persons hoard money, but they cannot use it rationally.

We once handled a social work case involving such a person. This elderly woman had lost some of her possessions in a flood and had applied to the agency we represented for disaster relief. She complained, among other things, that her apartment, still damp from the flood, was bitterly cold, and she feared that she might contract pneumonia. She had no resources whatsoever, she insisted. After a visit to her living quarters, where we found conditions to be deplorable, we gave her an emergency order for food and fuel.

Some days later we were shocked to receive a report from a local bank that this woman had a balance of several thousand dollars in her savings account. At this point, it would have been easy to think of this person as simply being dishonest, determined to get something for nothing. This explanation was much too simple, however. Investigation revealed that this woman was malnourished from lack of food, that she often had no fuel for heat, as on the day we visited her apartment, and that she was a familiar sight on the streets *begging* for food and money. And yet she had a sizable bank balance. In other words, this woman was neurotic about money and her behavior could not be understood if one approached it assuming that she was a normal person. Actually, she was the perfect miser type, the kind one reads about in the newspapers every now and then.

Does this mean that very many persons are like this? No, not exactly, but don't be too surprised to find that otherwise normal people may have some of this in their make-up. We once knew a man, worth about a hundred thousand dollars (old-fashioned dollars, before the inflation of World War II), whose wife was still using an outmoded ice-box long after all the neighbors had electric refrigerators. This man would also drive twenty miles to save ten cents on a quart of ice cream. The interesting thing is that otherwise he was a very conventional person, good to his wife and children.

When this man died, incidentally, his wife immediately purchased the largest electric refrigerator she could find, plus all the other things she had been denied all her married life. At her death, several years later, very little was left of the small fortune, but she had enjoyed every dollar of it.

This man, however, was not a miser; he at least kept his house warm and provided the necessities of life for his family. He would be described as "peculiar" or "close with money" by most persons.

If we visualize the spending habits of men and women as forming a continuum, at one end would be found the types already discussed, the hoarders, while at the other end would be the spenders, the persons who believe that you should never leave until tomorrow what you can spend today. Let's take a look at this pattern, and then we will be ready for the so-called "normal" person, if there are any.

The spenders, in their own way, are just as interesting as the hoarders, and almost as complex. A young wife, for example, once consulted us about her marriage. Her basic complaints about her husband were all related to his spending habits. They had been married only a few months, and still did not have their furniture paid for, when the young husband purchased a new car, plunging them into debt an additional $1,500. And this in spite of the fact that his salary was rather modest and showed no signs of a sudden increase. Furthermore, the husband had not consulted the wife about the purchase, probably because he sensed that she would object.

Their marriage survived this crisis, perhaps because their first baby was on the way, but this was only the beginning. Before the $1,500 had been paid off, the husband traded the car in on a new and more expensive model, also without the wife's consent.

The final blow came two years later, when the husband signed a note for $900 to buy a used airplane. At this point, the wife had reached the end of her tolerance and returned to her parents. At our last contact, she was planning to divorce her husband.

What can be said about such persons? What is wrong with them? Are they normal or not? Is this a neurosis? In his famous book, *The Mature Mind*,[18] a best-seller during recent years, Overstreet argues that such persons are immature: that is, they have not grown up emotionally but are like children. They are irresponsible and unable to face reality (such as their income). Some of our famous entertainers, faced with such problems, have employed personal business managers who handle all the individual's income, giving the person a weekly or monthly allowance. There is reason to believe that less famous persons would find a similar arrangement to their advantage.

Overstreet's diagnosis of immaturity may be sufficient to explain some of the spenders, but it seems to us that some of these persons must be approached in another way, from a more psychiatric frame of reference. In other words, some of these spenders are emotionally ill and are using money to buy affection or prestige. The following case illustrates this type of person.

In this situation, the husband is a young attorney, about thirty-five years of age, earning approximately $12,000 a year, which is not bad for a lawyer of that age bracket. His wife, however, spends about $15,000 a year, so that the husband has been in a financial crisis ever since he graduated from law school. At one point in the crisis he consulted us about his problems and the following picture emerged.

This man is a junior partner in a law firm, so that he has the lowest income in the group. In addition, most of his work is with wealthy clients, some of whom have become his friends. As the result of all this, he and his wife move in a circle of associates and friends all of whom make two or three times as much per year as he does. This does not seem to bother the man very much, but it has had a very disturbing effect on the wife. She feels that the firm is being unfair to the husband, that they should be paying him 15 or 20 thousand per year, and she fails to see that the senior partners in the firm are much older, or that they have developed the firm over a long period of time. She feels that the wives of these other men look down at her, and they seem to make her feel inferior.

This has resulted in the wife's insisting that they sell their relatively new home and purchase one in a new development; they had to join the most expensive country club in the city; the children had to attend a private country day school; the wife demanded a convertible car for herself ("if only a Ford"); all their clothes have to be purchased at exclusive shops; and so on *ad nauseam*. They are now in a state of chronic debt and the husband is desperate.

Interestingly enough, the wife does not come from a wealthy background. Another strange fact is that the couple were apparently able to live on a very modest income while the husband was in law school, during which period the wife worked.

Our belief is that this wife is emotionally ill and we suggested that the husband consult a psychiatrist. It seems clear that the wife is attempting to *buy* love and acceptance, that her feeling of security or her conception of herself has been severely threatened, perhaps as the result of her marginal position in the status system of this new community.

This may seem like an abnormal case, but keep in mind that

this woman is a good wife and a good mother, except for this one area, and she has always been considered to be a normal person.

What is normal behavior? How many persons can be put under that time-worn label? Are you normal? Is your boy or girl friend?

Perhaps we should simply label all this as human behavior, which it certainly is. None of the persons cited in this chapter has ever been diagnosed as mentally ill, nor have any of them ever received psychiatric treatment. With the exception of the elderly woman beggar, all of them have been respected members of their communities. These persons are not stupid either, but on the contrary are intelligent, some of them college graduates. It does not seem possible to determine, on the basis of present research, the proportion of the general population that may have relatively deep emotional conflicts about money. Psychiatrists, however, seem to believe that *all of us* have some elements of this behavior in us. In other words, they stress the fact that it is only the intensity of the emotion about money that distinguishes the so-called "normal" husband or wife from the so-called "abnormal" person.

4. *Money and rational behavior.*

In this part of the discussion we wish to explore the question: How rational is the average American man or woman in handling money?

If we look at the psychology used in advertising, it seems clear that the specialists in advertising believe that rational analysis plays a rather minor role in most consumer purchases. In an interesting novel, *The Hucksters*,[19] based on his own experience in advertising, Wakeman tells how people buy soap. His main point is that all facial soaps are basically alike, except for the perfume, the wrapper, and the advertising. As a result, the average person buys a particular brand of soap because he or she likes the radio or television program that features that soap, or they may like the perfume used in the soap, but all this has nothing to do with the *cleansing* ability of the soap. And soap is used, at least theoretically, as a cleansing agent. The soap tycoon in Wakeman's novel scoffs at the idea that one soap is better than another: "It's all made the same," he points out.

This same observation has also been made about cigarettes (which is the industry in which Wakeman actually had most of his advertising experience). For years, Consumers Union, a non-profit organization devoted to testing products for consumers, has claimed that its panel of smokers could not distinguish one major brand from another *while blindfolded*. This seems to indicate that most cigarettes do not have a distinctive flavor, but that preference is based on packaging and advertising rather than tobacco or flavor.

General Motors, which in recent years has dominated sales in the automobile field, has emphasized the appearance of its cars, leading the industry in new car design, such as the hardtop convertible and the wrap-around panoramic windshield. Chrysler, on the other hand, which has provided leadership in the mechanical engineering of cars, such as power brakes, but which has not been a leader in styling, has suffered severe losses in its sales position.

All this would seem to indicate that Americans do not buy cars primarily for *transportation* but for aesthetic and status purposes.

Used car dealers consulted by the writer claim that used cars sell on the basis of looks rather than on how they run. And they devote most of their reconditioning budget to improving the appearance of the cars, not their mechanical condition.

All this seems to add up to the conclusion that money is not spent in our society for purely utilitarian ends, such as transportation in cars, but that it is spent to purchase a variety of needs: beauty, status, ego satisfaction, etc. My conception of myself, for example, may depend upon the kind of car I drive; for a woman, clothes may be a basic factor. My household furnishings reflect my taste and income; my record collection or my books serve a variety of purposes.

Is there a male reader of this text who has never splurged on some item that he couldn't afford but which he "just had to have"? Perhaps a car? Or a suit? Or a trip? Or a party?

Is there a female reader who has never splurged on a dress? A suit? A trip? A beautiful pair of shoes? Or a gift for some loved person?

Let the ones who can answer "No" to these items cast the first stone. The rest of us will have to plead "Guilty."

A Gallery of American Husbands and Wives and Their Financial Idiosyncrasies

The purpose of the following is to illustrate the diversity of financial patterns among American married couples. Most of these couples are middle class, but a few of them might range above or below middle-class status.

During World War II we shared a room for several weeks with a millionaire, a chap who seemed modest in his expenditure patterns. His one luxury seemed to be long distance telephone calls, which he made almost nightly to his wife and children. One month, for example, he called home 28 times, and he told us later that his telephone bill averaged about one hundred dollars a month. In all other respects, however, his expenditures were not different from other men living in the building.

A man known to us who seems rational with money has an expensive weakness: beautiful cars. This man can resist any salesman except one selling the latest convertible. In the past ten years, this man has bought seven cars, each of which has cost over $3,000. Although this man owns a business himself and is usually considered to be shrewd, his car deals have not been good trades but have been vastly in favor of the dealer. In other words, he will sign almost any note to acquire a car he wants. But other than that, he is not loose with money.

A middle-aged social worker we know has an obsession that she and her husband will be paupers in their old age. As a result, they buy almost any insurance policy presented to them, which keeps them insurance-poor, but in other respects they seem typical in their finacial habits.

An elderly woman of our acquaintance has no resistance to house-to-house salesmen. Her cupboards are cluttered with

"I'll bet my folks live more beyond their income than yours do!"

Cartoon by courtesy of Barney Tobey and *Look Magazine.*

"amazing new cleaners" and similar items sold to her by three generations of such solicitors. Except for this extravagance, however, she is a very frugal woman.

A professor known to us buys more books than he can afford —at least more than his wife thinks he can afford. This seems to be this man's only luxury.

A woman acquaintance of ours admits that she spends too much money on her hair. She would rather eat less than miss her regular appointment at the most expensive beauty salon in her community. Need we point out that her conception of herself is closely related to the appearance of her hair?

Lower class persons, as every social worker knows, are apt to splurge on funerals, running up debts that plague them for years. Their rationale seems to be that "nothing is too good for the dead."

Low-income groups also tend to buy very lush and expensive furniture, such as bedroom suites, and very large television sets or other appliances. These items seem to carry considerable prestige in lower class subculture. Most of these families, of course, cannot afford such items, or at least could use the money to better advantage on other family needs, such as medical care.

A young physician once told us that he has to carry large sums of cash in his wallet; otherwise he feels inferior. It seems that he never had any money in high school or college and that all during this period of his life he felt inferior. So now that he is a monetary success, his wallet has become a symbol of that success. If he feels inadequate in a social situation, he pats his wallet and is reassured. And he is fully conscious of this entire defense mechanism.

What Is Money For?

We have been arguing that money is not always spent rationally in our society, that it often is used for ends that do not appear on the surface: a car, for example, is supposed to be purchased for transportation, but it would be hard to explain American car-purchasing habits on this basis. A car, to many persons in our society, is a thing of beauty, a symbol of social and financial success. As the Cadillac people put it: "For the man who has earned it."

In the traditional Puritan ethic in our culture, it was wrong or sinful to use money for nonutilitarian purposes (except for the support of the church), and to some extent this attitude still persists at some levels of our society. The Ford Motor Company, for example, in attempting to sell its new $10,000 Continental, has had to convince persons who can afford such a car that it is all right to own one.

In the writer's opinion, all these uses of money are functional, in the sense that they all meet certain needs of the individual, or the married couple, or the society itself.

As a matter of fact, the American economy would collapse if very many of us became pure utilitarians and purchased only the absolute essentials of life. In a sense, this is what happened during the economic crisis of the 1930's, when most families bought only food, clothing, and shelter.

Perhaps our main point in this part of the chapter is this: the American socioeconomic system is based on a constantly expanding standard of living, which means that most of our family units must be motivated to want things they do not possess at the moment. Our mass media, with their heavy emphasis upon advertising, function to create these new wants—air-conditioned homes, two cars, a college education for every child—and to make the system work, the advertisers must always be a few years ahead of the consumers.

At this point another economic device is introduced to bridge the gap between what the advertisers say we should have and what we can at the moment afford, and this gimmick is consumer credit or installment purchases. Over radio or television this takes the form of this message: "No money down and 36 months to pay." During the depression of the 1930's this used to be paraphrased to read: "One dollar down and the rest when we catch you."

Perhaps it is clear by now that we are critical of the purely utilitarian use of money in marriage and family living and are prepared to defend installment buying, certain types of extravagance, also going into debt on occasion. The next few pages will present, then, a somewhat unorthodox view of family finances.

A Defense of the Nonutilitarian Use of Money

In restaurants and other public places one occasionally sees a printed motto: IT IS LATER THAN YOU THINK. This, it seems to us, typifies the attitude some Americans have toward money. After two world wars and a severe depression, after alternate periods of economic inflation and deflation, many of our married couples have evolved a sort of day-to-day (or payday-to-payday) financial policy. In a sense, their point of view seems to be that of the soldier: "Let us eat, drink, and be merry, for tomorrow we die." Some of this fatalistic attitude about money may be the result of the atom and hydrogen bombs: the feeling that wide-scale catastrophe may be just around the corner. Some of it is a reflection of the idea that "you can't take it with you." Our income and inheritance taxes may be related to it. Even our emphasis upon youth could be involved, since we are inclined to justify almost any expenditure if it is for the children. And since old age holds little appeal for the average American, he may prefer to spend his money "while I can still enjoy it."

If we dig deep enough, we may discover that American spending habits are related to what the sociologists term the "secularization" of our value structure.[20] Essentially, this refers to the change from the Puritan conception of hard work as the good life to the modern emphasis upon leisure-time activities, vacations, and sports. To the Puritans, idle time belonged to Satan; to the modern secularists, it is the reward for hard work and may be enjoyed for its own sake.

Let us take two hypothetical boy friends, both of college age, and contrast their handling of money. Then let us ask the question: Which boy would the average girl prefer?

Boy Friend *A*, the utilitarian, does not send his girl a corsage for the big dance, because he believes that such money should be saved for a rainy day. Because of the added expense, he does not join a fraternity, believing this to be a waste of money. Although he has funds in the bank, he does not own or drive a car, because he can't afford it. At Christmas he gives a very modest gift, believing that the Christmas season has been overcommercialized.

Boy Friend *B* sends his girl a corsage for the dance, on the theory that women love flowers. He has joined a fraternity, even though it cramps his budget, because he believes that "fraternities are good for you." He spent last summer's earnings on a used car, even though he realized he couldn't afford it. He now has no savings, having joined the fraternity and bought the car, so he borrows twenty-five dollars from his roommate to buy his girl a nice Christmas present.

No doubt we could agree that Boy Friend *A* is going to save a lot of money before he dies, whereas Boy Friend *B* is headed straight for economic stress and strain. But which one will be more popular on the campus? And which one will the girls "go for"? We put our money on *B,* and we predict that most of the readers will too.

It might almost be argued that Americans are a nation of gamblers, that we always have been, from the days of the Revolution and the Frontier. The whole series of events out of which our nation developed was a colossal gamble, and this spirit is still a dominant theme in our civilization.

We are impressed by the fact that Franklin D. Roosevelt, the greatest spender in our history, was elected President four times, with overwhelming majorities, in spite of the opposition's frantic warning that the nation was headed for economic and moral disaster. It could also be pointed out that Landon, running on an economy ticket against Roosevelt in 1936, suffered the worst defeat of any

Presidential candidate, carrying only two states (Maine and Vermont).

It might also be argued that the advertisers are too much for us—they have us figured out, as it were. General Motors, for example, knows that the average American loves a beautiful car, regardless of how much gasoline it consumes. And even colleges have learned that American parents will mortgage the old homestead to give their children a good education. A great many colleges, as a matter of fact, now have a plan whereby tuition and other costs can be paid monthly, on the installment plan.

It is not uncommon for young couples today to pay for their babies in three or four installments: one third on delivery and the balance monthly.

All this should not be too surprising, since our free enterprise system is dedicated to the mass distribution of items that used to be luxuries. No other nation has ever spent as much money for research on consumer habits, or has ever rewarded the salesman as we do.[21]

The result of all this is that it is not hard to sell an American something he has been taught to want (such as a beautiful car). The only question is: Will he be able to pay for it?

If our analysis is basically sound, then we believe that young couples should not approach marriage with the assumption that they will keep out of debt; on the contrary, the trick is to learn how to use debt (credit) intelligently, so that it aids in the achievement of goals that have significance for the couple and (later on) their children. Thus we defend installment purchases, on the grounds that this is a well-established method of forced savings— that is, it prevents the couple's spending their income each month on purely expendable items (such as food), and gradually helps them to accumulate some capital equipment, such as a car, refrigerator, and other necessary items.

As a matter of fact, Americans have always bought their houses that way, and we see no reason why the same principle should not be extended to college educations, trips to Europe, power mowers, medical bills, and even funerals.

Some Suggestions for Couples Approaching Marriage

In concluding this chapter, it seems wise to suggest ways in which couples may explore their ideas and feelings about money before they marry. You may disagree with some or all of them. Our only hope is that you do not ignore them.

1. Do you both come from relatively the same social class background? This can most easily be determined by comparing the occupations of your fathers, the type of home and neighborhood lived in, educational level of parents, membership in country clubs, etc. If you are from very different economic backgrounds, explore systematically how this might complicate marital adjustment, and face these facts before marriage.

2. Find out what are your basic attitudes toward money. Do you agree on how to *spend* money? Try keeping a joint budget for a month or so (this is especially recommended for engaged couples). Do you both like to keep records of what you spend? Do you both have a savings account?

3. Make a careful comparison of how your families handle money. Does your mother do most of the buying? Who keeps the records (if any)? Do they buy things "on time"? Are they close with money or are they free spenders? Do you admire their handling of money or resent it? Does your boy or girl friend agree?

4. Analyze the spending and saving habits of your friends, and compare them with those of your boy or girl friend. Are there any striking differences? If so, discuss them and attempt to explain them.

5. One of the best clues to money handling is to observe what a person does with a sudden increase in income, such as a Christmas gift, or perhaps money earned during a vacation. Does he or she go on a splurge, or put some away for the future? Whatever is done, basic attitudes toward money will be revealed.

6. What a person *actually does* with money is more reliable than what he says his economic values are. If a girl, for example, claims that she is not extravagant in buying clothes, analyze her

wardrobe and its approximate cost. If a boy friend says he is a
free spender, observe him on the next big date. In this area of
behavior, people often say one thing but do another. The old motto,
"Actions speak louder than words," seems to be true.

A Final Comment

It seems to us that financial adjustment in marriage can
be profitably compared with sexual adjustment in marriage, in
the sense that both are inextricably related to the total relationship
between the husband and wife. In other words, if the marriage is
not doing very well, the conflict may very likely be expressed in
either sexual or financial terms. Thus a man who dislikes his in-laws
may complain about the cost of the Christmas gifts his wife gave
her family. Basically, one could call this an in-law problem, since
that is the core of the husband's feeling, but it is expressed as a
money problem. To carry the illustration one step farther, the wife
may react to the husband's complaint by not responding sexually,
at which point the in-law problem is expressed as a sexual problem.

This does not mean, however, that all conflicts over money
need to be explained on other grounds, as Burgess and Wallin
seem inclined to do,[22] but it does mean that financial problems
must be analyzed in the light of the total marital relationship.

Conclusion

In this chapter we have taken a long look at the function
of economic factors in marital adjustment. Basically, we have
rejected the view of some researchers in this field that money plays
only a minor role in marital adjustment, and an attempt has been
made to show specific ways in which money and its connotations do
enter into marital interaction.

In the next chapter we come down to earth, so to speak,
and discuss some of the mundane details of budgeting and its
relationship to marital adjustment.

References

1. Ernest W. Burgess and Leonard S. Cottrell, Jr., *Predicting Success or Failure in Marriage* (New York, Prentice-Hall, Inc., 1939), chap. 9.
2. Lewis M. Terman *et al.*, *Psychological Factors in Marital Happiness* (New York, McGraw-Hill Book Co., 1938), pp. 169–171.
3. *Ibid.*, p. 96.
4. *Ibid.*, p. 105.
5. Ernest W. Burgess and Paul Wallin, *Engagement and Marriage* (Philadelphia, J. B. Lippincott Co., 1953), p. 556. See also pp. 515–517.
6. Julius Roth and R. F. Peck, "Social Class and Social Mobility Factors Related to Marital Adjustment," *American Sociological Review*, 16 (1951), 478–487.
7. Harvey J. Locke, *Predicting Adjustment in Marriage* (New York, Henry Holt & Co., Inc., 1951), chap. 13.
8. William J. Goode, "Economic Factors and Marital Stability," *American Sociological Review*, 16 (1951), 802–811.
9. William J. Goode, *After Divorce* (Glencoe, The Free Press, 1956), chaps. 4 and 5.
10. August B. Hollingshead and Frederick C. Redlich, "Social Stratification and Psychiatric Disorders," *American Sociological Review*, 18 (1953), 163–169.
11. *Op. cit.*, p. 556.
12. *Ibid.*, p. 609.
13. See C. Hartley Grattan, "Buying on Time: Where Do You Stop?" *Harper's*, May, 1956; also William H. Whyte, Jr., "Budgetism: Opiate of the Middle-Class," *Fortune*, May, 1956.
14. See Whyte, *op. cit.*
15. See, for example, Karen Horney, *The Neurotic Personality of Our Time* (New York, W. W. Norton & Co., Inc., 1937).
16. Richard Brooks, *The Producer* (New York, Simon and Schuster, Inc., 1951).
17. See the portrait of the tycoon in Sloan Wilson's best-seller, *Man in the Gray Flannel Suit* (New York, Simon and Schuster, Inc., 1955).
18. Harry A. Overstreet, *The Mature Mind* (New York, W. W. Norton & Co., Inc., 1949).
19. Frederic Wakeman, *The Hucksters* (New York, Rinehart & Co., Inc., 1946).
20. See Howard Becker, *Through Values to Social Interpretation* (Durham, Duke University Press, 1950) for an analysis of secularization as a conceptual tool.

21. C. Wright Mills has analyzed these trends in his study, *White Collar* (New York, Oxford University Press, 1951).

22. This point was analyzed earlier in the chapter.

Suggested Readings

1. William J. Goode, *After Divorce* (Glencoe, The Free Press, 1956), chap. 4, "Socio-economic Factors and Divorce."

2. Harvey J. Locke, *Predicting Adjustment in Marriage* (New York, Henry Holt & Co., Inc., 1951), chap. 13, "Economic Factors."

3. C. Wright Mills, *White Collar* (New York, Oxford University Press, 1951), chap. 8, "The Great Salesroom." Mills examines the need for American families to purchase freely if our economy is to function properly.

4. Hazel Kyrk, *The Family in the American Economy* (Chicago, University of Chicago Press, 1953). There is a mine of information in this study for the interested student.

5. Allan Fromme, *The Psychologist Looks at Sex and Marriage* (New York, Prentice-Hall, Inc., 1950), chap. 8, "The Problems of Money and Work." This discussion analyzes some of the emotional states related to financial planning.

CHAPTER XX

FAMILY FINANCES

Introduction

It is the writer's belief that the financial problems of most married couples in America are due to emotional and cultural factors rather than to lack of knowledge of the techniques of budgeting or of financial planning. Along the same lines, we argue that obesity in our society is not due to inadequate knowledge of calories and where they come from.

However, for those who may need it or, better, for those who will *use* it, the following section will review the basic principles of financial planning and control for family units.

Financial Control

1. *Keep an accurate record of income.*

This may seem simple, but not every married couple can tell you what its total income was last year, especially if the husband or wife had a part-time job or any irregular source of income.

2. *Keep a complete record of all expenditures.*

This may not be possible for the entire year, but at least it should be undertaken for a trial period—say two or three months. This is the only way to get an adequate picture of your expenses.

In keeping such records, a simple and inexpensive account book will be found to be very helpful. These may be purchased at "Five and Ten" variety stores, or at an office supply shop. Some banks and consumer credit companies supply them free of charge.

3. *Designate some person as the bookkeeper.*

It is well to have one person responsible for the accounts, preferably someone who enjoys (or doesn't mind) such work.

4. *Segregate current expenses from savings or capital investment.*

Unless this is done, it will be difficult to determine how you are getting along. For example: a couple known to us always seem to be "broke," in spite of the fact that they both work and have an excellent combined income. At first we felt that they must be very poor at managing their income, but later on we discovered that they were making *two* payments per month on their house instead of just one; in other words, they had a ten-year mortgage plan instead of the customary twenty- (or even thirty-) year plan.

Another couple we know have an income almost as large as the one above but spend most of it on current expenses—food, recreation, clothes, etc. The two budgets have very little in common.

Businesses find it essential to segregate capital improvements (such as a new building) from current operating costs (such as wages paid out each week). Married couples will find this accounting practice helpful also.

5. *Keep your expenses within your income.*

This is the principle of the balanced budget. This does not mean, however, that you must pay cash for everything purchased. A married couple, like a business, are solvent if they can meet their obligations, whatever these may be.

This principle does mean, however, that your wants and purchases must be in some realistic relationship to your income. This is the rub, as we shall see later.

6. *Allow some margin of safety.*

In business, this is known as the contingency fund. Essentially, this refers to the fact that we must make some allowance for emergencies. It may be illness, loss of job, temporary unemployment, or a long visit from your relatives, but most married couples need some margin of safety in their financial plan.

This can be accomplished in either of two ways: (*a*) by a savings program, or (*b*) by limiting the use of credit, so that extra funds can be obtained (or items charged) if necessary. The latter procedure seems to be dominant these days.

These, then, are a few of the basic principles of budget control and financial planning. Let us now examine some of the folklore about family finances.

Folklore About Family Finances

As in most areas of behavior, there is a body of folk belief surrounding family finances. Some of the major ideas in this folklore seem to be the following:

1. *That you should never go into debt.*

According to this belief, married couples should always pay cash: "You should never buy anything unless you have the money to pay for it."

Apparently, not too many couples today take this belief

very seriously. If they did, the American economy would collapse. At the present time, about two thirds of our young couples at any given time are paying for something on the installment plan.[1]

2. *That the man should handle the money.*

This belief, fast dying out, goes back to earlier days when it was thought that men were "smarter" and "stronger" than women. In those days, women were regarded as children in financial matters and had to be looked after by their husbands. Father paid the bills, doled out the money, and in general supervised the family's finances.

Today, wives do most of the family shopping and are considered to be better bargain hunters than men. Husbands still have their fingers in the family purse, but their wives stand by and count what is taken out.

3. *That an increase in income reduces financial pressure.*

The average American earning $5,000 a year actually believes that his financial worries would be over if he could somehow get a raise to $6,000 a year. But if you talk to the $6,000 men, they are usually in financial difficulty also and are hoping to make $7,000 next year—"which should put us over the hump." More likely, the added $1,000 will put them in an even worse predicament, for they will suddenly feel rich, relax their usual controls, and plunge into deeper debt. Of course, if they could make $8,000 in a year or so (they think), "that would certainly end our financial worries." If you think this is so, talk to an $8,000 man and get his version of this modern fairytale.

The fact is that income itself is not necessarily the crucial item; our economic and social desires have to be *in adjustment* with our income if we are to escape financial pressure. But this adjustment is almost impossible to achieve in our socioeconomic system because of the simple fact that our entire economy is dedicated to the principle of *expansion,* and this means that consumers (you and I) have to be kept discontented with what we have. A contented consumer in the United States represents a problem; he is almost a traitor to the system.[2]

It is easy to see what most Americans will be yearning for next year or the year after: air-conditioned homes, two cars instead of one, television in every room, a college education for *every* child, bigger and better refrigerators and freezers, more travel—read the advertisements today and you will see what most of us will be struggling to pay for five or ten years from now.

Some married couples, of course, already have the items listed above, but don't worry, they are not forgotten. Have you seen the new $250,000 homes in *Fortune?* [3] They're beautiful! . . .

4. *That you never can get too much insurance.*

This can also be stated as "Insurance is your best buy." This belief rests on the delusion that the average American makes enough money to leave his wife and children comfortably fixed for the rest of their lives if anything happened to the husband-father. Yet a moment's thought will show that a man would have to carry at least $100,000 worth of life insurance to keep his family for 15 to 20 years after his death.

It is a fact that many young couples buy the wrong insurance policies, and some of them are kept insurance-poor by unrealistic insurance plans. During economic crises, such as that of the 1930's, millions of such couples lost their insurance because the premiums were too high. More will be said about insurance later in the chapter.

In this discussion of folklore about family finances, we have tried to point out that married couples need to see through the glittering generalities if they are to plan realistically. If they find a good real estate buy, for example, a stiff mortgage may be the best thing in the world for them. Actually, a family and its monetary problems can be compared to a small business: income, expenses, capital improvement, depreciation, taxes, all have to be planned for. This is one of the best approaches to the management of family financial affairs, in our opinion.

We are now ready to consider some of the basic monetary decisions facing most married couples.

Housing: To Buy or Not to Buy

Sooner or later, almost every married couple in our society has to face a series of basic questions about housing: Should they buy or continue to rent? And if they buy, how much can they afford to pay for a house? Should they buy in the suburbs or stay in the city? Is it best to invest in a new house or look for a good buy in an older house? These (and others like them) are very important decisions for any married couple. In the following discussion an attempt will be made to provide some points of view and some information about these questions.

1. *Should we buy?*

For most middle-class couples this question answers itself with the arrival of children: in order to provide a satisfactory home and play area for children, it is almost automatic that you have to become a homeowner (a mortgage owner, really), for the simple reason that adequate housing units are not usually for rent. Even if this may not be the case with the first child, the problem becomes more acute with each new arrival. Eventually, most couples will be forced to buy whether they wish to or not.

The real question, then, for most couples is *when* should we buy, and what kind of house? Let us see what light we can shed on these issues.

2. *When should we buy?*

Should we buy when we first get married? Or should we wait until the first baby arrives?

Well, frankly, the longer you wait the more your house will probably cost. Architects consulted by the writer report that building costs for the past decade have risen about 5 per cent per year.[4] This means that if you wait five years, building costs will very likely have increased about 25 per cent. In ten years, a $20,000 house may cost $30,000 (this has actually happened since 1945, as a matter of fact).

The truth is that the United States is committed to long-range inflation: our political parties are dedicated to maintaining "prosperity," trade unions are determined to win higher wages, and industry wishes to maintain profits. All this means that housing prices will have to increase, barring an economic crisis like the 1930's, and this seems extremely unlikely.

If we should be unfortunate enough to have war or another "Korean incident," property will very likely double or triple in cost, as it did in all our previous wars.

Looked at from the above point of view, the time to buy is *now* or as soon as possible. As a matter of fact, as this is being written, the cost-of-living index has hit a new all-time high, the steel industry has just granted a substantial wage increase and has announced higher prices for steel. And since the steel industry is a sort of economic barometer, we can be sure that another round of inflation has begun. This means that houses will go up. Why wait?

But, you say, "We aren't settled yet. My husband expects to be transferred next year. How can we buy now?" Well, the answer is simple: the chances are that you will *never* be permanently settled in our society. From 1941 to 1944, 17,000,000 Americans moved from one county to another.[5] From 1940 to 1950 up to 50,000,000 persons in the United States changed residences.[6] A real estate agent told us that he has sold the same house *seven* times since 1948, and every buyer had said he was looking for a place where he could settle down.

It is entirely possible that the average married couple will live in at least five different communities during their years of marriage. If they wait to buy a home when they are settled, it probably won't be until they retire to "Sunny Acres" in Florida or California.

It is true, of course, that some couples find it necessary to postpone the purchase of a home for various reasons (military service, no down payment, temporary job location, etc.), but it is also true that some of them have had to pay considerably more for their homes because of the delay.

3. *What should we buy?*

According to an FHA survey, about 55 per cent of the home purchases financed by that agency are for new homes.[7] The average FHA house contains 5½ rooms with three bedrooms and a garage. The suburb is preferred to the central city.

It should be remembered, however, that there are some excellent buys in older homes in some communities. Often these older houses offer more living space, more community services (such as bus lines), and easier access to work.

In choosing between the suburb and the city, don't forget to consider commuting costs. And remember that suburban taxes usually increase rapidly as schools are built, sewers provided, etc. If the wife expects to work, suburbs have many disadvantages for the employed woman: cleaning women are harder to get, for one thing, and transportation is often more difficult.

4. *How much can we afford to pay?*

FHA finds that a 15 per cent down payment is about average.[8] Thus, on a $12,000 house you should be able to pay $1,800 down, leaving you with a mortgage of $10,200. They also find that the average monthly payment (including principal, interest, and taxes) averages about 15 per cent of your monthly income.[9]

Traditionally, home mortgages ran for twenty years, but in recent years (beginning in 1954) the government has been experimenting with thirty-year mortgage plans. These, of course, allow couples with less monthly income to buy better houses. Many bankers, however, are critical of thirty-year mortgages and advise home purchasers to avoid them.

In buying a house, it pays to shop for the lowest interest rate. On a $10,000 twenty-year mortgage, for example, an interest rate difference of one half per cent (say 4½ per cent instead of 5 per cent) would mean a difference of about $1,000.

You may wish to know that real estate agents usually receive about 5 per cent commission on the selling price. Therefore, it is often possible to save money by buying a house advertised by the owner and sold direct by him. On the other hand, a good real estate agent can be helpful in comparing the value of different locations, etc.

Some young couples have purchased living units with rental income, on the principle that the tenant pays part of the landlord's housing cost. One couple known to the writer, for example, bought a new ranch style duplex, occupying one unit themselves and renting the other unit for $100 per month. Since the mortgage payment was $150 a month, they estimated that their own rent was only $50. And at the end of twenty years, they would own a building worth $20,000 to $30,000. Eventually, they planned to rent both units and buy a single home for themselves. As usual, however, mobility altered their plans: the husband took a position in another city and they sold the duplex to get the down payment for a nice house in their new community. They did, however, make a profit on the transaction.

In concluding this discussion, it is the writer's belief that family fortunes are made or lost according to the real estate success or failure of the married couple. This, therefore, is a problem worthy of your serious consideration.

Automobiles and the Vanishing Dollar

In a great many American families, the automobile represents the invisible leak and keeps the couple chronically broke.

For most American families, the car (or cars) has become a major budget item, absorbing as much as one fourth of the family income at certain income levels. We don't know how it was in the horse and buggy days, but we doubt if old Dobbin ever ate that much hay.

Here is a case study of one young couple and their dream car. The husband earns $4,200 a year. Two years ago, they traded their four-year-old model on a new hard-top convertible. In order to get a liberal trade-in allowance on their old car, they moved into a slightly higher priced car, telling themselves that "it wouldn't cost much more in the long run" (which is extremely debatable). They received $1,100 for their old car and the new one cost $2,700, leaving a difference of $1,600, payable in 24 monthly installments. The carrying charge at 6 per cent was $96 a year, or $192 for 24 months. Added to the $1,600, this made a total of $1,792. To this sum was added $84 per year for insurance, or $168, which made their total mortgage $1,960. Divided by 24 months, their monthly payment was $81.66.

This, however, was only the beginning. Now that they had a lovely new car (and "lovely" is the word for it), they enjoyed taking trips more, so that their gasoline bills have been rather high. The husband estimates that gas, oil, and lubrication averages about $25 per month, and this does not include the cost of several pounds of wax that he has lovingly bestowed upon his beautiful possession.

Adding this $25 to the monthly payment of $81.66, we find that the car is costing the young couple $106.66 per month.

But, you say, the car will be paid for in two years and they will have increased their net worth. This, of course, is true, but not nearly as true as one might think, because of a little item known as depreciation in the used car business. Actually, at the end of two years, when the car was paid for, the husband was offered $1,500 for it on a new one. Since he paid $2,700 for it new, the depreciation rate for the first 24 months was $1,200, or $50 a month. If we add this depreciation to the monthly cost of $106.66, we get a new figure for the cost of owning and operating the car of $156.66.

This thing seems to be getting out of hand, doesn't it? Since the husband's salary is $4,200 a year, or $350 a month, we begin to see that the car is absorbing a rather large chunk of his earnings. Actually, his take home pay is not $350 a month; with about $40 a month deducted for federal income tax, hospital insurance, and social security, his monthly check is about $310. We now see that the car is taking over half of his monthly earnings.

Fortunately, things aren't quite that bad, because the couple plan to drive the car four years, so they will not have any monthly payments for the last 24 months. Note, however, that the depreciation will continue (but at a lower rate), the insurance will continue, as will the monthly bill for gas, oil, etc. One can wager, however, that the wax bill will decline.

Reviewing these figures, one might deduce that this young couple could not afford this lovely car, and such a deduction would be correct. There was an out for them, as there often is for young couples, and it was this: they had no children as yet and the wife went back to work "until the car is paid for." They knew, of course, that the car might be too much for their budget and that the wife might have to go back to work, which she was prepared to do. Fortunately, they had *both* approved of buying the car; otherwise it might have been a source of conflict.

It should be obvious that this couple wanted this car very much, that it meant something to them. As a callous observer, we believe that they were both in love with the car, that a great deal of their satisfaction from owning it, driving it, and just looking at it, could be called *aesthetic*. We do not agree that they bought it to impress their friends, all of whom know what the husband's salary is (at least approximately). Furthermore, they admit readily that they have had to eat beans some months to meet the payments. Hence it seems to us that snobbery or prestige is a minor factor in the purchase.

What, then, was the complex of desires involved in this somewhat dubious financial decision? Well, in the first place, this young couple have not started their family yet, so that they did not have to plan as carefully as parents do. Furthermore, they had hoped to have a baby two years ago but this did not take place. The car, we believe, was purchased to fill a void in their lives when they learned that they could not begin their family at this time. Viewed from this point of view, we believe that the car's importance to them, *at this time,* can be understood.

Furthermore, the husband was expecting to be transferred to another community in the next year or so, and this prevented their buying a home of their own. If they had been free to buy a house, we doubt that they would have needed the car so badly.

How can one reduce the automobile item in the budget? Here are a few suggestions:

1. Trade less often. Depreciation rates (the big hidden cost in owning a good car) are highest the first two years, dropping off after that.

2. Buy smaller and less expensive cars. As a rule, the bigger and costlier cars are not only higher to begin with but use more gasoline and also depreciate faster (with some exceptions, such as Cadillac). In twenty or thirty years of marriage, you might be able to save $20,000 or so by sticking to the less expensive makes and models.

3. Buy a good used car instead of a new one. Depreciation savings would be considerable, but maintenance costs would be higher. The problem, of course, is to know a good used car when you see one.

A college professor known to us bought a used Chevrolet for $1,200, drove it two years, and then received $1,000 for it on a new car. His depreciation loss was almost zero for the two years. The catch is that he knew the previous owner of the car and knew it to be in good condition, as it was.

4. Don't live in the suburbs; your monthly commuting cost will be at least $25 to $35 if you drive every day. Explore the possibilities of living closer to your work, or form a car pool and share the commuting cost.

5. *Don't own a car.* This is undoubtedly the greatest savings device of all, but not many Americans have the willpower.

Three elderly couples known to us have never owned a car

in forty to fifty years of married life. They ride the bus, hire a taxi, take the train, or fly. They all own beautiful homes (paid for). But notice that none of them grew up after a car became a necessity instead of a luxury.

Medical and Dental Expenditures

Here is an item that can wreck a budget sooner than a doctor can say, "Send him to the hospital." Very often these bills come as a surprise, for very few of us plan on being ill.

Fortunately, most couples now find it possible to carry hospital insurance, often through their employer, and this covers the major hospital charges (but *not* the doctors' fees).

Young couples should know that most hospital insurance plans have a waiting period of a year or so before maternity benefits become effective. This may be a good point to keep in mind if you are planning a baby.

In most communities it is also possible now to carry insurance covering the fees of physicians. Some of these plans are fairly expensive but they at least should be investigated.

The big advantage of medical insurance is not that you save money, but that you can determine in advance about what your medical costs are going to be. Furthermore, they make it possible for us to spread these costs over a period of months or years, rather than face them all at once (when most of us would not have the money to pay them).

Couples with heavy medical or dental expenses should keep a careful record of all items as the federal government (and some states) permit you to deduct a proportion of these costs from your tax bill. We suggest you read a good income tax manual for suggestions about such deductions.

The new wonder drugs can be very expensive, so that this item can loom large in some months. With small children, the winter months are apt to produce infections of various kinds, at least in the North, so that one can almost predict some sizable drug items during that period. This is something to keep in mind when trying to anticipate monthly items. Incidentally, prescription prices are *not* uniform in most communities and considerable savings can be realized by choosing your druggist carefully.

Capital Equipment

Young married couples, like a new business enterprise, have a great deal of equipment to acquire. The following list, although incomplete, will give some idea of the capital equipment needed by an average middle-class couple sooner or later:

Car	Ironer (mangle)
House	Clothes dryer
Furniture	Power mower
Silver	Baby buggy (etc.)
China	Radio phonograph (plus records)
Refrigerator	Television set
Washing machine	Camera
Sewing machine	Luggage
Dish washer	Deep freezer

This may seem like a long list, and we grant that not every middle-class couple will possess all the above items, but the list is actually incomplete. A few minutes' reflection, for example, produces a second list:

Books	Hunting equipment
Electric toaster	Camping equipment
Automatic coffee maker	Fur coat for wife
Small radios	Porch furniture (or lawn furniture)
Electric mixer	Second car
Recreation room equipment	Boat
(ping-pong table, etc.)	*More* camera equipment, etc.
Golf clubs or fishing equipment	

If you think these lists are unreasonable, take an inventory of similar items in your own home, and then compare your list with that of your boy or girl friend.

The following is a list of possessions belonging to the writer and his wife—and keep in mind that college professors are by no means highly paid people.

1 car	1 dish washer
1 radio phonograph	1 electric mixer
142 records for above	2 carpet sweepers
2 small table radios	1 electric waxer
1 camera	1 set sterling silver dinnerware
1 fur coat	1 power mower
1 typewriter	400 books
1 refrigerator	9 pieces of luggage
1 clothes dryer	14 lamps
1 automatic clothes washer	etc.

This is part of an inventory compiled for an insurance policy and is by no means complete.

The main point involved is this: all the above items represent *capital investment,* things not *consumed* immediately but which do wear out or depreciate (at least most of them). Over a period of years any married couple, even the poorest, will have to buy some of these things, hence a place must be provided in the budget for them.

In a sense, these possessions represent SAVINGS, and yet they are different, for they do not represent liquid cash, and often they cannot be readily converted into cash. They have a great deal of utility and value for you, but not necessarily for anyone else.

It is suggested that items of this nature, long-term possessions, be segregated in the budget. From time to time it is useful to inventory such items and estimate their total value. This may be especially helpful if you have the feeling that "we aren't saving any money," a feeling not rare with married couples.

Life Insurance

A recent survey revealed that 96 per cent of the husbands living in a Midwestern metropolitan community carried life insurance.[10] The average man in this study had his life insured for an amount ranging from $5,000 to $10,000, but one fourth of the group carried policies in excess of $10,000.

The big question about life insurance is not *should* we buy but *what*. There are endless types of life insurance policies but they are by no means of equal value for all married couples. It is just as easy to make a mistake in purchasing insurance as it is in buying anything else.

The following suggestions have proved helpful to some couples:[11]

1. Investigate term insurance for additional protection during the early years of marriage when income is apt to be lowest. This type of policy has no savings program and hence can provide more *insurance* for less money. At age 20, for example, $1,000 of term insurance costs $9.07, whereas the same amount under a 20-payment life policy costs $32.06 (see Table 5, premium rates).

Term insurance, being pure insurance, has no surrender value, and the rate increases as you grow older. But it does provide more protection for less money.

2. Shop around for your insurance. Talk to several agents and compare their plans. Read a book on insurance. It is true that premium rates for life insurance are relatively uniform, but policies vary considerably in their various provisions. Don't buy until you have investigated what the different companies have to offer.

3. Don't be misled by dividends. Very often, insurance dividends are actually *refunds* on premium overcharges. Compute the *net* cost in comparing policies.

4. If you have GI insurance, keep it. It is impossible to buy life insurance at lower rates. You may wish to *change* your government policy but don't give it up. The straight $10,000 GI term insurance is one of the best insurance buys on the market.

5. Most life insurance should be carried on the main breadwinner, not divided equally between the wife, the children, and the husband. You need protection against loss of *income,* not loss of *life.*

6. Don't be *oversold* on insurance. As a form of investment, it is inferior in many ways to real estate or common stocks, because it does not protect against *inflation*. A $10,000 policy purchased in 1950, for example, may have a purchasing power of only $5,000 when it matures in 1970. But the same amount invested in real estate or common stocks might be worth $20,000 by 1970.

It is true, of course, that some investments prove to be unwise, but it remains true that life insurance carries no protection against inflation—and long-term inflation is a serious problem in our society, especially for elderly retired couples.

7. Keep in mind that there are various kinds of protection in modern society; if your wife has had technical or professional training, that is perhaps the best insurance she can have. If your house is paid for, that is a type of protection. If you are covered by social security, that also is protection.

Here is an illustration: suppose that a man has $20,000 insurance on his life (that is more than the average). Such a policy would support his wife and children for about 3 to 5 years at the most. But if the wife has a profession, she could eventually return to work and earn $75,000 to $100,000 in the next twenty years.

Table 5 offers some idea of the variety and cost of five basic types of insurance policies.

TABLE 5

ILLUSTRATIVE LIFE INSURANCE PREMIUMS [12]

Annual basis, participating, per $1,000.00 of insurance

Kind of Policy	Age at Time of Issue			
	20	30	40	50
5-Year Term	$ 9.07	$10.15	$13.35	$21.46
Whole Life Ordinary	19.68	25.42	34.45	49.33
30-Payment Life	25.07	30.21	37.90	50.93
20-Payment Life	32.06	38.21	46.56	58.98
20-Year Endowment	50.61	52.38	56.01	63.98

Income Taxes

In our society, federal and state income taxes are a major item in family budgets. In some cases, it is possible to save substantial sums by keeping accurate records and knowing what items are deductible.

Here is a case illustration: the wife of a college professor known to the writer has made herself an expert on the federal income tax regulations and has saved her husband several hundred dollars in federal taxes in the past five years. This woman sent to the United States Government Printing Office in Washington, D.C., and obtained a copy of their inexpensive (25¢) *Income Tax Guide,* a voluminous manual explaining what expenditures are deductible. After studying the manual carefully, she began to keep complete records of relevant expenditures. She also had several conferences with the federal income tax representative in their area. In a sense, this woman has made a hobby of income tax work, but it has proved to be a very lucrative hobby.

It might be added that this woman has never lost an argument with either the federal or state income tax bureaus; her deductions are based on official manuals and she has the expenditures properly recorded and documented.

It is a fact that most married couples pay higher income taxes than necessary. Get an income tax manual and learn to use it, or consult an income tax accountant. It will pay you to do so.

Gifts

Americans are dedicated to exchanging gifts. The following list will give you some idea how often gifts are called for in our society.

Weddings   Christmas (hundreds of people)
Wedding Anniversary   Father's Day
Birthdays (lots of them)   Mother's Day
Birth of baby   Funerals (flowers)
Graduation Gifts (high school and
    college)

Although these gifts are usually material in nature, their main function in society, as the anthropologist Malinowski has pointed out, is to *maintain and cement our social relationships*.[13] Hence the exchanging of gifts is not silly, as some cynics maintain, but serves a basic social purpose.

As a matter of fact, custom requires a pattern of reciprocity, as Malinowski makes clear,[14] so that the average person probably comes out about even over a period of several decades (assuming he doesn't get too many neckties he refuses to wear). From this point of view, gift exchanging is a pleasant form of lottery that is relatively inexpensive (on the reciprocity basis) and serves to remind our friends and our loved ones that our affections are as strong as ever.

The fact remains, however, that gifts can be a financial burden at times (Christmas in particular) and for this reason it is suggested that you segregate and record all expenditures of this nature.

It is very easy to fall into the habit of giving expensive gifts, even when they are quite uncalled for, and some married couples have their worst quarrels over problems of this sort. We recall a marriage counseling case in which the wife forced her husband to return an expensive watch he had given her for Christmas, on the grounds that they could not afford it (which they probably couldn't). A husband known to us grumbled so much about the cost of a sport shirt his wife had given him for Christmas that she removed the shirt from his bureau and took it back to the store (it had been charged, of course). Their relationships were a bit strained for a few days after this episode.

In another situation observed by us, a man got somewhat inebriated Christmas eve at an office party and bought his wife a fur coat on the way home. Although she loved the coat, she was appalled at the cost and suggested he return it, which he refused to do. She was also angry that he had bought the coat while drinking, which shows how critical wives can be, even when the recipient of a lovely gift. It was true, as the wife pointed out, that their budget did not allow for the purchase of a fur coat, but somehow the coat was finally paid for and the couple escaped bankruptcy. As a matter of fact, they are now relatively prosperous, and they often laugh about "the fur coat incident." It was not very funny at the time, however—at least not to them.

Some couples have found the Christmas savings plan, offered now by most banks, a useful device for avoiding what might be called "the Christmas blues." Under this plan, you decide how much you wish to save for next Christmas, then make weekly payments all through the year. Then, a few weeks before Christmas, you receive a check from the bank for your total savings. For some couples, this is just like finding the money, as they put it. Such accounts normally do not pay any interest, but since the money usually cannot be withdrawn until just before Christmas, you are protected against spending the money for some other purpose (such as your summer vacation).

Notice how easy it would be just to keep this money at home in an envelope marked CHRISTMAS, or to segregate it in your checking account balance, or to simply add it to your regular savings account, where it would draw interest. The fact is, however, that millions of couples have learned that they do *not* put money aside for Christmas unless they sign up for a Christmas savings plan. One can observe that these couples lack willpower or self-control, but the fact remains that millions of us are like that: we need a *forced savings plan* in order to save money.

Installment Buying

One of the great contributions of our society to the world is the installment purchasing system. Under this plan, you do not have to wait until you have saved enough money to buy something; you can have it now and pay for it later ("no money down and up to 36 months to pay"). This sales gimmick has all but revolutionized American life.

According to a recent study, American married couples in 1956 owed a total of 26 *billion* dollars for items brought home to be paid for later.[15]

Another study reveals that about half of all American married couples make an installment payment of some sort every month.[16] The bulk of these couples earn between $3,000 and $10,000 per year. Interestingly enough, about *two thirds* of our younger married couples are involved in installment purchases.[17]

In the 1950 decade, with jobs plentiful, only about 1 per cent of the couples were delinquent in their payments at any given time.[18]

In an interesting article for *Fortune,* Whyte has argued that installment buying has practically eliminated the old-fashioned budget among young middle-class couples.[19] He puts it this way: "They have become prey to 'budgetism.' This does not mean that they actually keep formal budgets. Quite the contrary; the beauty of budgetism is that one doesn't have to keep a budget at all. It's done automatically. In the new middle-class rhythm of life, obligations are homogenized, for the over-riding aim is to have oneself committed to regular, unvarying monthly payments on all the major items. Come the first of the month and there is practically nothing left to decide." [20]

According to Whyte, the new trend is not to be described as "pay-as-you-go" but as "pay-as-you-*went*." [21]

Whyte's observations are based on a study of the monthly expenditures of 83 couples with incomes from $5,000 to $7,500. In the writer's opinion, his conclusions, as stated above, are essentially correct.

There are a few basic roles to keep in mind when buying on the installment plan:[22]

1. Always make the largest down payment possible. This reduces the interest or carrying charge.

2. Always arrange to pay off the balance in as few months as possible, as this too reduces the interest charges. For example, don't take 36 months to pay for a car if you can do it in 24. The savings in this case would be about one third of the total charges.

3. Always *shop around* for consumer credit. Check to see if your firm has a Credit Union. If it does, this is probably your cheapest source of money. The next best source (assuming you have no wealthy in-laws), would normally be a regular bank. The most

expensive source, almost always, is the small loan agency or the store selling the merchandise.

4. Actually *compute* the installment costs before you buy. In some cases, the interest rate and fees will total 15 to 30 per cent, depending upon the laws in your state and other factors. These high interest rates are not readily discovered, but keep in mind that on the last month of the contract (say 24 months) you are still paying interest on the *entire* loan, even though by now most of the money has been repaid. At a Credit Union, however, you pay interest only on the actual balance left after the previous payment.

5. Pay cash if you can; it will save you a lot of money in twenty years.

Some Suggestions for Saving Money

When you face the facts, there are two basic ways in which families can improve their standard of living: (*a*) by earning more money; and (*b*) by spending their income more efficiently. We will leave the first to somebody else but are willing to venture a few suggestions on the second, recognizing, however, that home economists know more about this than we do.

Here, then, are a few suggestions for getting more for your money.[23]

1. *Consistent use of seasonal sales.*

The best-dressed college professor we know claims that he *never* pays full price for his clothes. "I always buy my summer suits in August and my fall ones in January," he says. "A suit that would cost me $75 in September will be marked down to about $55 by the end of the season. That's when I buy it." His shoes, shirts, overcoats, almost everything he wears, have been bought at marked-down prices. This man, incidentally, will not buy cheap or shoddy merchandise—only the better makes, but always on sale.

If you watch the market, almost anything you need (or

want) can be purchased on sale—television sets, various appliances, automobiles, sheets, furniture, etc.

A friend of ours bought a $3,000 car for $2,500 at the end of the season (just before the new models go on sale). Another friend found a television set marked down form $300 to $225 when the next year's models came out.

Some persons distrust sales, and perhaps for good cause. But careful shopping will help you determine when items have really been reduced. And that is the time to buy.

2. *Careful comparison shopping.*

This means that you should never buy until you have compared prices and quality in at least two different stores, preferably more. If you have not done this, how will you know when you find a good buy?

A few years ago the writer found almost $100 difference between refrigerators of the same size and carrying the same guarantee (five years on the cooling unit).

Mail-order houses often offer remarkable buys on fully guaranteed merchandise.

3. *Careful use of credit.*

In Whyte's study of middle-class couples and their spending habits, he was appalled at their lack of knowledge about interest rates or carrying charges.[24] Some of them (college graduates) were paying up to 36 per cent interest on car loans, even though the Credit Union at their place of employment charged only 6 per cent on similar loans. By shopping around for mortgages or loans, one can save a great deal of money over the years. Paying cash, of course, is even cheaper.

4. *Purchase of used items.*

Cars, houses, boats, children's bicycles, appliances, almost anything can be bought in good used condition if you try. It is true that some persons are snobs when it comes even to considering the purchase of anything not brand-new. This, of course, is their privilege, but it can be a rather expensive form of snobbery. "Looking down on the Democrats" would be cheaper.

5. *Avoidance of the luxury models.*

A hard-top convertible (they are not actually convertible, are they?) may cost up to $500 more than a standard two-door sedan. We grant that the hard-top has better styling (we like them too) but is the difference worth $300 to $500 to you? That is the sort of decision one has to make.

What you may not realize, however, is that the same price differential between the standard and deluxe models also is found in refrigerators, television sets, sewing machines, etc. In refrigerators, for example, you can pay up to $100 more for a butter "conditioner," "automatic" ice-cube dispenser, and similar frills, but the basic mechanical features of the two models are *identical*. The problem is to decide how much the extra features of the deluxe models are worth to you.

6. *Use of forced savings plans.*

Insurance companies, banks, stores, even the United States Government have discovered that the average American will not save money unless he *has* to. For this reason, most married couples need a forced savings program—that is, one which is automatic.

Here are some suggestions as to how you can utilize various types of forced savings:

a. Buy an insurance policy, as almost all of them (except term insurance) contain an automatic savings program. Most middle-class Americans would rather die than let their insurance lapse, so they are forced to save money.

b. Sign a payroll deduction plan for the purchase of government bonds. If your firm has a Credit Union, sign a deduction form which will automatically put a given amount of savings in the Credit Union every month. Some banks have a service whereby they will transfer a stipulated sum every month from your checking to a savings account.

   c. Buy a house. The monthly payment will include a certain amount on the principal. This is savings.

   d. Buy a car or some appliance on the installment plan (borrowing the money from a Credit Union if possible). This is an expensive way to save money, but it is nevertheless true that *someday* (you hope) the thing will be paid for and will belong to you. In other words, you will have saved some money (that is, you did not spend your whole income on consumable items but put a portion into capital equipment).

   A couple known to us had always wanted to take a trip to Europe but never seemed to accumulate enough cash to get beyond New York City. Finally, as middle age crept up on them, they borrowed the money from their bank and sailed off to Paris and Europe for the summer. Later on, the husband said: "I must say the monthly payments did seem pretty high—and somewhat ever-lasting—but we *did* get to Europe, thanks to good old First National Bank and Trust." Well, at least they *got there.*

7. *Careful scrutiny of expenditures.*

   Do you really need or want whatever you are thinking of buying? Would something else bring you or your family more satisfaction? Would your life suffer much if you did not buy it?

   All of us literally throw away money by cluttering up our lives and our houses with things we did not really want or did not need. Perhaps one can never hope to eliminate this type of expenditure completely in our gadget-conscious culture, but maybe its frequency can be reduced.

8. *Always consider quality as well as price.*

   Nothing (at any price) is a good buy unless it is well designed and well made. This must be kept in mind at all times.

9. *Use the services of consumer research groups.*

Both federal and state government bureaus publish numerous pamphlets (they call them "Bulletins") devoted to helping consumers get more for their money. The U.S. Government Printing Office in Washington, D.C., will send a list of the federal pamphlets if you request it. State governments will do likewise. These publications are either free or cost very little. You will find that your local public library has a collection of such material. On college campuses, the Department of Home Economics (if there is one) can give you reading material on consumer education.

Some colleges have a course called "Consumer Economics" that might be well worth taking.

There are two nationally known consumer research organizations whose services are available on an annual subscription basis. One of these is Consumers Union in New York City. The other is Consumer's Research located in Washington, New Jersey. Both of these organizations publish a monthly report on items they have tested, giving brand names, prices, and test results. They also publish a voluminous *Annual Buying Guide* containing a mass of information of interest to shoppers. Their subscription rates are reasonable (about $5 a year) and the chances are you will find their material interesting and well worth having.

It should be made clear that these organizations are completely independent of business firms and accept no fees from manufacturers or distributors. They also purchase all items tested on the open market.

In concluding this discussion, we think the following statement by Kyrk puts the basic point very well:

In essence [financial planning] is the method by which it is sought to insure that the income . . . secures what those who benefit from it want most. . . . It is an attempt over time to maximize the satisfactions derived from the allocation of income among its wide range of alternative uses. The perfect budget is one in which no dollar if moved to another use . . . would enhance the satisfaction derived from the total.[25]

It is obvious that very few (if any) of us will ever achieve the perfect budget, but there is no harm in trying. As the banks say, "The future belongs to those who plan for it."

References

1. C. Hartley Grattan, "Buying on Time: Where Do You Stop?" *Harper's*, May, 1956.

2. See William H. Whyte, Jr., "Budgetism: Opiate of the Middle Class," *Fortune*, May, 1956. Whyte argues that thrift today is un-American.

3. "The $250,000 House," *Fortune*, October, 1955.

4. This information was supplied by the firm of Knodle and Baucom, professional architects, Beloit, Wisconsin.

5. This figure is taken from Marvin B. Sussman, *Sourcebook in Marriage and the Family* (Boston, Houghton Mifflin Co., 1955), p. 154.

6. *Ibid.*

7. FHA report for 1954 summarized by the Associated Press, May 28, 1955.

8. *Ibid.*

9. *Ibid.*

10. 1956 survey of the Milwaukee area published in the *Milwaukee Journal*, April 15, 1956.

11. The following points are based on a lecture given to Sociology 60 (Marriage and the Family) at the University of Wisconsin in 1952 and 1953 by Dean Erwin A. Gaumnitz of the School of Commerce.

12. This table is based on standard insurance rates supplied by Professor Gaumnitz of the University of Wisconsin School of Commerce.

13. B. Malinowski, *Argonauts of the Western Pacific* (London, Routledge-Kegan Paul, 1922).

14. *Ibid.*

15. Associated Press news release written by Sam Dawson, October 5, 1955, based on data supplied by the National Consumer Finance Association.

16. Grattan, *op. cit.*

17. *Ibid.*

18. Dawson, news release cited above.

19. Whyte, *op. cit.*

20. *Ibid.*, p. 133.

21. *Ibid.*

22. These are based on Grattan, *op. cit.*

23. These suggestions are derived largely from the following sources: *Consumer Reports,* monthly publication of Consumers Union of United States, Inc., and *How to Buy More for Your Money* by Sidney Margolius (New York, Doubleday & Co., Inc., 1947).

24. *Op. cit.*

25. Hazel Kyrk, *The Family in the American Economy* (Chicago, University of Chicago Press, 1953), p. 324.

Suggested Readings

1. Hazel Kyrk, *The Family in the American Economy* (Chicago, University of Chicago Press, 1953). This is a classic in its field. Chap. 16, "Planning Expenditure of Income," is especially relevant for our purposes.

2. Sidney Margolius, *How to Buy More for Your Money* (New York, Doubleday & Co., Inc., 1947). This is an eminently readable and very practical book. The author claims that his approach to buying will reduce the cost of almost any item from 10 to 20 per cent.

3. *Buying Guide,* published annually by Consumers Union, 38 East 1st Street, New York 3, N.Y. If the student will read at random in this volume he will gain an insight into the value of consumer publications.

4. J. K. Lasker, *Your Income Tax,* published annually by Simon and Schuster, Inc., New York. This has become the best-seller in its field.

5. *Your Federal Income Tax,* United States Treasury Department, Internal Revenue Service, Publication 17, 25 cents. Revised annually.

6. Lillian M. Gilbreth, Orpha Mae Thomas, and Eleanor Clymer, *Management in the Home* (New York, Dodd, Mead & Co., 1954). This is an extremely well written and practical analysis of family finances and related matters.

CHAPTER XXI

WIVES WHO WORK

Introduction

One of the most difficult decisions facing young married couples today in our society is this: "Should the wife continue her employment after marriage? And if the answer is "Yes," then other questions have to be answered. How long should she work after marriage? Should they postpone having children so that she can work a year or so longer? How should her earnings be spent, if at all? Does working after marriage have a negative effect on marital adjustment? And then the big question must be faced: Is it possible, or desirable, for a wife to continue her job after the first child is born?

These are all vital and legitimate questions in modern marriage. We hope to deal with most of them in this chapter.

Some Historical Perspective

As a man, we must hasten to admit that married women in America, or in any society, have *always* worked. Certainly, the

American colonial wife put in a good long day, with her large family, her household tasks, and her myriad other chores around the homestead.[1] And it scarcely takes any imagination or a history major to realize that the frontier wife, one like Lincoln's mother must have been, was a very busy woman indeed.

However, the employment of the modern American wife-mother is of a different nature. For one thing, her job is *outside* the home, in a factory or office, whereas the work of the wife or mother in our earlier historical periods was usually on the farm. This means that the wife today is usually separated from her husband and children while she works, whereas the farm wife worked with or near other members of the family unit. It sometimes seems to us that this temporary daily separation may have positive value for the members of the modern family, but most books on the family seem to treat this modern pattern as a net loss. This assumes—not neces- sarily correctly so, in our opinion—that those families are stronger which are together most. While we have no way of knowing whether or not this was true of the colonial or frontier families, we have observed many modern marital and familial groups who seemed refreshed rather than weakened by this daily routine. Having been away from one another all day, and having had diverse experiences, the group is glad to be reunited at the end of the day, and they have a wealth of rich personal experience to share. We believe that most of the literature on the American family tends to reflect what is essentially a *rural bias*. Some characteristic of the rural family is selected, compared unfavorably with the related characteristic of the modern urban family, and the impression is left that the family of today has declined.

Let us ask a question: Is it true that the rural or frontier American family was stronger as a social unit because the members spent *all day every day* in close association? Is it not possible for persons to be too much together? Or are we reflecting a modern urban bias at this point?

This is a question not readily answered by reference to cur- rent research. It seems entirely possible, however, that family members can spend too much time together, and that some daily separation may be good for all of them. This is the point of view in a recent article defending the working mother.[2] The author states: "When her office day is done and my wife comes home to the boys, it is a meeting at the summit. . . . My wife is refreshed by the joy of seeing the boys and she is keyed to give them unbegrudgingly her ingenuity and patience. . . ."[3] Let us not assume, therefore, in this discussion, that *all* separations are detrimental to family life.

And so, with this brief aside, we return to the previous point, that in modern society the wife does not usually work alongside her husband or her children; in fact, the children often do not work at all. Whether this daily period of separation represents a net loss or gain for the family as a social unit has not been empirically demonstrated, in our opinion.

Another significant difference in the employment pattern of modern wives is that they work for wages or a salary, whereas formerly they were part of a mutual aid economic unit, such as a farm, and did not receive income as a separate individual. This, too, has been considered from the negative point of view by some writers, on the grounds that the two-income couple of today is not a closely knit economic unit, in that the husband and wife both receive individual pay checks. We also question this assumption and will deal with the point later in the chapter.

Some Facts

Whether men like it or not, whether women like it or not, and whether family sociologists like it or not, the trend toward wives working outside the home is very clear, as the table below indicates.

Note that, while the rate of increase is very uneven from one decade to another, there is only one decade since 1890 which shows a net loss in the percentage of married women working outside the home. This seems to indicate that the trend is not superficial or temporary but one that has deep sources of support in the nature of our society.

A 1955 study revealed that over ten million American wives now work outside the home.[4] This is approximately one out of four.

TABLE 6

EMPLOYED MARRIED WOMEN, UNITED STATES,
1890–1950*

Year	Per Cent Married Women Employed
1890	4.6
1900	5.6
1910	10.7
1920	9.0
1930	11.7
1940	15.2
1950	24.8

*Source: United States Census Bureau Reports.

Interestingly enough, this trend is *not* limited to urban wives but has spread to rural families also. By 1955, 26 per cent of farm wives were holding down outside jobs, perhaps as the result of the decline in farm prices.[5]

Contrary to popular belief, this trend (or revolution) is *not* limited to wives without children: in 1940 only 7 per cent of mothers with preschool children held outside jobs, but by 1955 this had increased to 18.2 per cent.[6] Another comparison puts it this way: since 1948 the percentage of mothers with small children employed outside the home has increased by *66 per cent*.[7] Can anyone still believe that this trend for wives (and mothers) to accept full-time jobs outside the home is temporary or due to the war? On the contrary, it represents a basic change in our marriage and family patterns, many of which are not perceived as yet.

Unfortunately, we have no adequate studies of the part-time employment of wives and/or mothers. Data on this might reveal a much greater trend than appears from information about full-time employment. Judging from our own observations, we guess that partial employment of wife-mothers is prevalent, but we also guess that this poses relatively few problems for families.

We also lack adequate information on the amount of time given on a volunteer basis by American wives. As we show later in this chapter, this may equal or even exceed full-time employment in some cases.

It appears that the general trend in this area of family behavior is well established. We predict that the trend is more likely to increase than decrease. Let us now analyze *why* married women are taking on this added economic role in their families.

Why Do Married Women Work Outside the Home?

We sometimes get the impression that people in the United States think that married women continue to work after their marriage because they *want* to: in other words, because they have a deep drive which compels them to continue punching the time clock long after the wedding bells have rung. The research data do not seem to support this assumption.

In 1939 a study of working wives revealed a very high negative correlation between a husband's income and the chances that his wife would be working outside the home.[8] For example, this study concluded that wives in the lower income levels were five times as likely to be employed as were wives in the middle income groups (in spite of the fact that low-income wives have more children and hence are less free to accept outside work). This, it seems to us, shows that American wives work for about the same reason that their husbands do: they need the money.

A 1951 study of employed wives twenty to forty-four years of age, with no children under eighteen, revealed the following: 55 per cent of the wives whose husbands earned $5,000 or less worked, but only 30 per cent were employed if the husband made $5,000 to $7,000; in the $7,000 to $10,000 income bracket, 8.6

Figure 7: Wives in the Labor Force by Income Level of Husbands,
United States, 1939 *

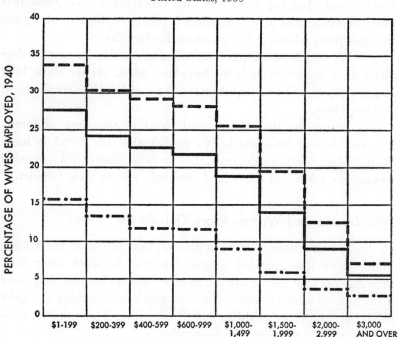

WAGE OR SALARY INCOME OF HUSBANDS IN 1939

━ ━ ━   WIVES WITH NO CHILDREN UNDER TEN YEARS OF AGE
━━━━   ALL WIVES
●━●━   WIVES WITH CHILDREN UNDER TEN YEARS OF AGE

It seems clear that as of 1939 there was a close association between the husband's income and the employment or non-employment of his wife.

* Source: Ruth Cavan, *The American Family* (New York, Thomas Y. Crowell Company, 1953), p. 19. Used by permission of the publisher.

per cent of the wives worked; and, surprisingly enough, in the $10,000 and up group, the percentage of wives employed *increased* to 21.1 per cent.[9] It appears that while most wives work for money, there are also noneconomic factors involved, just as one would expect to find in a study of why men work.

But, we may ask, do they need the money to survive, or to

live on a higher economic plane? The Lynds investigated this question in their two classic studies, *Middletown* and *Middletown in Transition,* surveys of a Midwestern urban community.[10] In general, they found that their employed mothers were working outside the home in order to enjoy a standard of living which otherwise their families could not attain. They wanted a nicer home for the family, a better car, perhaps a college education for the children. *Fortune* puts it this way: ". . . the American standard of living has become a built-in automatic 'drive' on the part of the American wife." [11] In other words, she works to earn money.

It appears that most American families feel that they could use more income. This is not hard to understand. We saw in the two previous chapters that our entire American economy depends on the desire of the population for a constantly expanding standard of living. In fact, the advertising in our mass media is planned to create desire for items that most of our families cannot *at the moment* afford. These are things that you and I will want for our children or our families next year, or the year after that. In this way, the family unit is exposed daily to very desirable things that the father's income will not permit the group to have. These things are not necessarily material items or household gadgets but include college educations, better medical care, finer homes, and more wonderful summer vacations for the whole family group.

Now, if we assume that the father's income is relatively fixed, it follows that there are really only two basic ways in which the family can resolve this dilemma: (1) give up the higher standard of living, or (2) the mother can seek a job. Statistics since World Wars I and II seem to indicate that the first alternative is less American than is the second.

Another alternative trend is for the father to have *two* jobs, this being made possible by the shorter work week. For those who oppose the outside employment of wives and mothers, it is essential to remember that the alternative for many couples is for the husband to get a second job. In some ways, this may be even more destructive of family life than is the wife's outside employment, judging by case studies by the writer. More will be said about this later.

Looking at this from a very broad point of view, it appears that the American family of the future will not only have two cars in every garage but two breadwinners in every home.

Figure 8: Employment Status of Married Women, United States, 1910–1949 *

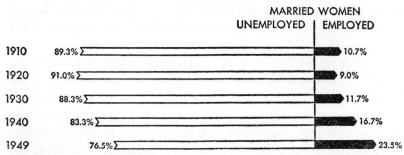

Here we see the long range trend for married women to work outside the home. The complete impact of this movement on the American family is not clear as yet.

* Source: Ruth Cavan, *The American Family* (New York, Thomas Y. Crowell Company, 1953), p. 105. Used by permission of the publisher.

Should Wives Work?

Sociologists are inclined to believe that behavior in our society—probably in any dynamic society—tends to change more rapidly than the moral sanctions supporting behavior. In other words, the ideology that will eventually justify the new behavior has not yet been developed, or at least not incorporated into the official moral system of the group. Essentially, this is a form of culture lag, a theory developed by W. F. Ogburn,[12] which holds that parts of a social system tend to change at differential rates, thus creating lag or maladaptation between the different parts of the system.

Seen from this point of view, the very clear trend for American married women to accept outside employment has created a culture conflict between the traditional economic roles of the married woman, which was to help her husband by excelling in supportive economic roles in the home (such as being thrifty) and her new economic role. Until the new pattern has become fully built into the ideology and mores of our culture, there will continue to be debate as to whether or not a wife should give up her job when she marries.

Back about 1900, when the first brave little band of wives went marching off to the offices and factories, there was essentially the spirit of the *pioneer* in this movement. The women who worked after the wedding bells had stopped tolling were fighting for a cause, the right of the wife or mother to work after marriage, if she wished to. Very likely these women had a good measure of the rebel in them and enjoyed their role of forging a new culture pattern. However, we suspect that the working wife of today has very little of the revolutionary spirit in her make-up. We doubt that the moral issue as to whether or not married women should work even exists for her. She works for the same reason that her husband does, which is, simply, to earn money for her family. She may enjoy her work, of course, as her husband may also enjoy his, but this is not the basic reason why she keeps her job. In a small study by the writer, roughly three fourths of 128 working wives said they would give up their jobs "tomorrow" if their families didn't need the money.[13] We suspect that the percentage would not be far different for husbands.

In this sense, the question, "Should wives work?" is no longer a sensible question. One might just as well ask, "Should husbands work?"

However, the situation regarding *mothers* working outside the home appears to be entirely different. There still seems to be great opposition to the mother devoting herself to a full-time job, especially if her children are very young. A survey made in the author's classes covering 249 young men and women, most of them from comfortable economic backgrounds, found both sexes to be overwhelmingly against (78 and 84 per cent respectively) a mother with preschool children working full time outside the home.[14] The same group, however, felt that it was entirely a personal matter whether a girl worked after her marriage before having children. In other words, the latter question had ceased to be a moral issue as far as this group was concerned, whereas the question of a mother working continued to be a moral issue.

Figure 9: Per Cent of All Women of Various Age Groups in the Labor Force, United States *

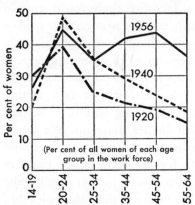

The outstanding trend in this chart is that of the older woman and her greater participation in the labor force in recent decades.

* Daniel Bell, "The Great Back-to-Work Movement," *Fortune,* July, 1956. Chart used by permission.

This matter of attitudes toward working mothers will bear some analysis.

Attitudes Toward Working Mothers

It is our contention that Americans at the present time tend to be ambivalent toward working mothers. On the one hand, they feel that children need their mothers, but on the other hand our economy needs mothers too. Our traditional attitudes tend to condemn the working mother—except the heroic widow struggling to support her large brood—but at the same time our modern economic system could not win wars or maintain high consumption levels without her. There seems to be considerable doubt, for example, that our economy could have produced to full capacity during both World War I and World War II if millions of mothers had not joined the labor force. Note that in both of these great crises in our society, mothers were urged, for good patriotic reasons, to forsake the kitchen sink for the welder's bench. But as soon as the wars are over, or as soon as economic recession sets in, the traditional attitudes become dominant again and people begin to feel that mothers should not work.

The fact is, however, that our economy would suffer a severe blow if working mothers were to withdraw from the labor force. Not only do we need their productive manpower, but our families have to have these double incomes to maintain their standard of living. Our installment sales owe a significant proportion of their volume to these working mothers. In the 1955 study cited above by the United States Census Bureau, it was discovered that the farm family *with a working wife* had "a median income 60 per cent larger than the family in which the wife did not pick up a pay check." [15] This reveals how crucial the double income can be in the current American economy.

It is our belief that husbands, relatives, neighbors, and the general public tend to reflect mixed emotions toward the working mother. As a matter of fact, the mother herself may feel the same way—glad at one moment that she *can* work, guilty at the next moment that she *does* work. Perhaps a case illustration will help at this point. We know a woman physician whose practice takes most of her time. Since this woman is also the mother of a small child, she has had to employ various persons to care for the youngster. At one time the author's child was attending a nursery school where the physician's child was also enrolled. In various discussions with the director of the school, it became clear that the director did not approve of this mother continuing her medical career. It was implied that the mother was being selfish and neglecting her child. The evidence the director cited to support her position was that the child was "maladjusted." We pointed out that some of the other children in this school, most of them from university faculty families, were not exactly outstanding in their social adjustment either, although most of their mothers did not work. This did not seem to impress the director. It had to be that the mother's working was *the cause* of the child's difficulties.

But note that here was a mother with elaborate and very expensive training, most of it with the full approval of society and partially at society's expense, in a field in which trained persons are badly needed, being condemned for practicing her profession. This, it seems to us, shows that the mother who chooses to work at the present time in our society will have to face many dilemmas, some of them insoluble as of now.

Is the Working Couple an Interdependent Economic Unit?

Historically, it can be shown that marriage in most human societies has involved fairly close economic co-operation between married partners. Nimkoff and others have stressed this in their analysis of the American colonial family of the seventeenth and eighteenth centuries.[16] The family, in that type of rural-frontier setting, was a sort of factory, producing and consuming a wide variety of economic goods. The operators of the factory, of course, were the married couple, plus their children and any relatives who might be living with the family. We happen to believe that this factory family has been highly idealized in American family sociology, but certainly it was a closely knit economic unit. It has been charged, by various writers in this field, that the modern family, and especially the two-income working couple type of family, is not an interdependent economic unit. We wish to challenge this point of view.

Actually, we think it can be shown that the modern working couple comprise a very highly integrated economic unit. They are both engaged in productive economic effort, just as the farm couple were in our earlier historical periods. They usually pool their income, just as the farm couple did. Inside the home, as Dyer's study shows, they share a number of activities, such as cooking, cleaning, shopping, all of which are at least semi-economic in nature.[17] If there are children of working age, they usually contribute their share toward making the unit effective.

What makes a group economically interdependent? We submit that one test is whether or not the members of the group can survive economically better as a member of the group or outside it. Our observation of working couples is that they live on a high plane, much higher than either of them could manage singly. In this sense, it seems to us, the working couple are economically interdependent: they need each other to maintain the level of living to which they have become accustomed.

It is true, of course, that either the man or the woman could *survive* economically if he or she chose to dissolve the partnership, but this was also true of the colonial family. A husband, in those early days, could always secede from his family if he so desired and join the westward migration, and a girl could always (or nearly always) move in with kinfolk if she so wished, or go into domestic service, or get another husband. With the shortage of women existing in those days, it was a very foolish man indeed who would leave his wife, unless she was completely impossible.

This modern family economic unit has been criticized, or held to be loosely organized, because it does not produce its own soap, make its own clothes, or brew its own medicine. This, it seems to us, is a rather silly type of criticism. We doubt very much that an American male in 1700 was dependent on his wife just because she kept him supplied with lye soap, any more than the modern male is tied to his wife because she keeps a supply of his favorite bath soap in the linen closet. From our point of view, both of these two types of wives and husbands are interdependent in the sense that they share economic activities, do things for each other, and live better as a pair than they could as single persons. The colonial man could also whip up a batch of soap if he had to, just as the modern man can stop at the supermarket and buy his own soap if necessary. But in both cases it is nice to have a wife to do this for you. Colonial wives and modern wives both could no doubt do many things for themselves which their men usually have done for them, but this does not mean that such wives are not members of closely knit marital unions. The basic test is whether or not we can live fuller lives within the marital group or outside it. In this sense we submit that the modern working couple represents a very tightly knit unit.

Kyrk, one of the authorities in this field, takes the same point of view. She writes:

> Far too sweeping statements have often been made regarding the former degree of self-sufficiency of the husband-wife, parents-children group. Further, the economic functions of the family have been identified with its productive function, leading to the conclusion that as its productive activity declined so did its economic significance. Actually the economic significance of the family arises not only from the tasks the members perform for and with one another but from the rights and obligations that the family relationship entails. The family may be less and less a productve unit, but it remains to no less an extent than before a unit of mutual responsibility. The size of the group whose members have mutual claims and obligations may have diminished and their relationship changed, but the family as an institution continues and performs its usual functions in this respect.[18]

It seems to us that the current marriage rate in the United States, now at or near its peak in our history, tends to support this analysis. If single persons could live more easily or better in modern society, one would expect to find some sort of decline in marriage rates. The tendency for divorced persons to remarry is also in line with our point of view, we believe.

Divorce Rate of Working Couples

If we grant the correctness of the preceding discussion and conclude that the working couple are a closely knit economic unit, it might still be asked: Isn't it true that the divorce rate is higher for marriages in which both spouses work? This is usually alleged to be the case, although it should be kept in mind that the research data on divorce in our society, strange as this may seem, are by no means adequate. But, even if we assume that working couples do have abnormally high divorce rates, does it necessarily follow that the basic factor involved is the employment of wives? We think not. For example, it is possible that the *childless* working couple pushes up the divorce rate for this group, in which case the basic variable would be the presence or absence of children, not the wife's outside employment.

It might also be true that divorce rates could be higher for working couples because, as a group, their marriages are not very old, and we know that the highest incidence of divorce comes in the first five years of marriage. Thus, a great many wives work only until children start to come, so that an abnormally large proportion of working couples not only are childless (because their family has not yet been started), but they are also more or less newlyweds, persons married less than five years. These two factors alone could account for any excess of divorces that working couples may show.

There is also a good possibility that the divorce statistics are themselves misleading. For example, a woman who decides to divorce her husband usually begins to look for work in anticipation of the whole or partial loss of her husband's support. In view of the fact that there is usually a lapse of several months between the time of actual separation and the final divorce action, most wives would be forced to go out and find a job to survive during this interlude. Then, when the divorce records are analyzed, it is found that both the husband and wife were employed *at the time of the divorce*. However, it is not known whether or not both spouses were employed during the period in which the marriage actually failed. This type of knowledge, it seems to us, is crucial before we can determine the role of the wife's outside employment in the causation of the divorce.

It might be pointed out that Locke, in his excellent study of happily married and divorced couples in Indiana, did not find the employment of wives to be a significant factor in marital success or failure.

In a more recent study by Goode, it was found that outside employment by the wife seemed to be characteristic of the divorced women in the sample.[19] Whether or not the wife's employment was a basic factor in this group of marital failures was not too clear. Goode makes this comment: "American family research has not yet disclosed the impact of the wife's job-holding upon the marriage."[20]

We do not mean to imply that the wife's working in our society *may* not be related to marital failure. Our point is that a number of factors (educational level, age at marriage, etc.) are very likely involved in the marital problems of this group. We shall see later (Chapter XXVI) that social class membership is closely related to marital instability in our society, and working couples tend to come from the lower social class levels. Essentially, we are taking the position that the wife's employment has not been *proved* to be a decisive factor in marital failure.

We are now ready to examine some of the problems of the two-income couple.

Financial Dilemmas of the Working Couple

One of the problems of the working couple is their tendency to become accustomed to a rather generous income before the husband's economic position warrants it. This may produce a difficult adjustment if they are forced to reduce their standard of living when the wife gives up her position to bear a child. We wish to point out, however, that there are a number of factors that will determine when and if the double income becomes a problem. These are as follows:

a. If the double income is unusually large, which could be the case if the wife's earning power is large—which it usually is not. This type of couple, of course, may wish not to give up the wife's income and seek some other solution.

b. If the wife's income is curtailed rather suddenly, as in the case of an illness. This might catch them with large installment payments or other financial obligations beyond the husband's income. Sometimes an unplanned pregnancy may operate in this fashion, although in this eventuality the wife can usually continue working for several months, allowing them to reduce their financial commitments.

c. If the double income is spent each month on current items, rather than being devoted, at least in part, to savings or the purchase of capital investment items, such as a home or heavy appliances. This is the sort of couple that may develop tastes too rich for the man's earning capacity. Many couples avoid this pitfall by using the husband's income for monthly costs and limiting the use of the wife's salary to savings or long-range investment purchases.

d. If the man's income is already at or near its maximum level while the wife is employed, then the couple may have problems when she quits. This, however, would seldom be true of middle-class college couples, most of whom would follow the pattern of having the wife work during the early period of the marriage while the husband was completing his professional training or establishing himself in his occupation. For a great many of these couples, the man's income would gradually come to equal or exceed what he and his wife formerly earned.

Unfortunately, we do not know of any competent research on these points, but it seems that none of these financial problems need be a great obstacle to the working couple. On the contrary, we predict that couples in which the wife *does not* work would show far more severe financial crises than do working couples. These latter, if they have any problems, are apt to have them in other areas of marriage. Let us turn to one of these.

Homemaking Problems of the Working Couple

We think it may be stated at the outset that most wives who are college graduates do not seem to dote on the routine aspects of housework, the dishwashing, the cleaning, washing clothes, ironing, and similar housekeeping chores. Maids who perform these duties in our society are not highly paid, nor are they required to have college degrees. It may even be true that the best household maids in our society are women with less than high school education. In any event, it is not too hard to understand that college-educated wives dislike routine household chores.

Thus, it seems to us, we may assume that wives who work are not the only middle-class women who have homemaking problems. Insofar as the cleaning and related tasks are concerned, we believe there is plenty of evidence that middle-class wives *as a group* tend to be maladjusted in this role.[21]

However, the wife who works finds herself in an odd social position: she has assumed a full-time economic breadwinner role while retaining her homemaker role, which for millions of American wives is a full-time job in itself. Thus, unless adjustments are made somewhere, by *someone*, the wife-worker will find herself with a grueling 12- to 15-hour day.

What is the solution to this knotty dilemma? The key, it seems, is the attitude of the husband toward sharing some of the homemaking tasks. In other words, whether the distribution of home chores is flexible. If the husband is a traditionalist, he will continue to expect his wife to do the shopping, cooking, dishes, cleaning, and all the rest. This sort of man, of course, should never permit his wife to work, but sometimes he does. The wife of such a man will usually be overworked and most likely will resent her husband's attitude.

If, however, the husband is consistently "modern" in his attitudes he will expect to help with the homemaking role in many different ways. For example, a study of married students at the University of Texas following the Second World War revealed that the typical husband of a working wife helped with food shopping, did some of the cooking, cleaned the apartment and even did the washing.[22] This, it seems is the pattern that is emerging as more and more wives continue working after marriage.

In a study of 129 two-income couples, Dyer discovered a definite trend toward partnership role performance in these family units.[23] This increased sharing of household tasks between husbands and wives may be one of the hidden gains resulting from the outside employment of married women.

In another interesting study, it was reported that employed wives organize their household chores more efficiently than do nonemployed wives. The report states: ". . . we have found that women who work at a full-time job away from home all day tackle their housework the same way they do their office work. They organize it efficiently and don't get bogged down in it." [24]

In the *Fortune* survey cited earlier, it was pointed out that a U-shaped curve describes the new employment history of the American woman: that is, she goes to work in large numbers while she is single (eighteen to twenty years of age), and remains on the job after marriage until starting her family (twenty to twenty-four); then she drops out of the employment picture until her children are well started in school (twenty-five to thirty-four), after which she resumes working (thirty-five to fifty-four).

What we are witnessing here, of course, is a merging of the male and female roles in our society. As the wife goes into the factory or office to help her husband support the family, the husband dons the kitchen apron, or mans the vacuum sweeper, to aid his wife with the household tasks. It seems to us that couples of this sort are going to emerge as some of the strongest family units in American society. These couples have flexibility and adaptability, traits that seem to be crucial for successful marriage in modern, turbulent society.

If our preceding discussion has any validity, it seems to follow that the marriage patterns being developed by the working couples in the United States may eventually emerge as the dominant patterns. In a sense, this is real equality of the sexes. Perhaps it is time that America began to respect these working couples instead of regarding them with mixed emotions. It may well be that this is the type of marriage partnership which can best withstand the pressures of modern living.

The Two-Job Husband

It is becoming increasingly clear, we think, that the average American family cannot sustain the standard of living the advertisers think it should have (or that the economy requires) on one paycheck. This means that either the wife has to work or the husband has to earn more money, unless the family wishes to lower its standard of living, a rather unpopular and somewhat unlikely possibility. To those who oppose the wife's working, we would like to suggest that the other solution to the problem (the husband's attempt to earn more money) may be even *less* desirable. Let us look briefly at the two-job husband.

The writer has no statistics on this pattern, but it appears to be fairly common. Here are some case illustrations:

1. A college professor works downtown five nights a week. He says his family cannot live on his college salary.

2. A high school teacher works at a supermarket from 5 to 10 every evening, plus all day on Saturday.

3. A meter-reader for a public utility works as a bartender six nights a week from 6 P.M. to midnight.

4. A store clerk manages a service-station from 7 to 12 six nights a week.

5. A married student at a college attends classes all day, then works in a factory until one o'clock in the morning.

These are only a few of the cases known to the writer. While some of these jobs might be called part-time, they often total 30 to 40 hours a week. All these men state that they could not meet their obligations unless they held two jobs. In almost every case, the wife is unable to work because of pregnancy or the presence of small preschool children. One of these men has recently been warned by his physician to give up his second job. So far, he has refused to do this.

What kind of family life do these men have? Our case studies, admittedly only exploratory in nature, are not very encouraging. The children see very little of the father, and the wife not much more. The husband-wife relationships appear to be inadequate. The husbands feel that they are in a rat race, as indeed they are.

It is admitted that the writer lacks adequate data on these families in which the husband-father has two jobs. But our preliminary case studies lead us to suspect that this attempt to balance the American family budget may be more destructive of marriage and family life values than is the outside employment of the wife-mother. This is a matter that deserves more attention than it has received to date.

Married Women Who Do Not Work

From our preceding discussion, it may appear that the cards are stacked against wives and/or mothers who work for wages or salaries outside of the home. This, however, is not necessarily the case. Let us look for a moment at the situation of the married woman who does not work.

For the past five years, the writer has been studying women who have given up their careers to "marry and retire." [25] To date, 56 of these middle-class women, all of whom have one or more children at home, have been studied. Out of the total group, 44, or approximately 79 per cent, feel that they have made a poor adjustment to their new career of homemaking and child-rearing. In other words, these women *who don't work* have their problems too. Let us try to see why it is that these women have troubles also.

In the first place, these women *miss their jobs*. This should not be too hard to understand. Most of us, if we enjoy our work, feel lost if we are separated from the job for any length of time. This was painfully evident to social workers during the depression of the 1930's as they observed the maladjustment of unemployed men. The writer himself interviewed hundreds of such men. The same problems have been observed in men as they face retirement after a lifetime spent in some factory or office. The women surveyed in our study show some of the same symptoms. They miss their companions at the office. Staying at home all day with small children, they miss adult companionship while the husband is away at work. They miss their weekly or monthly pay check. In a culture as materialistic as ours, this is no small loss. If they really enjoyed their jobs, then they miss the pleasure and satisfaction known to all who have ever enjoyed their work. Interestingly enough, one of our conclusions from this study is this: that women adjust to housekeeping, home management, and child-rearing in inverse proportion to the degree of enjoyment they received from their premarital occupation.

Many of the women in our study actually envied married women who had continued their outside employment. A majority of the women interviewed did not feel that they were doing an outstanding job as homemaker or child-rearer, many of them believing that they had been more efficient in their premarital economic roles.

Space will not permit us to discuss all the findings of this study.[26] Our main point is simply to challenge the generally accepted proposition that married women who give up their outside work are necessarily better adjusted in their marital and familial roles than are those women who try to combine family life and outside employment.

The Volunteer

Up to this point we have been analyzing the conflicts and pressures on women who work outside the home for wages or a salary. We think it essential now to indicate that women who volunteer their services to various community organizations may have identical problems; in fact, we have known situations in which their problems were even worse, partly because there is no 40-hour week for the volunteer. Unless she has the courage to say "No," she may find herself putting in 60 or 70 hours a week for different community groups.

Looking at these volunteers, we can see the weakness in the information, given earlier in this chapter, which revealed that the outside employment of wives tends to be associated with the husband's income. The weakness, of course, is that the table tells us nothing about the outside volunteer work of the middle- and upperclass women. Our experience indicates that these women have pressure and conflict also. Superficially, it may seem that these women are not obliged to engage in this outside work; that they are free of the social pressure that forces women of more modest income levels to work outside the home. This, we think, is not necessarily true. Social scientists, as well as other observers of our society, are well aware of the fact that informal pressures of various kinds can be and are applied to make persons "volunteer" for community service. College students are well aware of this too as a rule. The following case illustration will illustrate our major point in this discussion.

Case study of a "volunteer": The wife of a promising young dentist in a medium-sized city was asked by a certain woman in the community to accept the chairmanship of a drive to organize a clinic for crippled children in the city. The dentist's wife, a very capable woman, was inclined not to accept. Having two young boys, she found her time fairly well occupied. However, she hesitated to decline, partly because she was very fond of the prominent woman who had asked her to undertake the assignment. Furthermore, both she and her husband knew that community service of this type would be good for his professional practice, which was not yet fully developed. In addition, the wife had had some experience in this sort of work in another community (a fact known to the woman asking her to serve), and she felt confident that she could do the job well. And, lastly, she was interested in programs of this sort for crippled children. After considerable hesitation, the result of her fear that the project might take too much of her time, and after gaining her husband's support, she accepted. We think that one of the main reasons why she accepted was her desire not to disappoint the woman who had asked her, this person being very wealthy and influential in the city, plus being a very dear friend. We will leave it up to the reader to decide whether this woman volunteered for this nonpaying job or whether she was drafted.

In any event, the drive to raise funds for the new clinic proved to be a bigger job than anyone had anticipated (which seems to be typical of these volunteer positions) and the chairman soon found herself forced to work night and day, seven days a week, to keep the project from failing. She was forced to neglect her husband and children, especially at crucial points in the drive. Finally, as the pressure mounted, her husband became critical of the situation and asked her to resign. This produced a crisis in the marital relationship, which had never been too strong at any time.

The wife, by now, was frantic. Her pride, her desire to please her prominent friend, her dedication to the welfare of crippled children—all these made it impossible for her to resign until the campaign had been successfully concluded. When we interviewed her to discuss the marital crisis, this woman was under tremendous pressure.

We submit that this type of pressure is not at all rare for the woman active in various community causes. In a meeting with doctors' wives this past year, we were impressed by the pressure that *most* of them were under in their various community roles. As we indicated earlier, the paid worker has more protection than the volunteer against excessive hours. She also may have more sympathy and support from her husband, in that he can see the sense of his wife's working (they usually need the money), whereas the husband of the volunteer may feel that his wife is wasting her time.

It can be argued, of course, that the volunteer may have domestic help to assist her at home, but this is easy to overestimate. For example, in the group of doctors' wives referred to above, only two out of twenty-seven had full-time domestic servants. The rest had a cleaning woman one day a week, with a few also having help with the laundry. This is in line with the general trend for servants to disappear from most American homes.

In concluding this discussion, we have merely been trying to question the assumption, which we believe to be widely held, that it is the working wife who has the problems in modern American marriage. Our thesis is that wives who do not work have their troubles too; furthermore, that the well-to-do volunteers may also have to neglect their families occasionally.

Our Communities and the Working Mother

It seems to us that many of the problems of the working mother in our society can be traced to the fact that our communities are not designed for such mothers. To put it another way, our communities are organized for the convenience of mothers who do *not* work, rather than for those who do. Let us look at this point in more detail.

The following conditions seem to be to the disadvantage of the working mother in most (if not all) of our American communities.

1. Public school patterns: Our public schools do not accept children until they are five or six, depending on whether or not the local school system includes a kindergarten program. And since most five-year-olds attend for only half a day, a child must really be six before attending school becomes much of an aid to a working mother. This means that the mother has to find other ways of caring for the child during the day for a period of six years, a very difficult task.

Furthermore, the school day is not designed to help the working mother. The hour of 8:30 or 8:45, the time at which most urban schools begin in the morning, is too late for the working mother, since she usually has to leave for work before that time. Then, at the end of the day, school usually is over at 3:00 or 3:30, at least two hours, and probably three, before the mother can get home from her job.

The long school vacations, while nice for the teachers, create a serious problem for working mothers. Counting the summer recess, the child may be out of school about four months during the year. This makes it very hard for the working mother, unless she herself is a teacher.

It is well known, of course, that our basic school year pattern was developed for rural farm families and that it is poorly planned for the urban family. This is especially true of the urban family in which the mother is employed outside the home.

2. Privately operated nursery schools, as a rule, adhere to about the same hours as the public schools, also to the same vacation schedule. Furthermore, the fees of these schools are often prohibitive.

3. Working hours in stores and offices are not designed for

the convenience of the working mother. Usually, she has to be there too early and stay too late. The hours to be worked are often not flexible enough to meet her family's needs, such as the illness of a child. She may have to work full time or not at all, when she would really prefer half time or perhaps three-quarter time. Except for periods of extreme shortage of personnel, she can seldom arrange working hours to the complete satisfaction of her family.

4. Very few American employers, even our largest employers, provide any nursery care for small children, although this has become standard practice in such countries as Russia and Israel. Employers who have tried offering such facilities in the United States have found that the service makes it much easier to attract married women with small children.

5. Our state and federal income tax laws, with few exceptions, penalize the working mother by not permitting her to deduct added expense incurred as the result of her outside employment. The federal laws, however, are now being altered somewhat in this respect.

6. Last, but not least, the negative attitudes expressed toward the working mother. These have been discussed earlier in the chapter and we need not analyze them again.

Thus, we see that our society is not yet ready for the working mother. Our supermarkets and other stores have adjusted their shopping hours to accommodate her, but our nonprofit service agencies, such as our schools, have not yet recognized that the working mother exists. This is what Ogburn means by "culture lag." [27]

Planning for Wife's Employment After Marriage or Parenthood

If a girl believes that she will probably continue to work after marriage, or after becoming a mother, it is possible to plan intelligently for the combined career of wife-mother-breadwinner. Here are a few general principles, all of them based on interviews with employed wives.

1. Try to avoid jobs that will put very much pressure on

you. Employed wives are emphatic in their belief that such positions are especially dangerous for women whose first obligation is to the husband and/or children.

2. By all means choose an occupation that will give you at least Saturday and Sunday free for yourself and your family. In particular, try to avoid jobs that involve Saturday morning work or overtime on short notice. Just a few hours a week can be very important to the employed wife.

3. Try to select an occupation in which there is an acute (and long-time) shortage of trained persons, as this will permit you to be more selective in regard to hours, salary, time off, and many other working conditions important to married women. At the moment there are several excellent fields in which relatively permanent shortages exist, including nursing, social work, teaching, and secretarial work. Scarcity also permits mobility, which is important to wives also.

4. Be very careful *where you live* if you plan to work after children arrive. Avoid suburbs in particular. Residential areas that provide good public transportation may mean the difference between having a cleaning woman and not having one. It also will make it possible for you to get home on evenings when your husband may have to stay at the office. Availability of nursery schools or other schools is crucial. So is easy access to good shopping facilities. For many employed couples, an apartment or duplex may have real advantages over the single dwelling. Presence or absence of good baby-sitter material may also be related to the neighborhood you select.

The above four principles were reiterated over and over again in our interviews with employed mothers.

Conclusion

It is hard for Americans to accept fully the employed wife, yet her numbers are increasing and, like television, she appears to be here to stay. Indeed, the car dealers, the appliance salesmen, and a great many employers would be lost without her.

She has been viewed with alarm by at least two generations of ministers, social workers, and sociologists. As Bell states in the *Fortune* survey cited earlier: ". . . a whole host of pathologies, from rising delinquency to increasing divorce, is being charged to working women. Yet there is no evidence that these presumed social disorganizations are really caused by women working." [28]

The writer believes that the time has come to face the facts of life about employed wives and mothers, that we should attempt to revise our thinking and see how these married women can be aided, rather than hindered, in juggling their various roles.

References

1. For a good description of this, see Meyer Nimkoff, *Marriage and the Family* (Boston, Houghton Mifflin Co., 1947), pp. 68–82. Another excellent account is to be found in Stuart A. Queen and John B. Adams, *The Family in Various Cultures* (Philadelphia, J. B. Lippincott Co., 1952), chap. 12.

2. David Yellin, "I'm Married to a Working Mother," *Harper's*, July, 1956.

3. *Ibid.*, p. 36.

4. United States Census Bureau publicity release, published July 5, 1956 by the NEA news service.

5. *Ibid.*

6. These figures were taken from an excellent article on employed women by Daniel Bell, "The Great Back-to-Work Movement," *Fortune*, July, 1956.

7. *Ibid.*

8. This study is summarized in *The American Family* (U.S. Government Printing Office, 1949), p. 64.

9. See Bell, *op. cit.*

10. Robert S. Lynd and Helen Lynd, *Middletown* (New York, Harcourt, Brace & Co., 1929), also *Middletown in Transition* by the same authors and the same publisher, 1937.

11. Bell, *op. cit.*, p. 93.

12. This theory is developed in W. F. Ogburn, *Social Change* (New York, B. W. Huebsch, 1922).

13. Unpublished survey conducted in Madison, Wisconsin, 1952.

14. Survey of students in marriage courses, 1954–56. This sample was predominantly upper middle class in background.

15. NEA news release cited above.

16. See Nimkoff, *op. cit.*, also Queen and Adams, *op. cit.*

17. Everett D. Dyer, "A Study of Role and Authority Patterns and Expectations in a Group of Urban Middle-Class Two-Income Families," unpublished Ph.D. dissertation (Madison, University of Wisconsin Library, 1955).

18. Hazel Kyrk, *The Family in the American Economy* (Chicago, University of Chicago Press, 1953), pp. 4–5.

19. William J. Goode, *After Divorce* (Glencoe, The Free Press, 1956), pp. 71–74.

20. *Ibid.*, p. 71.

21. Considerable evidence to support this point of view has been presented by *The Ladies Home Journal* in an excellent series of case studies, "How Young America Lives," published in various issues during 1954–56.

22. Cited in Dyer, *op. cit.*

23. Unpublished doctoral dissertation cited above.

24. Survey conducted by the Lewyt vacuum cleaner firm, published in the *Beloit Daily News*, December 2, 1954.

25. This is a study of professional women who retired from their professions to have a family.

26. It is hoped to publish this material in the near future.

27. *Op. cit.*

28. Bell, *op. cit.*, p. 172.

Suggested Readings

1. David Yellin, "I'm Married to a Working Mother," *Harper's*, July, 1956. This is the most eloquent defense of the working wife-mother we have seen.

2. Daniel Bell, "The Great Back-to-Work Movement," *Fortune*, July, 1956. Most of the relevant data in this social revolution are collected in this study.

3. W. F. Ogburn and M. F. Nimkoff, *Technology and the Changing Family* (Boston, Houghton Mifflin Co., 1955), chap. 7, "More Working Wives." This is a very worthwhile summary of the material related to this trend.

4. Robert S. and Helen Merrell Lynd, *Middletown in Transition* (New York, Harcourt, Brace & Co., 1937), chap. 2, "Getting a Living," pp. 54–73.

5. Robert S. and Helen Merrell Lynd, *Middletown* (New York, Harcourt, Brace & Co., 1929), chap. 8, "Why Do They Work So Hard?"

CHAPTER XXII

HOW THE OTHER HALF LIVES: SUBCULTURE OF THE MALE

Introduction

In this chapter and the next, it is proposed to examine what we prefer to call male and female subcultures and their roles in marital interaction. It is a fact that boys and girls in most societies, including our own, spend the first ten to fifteen years of their lives in relatively distinct social worlds; it is also a fact that in marriage these two social worlds, which by then have been internalized in the personalities of the husband and wife, have to be fused, at least in part. In these two chapters, we wish to look at this fusion process and to examine its complexities.

In this first chapter, our attention is focused on the subculture of "the male animal," as Thurber and Nugent have labeled it,[1] but in the next chapter we turn the microscope on the female. Being a member of the masculine sex, the writer may be somewhat biased in his analysis, but an attempt will be made to be objective.

It should be clearly understood that we are not implying that all men are alike; on the contrary, men differ considerably, as do women, in the extent to which they reflect the subculture of their sex. Essentially, we are claiming that the *average* male will reflect the patterns to be described more consistently than would the *average* woman. After all, Russians are not all alike, but it is still true that Russia does possess a somewhat distinctive way of life. That is all we claim for male and female subculture.

Some General Observations on Male and Female Differences

We are all aware of physical differences between men and women, but we may be less aware of differences due to the separate social worlds experienced and occupied by men and women in our society. For example, we have interviewed unhappily married women who have complained about behavior on the part of their husbands that was almost universally characteristic of male behavior in America. One woman in particular objected to her husband's preferring to hunt (bears, in this case) with his old football buddies rather than to take his wife along as companion on such excursions into the woods. We suspect that this woman does not understand the American male very well, or her husband, either. We submit that her husband's behavior in this situation reflects the basic subculture of the American male at this point in our cultural evolution. Our point, in other words, is that this Mrs. *X* is complaining, basically, that she does not like American *men,* not just her husband. To put it another way, she is objecting to her husband's being normal.

We will admit, of course, that there are some husbands in our heterogeneous society who *do* prefer hunting bears with their wives (in fact, we know such a man), but we submit that such husbands are not typical in this era and that they are not easy to find.

From another point of view, the wife in this case is most likely atypical herself, in that *most* American wives today do not accompany their husbands on bear-hunting excursions.

The basic principle underlying this discussion is that there is a male subculture in every society, including our own, and that women will understand men in general, and their husbands in particular, much better if they have some realistic knowledge of and insight into this subculture.

Going back very briefly to our bear-hunting illustration, we submit that historically, in our society as well as in most others, hunting parties have been male prerogatives, and that there has developed a whole hunting complex that is essentially unknown to most women. It is true that some American women have been admitted to this part of the man's world, but we must not assume that this merging of the male and female social worlds (or subcultures) is by any means complete. Nor must we assume that *all* American men are happy about this merging process, or that all women are equally interested in participating in the man's world. In the marital situation under discussion, the problem (or conflict) developed out of the fact that the man was much more traditional than his wife in his attitudes toward females moving into male areas of behavior.

All this illustrates how rapid social change in modern America complicates courtship and marital adjustment. In this case, the wife's attitudes toward hunting and similar male activities were changing more rapidly than were those of her husband.

Sources of the Sexual Subcultures

The question might be asked: What is the source of these subcultures? Are these differences innate, because of hereditary factors, or do they develop from repetitive differences in male and female experiences in society? Margaret Mead has devoted many years to the attempt to answer this question, and her basic conclusion seems to be that most of the differences are the result of differential conditioning of boys and girls from birth on through adolescence and maturity.[2] From the point of view of this course, it really does not matter whether these differences are biological or cultural or both; the main point for us is that *the differences exist* and that they affect marital adjustment in our society.

It may help to point out that the greater part of the young person's life prior to marriage is spent in the company of his (or her) own sex. This may be less true in our society than in some others. Our educational system, for example, is more coeducational than has been the case in England. But does this mean that boys and girls, at any grade in school, actually inhabit the same social world? We argue that it does not. The two worlds may *overlap* more in America than they do in societies less modern, but it seems to us that the male and female subcultures continue to exist to a substantial degree, even in the United States of the twentieth century.

Some proof of this, it seems, can be seen (or felt) in the amazed reaction of the American public to the case of Christine Jorgensen. People seemed completely flabbergasted at the very idea that a *man* could become a *woman*. Part of this amazement, of course, was related to the physical transformation involved, but many of the news accounts commented extensively on the fact that Christine could wear make-up successfully, knew how to choose and wear attractive feminine clothes, and could even balance on high-heeled shoes. In other words, it was hard for the news reporters to believe that a person could learn the subculture of the other sex.

Marriage as an Entrance to the Man's World

Up to this point our discussion has attempted to show that there are essentially two different social worlds, that of the male and that of the female, in our society. We are now ready for the next point: namely, that marriage is often the first point at which a boy or girl attempts to really live (or try to live) intimately in the world of the other sex.

But you may think this generalization too broad. Isn't it true, you say, that a girl lives intimately with her father and her brothers? Doesn't she share the subculture of the male in her parental home? The answer is "Yes and no." It is true, of course, that the child learns something about the opposite sex from father or mother. It is likewise true that we learn (or should learn) something of the other sex from brothers or sisters. But there are severe limitations to this learning. Let us look carefully at these in the next few paragraphs.

In the first place, the smaller family of the modern era in America reduces the number of siblings of the other sex to which we are exposed. In fact, some of our smaller families may contain only children of one sex, as was demonstrated recently in one of our classes in which a fourth of the girls reported that they had no brothers.

Furthermore, the existence of broken homes must not be ignored in our society. In these homes the absence of one parent often eliminates exposure to a parent of the opposite sex.

There are other limitations to this type of learning also. The daughter, for example, does not enter the sexual world of her father; she does not share intimately (in most middle-class families) his financial matters; she is usually protected by her father and her brothers from the male world of the locker-room stories, the crude language, military experiences, etc.

In other words, we contend that a daughter or a sister does not share a man's world the way his *wife* does. If we are correct in this line of analysis, then it follows that marriage marks the first point at which the social worlds of the male and the female are thrown into intimate interaction. At this point, we have to understand not only ourself as a man or as a woman, we must understand the opposite sex as well.

We might add, incidentally, that our siblings and our parents are not always typical representatives of the behavior patterns of the opposite sex. We know a married woman, for example, whose father was a Methodist Sunday School superintendent for forty years. This man had never smoked nor drunk alcoholic beverages in his life; he probably had never kissed any woman except his wife; he very seldom spent an evening with men, except for meetings of the church board; he had never been in the armed forces; it is doubtful if this father had ever told or enjoyed male jokes. In other words, this father was atypical in many ways.

Now, all this is fine, except that this man's only daughter fell in love with and married the son of a very worldly traveling salesman! You can imagine that there were some exciting adjustments in this marriage.

Some Characteristics of Male Subculture

Although space will not permit a complete analysis of the subculture of the American male, a few of its more striking features will be presented. Perhaps the men in the class would like to complete the description.

We have already seen in previous chapters that women in our society are apt to consider their husbands as crude and oversexed, while husbands often believe their wives to be prudish and cold. The Kinsey group reports that American men like to talk about, look at, and participate in sex more so than (most) women.[3] Out of these differences has evolved almost entirely different sexual worlds for males and females in our culture. After marriage, these two worlds have to be merged, at least to some extent. Evidence has been presented in earlier chapters indicating that this merger is not always easy.[4]

Let us turn now to other illustrations of the social world of the male. We submit that tavern society is still basically a man's world. The world of the Elks Club, the American Legion, the Moose, are basically male worlds. Luncheon clubs, athletic clubs, veterans' organizations, hunting clubs—all these, within limits, illustrate a way of life that is essentially masculine in our society. We grant, of course, that women share more of this man's world today in the United States than they did fifty years ago, but we think it unwise for women approaching marriage to conclude that male society is now completely open to them, or to condemn their husbands for wanting to participate in the man's world, as he has been accustomed to doing since he can remember.

In the next few pages, we wish to give a few illustrations, from marriages known to us, of how this male society still functions in modern America.

During the war we knew a prominent attorney who was very much in love with his wife. Yet this man and his wealthy friends maintained a hunting lodge to which *no woman could ever be admitted*. These men thought that men and women should each have some social participation that was equal but separate, a type of segregation of the sexes. These men were all happily married, and they were willing for their wives to have a similar club for women only (as the attorney put it), but they were adamant about their wives sharing this last vestige of a man's world.

A man we know, a brilliant news editor, is extremely fond of playing poker, but only with men. He will not play with his wife or any other woman. He does not object to women playing poker by themselves, but he prefers to play his cards with men.

Many women today play golf with their husbands. Mrs. Eisenhower, however, has been quoted in the public press as saying that she has always felt that the President enjoys his golf games more when he plays with men. In fact, women are not admitted to the golf club in Washington to which he belongs. Yet the President is obviously a devoted husband and does not neglect his wife.

Mrs. Ben Hogan, wife of the champion golfer, has been quoted in the newspapers as having the same philosophy about golf as that of Mrs. Eisenhower.

To us, these illustrations tend to add up to an important point: it is unwise to approach marriage, even in modern America, with the assumption that modern marriages succeed to the extent that husbands and wives share more and more activities as a pair. We believe that this point of view ignores the existence of significant differences between men and women in America today.

Military service exemplifies the sort of thing we have been trying to describe in this chapter. With a relatively few exceptions, hardly any wives in our society have any realistic understanding of what it means to spend several years in the armed forces. This, of course, is no criticism of women; the world of the military has traditionally been closed to the female sex. Yet we argue that a man cannot spend three to five years of his life in the armed forces without acquiring certain behavior patterns and values that are significant for marriage. His vocabulary, his eating preferences, his sexual values, his need for male companionship—all these and many more facets of a man's personality can be related to military service. Even a man's conception of himself as a man can be related to his years spent in the armed forces.

The world of sports participation is another good illustration of the basic point of this chapter. While it is true that women in the United States today are increasingly active in many sports, such as golf, tennis, and bowling, the fact remains that two of our most popular mass sports, baseball and football, are closed to women competitors, at least on the interscholastic and professional levels. Although Negro players have finally been admitted to the professional baseball world as team members, this as yet has not been the case with *female* ball players.

The significance of the preceding material is simply this: that wives often find it difficult to understand the passionate reverence their husbands feel for their favorite baseball team (say, the New York Giants), the batting slump of the star they admire most (such as Willie Mays), or the latest trade of their chosen professional football team (such as the Cleveland Browns). What women often fail to realize is that the world of sports is a basic part of male subculture. In general male conversation, for example, it probably outranks even sex as a topic for discussion.

We believe it is difficult for women to understand why sports are so important to men in our society. In a sense, high school, college, and professional sports function as a symbol of adult manhood. We have noticed that men who won a high school letter in football will often refer to the fact with pride thirty or forty years later. This would be comparable to a middle-aged woman making a point of the fact that she was once elected Homecoming Queen. Somehow, such events operate as symbols of status. And they are not to be made fun of by members of the opposite sex.

If a man *failed* to earn a letter in high school football, that may become a major goal as his son nears high school age. Now, if the wife of such a man decides that the boy may not try out for football because he might get hurt, then the stage is set for trouble. We argue, in such a case, that the wife, reflecting female subculture, is probably not aware of how important this matter is to her husband, or to the adolescent boy, for that matter. In some ways, athletic success to a man might be compared to the importance of courtship success to women in our society. If a girl is too heavy, has unruly hair, or piano legs, her entire feminine world is threatened. Yet these things may mean nothing to her husband. He will probably be puzzled as to why his wife pays so much attention to such things. It is our thesis that wives are apt to react in similar fashion to matters that seem to be of deadly importance to men— whether the Dodgers or the Giants will get into the World Series, for example. And the man who has never played an inning of baseball himself is likely to be as avid a fan as the man who almost had a try-out with the Yankees (there seem to be thousands of such men in the United States). It is our point that each sex would do well to make some effort to understand the social world of the other sex. This is what we mean by the phrase, how the other half lives. Before concluding this chapter we wish to make a few suggestions as to how women can reduce the social distance between their feminine world and the masculine world of their boy friends or husbands.

How Can Women Understand This Man's World?

Perhaps the first point is this: *respect* for the man's world and a realization that you, as a woman, can never fully be admitted to this world. Try to realize that this failure to be completely admitted to your husband's world has nothing to do with you as an individual. As a matter of fact, he probably is sharing his subculture with you more than he has ever been willing to share with any other woman.

Our next point is that you must have some *determination* to understand your husband's world. This means that you must show interest when he is willing to share his masculine world with you. You must listen with respect when he and his male buddies (mystical brothers in this vast secret society of men) are talking about their world; and you must exhibit some intelligence (plus respect) in your comments about the male world.

And last, but not least, you must accept the way of life of your *own sex*. Otherwise, you will envy your husband his world and feel hostile toward it. Psychiatrists claim that many women in our society reject their roles as women and unconsciously (or consciously) wish they were men. Such a woman often gets into difficulty with her husband because of her desire to share the man's world completely—in other words, to be a man. Such social transvestites are not likely to be very happily married women. Failing to accept or respect their own sex, they often fail to respect the opposite sex as well.

In attempting to understand men, it should be kept in mind that men in our society vary considerably in their willingness to accept women into their masculine world. There are traditionalists who still feel that woman's place is in the home, but at the same time there are modernists who feel that woman's place is by her husband's side, no matter where he may be. It is important that girls understand *before* marriage which type (or subtype) of man they prefer and keep this in mind in choosing a husband.

There are many men in our society who *prefer men as companions to women.* In the last two decades we have studied many of these. Such men go out with girls, and even marry them, but when they have an hour or so of free time, they beat a straight line to the Elks Club or the Legion Home, without their wives. The man who works fifteen hours a day at the office is apt to be of this basic type also. We sometimes refer to such a man as "Elks Club Type Man," or "Hunting Type Man." Such men prefer to work with men, drink with men, talk with men, etc. They are apt to view women as necessary evils in life. A girl should not marry such a man unless she is confident that she can be happy with him *as he is.* Our observations of such men lead us to conclude that they are not easily reformed, partly because they do not wish to be reformed. They like their life as it is.

In an interview reported in the press, the wife of Rex Harrison, the famous English actor, was quoted as saying: "The greatest compliment Rex can pay me is to say that being with me is as good as being with a pal. He's a man's man. . . ." [5] It is our belief that a great many men in our society find their male friends more interesting than their wives. This is likely to pose problems in a culture that idealizes complete sharing in marriage.

On the other hand, there is another type of man who prefers women to men. We sometimes call this type "domesticated man." Such a man, when he has a spare hour or two, likes to spend it with his wife. He comes straight home from the office. If he has a drink before dinner, he has it with his wife. If he plays golf, he may invite his wife to play with him. He may even take his wife fishing or hunting with him. While his office buddies are down at the Moose Club celebrating the 100th anniversary of the FIRST MOOSE, this man is home painting the storm windows. In a sense, this man is not a full-fledged member of Male Society; he is a marginal man, overlapping the subculture of the male and the female. Such men may not scale the heights of economic success as well as their more masculine brothers, but for many women they make ideal husbands.

One last bit of advice to women on how to understand men: don't ask a potential husband if he likes children or if he likes home life, and take his verbal responses too seriously. Of course he likes children (almost everybody does), if he doesn't have to take care of them. He loves his home too, if he doesn't have to spend too much time there. The best way to answer such questions is to study the way a man actually spends his time, and what his best male friends do with their time. His choice of friends will often reveal what his basic values are.

There is evidence that men in the United States drink more than women; gamble more than women; go to church less often than women; pay less attention to clothes, etc. These differences will be examined in the next chapter.

Summary

In this chapter we have developed the thesis that the two sexes have different social worlds (or subcultures), that marriage is usually the first point in our lives when we attempt to share intimately the world of the other sex, that some marital adjustment problems are related to this attempt to mix the worlds of the two sexes, and that women would do well to gain some understanding of the man's world before marrying. We have also sketched in some of the relevant characteristics of the man's world in modern America.

In the next chapter we propose to analyze the subculture of the female in our society and to point out some of its implications for future husbands.

References

1. James Thurber and Elliott Nugent, *The Male Animal* (New York, Random House, 1940).

2. Margaret Mead, *Sex and Temperament in Three Primitive Societies* (New York, William Morrow & Co., Inc., 1935). See also her *Male and Female* (New York, William Morrow & Co., Inc., 1949).

3. See Alfred C. Kinsey *et al., Sexual Behavior in the Human Female* (Philadelphia, W. B. Saunders Co., 1953), especially chap. 16. Almost every chapter of this second Kinsey volume contains comparisons of male and female sexual behavior.

4. See chaps. IX, XVII, and XVIII.

5. *Time*, July 23, 1956, p. 46.

Suggested Readings

1. Pearl S. Buck, *Of Men and Women* (New York, The John Day Co., 1941). This little book contains some very shrewd observations on the relationships between men and women in our society.

2. Margaret Mead, *Male and Female* (New York, William Morrow & Co., Inc., 1949). This volume contains the results of a lifetime's research on the two sexes.

3. Charles Jackson, *The Lost Weekend* (New York, Farrar and Rinehart, 1944). This classic study of the male alcoholic is also a study of male-female relationships in our society.

4. James Jones, *From Here to Eternity* (New York, Charles Scribner's Sons, 1951). This best-seller of life in the Army is essentially a study of the American male. Women can learn a great deal from it.

5. Amram Scheinfeld, *Women and Men* (New York, Harcourt, Brace & Co., 1943). A considerable amount of factual information about the two sexes is to be found in this interesting volume.

CHAPTER XXIII

FOR MEN ONLY: FEMALE SUBCULTURE

Our Theoretical Frame of Reference

It may be well to restate our point of view, or what social scientists might term our "frame of reference," in this and the preceding chapter. Briefly, we have been maintaining that men and women occupy somewhat distinct social worlds in our society, and probably in most societies, and that marriage represents the first attempt, for most of us, to share this subculture (as we call it) of the other sex on an intimate basis. If we are correct in this point of view, it should follow that we can improve our understanding of the other sex (our future mates, in other words) by gaining insight into their way of life.

It is true, obviously, that all men and women are not exactly alike, but this does not invalidate the point of view presented here. No matter how typical or atypical a given boy friend may be, any girl should be in a better position to understand him if she has a knowledge of the male *in general* in our society. As a matter of fact, her very ability to determine how typical is any given boy will

496

depend, ultimately, on her understanding of American masculine behavior as a subcultural pattern.

This may be illustrated by reference to other studies in our high schools and colleges. For example, we study the French language and French culture, knowing full well that all Frenchmen do not speak or behave identically, because we realize that a general knowledge of what France is will be helpful to us in trying to penetrate the mystery of any given French man or woman. And this is precisely the same claim (or hope) we make for the material on masculine and feminine subculture presented in this chapter and the preceding one.

With this preface, let us plunge into the mysterious world of the American female, knowing that no man, and certainly not a college professor, will ever succeed entirely in dissecting this particular subculture. But let us try, at least, because we men will have to try to understand women once we are married, if not before, and we had best begin now.

Glimpses of the Feminine World

1. *Clothes.*

If you are a single male, the chances are that you know nothing, or next to nothing, about the cost and complexity of the average woman's wardrobe. You may think that you understand such things because you had a sister, or because you once helped your girl friend choose a sweater. But do you know how many pairs of nylon hose, at so much per pair, a girl needs to see her through the average year? When you see "Hose—$3.75" on your monthly department store statement, perhaps month after month, will you understand that this is typical, and not unusual, for well-groomed American wives?

And when you choose a well-dressed girl to be your wife, as you very likely will, will you remember what it costs to clothe such a woman in our society? If you can answer all these questions in the affirmative, then you need not finish reading this discussion.

One of the basic reasons why men find it difficult to comprehend the wardrobe problems of their wives is that American men, as a group, are a rather poorly dressed lot. The designers and manufacturers of men's clothing have been lamenting this sartorial neglect for decades. The other day, for example, we met a prominent and brilliant professor from one of our great universities. This man, who has an international reputation in his field, was wearing an ancient pair of unpolished shoes, with run-down heels and cracked leather prominent in the upper portion. His necktie resembled an old piece of colored string, while his shirt left much to be desired. A similar appearance on the part of a well-known professional woman is almost unthinkable.

It might even be argued, we think, that the average American man may very likely take more aesthetic interest in his car than he does in his clothes. To support this, we cite the fact that American men have been buying large numbers of fire-engine-red cars, and other brilliant shades too, for the past several years, but only recently have they been willing to purchase *and wear* red, pink, or other unusually colored dress shirts (we are not talking about sports shirts).

A man usually wears only brown or black shoes, and these he considers a perfect match for any outfit he might own. Women's shoes, on the other hand, come in endless shades designed to match the innumerable colors worn by women during the various seasons of the year. A wife may have to visit five to ten shoe stores before finding exactly the color she needs to match a scarf or purse. Her husband, however, may need to visit only one store to find the shoes he needs. And when he sees row after row of shoes in his wife's closet, he may very likely wonder why on earth she needs *so many* shoes. He may also be shocked at some of the prices asked for women's shoes—often several dollars more than men's shoes.

But this is only the beginning. Well-dressed women do not buy single items of clothing; they buy complete ensembles, consisting of basic dress or suit, shoes, gloves, hat, purse, scarf, blouses, sweaters, and so forth, all of which costs money.

Furthermore, well-groomed women recognize four distinct seasons, fall, winter, spring, and summer, each of which makes its separate demands upon her wardrobe. The good solid male, however, recognizes, at most, two seasons, winter and summer, and we know men who refuse to concede even this to Mother Nature. Is it any wonder these two groups may have some misunderstandings when they begin, for the first time in their lives, to share a common clothes closet and a joint checking account?

Women's hats, a subject of perennial humor for radio and television shows, are not nearly as funny for the woman who needs one for a particular costume or occasion. Afternoon teas, for example, *require* hats for women as a rule, as does church attendance for most women. A man is unusual if he has one hat today, whereas a woman may need several. Furthermore, a woman's hat hardly ever wears out; it is *discarded*. The rapid style changes reduce the hat to obsolescence within a season or two, but the styles of men's hats seem to last forever. Watch the next time you see a man place his old hat on the trash can with loving care. The sweat band will be mute testimony to many seasons of loyal service. In fact, if a man doesn't lose his hat, which he is very likely to do, it may be almost indestructible. With proper care and good dry cleaning, it is capable of several years' wear. One can hardly make the same comment about feminine headgear.

How many men, except husbands or department store buyers, realize the problem modern American women face in keeping their limbs well dressed? What man has ever had to run back into the house at the last minute because he snagged his stocking getting into the car? Or has had to borrow a pair of hose from his roommate before he could go to a college dance? These are not unusual events in the social world of women in our society.

A friend of ours, a modestly paid college professor, was horrified to learn that his fiancée had paid thirty-five dollars for a blouse. In fact, he hastened to assure her that such expenditures would be impossible once they were married and began living on his salary. One can understand his state of shock when it is realized that this man had never paid over $3.95 for a shirt in his life, and to him a blouse was merely a woman's shirt. Such is the innocence of the male in matters of this sort.

If a man has a good suit, he may wear it for years, and it would hardly occur to him that he should discard the suit because "all our friends have seen it so often." But women may be heard to say this. As styles change, as other women blossom forth in new outfits, a woman begins to feel that she has "nothing to wear." Almost every middle-class husband has heard his wife make this sad comment more than once. Yet his wife's wardrobe seems to be full of clothes, as it probably is. But, the wife will say, they are "out of style," or "I have worn them everywhere we have been this whole year." The husband may counter with the age-old masculine question, "What about that blue dress you look so good in?" Then the wife has to explain, very patiently, that this is winter, and the blue dress is a spring dress. At this point the husband usually gives up and retires to the comfort of the television set.

We are not just trying to be funny in this discussion. The little domestic drama we have just described has undoubtedly been played hundreds of thousands of times all over America, and often with considerable feeling on the part of both actors. We do not mean to imply, of course, that good sound marriages are destroyed by such events, but we do mean that lack of understanding of such problems keeps many husbands from being *better husbands*.

2. *Why do women have to dress so well?*

This is a good question. Do American wives, for example, spend so much time and money on their appearance because they enjoy this sort of thing? The answer is very likely in the negative. The plain truth is that our girl friends and wives are required to maintain certain standards of dressing and grooming if they are to compete successfully for husbands and fulfill their wifely roles after marriage. In a very real sense, then, it is we men who demand that our women devote time, money, and energy to make themselves attractive. If this is the case, then it follows that only the most ungrateful husband would fail to understand that feminine beauty demands a price.

Once an American girl is married, her appearance tends to reflect her husband's social position, which means that she has to measure up to the dressing and grooming standards of the women in that social stratum. Thus, if the other wives have nice fur coats, she becomes somewhat conspicuous if she does not have one also. To a certain extent, of course, this is also true of men, but their social status is less likely to depend upon their appearance than is that of their wives.

All of this may seem very much like "keeping up with the Joneses," as it is, but social standards are enforced in all human societies, and ours is no exception.

All of this, we think, adds up to a moral for men: if you don't like to pay for good-looking clothes for your wife, then choose the girl who does not pay much attention to such things, the sort of girl whose idea of a fine outfit is an old skirt and sweater and a new pair of walking shoes. There are women like this if you look for them. We do not think they are typical of middle-class American women, but they can be found.

Another possibility would be to marry a girl with money, but they seem to be scarce. If a girl has a good position, and retains it after marriage, that may also be a solution to the problem. Marrying a girl who *already* has a fine wardrobe, including a fur coat, has certain obvious advantages for the new husband.

We might point out that women, in their turn, are just as uninformed about some masculine expenditures as men are about women's clothing. The size of night club checks, for example, is often a complete mystery to women until they marry. A friend of ours took his wife to a well-known dine-and-dance spot to celebrate their tenth wedding anniversary. After dinner, they stayed very late, enjoying their night out, and their check increased as the band played on. The next morning the wife inquired what the total evening had cost. "About twenty dollars, if you include the baby-sitter," the husband replied. "But we can't afford that," the wife said. At this point the husband smiled, patiently, and explained that many of their big evenings during their courtship and honeymoon had cost even more than last evening, and then he added, "We couldn't afford it then either." He was not begrudging the money spent celebrating their anniversary, for he had known in advance about what such an evening would cost. His wife, however, was upset because she had never paid a bill of this sort and knew practically nothing about expenditures of this nature.

Biological Differences of Women

Up to this point we have been discussing feminine characteristics that seem to be largely the result of the differential conditioning girls experience as they are trained to be women in adult society. There is another complex of differences basically biological in nature which we believe men should know something about before they get married. Even though these are essentially physical in nature, there exists a body of folk belief about them which men absorb from their peer group as they move through that wilderness known as adolescence. Let us look at some of these factors and attempt to analyze their implications for marital adjustment.

1. *Sexual differences.*

In previous chapters, male and female sexual differences have been discussed at some length.[1] At this point it is only necessary to repeat that all the major research reports on sexual patterns in our society have reported deep and pervasive differences between males and females. It is not very clear, as yet, to what extent these differences are due to innate biological factors or to differential conditioning. Regardless of origin, however, the differences are real and do complicate marital adjustment, as we have already seen.

2. *Other physiological differences.*

To the average woman, menstruation is one of the facts of life that she has had to live with each month from adolescence through the menopause. The average man, on the other hand, never really grasps the full meaning of menstruation until he marries. That is, he does not realize what a basic factor menstruation is in the lives of women until he is intimately exposed to feminine sub-culture, something that seldom happens to a man until he marries. The fact that women often refer to their monthly periods as "the curse" gives some idea of how basic it is in their lives.

Some women, of course, are much more casual about their menstrual cycle than are others. But even for the girl who has no particular menstrual difficulties, it still is a factor she has to think about in scheduling her honeymoon or planning for a big "reunion" with her husband if he has been away for some reason. And each month millions of wives wait, anxiously or joyously, to learn from their menstrual cycle whether or not they are pregnant.

It seems to us that young men are often the victims of unfortunate conditioning regarding menstruation. Either they know almost nothing about it, or their knowledge has a sort of "behind the barn" emotional tone that doesn't help much.

This is not a book on human physiology, but we think the following points, at least, should be known to every prospective husband.[2] Women vary tremendously in their menstrual patterns. Although the majority may accept it and experience no particular discomfort, there seems to be a significant proportion of wives who find this to be almost a monthly burden, both physically and psy-chologically. Some of these wives begin to show signs of discomfort and/or disturbance a day or two before the period begins and may not return to normal until a day or two after the period is over. Thus, with these women, from seven to ten days a month tend to revolve, more or less, around their menstrual cycle. It may be, of course, that some of these women are neurotic or maladjusted, but regardless of the label we attach, the problem remains the same. Obviously, such women should seek medical aid, but most of them have already consulted physicians about such problems by the time they have married.

The point we are leading up to is this: most men, with the

possible exception of some male physicians, have not the slightest idea of how complicated the female reproductive system is. It is only after marriage that most men realize that the cervix, the uterus, the Fallopian tubes, and the ovaries are basic parts of the female organism and that these may all cause difficulty for married couples at some time or other.

The male reproductive system, in contrast, seems simple. Except for the prostate gland, most men seem to live out their lives without any particular complication related to the reproductive organs. This seems to be much less true of women.

So far we have said nothing about the menopause, yet many wives seem to experience difficulty during this period, usually in the middle forties, when their reproductive cycle is about to end. Obviously, men have no real understanding of what this is, with the possible exception of a few medical specialists.

Pregnancy is another female specialty we have not covered, although this will receive some attention in a later chapter. Some wives breeze through a pregnancy as though it were nothing at all, while others may be miserable most of the time. It is easy for men to smile at the woman who has "morning sickness" (nausea) and label it "psychosomatic," but the fact is that pregnancy affects women in very different ways. And who can doubt that, for some women, the entire nine months is a rough time?

3. *Women and their diets.*

Some wives, it seems, are forever "trying to reduce," as the saying goes. When not actually on a diet, they are still "trying to control my figure," as they put it. This sort of thing often puzzles men, who are more apt to eat what they want and let the pounds be damned. The next time you go through a cafeteria line, observe the difference in food choices of men and women. The women, as a rule, take the salads and the low-calorie dishes, whereas the men are the meat and potatoes type.

This sort of behavior is strictly the result of subcultural conditioning. From adolescence on, or even before, middle- and upper-class girls are urged by their mothers, their relatives, and their boy friends to "watch your weight." The writer's sister, for example, struggled valiantly all through high school to attain what the advertisers call a "reasonable facsimile" of the Hollywood figure, while at the same time her adolescent brother was cramming himself with ice cream and cake, trying to gain twenty pounds to please the football coach! This, it seems to us, symbolizes the basic difference between male and female eating habits.

The truth is, of course, that the Hollywood figure does not come naturally to most American women. Since the motion picture screen makes people look heavier than they are, it is necessary for movie actresses to be underweight if they are to look slender in their films. This poses a real hardship on the average girl when she tries to look just as slender.

In a sense, the average attractive middle-class wife fights a constant battle of the bulge as she tries to satisfy the cultural ideal of the slender woman and at the same time be an eating companion to her husband.

If we may judge by the rich pastries and other desserts featured in the women's magazines, women like to eat as well as men do. The resulting dilemma has created a billion-dollar industry in garments (some of them like strait jackets) designed to permit American women to have their cake and their husbands' approval too.

We cite all this as just another bit of feminine subculture that the new husband will have to get used to living with.

In defense of the women, however, we think it only fair to point out that obesity is one of the major diseases of the American male, and that our wives now outlive us by four or five years. The old saying, "he dug his grave with his own teeth," is not entirely without support in modern medicine.

4. Women and their emotions.

We might as well face it: the average wife seems to need a good cry every so often. For various reasons, this is very disturbing to husbands. It makes them feel guilty, whether or not they have done anything to be guilty about. When a woman cries, there is always the implication that some brute of a man (in this case, the husband) was responsible for the tears. We recall seeing a woman sobbing in a railroad station during the war while a man walked away from her. Our immediate response, like a reflex, was to identify with the woman and wonder what *the man had done to her*. In fact, of course, she might just have broken his heart, for all we knew.

One of the reasons why husbands feel so confused and frustrated when their wives cry is that men are taught not to cry in our society. Hence, men have relatively little experience with crying until they get married. A male friend of ours, for example, now in his forties, claims that he has resorted to tears only twice in the last twenty-five years—once, in high school, when he failed to catch a crucial pass in the last minute of an important football game, and then, in college, when his mother died. We doubt very much that many women could claim a similar record.

Incidentally, little boys cry just as often as little girls, if not oftener. The differential pattern between boys and girls in the use of tears seems to develop during adolescence, when the boy is urged to be "big and strong and *brave*."

It is interesting to note that men are permitted a much freer display of emotion in French, Spanish, and Latin American cultures. We all know that two French males, when reunited after a long separation, will embrace, kiss each other, and very likely cry a little bit before settling down to mundane matters. This, of course, is typical feminine behavior in the United States. Most of us would view with some alarm similar behavior between two American men. In fact, their sexual normality would even be questioned by some persons. Thus we see that male and female patterns of expressing emotion are probably not innate but are learned.

Actually, it has not even been established that women are necessarily *more* emotional than men; it may be that they simply *express* their feelings more overtly than men do in our culture.

In defense of women, if they need any defense on this point, it can be pointed out that they seem to have fewer ulcers than men, a fact that very likely can be related to their expressing, rather than repressing, their feelings.[3] They also seem to have less mental illness than men, and they usually outlive their husbands. Modern psychiatry, in particular, emphasizes the expression of emotion, in suitable ways, as an aid to mental health. From this point of view, husbands shouldn't condemn their wives for crying; they should *join* them.

What should a husband do when his wife begins to cry? Well, we suggest you watch how women console each other when one is overcome with emotion. Usually, it seems to us, they put their arms around their crying friend, hold her close, whisper consoling words, and *allow her to cry herself out*. Then, when the flood subsides, they offer a handkerchief or tissue, followed by fresh powder and lipstick. We doubt very much that any man can improve very much on this routine.

Other Female Differences in Our Society

The following feminine characteristics deserve brief mention, we believe.

1. *Women and religion.*

There seems to be some evidence that wives tend to be more devout in their religious behavior than their husbands in our society. If this is true, it indicates a subcultural difference that men should be aware of as they approach marriage. We know a young man, for example, who is really an agnostic in his basic attitude toward religion, although he calls himself a "watered-down Protestant." A few years ago he fell in love with a charming girl, who happens to be very devout in her Protestant faith. It was not until after their marriage that this young man realized how much religion meant to his wife.

2. *Women and their children.*

Geoffrey Gorer, the English anthropologist, has described American child-rearing patterns as a "Mom complex." [4] His main point centers about the fact, which is hardly debatable, that American mothers spend much more time with their children than the fathers do. We doubt that this pattern is limited to the United States. More likely, it would be found in any urban-industrial socio-economic system in which the father's employment takes him out of the home several hours each day while the mother cares for the children at home.

This may not seem relevant to our discussion, but the fact is that married couples sometimes develop basic conflicts related to this intense preoccupation of the mother with her children. The husband, with his outside work and interests, may feel that his wife is becoming a slave to the children, which, to some extent, she usually is. The wife, on the other hand, may decide that her husband isn't interested in the children.

The fact is, of course, that there is a real difference here between the role of the husband as a breadwinner and the role of his wife as a rearer of children. Somehow, each must gain some insight into the role and subculture of the other sex. This will be elaborated upon in a later chapter.

3. *Women and liquor.*

Some of you have undoubtedly seen the classic film on the alcoholic, *The Lost Weekend,* or you may have read the novel, by Charles Jackson, upon which the film was based.[5] It is our belief that it was no literary accident that the main character in the novel and the film is a man. The truth is that the excessive use of alcohol is much more often a male pattern in our society than it is female, although the number of female problem drinkers in the United States has been increasing in recent decades.

For various reasons, many wives seem to be almost allergic to masculine drinking patterns, resenting bitterly each hour or evening their husband spends at his club or tavern "with the boys." We believe it is important for future husbands to know this. Even mild drinking patterns that girls tolerate in their boy friends, as seems to be the case on many college campuses, may be very annoying to the same girl after marriage. As in *The Lost Weekend,* there is a long history in Western society of wives and their children being neglected or abused as the result of the husband's drinking habits. Perhaps this is one of the reasons why wives resist such male tendencies so strenuously.

4. *Women and worry.*

An impressive group of specialists, including psychiatrists, consulting psychologists, and medical practitioners in general seem to believe that women are more likely than men to be "worry warts" in our society. Numerous volumes have been published to this effect in recent decades.[6] Behind this belief is the theory that women are confused and full of conflict because of the rapid change in their position in modern society. Our own belief is that this theory has not been adequately supported by good systematic research. It very likely is true that psychiatrists and consulting psychologists see a great many frustrated and maladjusted females, but this hardly constitutes a good random sample of American women. If we judge by mental illness rates, suicide rates, crime rates, or similar indexes, the data do not support the idea that women are more frustrated than men in modern civilization.[7] This much is beyond question: for a so-called "maladjusted" sex, they certainly live a long time—several years longer than the "adjusted" sex.

At the same time, husbands are often heard to say, "My wife worries about everything." We have a hunch that these wives are largely the traditional type of American wife, the wife who did not work outside the home or participate actively in community or societal affairs. Since that type of woman could not work actively to solve her family's problems but had to depend on men for solutions, she was forced to stay at home and "worry" about things in general. The modern soap opera reflects this type of woman.

Our personal belief is that the period of major adjustment for American women began during World War I and ended with the generation that married during and after World War II. The young wives we interview these days are not the worrying type.

Neither are they the chronic nagging type, a pattern of female behavior very common in grandmother's day.

5. *Women and security.*

It seems to be rather widely believed that women need security more than men do. The term "security," apparently, refers to emotional, affectional, or economic dependability in one's environment. Personally, we are not impressed with this belief. Child psychiatrists for decades have been reporting that *all* children, regardless of sex, require various kinds of security for normal physical, emotional, and intellectual growth, and we see no reason why adults should vary greatly in this respect. It is true, of course, that in some areas of living, such as premarital sexual behavior, the girl, because of biological differences, runs a much greater risk than the boy. In this sense, the girl may need more security in courtship than the boy. In fact, the whole courtship system, with its taboo on female overtures, may put the girl in a position whereby she feels threatened (or insecure) more easily than the boy.

Since mothers in our society usually keep the children in the event of marital failure, it very likely is true that women prize security or stability in their marriages more than men do.

In the sense discussed in the preceding paragraphs, it probably is true that there is a differential demand for security between men and women in our civilization. Let us not forget, however, that the modern male seems to crave security too, as Mills points out in his provoking study, *White Collar.*[8] In our opinion, the female subculture is not too different from that of males in this area, except for the special circumstances referred to above.

6. *Women and money.*

Although systematic data are not at hand, it seems likely that men and women are inclined to use money for somewhat different purposes in the United States. One wife put it this way: "My husband always wants a new car. He never seems to realize that rugs wear out, or that drapes need to be replaced. And he considers it absolutely sinful to spend money on new slip-covers for the furniture."

Another wife told us this: "My husband always gets upset when the children have their teeth fixed and a big dental bill comes in. He seems to regard modern preventive dentistry as a racket. But if *he* needs a new power-tool for his basement workshop, that's all right. He also likes expensive fishing rods."

Husbands, for their part, complain that their wives are "always redecorating the house"; they spend too much money on clothes; or perhaps they are accused of "wasting money on the kids."

If there are basic differences in male and female values in our culture, then one would expect to find these differences reflected in the uses of money. We suggest that you explore this topic with your parents or some other married couple.

7. *Women and their families.*

As we saw in an earlier chapter on in-law relationships,[9] there seems to be some research evidence to support the notion that married women in our society remain closer to their families than do their husbands. This can easily become a focus of conflict when a marriage is not going well. As one married student told us: "Every time we have a little spat she runs home to her parents." As Komarovsky has shown,[10] there is very likely a real difference between the son and daughter emancipation process in our culture: the boy should become a man, whereas the girl needs to be protected. After marriage, differences of this sort can be very irritating.

Summary

In this chapter we have been trying to give future husbands a more realistic understanding of the opposite sex. The concept of subculture has been employed to make the material more specific.

We hope no one will misunderstand us and conclude that we are so naïve as to believe that all women are alike. On every point covered in this chapter, it is freely granted that any given wife may not fit the pattern we have been describing. But that does not render useless the basic point of view. If a man is to know whether his wife is normal or not, something we all like to know, then he must have some systematic knowledge of what women in general are in our society. To some extent, the quality of any given marriage will reflect the ability of the husband to understand the social world of his wife, to see life from her point of view. If he feels that women have it soft in modern society, that taking care of children is a snap compared to a rough day at the office, then he is apt to be in for trouble.

In a sense, the adjustment of men in marriage reflects their ability to accept women as a distinct social group, to recognize their right to be women and to be different from men.

As a starter, we suggest to young men that they analyze their attitudes toward the other sex: Do you think most women are stupid? Do you feel that they are silly? Do you regard them as lousy drivers? If you have attitudes of this sort, it might be well to begin revising them. It may be hard to live successfully in modern equalitarian marriage unless you respect the opposite sex.

References

1. See Chapters XVII and XVIII for a detailed analysis of sexual sub-cultures.

2. One of the best books in this area is Amram Scheinfeld, *Women and Men* (New York, Harcourt, Brace & Co., 1943). His approach, however, is somewhat different from ours in that he is not analyzing subcultures as such but emphasizes physical and psychological factors in his analysis.

3. See Ashley Montagu, *The Natural Superiority of Women* (New York, The Macmillan Company, 1953), chap. 6, for a discussion of male and female emotions.

4. Geoffrey Gorer, *The American People* (New York, W. W. Norton & Co., Inc., 1948), chap. 2, "Mother-Land."

5. Charles Jackson's novel, *The Lost Weekend* (New York, Farrar and Rinehart, 1944).

6. See, for example, Ferdinand Lundberg and Marynia F. Farnham, *Modern Woman: The Lost Sex* (New York, Harper & Bros., 1947).

7. Montagu does not find American women to be more maladjusted than American men. See his study cited above.

8. C. Wright Mills, *White Collar* (New York, Oxford University Press, 1951).

9. See Chapter XV for a review of the data on wives and their relationship to their parents.

10. Mirra Komarovsky, "Continuities in Family Research: A Case Study," *American Journal of Sociology*, 62 (1956), 42–47.

Suggested Readings

1. Christopher Morley's novel, *Kitty Foyle* (New York, Grosset and Dunlap, 1929) is one of the finest studies of female subculture we have seen.

2. Ashley Montagu, *The Natural Superiority of Women* (New York, The Macmillan Company, 1953). This study explodes very effectively a great many myths about women in our society. Well written.

3. Simone de Beauvoir, *The Second Sex* (New York, Alfred A. Knopf, Inc., 1953). Although somewhat voluminous, this book contains some deep insight into male-female relationships in Western society.

4. Amabel Williams-Ellis, *The Art of Being a Woman* (New York, Longmans, Green & Co., Inc., 1951). Men will find this little volume helpful in trying to penetrate the woman's world.

5. *The Ladies Home Journal* (or any of the major women's magazines) is an excellent source for men interested in understanding the world of the female.

CHAPTER XXIV

PREGNANCY AND REPRODUCTION

Introduction

In our society the birth of the first child seems to be the very culmination of marriage. Parents as well as grandparents celebrate the joyous event; the mother receives flowers, the father dispenses cigars to his friends, and presents are bestowed upon the child. The minister appears at the hospital and registers the infant in the Cradle Roll, uncles and aunts arrive to see the new baby, and the local "Dydee Dan" sends congratulations and his offer to "take the dirty work out of parenthood."

In a community known to the author, the first baby of the New Year received over $300 worth of merchandise, plus getting his picture on the front page of the local newspaper along with those of his proud parents.

It is no accident that our greatest secular-sacred festival, Christmas, celebrates the birth of a baby.

In a child-centered culture such as ours, all this is understandable. It is almost a sin in the United States not to want children or not to like them. For segments of our population, marriage

514

itself would have relatively little meaning were it not for the presence of children.

All of this simply means that in this chapter we are examining one of the great events in modern marriage—indeed, it may even be true that the arrival of the first child in our society actually symbolizes final and complete maturity as an adult. One gets this impression sitting in the hospital near the delivery room as the soon-to-be fathers wait for the good news. And this impression is not dimmed by visiting a new mother as she receives the congratulations of her friends and her family. In many societies, of course, a wife is not considered a successful woman until she has her first child, and some of this seems to have survived in modern America. In men's talk, it is not unusual to hear a man say to a new father, "Now you can call yourself a *man*."

All this may be seen in reverse in the couples unable to have children, the so-called sterile couples in our society. These often seem to feel deprived or incomplete until the wife succeeds in becoming pregnant or they are able to adopt a child. Even though the childless couples are often the happiest couples, according to the marital adjustment studies,[1] the fact remains that they are usually regarded as tragic in our society. The fact that childless couples have higher divorce rates than couples with children indicates the powerful impact of the child on modern marriage.[2]

From a sociological point of view, as Kingsley Davis has pointed out, marriage as a social institution has as one of its main functions the provision of a stable social group for the care of the young infant.[3] This points up the basic importance of the child in *all* human marriage systems and not just in the United States.

In this chapter, then, we will be analyzing some of the most significant events in your marriage and mine—the achievement of conception, the adjustment to pregnancy, and the assumption of the responsibilities, the heartaches, and the joys of parenthood.

Let us look first at conception and its opposite, sterility, and then we will proceed to analyze the adjustments that usually accompany pregnancy.

Achieving Pregnancy

In a very real sense, conception is an achievement, and one soon realizes this when interviewing couples who have been unable to have a child—and this includes about 17 per cent of the urban couples in our society.[4]

It seems odd that conception should be difficult for so many married couples in the United States, especially in view of the fact that as youngsters we are taught that pregnancy will most certainly result if a girl goes too far with a boy. Married couples, as a rule, do not find this to be the case. In fact, it is not rare to meet couples who required a year or more to achieve conception.

It is important to keep in mind throughout this part of our discussion that on any given day (or night) as many married couples may be trying to *achieve* conception as are trying to *avoid* it. This may be an overstatement, but the current birth rate lends strong support to our assertion.

Planning for Parenthood

It seems clear that the majority of American couples resort to some method of birth control. During the economic crisis of the 1930's, there was an essentially negative tone to the birth control movement in the United States: its main aim was to *prevent* unplanned pregnancies. In recent decades, however, the movement has embraced the total problem of planned parenthood and concerns itself with problems of sterility as well as fertility. A study of married couples in Indianapolis revealed that failures in this area include failure to conceive at the time desired as well as the failure to prevent unplanned conception.[5] Let us discuss first the problem of *prevent* or *controlling* pregnancy, after which we will analyze the problem of *achieving* pregnancy.

For most American couples, excluding some of our very devout religious couples, birth control is essentially a medical problem.[6] Most marriage counselors recommend that the girl consult a woman's medical specialist, usually a gynecologist or an obstetrician, for the prescription of appropriate contraceptive methods. At the same time, the physician can examine the wife-to-be and may detect any physical abnormalities that might interfere with normal sexual intercourse and/or pregnancy. In most communities this examination and prescription should not cost more than $10 to $20. Some general practitioners also provide this service. In the larger urban communities, there are usually clinics that specialize in this work.

It appears that some husbands are not always co-operative in the use of birth control devices, especially any which they consider to interfere with the sex act. For this reason, it is essential that the method adopted be understood and accepted by *both* the man and the woman. If possible, it would be a good idea if the man could accompany his bride to the doctor's office when she receives instructions about contraception.

Many couples wish to read about the control of fertility before marriage. The readings at the end of this chapter contain excellent discussions.

It should be emphasized that *none* of the present-day birth control methods is completely *foolproof*; that is, they all require some intelligence, some maturity, and considerable control of the sexual impulse. Couples that drink excessively, for example, are apt to find all the methods less than perfect. The writer knows personally a number of couples who conceived in spite of the best medical advice. It may be, as the birth control clinics claim, that the best methods are 95 to 100 per cent efficient; the trouble is that the couples using them *are not*.[7]

This poses, of course, some real problems for the couple who feel that they must be absolutely sure that there will be no pregnancy during any given year.

The Problem of Sterility

It is not hard to imagine the acute disappointment or the feeling of failure that often overcomes the young couples who fail to achieve parenthood. Perhaps the following case, taken from the writer's counseling experience, may help to illuminate this American tragedy.

A young couple, married five years, consulted us about their marital problems. Among other things, it appeared that they both were bitterly disappointed at not having had any children. In addition, the husband's family (his mother in particular) had decided that the failure to conceive was due to the wife being a neurotic, and there was some evidence that the mother and sister-in-law had encouraged the husband to seek a divorce.

Actually, this was not a bad marriage at all. When the in-laws left them alone, and when they could forget about their failure to have a baby, the young couple got along very well. Their courtship had been adequate and there were many areas of deep compatibility. We could find no evidence of neurosis in the wife and her whole history of college and work indicated good personal adjustment. She did have, however, a great deal of hostility toward her mother-in-law; she was also beginning to develop a complex about being sterile.

This couple had consulted local physicians about their inability to conceive without receiving too much help. At our suggestion, they made an appointment with a fertility clinic in a large city in the area. This examination revealed that the husband had a very low sperm count—in other words, that his production of sperm was far below average. The sperm were also relatively sluggish and inactive. In general, the husband's total physical condition was such that conception seemed unlikely. Interestingly enough, the wife's examination revealed nothing that might prevent conception.

After this consultation, the marital situation improved considerably. For one thing, the husband gained some insight into his mother's attitude toward his wife. His health also improved under a plan of treatment worked out by the clinic. Among other things, he received male hormone shots, also medication for a low metabolism rate.

Eighteen months later, the wife called us to announce, very happily, that "we are pregnant." They now have two children and seem happy. There still is a mother-in-law problem but it seems under control.

In this case, we see that couples can become upset over failure to achieve conception. We see also that relatives and friends often do not help the situation by their comments and jokes. Actually, this is not usually a joking matter; it involves too many emotions to be funny.

We see also in this case that sterility is very often an illusion, or at least temporary. The Planned Parenthood Federation of America, as a matter of fact, claims that at least *half* of the childless couples in America are capable of achieving conception under proper medical care.[8] All of us know couples for whom pregnancy has occurred years after they had given up hope. One couple known to the writer failed to conceive in ten years of marriage, despite what they described as frequent sexual relations. They both appeared to be in excellent health, physically and mentally. Their marital adjustment was excellent. A well-known specialist in New York City was consulted in the fifth year of marriage and diagnosed the wife as sterile—her Fallopian tubes were "completely closed," thus making normal conception impossible.

At the end of the husband's military service this couple concluded they would never have any children by the normal process and applied to an adoption agency. Three years later they finally obtained a baby girl for adoption, and eighteen months later the wife was pregnant. They now have two lovely little girls and are one of the happiest couples we know.

It seems obvious that no couple should accept the verdict of sterility without expert medical consultation—and even then with some reservation.

The truth is that there is still a great deal of mystery as to why some couples conceive while others do not, or why a couple will be "sterile" for several years and then conceive.

A divorced woman interviewed by us cited her experience:

in her first marriage she had tried for three years to become pregnant with no success. In her second marriage, however, she had conceived within six months, but so had her former husband with his second wife. Thus it appears that two persons may be potentially fertile but not with each other. It is possible, of course, that this woman would have conceived with her first husband had they remained married long enough.

Adoption as a Substitute for Biological Parenthood

Fortunately, the experience of rearing a child is not limited to married couples able to produce children; through adoption, a great many childless couples are able to become parents also.

There is a great deal of folklore about adoption, most of it misleading. If you work through a recognized professional adoption agency, there is every reason to believe that adoption can be a positive experience for both the child and the adoptive parents.[9]

Actually, the main problem is that there are not enough infants or young children available for all the applicants. For this reason, it is advisable to apply before you are too old for consideration, and it may be wise to consult more than one agency. Some physicians can also be helpful in obtaining a child for adoption.

It seems clear that most adoptions turn out very well, which is as much as or more than can be said of so-called "natural" parenthood in our society.

Artificial Insemination

Modern science has made it possible for some couples to conceive through a technique known as "artificial insemination." In this technique, the husband, if possible, or a donor, contributes sperm, introduced into the wife's reproductive tract by medical means. This assumes, of course, that the wife is capable of going through a normal pregnancy.

When the husband is sterile and unable to provide the necessary sperm, an anonymous donor may be used, as in blood bank procedure. This appears to be a very questionable practice, however, for several reasons: the mother may feel that the child is *hers,* since the father has had no biological parent role; the husband may feel that the child is not really his, which it is not in a biological sense. There may also be legal difficulties since at least one judge, in Chicago, has ruled that children born of sperm from a donor other than the husband are illegitimate. This decision will very likely be altered as time proceeds, but at the moment it presents many knotty legal problems. Some religious groups also do not approve of this practice.

In view of these negative factors when an anonymous donor is used, it seems likely that adoption would prove more satisfactory for cases in which the husband cannot provide the sperm for artificial insemination.

Adjusting to Pregnancy

In recent years, there has been a renewed emphasis upon the fact that pregnancy and childbirth are normal experiences, not to be feared or approached with anxiety. It seems to us that a good deal of this discussion begs the question, or at least avoids it. One could just as logically point out that death is also normal, but this does not alter the fact that we all have to adjust to death when it strikes our family or our friends.

The truth is that life in all societies is punctuated by certain events, or rites of passage, which symbolize our maturation and movement from one life stage to another. In our own society, these events or special occasions include being baptized and/or confirmed in the church of our family, our first day at school, graduation from high school or college (or both), our first real job, our wedding day, and the birth of our first child. It *is* a very joyous and wonderful day (or night) for most parents, at least for those possessing a marriage license, and we see no reason for deflating the event.

In a very real sense, as we stated earlier, the arrival of the first child symbolizes several things in our society: it makes the father a man and the mother a woman; it reaffirms our adult status in our community; in the case of the first grandchild, it creates two sets of grandparents; it alters our military draft status; employers begin to regard us as more stable or more mature; and even the Bureau of Internal Revenue has to alter its records.

Can anyone who has been a parent ever forget the excitement of the day or night when the first baby arrived? The terrible feeling of responsibility as you carried the first one out of the hospital and headed for home? Or the first illness? This is obviously normal, but it is also *singular* and *extraordinary*; it happens only once in a lifetime, since subsequent births will have a somewhat different meaning.

The Pregnant Father

Almost inevitably, most of the attention and concern during pregnancy focuses on the mother and the infant-to-be, but from a sociological point of view the father is just as pregnant as the mother; after all, he did have *something* to do with the conception and he is also an *expectant* parent. Moreover, it is not unusual for him to gain as much weight as the mother during the gestation period; we have often heard the remark, "Who's going to have this baby?" regarding the father's swelling waistline.

The answer, of course, is that they *both* are having a baby, not just the mother. Let us look, then, at the adjustments required of the father as the young couple go through their first pregnancy.

1. *Economic adjustment.*

In modern marriage, the average young man does not assume any great economic weight at the point of marriage; in fact, with his wife employed full time he often "never had it so good" before. With two pay checks each month, plus the economy of sharing food and rent, the young husband may feel more secure financially than ever.

This is only a temporary situation, however, to be rudely

interrupted by pregnancy. As the months roll by and the delivery date slips up closer and closer, there comes the day when the girls at the office give their shower for the baby and the little mother brings home her last pay check. In middle-class subculture, with its taboo on mothers working during the early years of childhood, this may be the last money earned by the mother for ten or more years. In other words, from now on the financial burdens of the family rest squarely on the shoulders of the young husband.

We believe that this added economic responsibility can be a fairly sudden and severe adjustment for some expectant fathers. He now needs to think of increasing his life insurance, perhaps of buying a house, getting a promotion, etc.

In many cases, of course, he and his wife have been saving money for this event and have a nice savings fund to tide them over any emergencies. Some will have purchased a home and acquired the more expensive appliances (and a car) before their family was begun. And, as Sussman has shown, there is a helping pattern in middle-class families which stands ready to aid the young couple if necessary,[10] and there is nothing like a grandchild *Amen* to open the parental purse!

Nevertheless, we believe that young wives should be alert to signs of financial worry in the expectant father and lend him any psychological support he may need. Restraint in buying things for the new baby is one way to help. A modest budget for maternity clothes might be a relief also.

2. *Sexual adjustment.*

It may very well be that the early childless years of marriage represent the epitome of sexual satisfaction for the average American male, although the research data on the point tend to be inconclusive. On logical grounds, it seems that these carefree years of marriage represent essentially a continuation of the honeymoon, a sort of "playing house" period. If this is so, then one would expect sexual relations to play a rather prominent role during this pre-parental stage of marriage.

With the coming of pregnancy, however, with its physio-

logical adjustments and its added fatigue, one expects some deterioration in the frequency and intensity of the sexual relationship.
In a survey of 228 young college married couples in 1949, all of
whom had had their first child within the last two and a half years,
Landis and Poffenberger found that about one fourth of the couples
felt that pregnancy had had an unfavorable effect on their sexual
adjustment.[11] Interesting enough, 58 per cent reported "no effect"
on their sexual adjustment, while 17 per cent of the wives and 19
per cent of the husbands felt that the effect had been favorable. In
general, this study concluded that couples with a good sexual
adjustment before pregnancy had a good adjustment during and
after pregnancy.

If we assume this study to be essentially sound, it indicates
that about one fourth of the couples going through pregnancy for
the first time will have to adjust to some sexual deprivation. When
we add to this the fact, previously analyzed, that men seem to
take their sex more seriously than women in our society, it appears
that the husband will usually feel this deprivation more intensely
than the wife. If the marriage is good, and if the husband really
wants a child, then the adjustment should not be too difficult. In
the absence of these qualities, however, some repercussions may be
expected.

Unfortunately, some wives seem to use pregnancy as an
excuse for avoiding sexual relations—these, of course, for the most
part, being wives who do not enjoy sexual relations at any time,
pregnant or otherwise. There are some women, however, who find
child-bearing so difficult that sex becomes unthinkable, even though
they normally enjoy it.

Thus it seems likely that some sexual adjustment to pregnancy will have to be made by the average couple, that the husband
may feel this more than the wife, but that most couples will not
find this adjustment to be too difficult. As the Landis study shows,
most husbands tend to identify with their wives during pregnancy,
in the latter months especially, and this tends to reduce their sexual
demands or wants, at least temporarily.

3. *Role adjustments.*

The change from being only a *husband* to a *husband-father* does not begin at the birth of the baby; on the contrary, it begins with the discovery of pregnancy, if not before. It is important that the young husband realizes this: that his attitude and interest during the long gestation period is often the clue as to what sort of father he is going to be after the baby comes. Moreover, his behavior will determine to a considerable extent how well the wife goes through pregnancy.

Here are some suggestions as to how a husband can be helpful during this period:

A. By showing that he is *pleased* about the pregnancy; not just accepting it but being enthusiastic about it.

B. By reassuring his wife of his love for her. Some wives develop rather odd ideas about themselves, especially during the later months of pregnancy, and need more love than ever.

C. By helping with the shopping, dishes, and the housework if his wife seems fatigued or does not feel well at times.

D. By being considerate in his sexual desires if his wife is not as ardent as usual.

E. By limiting his evenings out, and his week-end golf, in order to spend more time with his wife.

F. By taking a lively interest in the whole process of becoming a parent—in the weekly changes as the fetus develops, in the reports from the doctor, in the plans for the nursery, in the discussion of names, etc. In all these ways a husband can show his wife that he intends to be the father she thought he would when they were married.

We believe an occasional visit to the obstetrician with the wife is good for "pregnant" husbands. We shall never forget our own first experience of this sort. As we took our place in the waiting room, it seemed to us that we had never seen so many pregnant women in our life—all shapes and sizes. And for some reason, we felt a little proud that we were the only man in the place

—almost as if we were the only husband interested enough to come. The talk with the doctor was most interesting, and he seemed to be glad to see a man for a change. The real climax of the visit, however, came when we emerged from the consulting room and a woman in the waiting room, a friend of ours, asked: "Well, did the doctor find *you* were pregnant *too*?" Our exit was a bit confused. But we still recommend the trip.

In concluding this discussion of the expectant father, we repeat that he too goes through the pregnancy, and that he too has many adjustments to make. A little attention in his direction would not be amiss.

The Pregnant Mother

The reactions to pregnancy, both physiological and psychological, vary tremendously from one woman to another.[12] Some seem to feel wonderful, better than usual, and seem to enjoy almost every minute of the gestation period. They are thrilled and elated at the very thought of becoming a mother and walk down the street with an angelic look on their faces. They enjoy the growth of the baby inside them, the attention they receive, the whole atmosphere of creation and expectancy. These seem to be natural mothers; it is almost as if they were specially designed for pregnancy and childbirth.

There is another type of woman, however, who finds the whole experience difficult and exhausting. She starts off with nausea and vomiting during the early months, feels a little better during the middle months, and ends the last month or so tired and utterly exhausted.

One observes this same variation after delivery as well; some mothers recover quickly from the delivery and feel fine, whereas others seem to need several months to recover their full strength.

It has become fashionable, in these days of psychosomatic medicine, to refer to the women who find pregnancy and childbirth difficult as neurotic, with an implication that they didn't want a baby in the first place. There is hardly enough research data to support this point of view, and it undoubtedly does many women an injustice. Once the baby is born, many of these women become excellent mothers; it is the *physiology* of childbirth that bothers them and not the prospect of motherhood.

Recognizing, then, the wide variation in reaction, we suggest that the following areas of adjustment are the most important.

1. *Giving up the job.*

The average middle-class wife will have held a job during the early years of marriage as a way of helping her husband establish himself in his business or profession. This means that one of her adjustments to pregnancy will be the cessation of outside employment. For most wives, this may not be very difficult; it may even come as a relief. But for the women who enjoyed their work, the long days at home can be rather lonely until the baby comes.

In many cases, if the wife feels well, it probably is best to continue working for the first few months. This will keep her busy and may help to shorten the waiting period. It may also relieve the young husband of some financial pressure, at least temporarily.

Actually, most of us miss our job, almost any job, when we first give it up. We have had friends at the office, the work has provided a certain pattern for our daily living, and we are apt to feel somewhat at loose ends when we first stop working. It will be necessary for some wives to keep busy during this transition period so that they don't become lonely and feel out of touch with what is going on in the community. Husbands can be helpful during this period by spending evenings and week ends at home, bringing home the local gossip, and seeing that their wives have enough to keep their minds occupied.

2. *Physiological adjustment.*

Perhaps the greatest aid to a pregnant woman, next to a good husband, is a competent and understanding physician. Since most of us are not qualified to evaluate a doctor's medical knowledge and skill, it seems best to consult friends and acquaintances who have had babies recently. A good physician can be helpful during the pregnancy if problems arise, but this becomes even more true as the delivery date approaches. The wife, and the husband also, will be more confident and relaxed if they have faith in their physician.

It is important not to wait too long before consulting a physician, not more than six or eight weeks as a rule. He can then establish whether or not pregnancy exists and prescribe diet, rest patterns, etc.

A great many American women worry about their "figure" during and after pregnancy. Although some gain in weight is inevitable, this can be held to a minimum by proper diet, and this in turn will assure a return to the prepregnancy figure after the delivery. Since husbands admire a trim figure, they should be willing to help the wife control her appetite during pregnancy. If your husband is overweight, put him on a diet too.

It should be remembered that pregnant women, especially during the last few months, tire easily, and this necessitates control of work and social engagements./Amid all the showers and the other activities preceding the delivery, it is essential to get plenty of rest.

3. *Role adjustments.*

We have already pointed out one basic role adjustment, the shift from breadwinner to the combined housewife-mother role.

As the pregnancy approaches its later stages, there will be additional role realignments. The wife, for example, will usually find that she has to curtail her companionship role with her husband —bowling with him, or going fishing, or painting the house. If she has been accustomed to going with her husband on business trips, this may not be as easy now that she has to think of the baby as well as herself and her husband.

Community roles, such as holding office in various clubs and welfare organizations, may become a burden and have to be dropped temporarily.

In sum total, we are simply saying that motherhood will have a profound effect on the life of the average American woman, far more than she probably realizes as yet. It is not meant or implied that she will be sick and unable to carry on her usual activities if she wants to badly enough; the point is that she will begin, perhaps without being fully aware of it, reorganizing her life in preparation for motherhood. Interests and activities that have deep significance, such as church attendance for some women, will not be curtailed at all; but less important things, such as improving her golf game, will tend to be neglected or discontinued altogether for the present.

Some women find this a good time to *review* and *re-evaluate* their various interests, to sort out the really important activities from those that have little significance. If you wish to try this, we suggest you read, or read again, Anne Lindbergh's little masterpiece, *Gift from the Sea,* in which she attempts to put her life in order, so to speak.[13]

In summary, we point out that there are no data to suggest that most American wives are not able to make all the above adjustments with relatively little difficulty. After all, most of these women have been looking forward to motherhood and are usually more or less prepared for it, or at least they think so at this point. We shall see in the next chapter, however, that not nearly as many of them are as sure they were prepared to be mothers once they begin child-rearing itself (that is, once the baby has actually arrived).

Let us not delude ourselves, though, that pregnancy is always regarded as an unmixed blessing in our society; some young couples are not ready when the first pregnancy announces itself; some wives (and/or husbands) are not well adjusted personally and may be disturbed by the thought of parenthood; and some marriages have already begun to fail when the young wife discovers she is pregnant. And later on, when the couple feel that their family is completed, only to discover that the stork has his eye on them again—this can be traumatic in many cases. Most abortions in our society, after all, are performed on *married* women, not single ones.[14]

Thus we see that pregnancy, in itself, has no single meaning for married couples. Physiologically, psychologically, and socioeconomically, it can range from the heights of ecstasy to the depths of gloom and despair. It is at this point that the basic importance of an adequate courtship and good marital adjustment begin to become fully clear: now that the deep responsibilities of parenthood stare them in the face, the young couple are forced to take a good long look at their marriage. If what they see is good, then pregnancy should come as a blessing. But if what they see is not good, then the event has an entirely different impact.

This is exactly what is meant when we say that *preparation for child-rearing begins back in courtship,* when we select our future partner in parenthood. It is well to keep this in mind.

Some Random Suggestions

The following points are based largely on the writer's personal experience and discussion with middle-class married couples. The student should regard them as *opinions* and evaluate them as such.

1. *Maternity clothes.*

We believe that the better-looking women in our society, at least at the middle- and upper-status levels, have some trouble visualizing themselves pregnant. As the figure begins to change, these women begin to feel the need of expensive maternity clothes, and the more they cost, the more they seem to do for these women, at least psychologically. It is odd that our society cannot look with satisfaction on a stomach "swollen with child," as the saying goes, but we have yet to see such a woman featured in any of the mass magazines edited for women. Television, however, has displayed the pregnant profile, so perhaps the advertisers may follow suit.

It is interesting to note that a nice maternity outfit purchased at one of the better stores can cost *more* than the delivery of the baby itself.

2. *Baby clothes.*

Most couples, at least with the first baby, cannot resist buying some nice things for the baby to wear. The truth is, however, that your parents, other relatives, and friends like to send such items as gifts, so why not save your money and avoid frustrating the grandparents? Another excellent reason for not spending a great deal of money on baby clothes is that infants *grow so fast*; in no time at all, they have outgrown most of the items purchased.

3. *Baby equipment.*

It is possible to spend a sizable sum on various items of equipment for a baby—crib, weighing scales, bottle sterilizer, etc. On the other hand, it is usually not necessary to invest a great sum in such items for three reasons: (1) They are usually available in good used condition; (2) They can often be borrowed from relatives or friends; and (3) Some of them are often received as gifts. Oddly enough, there seems to be no stigma attached to buying or borrowing used baby equipment. Many couples, of course, will wish to "shoot the works" in buying for the first child, and if you are planning to have several children, it is wise policy to buy only good sturdy equipment that will survive more than one child. However, if you are short on cash when the first baby arrives, we submit that the essential items can be obtained without great expense.

Should All Married Couples Plan on Having Children?

Some groups believe that this decision rests with God. Aside from religious values, the writer is convinced that some married couples might well decide not to have children. In addition to certain obvious medical conditions that more or less preclude parenthood, there are some married persons who do not seem well equipped for parenthood; their emotional make-up does not lend itself to the rearing of children. An extremely self-centered husband, for example, will regard a baby as competition, and he may feel hostile toward the wife for having brought the competitor into the family. Such men seem unable to share the wife with a baby.

And there are certain immature and neurotic women who should never attempt motherhood, in our opinion.

This, of course, is a delicate subject. In our marriage counseling practice, however, we have had several cases in which the husband and wife got along reasonably well until children were born, after which the marriage seemed to deteriorate rapidly. Just as we argued in an earlier chapter that not all adults should attempt marriage, so do we also argue that some couples should not attempt parenthood. We suggest that your class debate this question to bring out the various issues involved.

By all means, avoid regarding parenthood as a magical solution to marital problems. As Burgess and Wallin point out, the adjustment to parenthood tends to follow the patterns of marital interaction established before the arrival of children.[15] In other words, don't expect your marital problems to disappear just because you had a baby. It is undoubtedly true that childbirth tends to delay or prevent divorce, but this does not mean that the problems are *solved*. We will have more to say about this in the next chapter.

Summary and Conclusions

We believe the following general observations are helpful in understanding the first pregnancy in modern marriage.

1. This event marks the end of the couple-centered or honeymoon stage of marriage and the nine months' gestation period constitutes a period of transition into the second stage of marriage, parenthood.

2. In some ways, the first pregnancy and the resulting parenthood actually represents the last step in the assumption of full adult responsibilities in our society, as in most human societies.

3. Pregnancy cannot be understood from the purely physiological point of view. It has emotional, economic, marital, familial, and community dimensions. This can best be apprehended by re-

garding the *couple as pregnant*, not just the wife. The phrase, "the pregnant couple," best expresses this point of view.

4. Americans are no longer concerned primarily about *preventing* conception: at any given moment, there is also a large number of married couples hoping to *achieve* conception.

5. Finally, the first pregnancy retests the marriage and results in a re-evaluation of the marital relationship. And the results of this will determine to a considerable extent the acceptance of pregnancy itself.

References

1. This material is reviewed in Harvey J. Locke, *Predicting Adjustment in Marriage* (New York, Henry Holt & Co., Inc., 1951), chap. 8.

2. See William J. Goode, *After Divorce* (Glencoe, The Free Press, 1956), chap. 21 for a discussion of this point.

3. Kingsley Davis, *Human Society* (New York, The Macmillan Company, 1949), chap. 15.

4. As of the 1950's, roughly 15 per cent of all married couples in the United States were childless.

5. There is ample evidence that the control of conception is by no means perfected as yet in our society. See Robert B. Reed, "The Interrelationships of Marital Adjustment, Fertility Control, and Size of Family," *Milbank Memorial Fund Quarterly*, 20 (1947), 382–425.

6. See *Planned Parenthood* by Abraham Stone and Norman Himes (New York, Viking Press, 1951).

7. In the study by Reed cited above, over one fourth of the 1944 couples studied had experienced unplanned pregnancies.

8. See John Rock and David Loth, *Voluntary Parenthood* (New York, Random House, 1949), chaps. 4 and 5.

9. See Lee and Evelyn Brooks, *Adventuring in Adoption* (Chapel Hill, University of North Carolina Press, 1939) for a very helpful discussion of adoption as a way of achieving parenthood.

10. Marvin B. Sussman, "The Help Pattern in the Middle-Class Family," *American Sociological Review*, 18 (1953), 22–28.

11. Judson T. Landis, Thomas Poffenberger, and Shirley Poffenberger, "The Effects of First Pregnancy Upon the Sexual Adjustment of Two Hundred Twelve Couples," *American Sociological Review,* 15 (1950), 767–772.

12. We are indebted to Elmer Wessel, M.D., obstetrician, Plattsburg,

New York, for some of this material on the diverse reactions of women to pregnancy.

13. Anne Morrow Lindbergh, *Gift from the Sea* (New York, Pantheon Press, 1955).

14. Harry Elmer Barnes, *Society in Transition* (New York, Prentice-Hall, Inc., 1952), pp. 73–75.

15. See Ernest W. Burgess and Paul Wallin, *Engagement and Marriage* (Philadelphia, J. B. Lippincott Co., 1953), chap. 21 for a thorough review of the evidence that children do not solve marital problems.

Suggested Readings

1. John Rock and David Doth, *Voluntary Parenthood* (New York, Random House, 1949). This book combines the knowledge of the physician with the writing skill of the professional public relations specialist. It is an excellent discussion of sterility, birth control, and related matters.

2. Abraham Stone and Norman Himes, *Planned Parenthood* (New York, Viking Press, 1951). Now in its tenth printing, this is a classic in its field. Extremely practical and readable.

3. Grantley Dick Read, *Childbirth Without Fear* (New York, Harper & Bros., 1944). This book describes the method of bearing children without anesthesia.

4. John J. Kane, *Marriage and the Family: A Catholic Approach* (New York, Dryden Press, 1952). This contains an excellent presentation of the Catholic point of view on parenthood.

5. Lee and Evelyn Brooks, *Adventuring in Adoption* (Chapel Hill, University of North Carolina Press, 1939). Very helpful analysis of the adoption process for couples unable to achieve conception.

6. William H. Genné, *Husbands and Pregnancy* (New York, Association Press, 1956).

CHAPTER XXV

CHILD-REARING IN MODERN SOCIETY

Introduction

It seems to be true that most American couples look forward with joy to the arrival of children. The current boom in our birth rate testifies to the deep desire for and anticipation of children. When one reflects on the cost and complexity of child-rearing today, the birth statistics become even more impressive.

At the same time, however, there is also considerable evidence that these same young parents are often less joyous once the children descend upon them—not that they regret having them but that they are confused and frustrated as to *what to do* once the children arrive.

For the above reason, we begin our discussion by raising the question as to how adequately college graduates today are prepared for parenthood. We then move into the question as to what is actually known about rearing children in our society, after which the author presents a few ideas of his own for the reader's consideration. We conclude the chapter with an attempt to formulate a philosophy of child-rearing in modern society.

535

Figure 10: Number of Children Under Age 18, United States, 1900–1954,
Projected to 1965 *

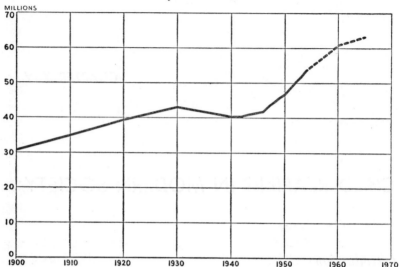

It seems obvious from the above figures that childrearing will be a major concern of American married couples in the decades ahead.

* Source: *Statistical Bulletin,* Metropolitan Life Insurance Company, February, 1955.

Are College Graduates Prepared for Parenthood?

In many societies, and sometimes in our own, older children acquire considerable experience in handling children by reason of their responsibility for younger brothers and sisters. This was true of the colonial family in the United States, also of the later farm family.

Because of the extremely low birth rate in America during the 1930's, very few college students today have had much responsibility for younger siblings. And this is especially true of students from middle- or upper-class backgrounds.

Let us not be romantic about this, however, and assume that minding a younger child constitutes adequate training for parenthood. After all, most parents from our lowest economic levels have had the benefit, if such it is, of this training and do not appear to have profited too much. As a matter of fact, it may be that no experience at all in handling children may be better than the child-rearing practices picked up by some boys and girls while taking care of their younger brothers and sisters. The writer knows of no empirical study of this matter.

For a great many college girls, baby-sitting has undoubtedly replaced the older pattern of caring for young siblings. Insofar as this consists of mere sitting with children after they have been put to bed by the parents, it appears that relatively little is learned about children's behavior and the handling of their problems. In many cases, however, the term "sitter" is a complete misnomer, when the job consists of caring for an active child during its waking hours, and one expects that experience of this kind provides considerable opportunity for real learning.

In one study made in the writer's classes, it was found that over 90 per cent of the girls had had rather extensive experience as sitters. One girl had cared for seventeen different children ranging from six months to five years of age. Her experience had covered a period of nine years. Although she felt that her baby-sitting experience had been eminently worthwhile as preparation for parenthood, she also felt that she had learned more about *parents* than she had about children.[1]

Another girl in the same study reported that the children she had cared for as a sitter had behaved so poorly that her desire for children had been somewhat dampened.

It appears that baby-sitting has become a fairly general type of experience in our society for high school and college girls, but its net value as preparation for parenthood is difficult to assess at the moment; this would make a worthwhile project (or term paper).

Brief and inadequate as this discussion has been, it was revealed that young people today, largely girls, have had *some* contact with small children, in spite of the small families of the 1930's. Whether this experience has been helpful or not, however, we do not know. Its net effect may even have been negative as a preparation for parenthood. But this may also have been true of the earlier pattern of older children caring for their younger brothers and sisters.

It appears that only a small percentage of college graduates have had any formal training in child psychology, child development, or child-rearing. One survey of Senior women in a liberal arts college by the writer revealed that less than 15 per cent of these women had taken a course directly aimed at preparation for parenthood.[2] A majority of these students wished they had had formal training in this area.

All this boils down eventually to the same point: that young people today are not receiving adequate preparation for parenthood. Except for a relatively few home economics or education majors, this seems to be almost universally true of college men and women. We are not assuming, please note, that the situation was any better *yesterday,* for we are not convinced that it was.

If it is true that college graduates in our society are not adequately prepared for parenthood, why is this so? What characteristics of our society account for this state of affairs?

A much broader question might also be asked: Does *any* society adequately prepare young people for parenthood? It may well be, as a matter of fact, that no society accomplishes this task, for the simple reason that it may be impossible. If this should prove to be true, we may be criticizing our society and its culture unduly. In a recent book, *Childhood in Contemporary Cultures,* edited by Margaret Mead and Martha Wolfenstein,[3] it is pointed out that the Soviet Union has failed to develop an adequate philosophy for rearing children in the modern world. This leads one to suspect that our society is not alone in its failure to prepare young people for the multiplicity of adult roles in our complex civilization. It is important, we believe, that the student maintain some cross-cultural perspective in considering such matters.

The writer's work in social science leads him to suggest that the following characteristics of our society make it extremely difficult, if not impossible, to train college students adequately for parenthood:

1. *Social class mobility.*

As Allison Davis has pointed out, there are deep and pervasive differences in child-rearing philosophy and techniques between the various social class subcultures in our society.[4] When one combines this with the American custom of children moving up a notch or so in the social class system, it becomes clear that a considerable proportion—at least one fourth—of American parents are in no position to transmit child-rearing principles or practices to their children. This is seen clearly when grandparents attempt to suggest child-rearing techniques to their married sons or daughters: the grandmother is often of a working-class background while the daughter has moved up into the middle class. To some extent, this is merely rapid social change, as we shall see in a moment, but it is also *social class mobility.*

2. *Rapid social change.*

When a society changes as rapidly as ours, parents are not sure that they are *qualified* to prepare their young men and women for parenthood. They feel that their beliefs and practices have become outmoded, as indeed they have. In an interesting study, "Trends in Infant Care," Martha Wolfenstein has clearly demonstrated the wide shift in child-care philosophy and method in the United States since 1914.[5] In a very real sense, child-rearing practices in our society have the essential characteristics of a *fad*: they reverse themselves every few years, destroying any real continuity from one generation of parents to the next. Under such circumstances, it is extremely difficult if not impossible for parents to make any real contribution to the preparation of young people for parenthood. And when this is combined with social class mobility, the break between generations is complete.

3. *Emphasis on "youth" in our society.*

As a society dedicated to progress (whatever that may be), it is inevitable that youth be emphasized in the United States. It is not always clear, however, that a price has to be paid for this emphasis, such as the current neglect of elderly persons, well documented by social workers and economists. This emphasis, or glorification of youth, has a tendency to make parents, grandparents, and even middle-aged professors feel hopeless in trying to help young people prepare for adult roles. For example, it is very common for parents, in discussions of sex education, to say of their high-school youngsters: "Oh, they know more than I do anyhow." Actually, this is not so in most cases, and many of these parents have considerable knowledge about sex and marriage that could be helpful to young persons approaching marriage. It is almost as though parents and older people in general in our society have developed an inferiority complex.

In his classic analysis of social change in our society over the past fifty years, *The Big Change,* Frederick Lewis Allen has pointed out that some of this feeling of inferiority is undoubtedly the result of children today having more formal education than their parents.[6] This, plus the rise of the various mass media, especially television, contributes to the feeling of parents and older people that "young people today think they know everything."

4. *Lack of scientific knowledge about child-rearing.*

The work of Sewell,[7] Orlansky,[8] and Wolfenstein[9] supports the proposition that we really have no reliable body of knowledge about child-rearing and related parenthood roles in our society; that the research to date has been poorly designed and lacks adequate controls; that your guess is as good as the next parent's, even if he does have a doctor's degree in child psychology.

If this is the true state of affairs, and the writer believes it is, then how can we transmit any body of knowledge, except folklore, to the next generation of fathers and mothers? This may explain why high schools and colleges have been reluctant to teach courses in child-rearing, confining themselves to marriage courses for the most part. Certainly, the lack of adequate research data is a major handicap to any teacher or professor who attempts to teach parenthood courses.

5. *Institutional conflict.*

It is not at all clear at the moment, at least to the writer, which of our basic social institutions has the major responsibility for preparing young persons for parenthood—the school (or college), the church, the government, or the family. Catholics apparently believe that the family should assume this responsibility, but in non-Catholics one finds a strong tendency to let the high school and/or college take over the job. Often, neither institution seems to be doing much in this area.

To summarize our discussion to this point: we have suggested that college students (as well as other young persons) are not being adequately trained for parenthood in our society; furthermore, that the very nature of our social system makes it extremely difficult to accomplish such training. We now proceed to the question as to *when* (what age) preparation for parenthood is most practical.

At What Age Can Parenthood Training Best Be Accomplished?

It is true, of course, that *informal* training for parenthood begins at birth: our personality formation, our attitude toward the outside world, all this may be thought of as training for parenthood.

The real question, then, is this: At what age should *formal* training for parent roles take place? In the opinion of the writer, the teachable moment for this does not occur until the married couple are actually parents. In other words, we believe that the romantic complex surrounding child-rearing is so thick and pervasive that couples without children are not able to learn very much until they face the problems themselves.

If we are correct in this belief, then it follows that high schools and colleges play a minor role in parenthood preparation, as indeed they do today. The main burden falls on adult education agencies, such as the PTA, and our mass media. Churches, social work agencies, adult education centers, the better mass magazines— these would have to lead the way. This appears to be the situation today.

Parents can learn a great deal from each other by means of informal discussion and group study. The main value of this experience seems to be the perspective it gives the parent—seeing that other parents have similar problems, that your child is normal, etc.

For the readers of this book, then, we suggest that you not consider yourself as being adequately prepared for parenthood when you graduate from college; that you explore the resources in your community as you enter parenthood—your library, the PTA, various discussion groups, films, etc. As your children mature and enter different stages of development, you will find it necessary to study those stages too. In this way, your growth as a parent will match the growth of your children. Furthermore, you will not be encumbered with a rigid set of practices which by that time will be outmoded anyhow.

What Do We Really Know About Child-Rearing?

Reading the mass magazines in our society, or listening to talks on child-rearing, one gets the impression that a great deal of tested knowledge has been accumulated about child-rearing in our culture. For example, it is often stated that the only child is usually selfish and not well adjusted; that breast feeding is better for children than bottle feeding; that children should not be weaned early as this will produce certain negative personality traits, and so forth.

Now, the amazing thing is that social scientists cannot find the research that is supposed to prove these assertions. Even the only child, to take an extreme example, has not been sufficiently studied to conclude that only children are less well adjusted than are children from larger families.[10] The writer has studied only children in his college classes for the past ten years and has found very little evidence that they are not well adjusted; and what is even more interesting, we have found very little evidence that such children are selfish or egocentric.

In view of this odd situation—all sorts of theories being

propounded as if they were *proved*—the writer thinks it wise to devote some space in this chapter to a review of the critiques of child-rearing theory in the United States. We may then be in a better position to set forth a general philosophy of child-rearing

LOOK   BILL HARRISON

"How much longer do we have to be buddies?"

that has some consensus behind it, and may have some value for the reader.

The Work of Orlansky

In the *Psychological Bulletin,* a publication of the American Psychological Association, Orlanksy of Yale University, published in January, 1949, a major review and criticism of the research on child-rearing published up to that date.[11] In this study, entitled

"Infant Care and Personality," Orlansky reviews 149 articles and/or studies of child-rearing, his major interest being to determine the scientific adequacy of the work to date.

It is important to realize that Orlansky was not attempting to formulate a new theory of child-rearing but was primarily interested in weighing the methodology and the adequacy of the research available to support the existing theories about infant care and child-rearing. It should be remembered also that he was not attempting to show that current theories are *wrong,* but to determine whether their supporting data were *adequate.*

Reading this careful analysis, one cannot fail to be impressed by the methodological weakness of the vast majority of the 149 publications reviewed. In almost every case the sample was inadequate, certain variables were not controlled, or the results could be interpreted by the use of a different theory.

A good example of the lack of adequate data on child-rearing practices can be seen in reference to bottle-feeding versus breast-feeding. Physicians, in particular, have tended to urge mothers to breast feed their babies, implying that the child would be better off if the mother did so.

Orlansky, however, failed to find any adequate data to support the theory that breast feeding is superior. He quotes a study by the National Research Council as follows:

Although there is a voluminous literature on the subject of the emotional value of breast feeding to both mother and baby, it is regrettable that concrete evidence on this point is difficult to obtain. This is particularly regrettable in view of the rather emotional treatment the subject is receiving in both professional and lay circles. The necessary evidence will have to come from long observations on the development of the personalities of both breast-fed and artificially fed infants.[12]

This is typical of what Orlansky found when he subjected the data on child-rearing to rigorous analysis. It may well be, of course, that some or all of the theories are sound, including that of breast feeding. Orlansky's point was that as of 1949, when his evaluation was published, the theories had not been proved to be correct.

The Work of Sewell

In 1952 a detailed field study of infant training was published by Sewell of the University of Wisconsin.[13] Using a carefully selected sample of 162 farm children, age five to six, Sewell attempted to control all the basic variables affecting personality development except that of infant care practices—method of feeding, weaning practices, toilet-training systems, etc. His main objective was to test the theory propounded by a great many psychiatrists, especially the psychoanalysts, that infant care practices tend to determine the basic personality characteristics of the child.

Sewell's field staff conducted very complete interviews with each of the 162 mothers as to the practices they had followed in infant care. Then, after these five-year-olds had begun school, they were given a battery of tests to measure their personal and social adjustment. In addition, their teacher was asked to rate each child on an adjustment scale.

It should be remembered that these children were all of the same socioeconomic environment, farm children of the same community and the same social class. All the marriages were unbroken, and the children were all of the same age.

Sewell's findings are impressive: *he did not find that different infant care practices produced any significant differences in the adjustment of the child at the first grade level.* He states his basic finding in this way: "Certainly, the results of this study cast serious doubts on the validity of the psychoanalytic claims regarding the importance of the infant disciplines and on the efficacy of prescriptions based on them." [14]

Sewell seems inclined to believe that it is the *total* situation in the home and family that determines personality formation and not some specific practice such as early or late weaning.

Sewell himself admits that his study leaves most of the

questions unanswered. But he agrees with Orlansky that the existing theories of child-rearing *still need to be proved*.

The Work of Wolfenstein

Since 1914 the United States Children's Bureau has published several editions of a widely distributed pamphlet called *Infant Care*. Altogether, there have been nine editions of this publication, all of which have represented the best thought of that particular era on child-rearing during the early years.

In 1953 a well-known student of child psychology, Martha Wolfenstein, took the trouble to study the various editions of this booklet, in an effort to determine how *consistent* child-rearing advice has been since 1914.[15]

Her basic conclusion is this: that there has been no consistent pattern of child-rearing in our society during the past several decades, judging by the advice given to parents in this booklet. In one decade parents are urged to be firm with a child who masturbates, but a few years later we are told that this is normal. At one point mothers are urged to wean their baby early, but a few years later gradual or late weaning is advocated. And so on through the list of infant care practices.

Perhaps we should point out that this is not a criticism of the Children's Bureau; the point is that there has been no adequate research data base for these child-rearing practices during these decades, so that they have fluctuated from year to year.

In commenting on this paper, Sussman has this to say:

With each passing year new findings from research on child raising are offered to parents. Child-rearing practices seem to change as do fashions in women's clothes. Each method of rearing—breast or bottle feeding, self-demand or scheduled feeding, self or forced toilet training—is claimed to have special psychological significance in the development and growth of stable personalities. How are parents to act in the face of so many conflicting data and opinions on bringing up children? [16]

In concluding this review of the work of Orlansky, Sewell, and Wolfenstein it seems to us impossible to reject their major finding: that *as yet* our theories about child-rearing must be regarded as *opinions* or *hypotheses* not based on adequate research. This is not to say, however, that some or all of these theories may not be correct. The only point is that as yet their soundness has not been scientifically established.

Do Parents Actually Lack "Knowledge" of Child-Rearing Principles?

One gets the impression from magazine articles and books that parents *do not know* the principles of good child-rearing. These discussions seem to assume, in other words, that the main problem is *ignorance* or lack of knowledge. The remedy, of course, is obvious —more knowledge.

The writer believes the above assumption to be fallacious and misleading. Our own position, based on fifteen years' work with parent education groups, is just the opposite: that parents *do* know the basic principles of good child-rearing and that the main problem is their *inability to live up to what they know*. If we are correct in our belief, then *more knowledge* of high child-rearing principles and practices will not help; in fact, it will *hurt,* for it will increase the parents' feeling of frustration and failure, already too great in many cases. The rest of this section will be devoted to examining the points stated so far.

Knowledge of Child-Rearing Principles

For the past several years we have questioned parents in our parent education classes about the principles of good child-rearing. Our data indicate that at least 90 per cent of the mothers with a minimum of a high school diploma are familiar with the generally accepted principles of good child-rearing.

The following is a list of the principles of which these mothers are aware:

1. Don't lose your temper.
2. Be consistent. Don't vary from day to day in your handling of the child.
3. The child needs security.
4. Insecurity is the major problem in maladjusted children.
5. Love your child.
6. Punish *the act,* not the child.
7. Be impartial and fair in handling your children.
8. Sexual curiosity is natural and should not be punished.
9. *Never* play one child against another, or one parent against another.
10. Children *know* how you feel toward them, even if you say nothing.
11. Every child is unique and must be individualized.
12. Don't *spoil* your child. He has to face reality sooner or later.
13. Be patient. The good parent is like a good teacher.
14. Children, like adults, are complex. You have to observe and study them closely if you wish to understand them.

This list could be expanded almost indefinitely, but we believe the main points have been presented.

Now it is our contention that most "experts" on child-rearing would agree with the vast majority of the above principles. A few might quibble about one or two points, but the agreements, we feel, would far exceed the disagreements. We might add that our own training in psychiatric social work and our later training in social science would lead us to endorse the above list whole-heartedly.

We will go one step further and say this: in the papers written for us about their families by our students, the above principles of good child-rearing are prominent in the well adjusted or well organized families. This is decidedly less true of the descriptions of unhappy or maladjusted families.

If our material is any good, it supports the contention that most fathers and mothers *do know* how they *should* rear their children. The basic problem is that they cannot live up to their standards.

Perhaps an analogy might help at this point. It is well known that too many Americans are overweight. Articles and books on "How to Lose Weight" appear daily, but the vast majority of our fat people continue to be too heavy. *Why?* Is it because they don't know *how* to lose weight? Of course not. Almost everybody knows that to lose weight you simply cut down your daily intake of high-caloric foods: in other words, eat less pastry, more lean meat, drink less beer, etc. The problem, then, is not ignorance but inability to put into action what we know.

Going back to parents and child-rearing, we are now ready to pose the big question: *Why* are parents unable to practice what they preach? This is the next step in our analysis.

Why Are Parents Unable to Live Up to Their Child-Rearing Principles?

In our own work with parents, we have gradually come to focus on this phase of parent education, believing this to be more fruitful than a discussion of the principles themselves. On the basis of this experience, we suggest the following major obstacles that frustrate fathers and mothers and often defeat their efforts to be good parents.

1. *The standards are too high.*

We believe that one of the problems with modern parents, especially middle-class parents, is that they attempt the impossible. They have read so many articles by "experts" and have heard so many lectures that they have internalized impossible goals. For example, the idea that a parent should "never lose his temper" is not practical for most human beings, nor is the belief that one should always be consistent in handling children. This too is not feasible for most of us.

In a great many cases, these high standards lead to a feeling of failure, even in parents who appear to be doing well with their children.

If our analysis is correct, then one of the goals of parent education is to make the goals and practices *more realistic,* more practical.

2. *Personal problems in one or both parents.*

It hardly needs to be argued that our society puts a lot of pressure on the individual. Various studies indicate that on any given day one out of every three or four Americans is struggling with some fairly severe personal problem, psychiatric, economic, sexual, occupational, marital, etc.[17] This leads one to suspect that in any given family at any give time one or both parents may be under considerable strain, thus preventing their living up to their full potential as parents.

One can see this very clearly in detailed case studies of families: the father barks at the children because things are not going well at the office; mother loses her temper on the days that she is not feeling well; both parents fail to live up to their child-rearing standards if there has been a marital crisis.

Most of this is inevitable—one cannot live in a vacuum—and young parents should be taught that such failures are to be expected. It may be that their frequency and their impact on the children can be reduced, but it is unrealistic to expect fathers and mothers to be at their best every day, 365 days a year. We don't expect this of employees in our society, so why hold parents to impossible standards? After all, even Ted Williams doesn't hit like a champion *every* day. What we need for parents is a sort of batting average (not *beating* average) similar to that in baseball. Otherwise, we are always judging them against a mythical perfection. And this is destructive.

3. *Marital conflicts.*

It seems obvious that marital tensions seriously handicap most parents in doing a good job with their children. Note, however, that we are not referring to divorced or separated couples but to couples *living together in conflict*. Once the conflict has been resolved, either parent may do an excellent job.

There has never been an adequate survey of marital adjustment in the United States, using a random sample. The several studies we have seen all seem to be biased in favor of the adjusted couples. It is known, of course, that about one fourth of our current marriages end in divorce, but it becomes increasingly clear that the lower income groups have more than their share of divorces, separations, and desertions.[18]

We know also that divorce in itself is a very poor index of total marital adjustment in any modern society, for the simple reason that a significant proportion, perhaps the majority, of poor marriages never reach the divorce court.

Our own survey of the marital adjustment of college students, mostly middle class, shows that approximately 80 per cent of these students rate the marriage of their parents as good or very good. This is not too far from what Terman found in his survey of middle-class couples in California in the late 1930's.[19]

It seems safe to assume, then, that at any given time *at least* one fifth of American parents may be handicapped in rearing their children by marital problems. These overlap, of course, with those having personal problems as discussed in the preceding section, but the two groups are by no means synonymous. A mother, for example, may be perfectly capable of rearing her children *alone* but unable to do it while living in an unsatisfactory marriage.

Our figure of 20 per cent would be far too low if we were discussing the *average* American marriage; we use the lower figure only when referring to middle-class groups.

4. *The nature of the human infant.*

For decades, psychoanalysts and other psychiatrists have tried to present a more realistic conception of the small child—his tremendous emotions, his utter dependency, his complete egocentrism. As yet, it appears that the efforts of these specialists have been largely in vain. Young Americans still approach parenthood with a very romantic notion of what babies are—wonderful "bundles of joy" dressed in pink or blue. They *are* sources of joy, of course, but they are also sources of anguish and frustration and heartache.

For example, when a mother tells herself that she must never lose her temper, she is doing one of two things (if not both) : overestimating her self-control and/or underestimating the ability of children to disturb parents.

Thus, in the long run, parents find that they cannot live up to their child-rearing principles because they did not know what children are. As adults, of course, we have no memory of what we were as small children, and our parents tend to look back on those years with a nostalgic glow, which means that we seldom have any realistic notion about children until we have them ourselves.

This may sound a bit gloomy to young readers. We do not intend it so; we are referring only to *normal* children and not to abnormal behavior problems.

5. *Societal pressures.*

We are all familiar with the stress that economic factors can place on parents—the pressure exerted on a father by his job, the depression of spirits related to too many unpaid bills, the threat of unemployment or business failure.

But there are other societal forces impinging on parents also —the threat of war, racial and religious conflicts, demands of various organizations to attend meetings, etc.

We obviously live in a complex social world, and not one designed especially for the easy rearing of children. In detailed case studies one can see clearly how some of these societal forces handicap parents.

Summary to This Point

In this discussion we have tried to establish two basic points: (1) that most parents *do* know the basic principles of good child-rearing; and (2) that their main problem is living up to these principles, owing to the operation of several factors, as analyzed above.

If we are correct in our analysis—and we recognize that many competent persons will disagree with us—then it follows that the major job in helping parents will have an indirect focus: helping them understand *themselves,* helping them resolve marital problems, reducing societal pressures and strains, etc. At the end of this chapter we will present a philosophy of child-rearing we believe to be compatible with the basic points advanced so far in this discussion.

Let us now take a brief look at the roles of fathers and mothers in modern child-rearing.

The Role of the Father in Modern Child-Rearing

Winch's research has demonstrated rather conclusively that middle-class young people, regardless of their sex, feel closer to their mothers than they do to their fathers.[20] Although this may not produce any particular maladjustment, it does tend to support the charge of Gorer and others that American youngsters tend to have a "mommy" complex.[21]

It may be, of course, that children in *most* societies tend to be closer to their mothers, owing to the simple fact that child-rearing is usually a major responsibility or role of the mother. Her household chores normally keep her closer to the house, where she is in close contact with the children, at least during the early formative years. When we combine this with breast feeding, it is easy to see that fathers tend to be on the edge of the family as the young child sees or feels it.

In American culture, there seems to be a norm or value which says that we should love our parents equally, just as they should love their children equally. So far, we have not achieved this ideal of equal love for parents. Is there any way of getting *closer* to the ideal?

Perhaps the following case will illustrate the problem. A college woman, a Senior, writes: "I can never remember being close to my father. My earliest memories are of my mother and I doing things together. I have no recollection of my father bathing or feeding me. It was my mother who took me to my first circus, my first movie, and to Sunday School. I would like to love my father the way I do my mother but I don't know how—he has always been too remote. To this day, I can hardly carry on a conversation with him."

"Same as the last three times—the bees make honey and the birds lay eggs, and then he fades off to fill that pipe of his."

If we analyze this case, we find that the father held a very difficult position involving considerable responsibility all during this girl's childhood. His hours were long, he often worked nights and week ends. By the time he got home, the daughter was often in bed. Furthermore, this man's job took so much out of him that he had very little to give his daughter when he did spend time with her.

It is probable that personality factors also hampered this man in his parental role, but the occupational pressure certainly was a major roadblock preventing any very deep relationship from developing.

This girl feels guilty that she has such a superficial relationship with her father. But she has been helpless so far to do anything about it.

In a sense, this is one of our American tragedies—that the father spends so much time earning a living that he forfeits his rights as a parent.

The author believes that a great many young couples would like to prevent this one-sided relationship developing in their children. The following suggestions may help.

1. Avoid exclusive breast feeding, as this excludes the father completely from the nursing experience, which we know has great emotional significance for the child.

Bottle feeding, with the father taking as many turns as possible, should help to establish a deeper bond at the beginning between the father and the baby. This assumes, of course, that the father is interested.

2. Avoid by all means having the father be the major disciplinarian. Since the mother is the source of much gratification for the child, she is usually in a better position to punish or deny than the father. The old pattern of "just wait until your father gets home" will hardly help the father become a love object.

3. Try to plan the child's routine so as to maximize the father's participation. Perhaps the father could get the youngster up in the morning, or put it to bed at night. The week-ends could be utilized as times when the father might bathe and dress the child. A regular play period with the father is possible in some families.

4. Allow the father to take the baby or child out alone on week-ends or holidays, to give them a good chance to get acquainted.

In all this discussion, we have been assuming that the mother *wants to share* the child (or children) with the father. Actually, this does not always appear to be the case. Some women seem to need to pull the children very close to themselves and resist the father's attempts to break into the select circle. This is common, it seems, when there is marital discord.

When both parents wish to relate themselves equally to their children, we believe it can usually be accomplished. In our society, however, this does not result automatically but must be achieved. The writer believes this particular goal to be worth the effort.

The Mother in Modern Child-Rearing

If we limit ourselves in this discussion to middle-class mothers, their problems in child-rearing seem to be basically different from those of the father. The father's problem is to get into the child-rearing act, as it were, whereas the mother's problem is that she is in the act *too much,* especially during the formative preschool years. She spends 12 to 15 hours daily with the child, day in and day out, until it goes to school. The infant is fed, bathed, changed, and played with by the mother almost exclusively, the father's occupational role preventing his being home much during the child's waking hours. This pattern often leads to the following problems.

1. *A "mommy" complex.*

The child is too dependent on the mother and has a woman's conception of the world. This seems to be less than ideal, although not necessarily disastrous.

2. *The mother is overexposed to the child.*

She is with them too much and loses perspective. She also becomes fatigued and overexposed, which reduces her effectiveness in handling the children. At times, in severe cases, she begins to think of herself as a bad mother. An unpublished study of the author's indicates this to be a fairly common problem with middle-class mothers.[22]

3. *The mother may have difficulty emancipating the child at adolescence.*

If the mother dedicates her life to her children, she may have difficulty giving them up, especially in the relatively small middle-class family. Unless she can restructure her life and acquire outside interests, such as a job, she may feel like the prematurely retired man—retired *to what?* Unless she is careful, she will find herself clinging to her children, extending their period of dependency, or interfering in their adult lives.

4. *Any "problem" or deficiency in the mother is communicated to the child.*

It seems obvious that an ill or emotionally disturbed mother will have deep impact on the child under this system of child-rearing, especially during the preschool years. This means that her physical and mental health are crucial for the well-being of the child.

Some Suggestions for Reducing These Hazards

We do not delude ourselves that any five-minute course in child-rearing will eliminate the problems cited above. Indeed, these problems result essentially from the *basic social structure* of our society, in our belief, and not from neurotic or maladjusted mothers. If our view is correct, it means that mothers have to plan carefully if they are to escape these pitfalls—in other words, they have to connive or conspire to *beat the system.* How can this be done, at least in part? We do not pretend to have all the answers, but the following suggestions may help.

1. *Recognize the hazards.*

It is an axiom in social work and social science that little can be done about any personal or group problem until the problem is identified and accepted. Let us, therefore, begin to accept the fact that *some* mothers are with their children too much; that not all mothers can take the confinement of rearing small children; that not all mothers are especially well suited for rearing children; that children benefit by being in contact with a variety of adults; and that social institutions other than the family (the nursery school, for example) [23] also have a contribution to make to the rearing of the

preschool child. Unless and until the above principles are recognized
and accepted, it is unlikely that anything will be done about the
"mommy problem" in our society.

2.   *Restructure community life to help mothers.*

In our opinion, this involves not only the revision of attitudes
toward mothers (the working mother, for example), but also the
provision of services and agencies designed to help mothers. This
might include co-operative neighborhood nursery schools, church
nursery schools, more kindergartens (both public and private), more
part-time jobs for mothers who need to work or who feel better
when they work, and more discussion clinics for mothers to give
them greater perspective on their motherhood role.

The writer sincerely believes that the mother is the "forgotten man" in our society.[24] Perhaps it is time that we stop condemning
her and begin trying to help her.

A Philosophy of Child-Rearing

In a previous section of this chapter, we have presented
evidence that present research is not adequate to specify the
exact techniques of child-rearing—how to feed, how to discipline,
etc.

In the present section, then, we are faced with the problem
of trying to develop a philosophy of child-rearing without the
benefit of adequate data. It seems wise, therefore, to warn the
reader that the principles to follow do not pretend to represent the
findings of scientists; instead, they represent the author's opinions
about child-rearing in modern society. These opinions are based on
several years' experience leading parent education discussion groups,
interviews with several hundred parents and their children as a
family social worker, plus reading term papers from over two
hundred college students describing their families and the child-
rearing practices of their parents. It is recognized that some equally
(or more) competent persons would not accept all the statements
below.

1. *The quality of your marriage is the most important single factor in child-rearing.*

If you and your marriage partner can get along well and meet each other's basic needs, we doubt very much that you will experience any serious child-rearing problems. If you do, you can get technical help from books, teachers, social work agencies, and child guidance clinics.

2. *The personal adjustment of the parents is the second most important factor.*

This, obviously, is closely related to the point made above, although the two are not always synonymous.

We do not imply that a maladjusted parent can *never* do a good job rearing a child, or several children, but we do mean that being well adjusted yourself makes it a lot easier to rear children successfully.

Taken together, these first two principles underscore this point: *don't focus your concern on child-rearing itself.* Instead, do what you can to improve your marriage and the personal satisfactions of you and your spouse.

3. *Children are not as fragile as you think.*

Orlansky states this very well when he points out that there is a margin for error in child-rearing.[25] Parents do not have to be perfect by any means; children very often turn out well in spite of serious family problems. As one pediatrician put it to us when we brought our first baby home from the hospital: "Don't be afraid to handle them—they're pretty tough."

If the above were not true, it would appear that our rate of personality breakdowns would be higher than it is.

4. *Parents are not responsible for everything that happens to children.*

Orlansky concludes that constitutional or genetic factors probably play a greater role in children than we think, although our knowledge of this as yet is very poor.[26]

We know, of course, that the child's peer group has great impact, especially during the adolescent years.[27]

Certainly, in an urban society, with its mass media and its complex social forces, we cannot assume that parents are as influential as they were in the rural-village society of our ancestors. Parents today are *only one* set of factors determining the ultimate fate of the child.

5. *And, finally, there is considerable luck or chance in the rearing of children.*

It is our firm belief that some children turn out poorly in spite of excellent family environments, while others become happy and useful citizens in the face of overwhelming odds.

We believe that parents need a concept of fate (or *faith*) in rearing children today. They do the best they can and then pray, or hope. One cannot do more.

References

1. This was a study of baby-sitting as preparation for parenthood. The sample was made up of college women in their Senior year. Twenty students were included in this exploratory project.

2. Of 421 Senior college women surveyed by the writer, less than 15 per cent had had any formal training for parenthood. Most of them felt this to be a serious lack in their education.

3. See Margaret Mead and Martha Wolfenstein, *Childhood in Contemporary Cultures* (Chicago, University of Chicago Press, 1955).

4. W. Allison Davis, "Child Rearing in the Class Structure of American Society," in *The Family in a Democratic Society*, Anniversary Papers of the Community Service Society of New York (New York, Columbia University Press, 1949), pp. 56–69.

5. See Martha Wolfenstein, "Trends in Infant Care," *American Journal of Orthopsychiatry*, 33 (1953), 120–130.

6. See Frederick Lewis Allen, *The Big Change* (New York, Harper & Bros., 1952).

7. William H. Sewell, "Infant Training and the Personality of the Child," *American Journal of Sociology*, 58 (1952), 150–159.

8. Harold Orlansky, "Infant Care and Personality," *Psychological Bulletin*, 46 (1949), 1–48.

9. Wolfenstein, *op. cit.*

10. Orlansky, *op. cit.*

11. *Ibid.*

12. Orlansky, *op. cit.*, p. 3.

13. Sewell, *op. cit.*

14. *Ibid.,* pp. 158–159.

15. Wolfenstein, *op. cit.*

16. Marvin B. Sussman, *Sourcebook in Marriage and the Family* (Boston, Houghton Mifflin Co., 1955), p. 167. This is a comment by Sussman on the Wolfenstein study cited above.

17. This data is taken from John A. Clausen, "Social Science in the Mental Health Field," *Items* of the Social Science Research Council, 9 (1955), 37–40.

18. For a thorough review of the data on divorce, see William J. Goode, *After Divorce* (Glencoe, The Free Press, 1956).

19. Lewis M. Terman *et al., Psychological Factors in Marital Happiness* (New York, McGraw-Hill Book Co., 1938).

20. Robert F. Winch, "The Oedipus Hypothesis," *American Sociological Review*, 16 (1951), 784–793.

21. The classical discussions of the "mom complex" are to be found in Geoffrey Gorer, *The American People* (New York, W. W. Norton & Co., Inc., 1948), chap. 2, and Philip Wylie, *Generation of Vipers* (New York, Rinehart & Co., Inc., 1942), chap. 11.

22. This material is based on a study by the writer of overexposure to small children on the part of middle-class mothers. This is as yet unpublished.

23. One of the most promising developments in the child-rearing field is the growth of the co-operative nursery school movement. See Katherine Whiteside-Taylor, "Cooperative Nursery Schools," *Marriage and Family Living*, 17 (1955), 302. For a discussion of the attitudes of young mothers toward nursery schools, see Elise Boulding, "The Cooperative Nursery and the Young Mother's Role Conflict," *Marriage and Family Living*, 17 (1955), 303–305.

24. For a discussion of the young mother as "the forgotten man" in our society, see the *Ladies Home Journal* article, "The Plight of the Young Mother," February, 1956. This is part of an excellent series of studies called "How Young America Lives."

25. Orlansky, *op. cit.*, p. 13.

26. *Ibid.*, p. 42.

27. See James H. S. Bossard, *The Sociology of Child Development* (New York, Harper & Bros., 1948), chap. 21.

Suggested Readings

1. Benjamin Spock, *The Pocketbook of Baby and Child Care* (New York, Pocket Books, Inc., 1946). Millions of copies of this classic have been sold to young parents. This has become the "Bible" on infant care for modern Americans.

2. Martha Wolfenstein, "Trends in Infant Care," *American Journal of Orthopsychiatry*, 33 (1953), 120–130. This is reprinted in Marvin B. Sussman, *Sourcebook in Marriage and the Family* (Boston, Houghton Mifflin Co., 1955), pp. 167–175. This is an extremely interesting article.

3. William H. Sewell, "Infant Training and the Personality of the Child," *American Journal of Sociology*, 58 (1952), 150–159. This is also available in Sussman, *op. cit.*, pp. 175–184.

4. Harold Orlansky, "Infant Care and Personality," *Psychological Bulletin*, 46 (1949), 1–48. The better student will find this rewarding.

5. Della D. Cyrus, "What's Wrong with the Family," *Atlantic Monthly*, 178 (1946), 67–73, and "Why Mothers Fail," *Atlantic Monthly*, 179 (1947), 57–60. Excerpts from these two articles may be found in Judson and Mary Landis, *Readings in Marriage and the Family* (New York, Prentice-Hall, Inc., 1952), pp. 392–402. Ths is a very down-to-earth discussion of motherhood in modern society.

6. Shirley Jackson, *Life Among the Savages* (New York, Farrar, Strauss & Young, Inc., 1953). This is a semihumorous account of child-rearing as experienced by two young college graduates.

7. Elinor Goulding Smith, "The Absolutely Complete Book of Perfect Housekeeping," *Ladies Home Journal,* March, 1956. This is a hilarious account of how one middle-class wife-mother approaches home management and child-rearing.

8. Robert O. Blood, Jr., "Consequences of Permissiveness for Parents of Young Children," *Marriage and Family Living,* 15 (1953), 209–212. An interesting study of parents who did not believe in harsh discipline.

9. Lillian M. Gilbreth, Orpha Mae Thomas, and Eleanor Clymer, *Management in the Home* (New York, Dodd, Mead & Co., 1954). An attempt to apply scientific management to child-rearing and household planning.

10. *Child Study,* a quarterly journal for parents published by the Child Study Association of America. In the writer's opinion, this is the finest magazine in the parent education field. Subscription rates may be obtained by writing the Association at 132 East 74th Street, New York 21, N.Y.

CHAPTER XXVI

MARITAL FAILURE

Some Perspective on Divorce

So much has been written about the divorce problem in the United States that one sometimes gets the impression that other societies do not have this problem. The truth is, however, that all societies have to recognize the fact that some marriages will fail, for the simple reason that no marriage system is perfect.

In a very interesting cross-cultural survey of divorce a few years ago, Murdock discovered that marital failure is recognized in primitive as well as modern societies, and that practically all human societies have had to work out ways of dealing with such failures.[1] He also concluded that some primitive or preliterate peoples have a marital failure rate much higher than that of the United States. R. F. Fortune, in his study of the Dobuans, a group living in the South Pacific, discovered that practically all their first marriages failed, a rate that makes ours seem modest.[2]

If we accept Murdock's conclusion, then, that this is a universal human problem, the next question becomes: *Why?* Social science research is not able, as yet, to give a very satisfactory answer

Figure 11: Cross-Cultural Perspective on Divorce—Divorces per 100 Marriages for Selected Countries *

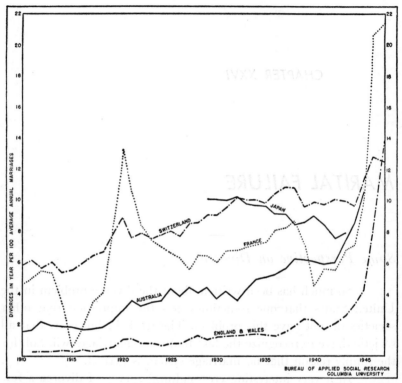

BUREAU OF APPLIED SOCIAL RESEARCH
COLUMBIA UNIVERSITY

This chart shows that the United States is not the only society faced with a rising divorce rate.

* Source: Kingsley Davis, "Statistical Perspective on Marriage and Divorce," *The Annals* of the American Academy of Political and Social Science, 272 (November, 1950), 9–21.

to this question, but it may not do harm to mention a few possible explanations.

1. In the first place, on what grounds should one assume that a certain proportion of marriages in any society would *not* fail? That is, what would lead us to assume that any marriage system would be perfect? Is it not true that we expect some ratio of failure in all the other social institutions in any society—the economic sys-

tem, the political system, and so on? And if this is so, why should it be different for the marriage system?

A good illustration of this point may be seen in the attitude of the Catholic church in our own society. While it is true that this particular group does not permit divorce and remarriage, it is not true that the Catholic church is naïve enough to expect that all marriages within this faith will be successful. As a matter of fact, the church recognizes the right of married persons to separate under certain circumstances, even though it does not sanction divorce and remarriage.[3]

Looked at from this perspective, it is really not surprising that a certain proportion of marriages in our society, or in any society, should fail. It would be much more surprising if they all succeeded.

2. Even if the institutional or structural system of courtship and marriage were relatively foolproof, this still would not completely prevent marital failure, for the reason that not all persons would make maximum use of the structure. In the United States, for example, there is reason to believe that our marital failure rate could be significantly reduced if all groups would make maximum use of our engagement system, but they do not. Thus the system or structure is not being utilized to the highest degree.

3. No matter how good the marriage system, some individuals will be defective or abnormal (psychotics, for example) and this will produce a certain percentage of marital failures. This is perfectly obvious in our society when one thinks of all the deviant types, the mentally deficient, the alcoholics, the psychotics, the sexual deviants, the criminals, etc. All complex societies have a certain proportion of these.

4. Even granting a good courtship and marriage system, and assuming relatively normal men and women, some marriages would still fail as the result of severe strain imposed by the larger society itself. Wars, economic crises, social revolutions—deep cultural crises always break up a certain proportion of marriages. This can readily be seen in our own society.

Figure 12: Marital Dissolution by Death and Divorce, United States, 1890–1948 *

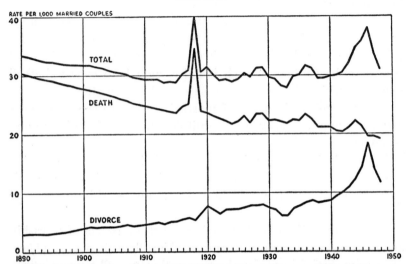

RATE PER 1000 MARRIED COUPLES

TOTAL

DEATH

DIVORCE

1890   1900   1910   1920   1930   1940   1950

This chart shows the effects of World Wars I and II on marital stability rates in our society. It also shows how divorce has replaced death as the breaker of marriage for young and middle-aged couples in the United States.

* Source: Louis I. Dublin, *The Facts of Life from Birth to Death* (New York, The Macmillan Company, 1951), p. 64.

5. And, finally, it might be argued that human nature itself is not completely compatible with permanent marital unions. There is some evidence, for example, that the sexual drive in humans is not easily conditioned to support long-term marriages, and this becomes especially relevant in a society such as ours which expects lifetime sexual monogamy.

Space does not permit us to explore any of these ideas any further, but we trust that enough has been said to convince the reader that the general problem of marital failure is by no means unique to the United States. On the contrary, it is as old and as universal as human marriage itself.

If we grant the general propositions advanced so far, it then becomes necessary to inquire as to what patterns or social structures have been developed to handle marital failure. Let us look at those to be found in our own society, since this is essentially a book about marriage in the United States.

1. *Annulment.*

This is an interesting legal device by means of which a marriage is canceled, the man and woman being restored to their single state, as it were.

To qualify for an annulment, it must be established that the marriage was invalid when the original ceremony was performed: for example, one of the parties might have been married already to another person, thus being guilty of bigamy. The innocent party could then file for an annulment. As a rule, fraud and/or deception of some kind are usually present when annulment is granted.

It should be understood that from a legal point of view an annulment is quite different from a divorce; in the former, the parties were never married in the eyes of the law.

The Catholic church grants annulments for certain reasons, thereby permittting the parties to contract a valid marriage.

Annulment is often resorted to in states such as New York in which it is difficult to obtain a divorce.

2. *Desertion.*

This is sometimes referred to as "the poor man's divorce." In this situation, one party simply walks off—or *runs* off, as the case may be. There is no legal or religious sanction whatsoever.

It appears that desertion is much more common at the lower income levels.[4] In some ways, it is a more serious problem than divorce itself, because more children are usually involved (owing to high birth rates at this income level), and because there is no supervision by the court, as there is in divorce. Desertion may also be more traumatic than divorce in that it is often unannounced, and it is also *unilateral,* whereas divorce usually is bilateral and hardly comes as a surprise.

One does not read much about desertion, but family social workers are extremely familiar with it.

3. *Separation.*

This term normally implies a bilateral or mutual agreement to live separately. It often involves a legal settlement similar to that granted in divorce actions. Separation does not, of course, carry the right to remarry. In both separation and desertion, this legal inability to remarry creates major problems, as these men and women often meet someone else they care for. This tends to produce illicit unions and illegitimate children, at least in some cases.

Catholics may obtain the right to separation under certain conditions.

4. *Divorce.*

In this solution to marital failure, one member of the marriage petitions the court to dissolve the union, presenting evidence that the other party has violated some provision of the statutes governing divorce in that state. If the court accepts and grants the petition, the marriage is dissolved. In some cases, the woman resumes her maiden name. The court usually approves a settlement of any property held in common. The court also determines who shall have custody of the children, if any, and who shall support them.

Divorce is now granted in all 48 of our states, although the grounds or acceptable legal reasons for divorce vary widely from one state to another. In general, the older states are less liberal in their divorce laws than are the states admitted to the Union at a later date.

Many persons do not realize that the federal government has no jurisdiction over divorce, this matter being regulated entirely by the states. Since there are 48 different sets of statutes on divorce, a certain amount of confusion is to be expected.

5. *Marital reconciliation.*

Persons who do not accept divorce as a solution to marital problems are strong in their advocacy of marriage counseling or its equivalent. Most churches strongly urge this as an alternative to separation or divorce. It is not clear as yet what proportion of our marital failures might be prevented by adequate counseling, but it seems to be clear that this has never been tried by the majority of our divorced couples—judging by the research of Goode,[5] to be presented later.

Some Folklore About Divorce

In spite of the fact that divorce is by now a fairly common occurrence in our society, there still is a great deal of misinformation and folklore about it. The following seem to be some of the main items in this folklore:

1. *That the United States has the highest divorce rate in the world.*

This is hardly true. Many primitive or preliterate societies have divorce rates exceeding that of the United States. In the 1920's Russia's divorce rate was probably higher than ours. At the present time England, Germany, and Japan appear to have divorce rates as high or higher than the United States.[6]

2. *That our divorce rate is increasing.*

This is true if you view the trend over a period of several decades—since 1900, for example—but it is *not* true for the last decade. Our divorce rate has actually declined somewhat from its peak at the end of World War II.

3. *That American divorce laws are getting "easier."*

As a matter of fact, divorce laws have not changed very much in recent decades—certainly not enough to account for the rise in divorce rates. In New York, for example, our most populous state, adultery remains the only grounds for divorce.

4. *That marriages can be dissolved by mutual consent.*

This is not true. In theory, if not in fact, every divorce case represents a lawsuit in which an innocent party sues the other party.

What actually happens, however, is that the spouse being sued usually does not contest the suit, and this makes it appear that the divorce was by mutual consent.

Stated in legal terms, marriage is not a partnership in the eyes of the law and hence cannot be dissolved merely by the two partners giving consent. There must be some grounds for the action, that is, some offenses recognized by the particular state as sufficient to justify divorce.

5. *That the grounds for divorce actually explain the cause of marital failure.*

Perhaps you have read in the paper that some Hollywood star has been granted a divorce on the grounds of cruelty. This does not mean that any cruelty was actually involved, at least not in the sense that the term is usually used. All it means is that the attorney decided that this would be the easiest way to get the divorce. If the same divorce had been granted in New York, the paper would have reported the grounds as adultery, for New York will not grant a divorce for cruelty alone.

Thus, we see that the legal grounds for divorce have very little relationship to reality. No social scientist or marriage counselor would accept them today as the cause of divorce.

6. *That the federal government should do something about divorce.*

Many Americans do not realize that the federal government has absolutely no jurisdiction over divorce laws, this power belonging to the 48 states. For this reason, we have no uniform divorce laws. The federal constitution does require, however, that each state recognize legitimate divorces granted by all the other states. Otherwise, there would be complete chaos.

7. *That middle- and upper-class couples have the highest divorce rate.*

Goode, Schroeder, and others do *not* find this to be the case.[7] It now appears certain that low-income groups have the highest divorce rate in the United States—in particular, the couples who do not complete high school.

8. *That lawyers could prevent a great many divorces if they attempted more marriage counseling.*

Although this sounds logical enough, there is a serious flaw in the proposal, namely, that attorneys are usually consulted *too late* for effective counseling. By that time the marriage is not failing; it has failed.

Actually, ministers and church staffs are in a much better position than lawyers to do effective marriage counseling. Family physicians and psychiatrists are also in good positions to help prevent divorce.

9. *That the rural divorce rate is far below that of the city.*

This may still be true in many states, but since 1940 the rural rate has shown a tendency to catch up with the urban rate. In Wisconsin, for example, the rural rate appears to be about as high as the urban rate since World War II.[8]

10. *That a "great deal" is known about divorce.*

One would expect to find a mass of research related to a social problem regarded as seriously as divorce is in our society, but the fact is that we know relatively little about who gets divorced and why. In the past twenty or thirty years, only two major field studies of divorce in the United States have been published, those of Locke and of Goode.[9] This seems incredible, but is true, nevertheless.

Interestingly enough, the federal government is not even able to get all the states to report their divorce statistics, so that even the national trend has to be estimated. It is little wonder that our society as yet has made relatively little progress in understanding or attacking this problem.

One could cite other misconceptions about divorce in our society, but perhaps the above will help the reader see this problem in greater perspective.

We are now ready to review the research studies of divorce published to date.

Empirical Studies of Divorce

It seems very odd that a problem as disturbing to Americans as divorce has received relatively little attention from research groups, but this is the case. All in all, the data required for a systematic analysis of divorce in our society are simply not available at the present time. It will be necessary, therefore, to leave unanswered many of the basic questions.

Our procedure in this section will be to review the research on divorce that seems best suited to help us understand it. At the end of the chapter we will attempt a few generalizations.

1. *The work of Schroeder.*

In 1939 Schroeder published an interesting study of divorce in a city of 100,000 (Peoria, Illinois).[10] He came up with some very interesting conclusions:

A. That divorce rates do not necessarily increase as the size of the city increases, as many people think. Peoria, for example, has had a higher divorce rate than Chicago for several decades.

B. Divorce rates in Peoria are *highest* in the *lowest* income areas of the city. As a matter of fact, the divorce rate in Census Enumeration District 55 (a high-income area) was only *one sixth* what it was in District 69 (a low-income area).[11]

In view of this striking discovery, it is interesting to note that most Americans still seem to believe that middle- and upper-class couples have the highest divorce rate. In a 1955 study by Goode (to be reviewed later), he points out that this myth still survives in America.[12]

Note that the difference in rates from one income area to another was not small; it was pronounced.

C. Divorce is significantly higher among persons who do not belong to a church.

D. Divorce rates are highly correlated with delinquency rates, the two being found together.

Since Schroeder's study was well designed, there seems little doubt that divorce is related to low social status, even though the precise dynamics are not very clear.

2. *The work of Kephart and Monahan.*

In 1952 the above men published an extremely interesting article, "Desertion and Divorce in Philadelphia," in which they pointed out that desertion as a type of family disorganization merits

Figure 13: Divorce Rate for Married Couples with and without Children under age 18, according to Duration of Marriage, United States, 1948 *

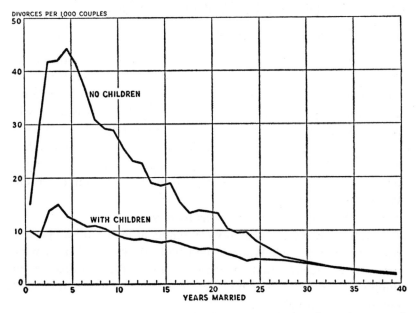

It appears that children retard the divorce rate during the early years of marriage. This does not mean, however, that children *solve* marital problems—they may merely prevent divorce.

* Source: Louis I. Dublin, *The Facts of Life from Birth to Death* (New York, The Macmillan Company, 1951), p. 71.

more attention than it has received.[13] Their specific findings were as follows:

A.   In the past thirty years there have been *almost twice* as many desertions as divorces in Philadelphia. Yet most of the public concern has been and is about the divorce problem.

B.   Children are involved in 75 per cent of the desertion cases in Philadelphia as compared to only 42 per cent of the divorce cases. Here again, desertion is more serious than divorce.

C.   In Aid to Dependent Children cases (mothers with minor children receiving public assistance) in the state of Pennsylvania, divorce accounts for only 5 per cent of the cases, whereas desertion accounts for 33 per cent.

This study makes it very clear that divorce is only one facet of the marital failure problem in the United States.

3.   *The work of Waller.*

One of the oldest studies, published in 1930, is still one of the most provocative: *The Old Love and the New*,[14] written by the late Willard Waller, probably the outstanding observer of the American family up to now. We recommend this book to persons who wish to acquire some insight into the dynamics of divorce.

Waller's method was that of the intensive case study. It is not known, of course, how typical his cases were, but the recent statistical study by Goode does not, in the writer's opinion, contradict Waller's basic conclusions.[15]

The major findings were as follows:

A.   Divorce is essentially *traumatic,* at least until a new love relationship is formed. Waller's data flatly reject the idea, so widespread in our society, that Americans can go through a divorce and think nothing of it. There may be a few deviants who can do that, but not most Americans.

B.   That divorce involves a profound disruption of the person's life: his living arrangements, his sex life, his recreation, his circle of friends, his financial affairs, etc. This is one of the reasons why divorce can seldom be easy.

C.   That a significant proportion of his divorced persons

regretted their divorce. These persons felt that their divorce had been too hasty or perhaps unnecessary. This particular finding has recently been questioned by Goode (see below).

D. The only real cure for a divorce is a new love affair. The current remarriage rate of divorced persons lends ample support to this observation.

Figure 14: Chances of Eventual Marriage for Single, Widowed, or Divorced Persons, United States, 1940 *

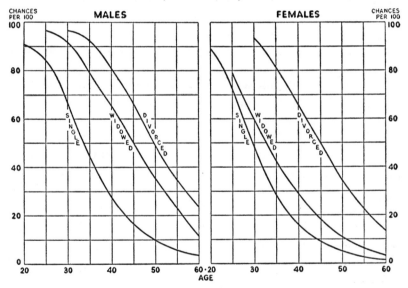

This chart points up the interesting fact that divorced and widowed persons are preferred to the "never married" group as marriage partners in the middle and later decades.

* Source: Louis I. Dublin, *The Facts of Life from Birth to Death* (New York, The Macmillan Company, 1951), p. 47.

E. That marriage on the rebound is a very real hazard for the divorced person in our society.

4. *The work of Monahan.*

It is very important that we know how remarriages of divorced persons compare with first marriages. Monahan attempted to discover the answer to this crucial question in a study of remarriages in Iowa and Missouri.[16] Although his data include the widowed as well as the divorced, Monahan's findings apply largely to divorced persons.

A. Remarriages are *less* stable than first marriages.

B. The probability of divorce *increases* with each subsequent marriage.

C. Men and women do not differ significantly in this respect; in other words, divorced or widowed women are no better marital risks than divorced or widowed men.

5. *The work of Locke.*

In 1951 Locke published a marital prediction study in which he compared 200 divorced couples with 200 happily married couples.[17] Although this was not intended primarily as a study of divorce, it nevertheless constitutes one of the best studies of this problem yet published. For one thing, Locke's sample, covering a single county in Indiana, was much more representative than most of the previous samples used in marriage and/or divorce studies.

Locke's most interesting findings seem to be the following:

A. "The alienation process is generally a slow cumulation of conflicts and disagreements, accompanied by the psychological withdrawal of one or both spouses. If the course of the alienation process is far advanced, the spouses tend to express derogatory attitudes toward each other, tend to have many complaints about the mate and the marriage, and tend to exaggerate the deficiencies of the mate and the marriage." [18] In other words, Locke rejects the theory that marriages crack up suddenly.

B. Divorced couples have usually had an inadequate courtship, whereas happily married couples have actually begun their marital adjustment process before the marriage even takes place.

C. The presence or absence of children is not significantly related to marital failure.

D. The outside employment of the wife was not a significant factor in the divorces in this study.

E. Divorced women are not a poor risk for a second marriage, but divorced men are. Locke's finding about women is contrary to general belief.

F. Unconventional behavior patterns are related to divorce
—such items as not belonging to a church, being married by a civil
justice instead of a minister, etc.

G. Differences in religion were not a significant factor in
these 200 divorces.

Locke has additional data but these seem to be his outstanding conclusions. He definitely challenges a number of widely held
theories or beliefs about divorce: that children prevent divorce;
that divorcees are poor marital risks; that a wife's outside job is a
cause of divorce; that religious differences often cause divorce; etc.
We shall see below, in the study by Goode, that most of Locke's
findings seem to be confirmed.

6. *The work of Goode.*

In 1955 Goode published the most systematic field study
of divorce yet available in his book, *After Divorce*.[19] This study,
made in Detroit after World War II, focuses on 425 divorced
mothers twenty to thirty-eight years old. The sample was carefully drawn from the official records in Detroit, thus avoiding the
pitfall of interviewing volunteers (who usually are not very
typical).

One of the serious limitations of this study is that all the data
were obtained from the wives; none of the husbands were included
in the interviewing. Hence this survey, excellent as it is, gives us only
the woman's version of divorce.

The methodology of this study appears to have been unusually rigorous. For this reason alone, it is interesting to compare
Goode's conclusions with those of the preceding studies, also with
popular belief.

The major findings are as follows:

A. Goode agrees with Waller that divorce in the United
States, even today, involves a major readjustment of the divorced
person's life. In other words, it is no picnic and is not viewed lightly
by those who have gone through it—at least not by the vast bulk of
the 425 mothers in this study.

Note, however, that Goode's sample excluded divorced

women *without children,* for whom the experience should have been less difficult. His study also does not show whether the husbands suffered as much as did the wives.

B. The trauma or shock *precedes* the divorce itself, going back to the earlier period when the marriage was failing.

C. Once the battle is over and the decision to divorce made, there is usually a feeling of relief. Most of the women in this study did not regret their divorce.

D. Of the women who had remarried by the time of the study, about 90 per cent thought their second marriage was better than the first. It is possible, of course, that this was essentially a defense mechanism; in order to justify all the trouble related to getting a divorce, one might have to believe that the new marriage was an improvement. It seems that we still need to know a lot more about second and subsequent marriages.

E. Sexual maladjustment was *not* a major cause of divorce in this study, at least not in the opinion of the wives. It is well known, however, that sexual response in marriage is more important to husbands than wives, so that a study of the husbands in this sample might reveal sex to have been more of a problem than the wives thought.

F. Low-income groups in this study definitely have higher divorce rates than do middle- or upper-income groups. Goode devotes considerable attention to this matter and his findings should help to dispel the myth that higher income groups have higher divorce rates. Note that his findings completely support the earlier conclusions obtained by Schroeder in his study of Peoria, Illinois, cited earlier in this discussion.

G. Negroes in Detroit have a significantly higher divorce rate than the white population.

H. Marriage before twenty years of age was typical of the divorced women in this study.

I. Failure to complete high school was characteristic of the husbands in this sample.

J. These couples did not make adequate use of the engagement stage in our courtship system to test their compatibility. Seventy-one per cent were engaged for less than six months, while 19 per cent had no formal engagement.

It was not true, however, that these couples were the victims of whirlwind courtships; 70 per cent knew each other at least a year before marriage. Their total courtship, nevertheless, appears to have been inadequate, as it was also in Locke's study.

K. A significant proportion of the parents had disapproved of these marriages—40 per cent of the wives' parents and 25 per cent of the husbands'. This supports the finding of Burgess-Wallin that parents, and especially the girl's parents, are in a good position to predict the outcome of the average marriage.[20]

This finding also points to a serious weakness in the American courtship system : giving the parents an adequate voice in the marital plans of their children. This seems to be especially true of low-income groups.

L. Goode does not agree with Locke that outside employment of the wife is not associated with divorce. Forty-two per cent of these divorced women held full-time jobs during most of their married life.

Actually, Goode seems to believe that *economic factors in general* were basic in these marital failures. If we look at the husbands, for example, 51 per cent did not have steady jobs; 64 per cent of them earned less than $60 a week (not very good for Detroit) ; a considerable proportion of them had not completed high school. One gets the general impression that these husbands were socially inadequate. And since the wives had chosen them (or been chosen) for marital partners, it seems that these couples tend to represent that segment of our population which social scientists have come to call "the underprivileged." If this is correct, then divorce begins to resemble many of our other social problems.

M. Goode's study does *not* support the widely held belief that divorce is bad for the children. His divorced women reported that, on the average, their children were less disturbed living with one parent in peace than with two parents at war.

N. Most of his divorcees reported that they would rather be divorced than unhappily married.

O. Most of the divorced women in this study did not become social outcasts but retained their previous circle of friends.

P. Divorced mothers usually have severe economic problems —their former husbands seldom are able, or willing, to support them and their children. It should be remembered, however, that most of these husbands were not good breadwinners at *any* time, married or divorced.

Q. And, finally, Goode is critical of any simple explanations of divorce. He is of the opinion that marital failure is usually the result of a complex interplay of several sets of factors—economic, psychiatric, cultural, etc.

7. *The work of Bernard.*

In 1956 Bernard published a study of 2,009 remarriages.[21] Although her data include the widowed as well as the divorced, the bulk of Bernard's findings are applicable to the remarriages of the divorced group.

Her most interesting findings appear to be the following:

A. That about 80 per cent of the remarriages in her sample appear to be successful. She comments: "It is the surprising amount of reported success in remarriage, not the amount of failure, that seems to require explanation." [22]

B. It is not true, as some psychiatrists have argued, that "divorce won't help." [23] Bernard estimates that as many as two thirds of our divorced population may benefit from their divorce— that is, find a more compatible partner.

C. Remarriage, on the average, is not only successful for the married couple but also for their children. Bernard and Goode are in agreement on this point.

D. That remarriage in our society has *not* increased appreciably in the last century, as the decline in death rates has offset the increase in divorce.

E. That social class or socioeconomic factors are highly associated with remarriage rates—in other words, that low-income marriages are the least stable in our society.

Discussion of Research Findings

While recognizing that the research on divorce is still inadequate, it begins to appear that this problem is essentially a low-income group phenomenon. Bernard, for example, reports that only 5.8 per cent of college graduates have ever been divorced.[24] It appears that the proportion of divorced college graduates is only about half that of the general population.[25] This type of data makes one suspect that the psychological or psychiatric approach to marital failure may be somewhat inadequate, and that this problem must be seen in its socioeconomic context.

The research to date also challenges the old notion that "divorce is bad for the children." It is undoubtedly true that children derive unlimited benefits from *good* marriages, but does it follow that they also benefit from the preservation of *poor* marriages? It does not appear so.

And, lastly, the current research challenges the psychiatric notion that marital failure is largely the result of personality deficiency and that the subsequent marriages of divorced persons would be doomed also. It is true that second and third marriages as a group have fairly high failure rates,[26] but it also appears that a substantial majority of remarriages are successful.

It is interesting to note that, in Popenoe's study of 200 divorced couples who remarried each other, 48 per cent of these reunions were rated as "happy." [27] While this is a respectable showing, it appears that these couples might have done even better if they had chosen a new partner, judging by the Bernard data cited above.

The Process of Marital Failure

There appears to be a belief in our society that marriages break up all at once or suddenly. The research does not support this view. Locke, as we have seen, in his study of 200 divorced couples in Indiana, reported a *slow* process of deterioration, with many crises, each of which was followed by a lower level of adjustment.[28] Locke's data would support the view that just as time is required to *build* a love relationship, so is time required to *tear it down*.

Koos and Hill, in their studies of general family crises (not divorce specifically), report a similar process of gradual decline in the level of organization or adjustment.[29]

In his recent study of 425 divorced mothers in Detroit, reviewed above, Goode also was unable to identify any sudden pattern of marital failure.

Waller's study of the 1920's supports the same point of view.[30]

The process might be diagramed as in Figure 15.

Figure 15: Schematic Drawing of the Process of Marital Failure *

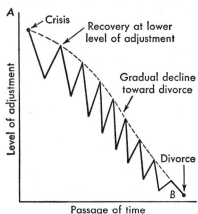

* This is based on the work of Reuben Hill, *Families Under Stress* (New York, Harper & Brothers, 1949), also that of Harvey J. Locke, *Predicting Adjustment in Marriage* (New York, Henry Holt, 1951).

Beginning at some point in time, not usually identified by the couple, the relationship begins to deteriorate. In some couples, this may even antedate the marriage itself. As the conflicts increase, the couple usually struggle to resolve their problems, and to some extent they succeed. But, as the graph shows, the level of recovery keeps dropping, so that each crisis leaves them with less reserve than before.

At some point, also not well defined as a rule, one (or both) of the partners becomes *indifferent*. This often gives a false sense of improvement because the quarrels and the conflicts seem to subside. Actually, this is the beginning of the end and means that the person (or the couple) has ceased to care what happens. At this point the final break or separation may come at any time. This is when they usually consult a lawyer.

It may be that in some cases one partner reports that the failure was sudden, but this usually means only that this person was unaware of what was happening to the marriage. It also happens that some couples will not admit that their marriage is failing and keep whistling in the dark. Then one day (or night) one or both of them "suddenly" sees the futility of their relationship. This seems to be the pattern most popular with dramatists as it lends itself well to the needs of good theater. Ibsen, for example, utilizes this form in his famous play, *The Doll's House*.[31] In actuality, however, the majority of divorced couples knew their marriage was failing but found themselves helpless to halt the deterioration process.

Implications of This Analysis

If the social scientists are correct in their analysis of this gradual process of failure, then it follows that marital counseling, to be effective, must be initiated fairly early in the pattern of decline. This supports our earlier assertion that lawyers (and divorce courts) are in a very poor position to do effective marriage counseling.

It appears that any really successful program in preventing divorce will have to come to the same conclusion as the tuberculosis, heart, and cancer campaigns, namely, that *successful treatment depends on early diagnosis*. Notice, however, that this runs counter to the current practice of *concealing* marital problems. It appears that in this regard we are facing the same problem encountered by the tuberculosis and venereal disease campaigns of several decades ago. It seems obvious that the education of the general public in how to identify the early signs of marital failure has only begun.

It is also apparent that *as of now* we do not have sufficient treatment facilities even for those who recognize their problem and are willing to accept help. It appears that most physicians are too busy to take on this job, even if they had the training, which they usually do not. Ministers, already overworked, appear to be handling more cases than any other professional group.

In the opinion of the writer, most marriage problems do not require the services of a psychiatrist in that mental illness is not normally involved. Furthermore, the majority of couples cannot afford a psychiatrist, even if one were available, which they usually are not.

Professional psychologists are well equipped to help most couples, but they are not numerous and their fees are apt to resemble those of the psychiatrist.

The modern professionally trained social case worker is able to alleviate a great many marital conflicts, but the general public as yet is poorly informed about this professional group. And as Koos showed in his revealing study of New York City families, there is considerable prejudice against social workers as a group.[32] There is also some stigma still attached to consulting a social work agency. The writer believes that the greatest potential agency for the early treatment of marital problems is the urban church, but it remains to be seen whether or not the church will see this opportunity, or will have the resources to tackle it.

Since there seems to be a strong trend toward group practice (clinics) in modern medicine, and since doctors are usually too busy to do marriage counseling themselves, it is to be hoped that some clinics will see fit to add marriage counselors to their staff, either social case workers or clinical psychologists. As conservative as they are, physicians in the last few decades have shown a willingness to turn over certain duties to nurses, laboratory technicians, occupational therapists, medical social workers, and nonmedical hospital administrators. Maybe it is not impossible that they will also see the wisdom of adding the marriage counselor to their growing list of associates.

Summary and Conclusion

In this discussion we have seen that the general problem of marital failure is by no means peculiar to the United States. In an earlier chapter, you may recall, we also saw that the divorce rate in itself is not adequate evidence of the functioning or malfunctioning of our marriage system.

The empirical research reviewed in this discussion, meager as it is, certainly indicates that there is no single cause of divorce in our society. Furthermore, this research indicates that marriages do not disintegrate suddenly; as a matter of fact, marital failure is a long process and often precedes any real insight by the partners themselves. This finding makes it all too clear that effective treatment of marital discord depends upon early diagnosis and willingness to seek help.

It is odd, but true, that most couples are unable to solve serious problems by themselves; like two fighters in a clinch, they need an impartial referee to separate them. As a rule, family members and friends are not well qualified for this job—they are too partial to help the participants gain insight. For this reason, professional outsiders seem to do best—ministers, social workers, physicians, etc.

It must be admitted, however, that some of the marriages in our society are hopeless, and that no counselor can solve their problems. In those cases, it seems that separation and divorce (religion permitting) are the only solutions. Even the children may be better off with one parent than living under daily conflict.

In the last analysis, as Waller and Goode suggest,[33] the only remedy for a broken love affair in our society is a *new* love affair. It is to be hoped, however, that the new relationship will be more adequately tested before marriage than was the old.

References

1. George P. Murdock, "Family Stability in Non-European Cultures," *Annals* of The American Academy of Political and Social Science, 272 (1950), 195–201.

2. Reo F. Fortune, *Sorcerers of Dobu* (New York, E. P. Dutton & Co., Inc., 1932).

3. John L. Thomas, *The American Catholic Family* (New York, Prentice-Hall, Inc., 1956).

4. William M. Kephart and Thomas P. Monahan, "Desertion and Divorce in Philadelphia," *American Sociological Review,* 17 (1952), 710–727.

5. William J. Goode, *After Divorce* (Glencoe, The Free Press, 1956), pp. 155–156.

6. Goode, *op. cit.,* p. 11.

7. See Goode, *op. cit.,* chap. 4, for a complete review of the relationship of socioeconomic factors to divorce in our society. The most intensive study is that by C. W. Schroeder, *Divorce in a City of 100,000 Population* (Chicago, University of Chicago Press, 1939).

8. See Jessie Bernard, *Remarriage* (New York, Dryden Press, 1956) for a review of urban and rural divorce trends. Unfortunately, this study did not become available until the bulk of this text had been written.

9. In recent years, the study by Goode, cited above, has been the only major field study of divorce in our society. However, the work of Harvey J. Locke, *Predicting Adjustment in Marriage* (New York, Henry Holt & Co., Inc., 1951), although not primarily a study of divorce itself, contains a great deal of useful data about marital failure. More recently, the work of Jessie Bernard, *op. cit.,* has also helped to understand divorce in our culture. One can still say, however, as Goode does, that this important American problem received practically no attention from American social scientists from about 1930 to about 1950.

10. Schroeder, *op. cit.*

11. *Ibid.,* pp. 36–43.

12. See Goode, *op. cit.,* for a refutation of the myth that middle- and upper-income groups have the highest divorce rates in our society.

13. Kephart and Monahan, *op. cit.*

14. Willard Waller, *The Old Love and the New* (New York, Liveright Publishing Corp., 1930).

15. Goode, *op. cit.*

16. See Thomas P. Monahan, "Divorce by Occupational Level," *Marriage and Family Living,* 17 (1955), 322–324; also his study, "How Stable Are Remarriages?" *American Journal of Sociology,* 58 (1952), 280–288.

17. Locke, *op. cit.*

18. *Ibid.,* p. 358.

19. Goode, *op. cit.*

20. See Ernest W. Burgess and Paul Wallin, *Engagement and Marriage* (Philadelphia, J. B. Lippincott Co., 1953), pp. 560–562.

21. Bernard, *op. cit.*

22. *Ibid.,* p. 269.

23. See Edmund Bergler, *Divorce Won't Help* (New York, Harper & Bros., 1948).

24. Bernard, *op. cit.*, p. 81.

25. Ernest Havemann and Patricia Salter West, *They Went to College* (New York, Harcourt, Brace & Co., 1952), p. 41. We are indebted to Bernard, *op. cit.*, for this reference.

26. For the details on remarriage failure rates, see the studies of Goode and Bernard cited above.

27. Paul Popenoe, "Remarriage of Divorcees to Each Other," *American Sociological Review*, 3 (1938), 695–699.

28. Locke, *op. cit.*, p. 358.

29. See Earl Koos, *Families in Trouble* (New York, Columbia University Press, 1946), and Reuben Hill, *Families Under Stress* (New York, Harper & Bros., 1949).

30. Waller, *op. cit.*

31. Henrik Ibsen, "The Doll's House," *Plays* (New York, Tudor Publishing Co., 1936).

32. Koos, *op. cit.*

33. *Op. cit.*

Suggested Readings

1. William J. Goode, *After Divorce* (Glencoe, The Free Press, 1956). The serious student will find this study extremely worthwhile.

2. Willard Waller, *The Old Love and the New* (New York, Liveright Publishing Corp., 1930). Based on intensive case studies, this little book can aid the student in understanding the process by which marriages fail.

3. Jessie Bernard, *Remarriage* (New York, Dryden Press, 1956). Although this study does not limit itself to the remarriages of divorced persons, it contains a great deal of material helpful to the student who wishes to gain some perspective on divorce and the process of remarriage in general in our society.

4. Kingsley Davis, "Statistical Perspective on Marriage and Divorce," *Annals* of The American Academy of Political and Social Science, 272 (1950), 9–21.

5. George P. Murdock, "Family Stability in Non-European Cultures," *Annals* of The American Academy of Political and Social Science, 272 (1950), 195–201. The interested student will find other worthwhile articles on family stability in this issue of the *Annals* as the entire number is devoted to this problem.

CHAPTER XXVII

MARRIAGE AND MATURATION

Introduction

For most Americans, marriage symbolizes the end of adolescence and the beginning of adult responsibilities. Newly wed persons begin, often for the first time, to notice the cost of living: food prices at the supermarket, rental levels, fuel oil prices, etc. When the first child arrives, they may suddenly become concerned about the "school problem" in their community, or the need for a neighborhood playground. Interest in political issues often coincides with the age of marriage in our society also.

In a very real sense, it seems to us, the young American begins to really grow up when he marries. It is this social maturation aspect of marriage and parenthood that we wish to analyze in this concluding chapter. Essentially, the purpose of the discussion will be to give the student some long-range perspective on the developments he can expect as his marriage matures. To do this, we will employ the life cycle technique developed by Glick for the analysis of the American family.[1]

Perhaps it should be made clear that we are not implying that unmarried adults (the male and female bachelors) in our society are not mature because they do not marry. We believe that social maturation in these persons results largely from two experiences: (*a*) the assumption of adult occupational responsibility; and (*b*) the assumption of family responsibility, either for elderly parents or younger siblings. In a very real sense, these persons *are* married to their jobs and/or their families of birth.

With this apology to the bachelors, let us look at the average American middle-class married couple as they move through life together.

Life Cycle of Marriage

1. *The preparenthood stage.*

After the wedding reception and the honeymoon are over (but not forgotten), the young couple move into their apartment and begin to assemble furniture, life insurance, clocks, phonograph records, and the other essentials of middle-class married life. The young wife will normally be employed at this point, also learning how to cook. Sex is apt to be rather pervasive at this time, a sort of extension of the honeymoon.

In many ways, this is one of the most pleasant interludes in the average American's life, almost as carefree as high school or college but with sex (complete and legitimate) added, plus home cooking. As one of our married students in this stage once described it: "It is almost like *playing house,* the way we used to as children. 'You be the Daddy and I'll be the Mommy.' It's a very nice way to live."

Like all good things, however, this carefree stage has to end, at least for the vast majority of young couples, and we then move into the next stage. "At present, almost one half of our couples have a child before the third year of marriage and about three fourths are started on their family life within the first five years." [2] For about 15 to 20 per cent of our married couples, however, who do not become parents, this stage continues more or less indefinitely.[3]

2. *Preschool parenthood.*

With the first pregnancy, the young couple leave the delightful land of the honeymooners and head for the world of the pediatrician. Instead of reading the comics they are more apt to be found with a copy of *Dr. Spock* (the classic authority on baby care in our society).[4]

This stage may last for five years or twenty, depending on how many youngsters they have and how close together they arrive. As of the 1950's, the average (median) couple had their last child by the end of their sixth year of marriage. It is interesting to note that the span of childbearing has been cut almost in half in the last two generations.[5]

In many ways, these are apt to be rather rough years for most young couples. For one thing, the husband will still be working hard to establish himself in his occupation, which means that his hours may be long and his income moderate. In a sense, this is unfortunate, for his small children and his wife need both his time and his money during these years. Housing needs, for example, are very real during this stage, and housing costs money. Most young couples will be moving out of their apartments at this time and heading for the suburbs. The household appliance bills are apt to be high as the babies arrive—an automatic washer, an electric dryer, an ironer, dishwasher, etc. And more life insurance is often a good idea. Thus, for the young husband-father, these years are not apt to be very easy. His employer (or his profession) and his family will often want him at the same time. And *everybody* will want his money.

For the young middle-class wife-mother, these preschool years involve long hours with the babies, hard work around the house, and a good deal of social isolation. She gives up her job and becomes a mother. In many ways she has not been adequately prepared for these years. She is also worried at times about the great responsibility involved in her role as major child-rearer during this period—whether she is doing a "good job" with the children. And, indeed, her work with the children during their preschool years *is* crucial in our society.

To balance the hard work of these years, there is, of course, the thrill and joy of being a parent—of holding your baby in your arms, of putting a small child to bed, of watching children in their daily growth. This is apt to be the period that parents feel most nostalgic about years later when they get out the baby pictures and look back at the exciting preschool years. But while they were struggling with the colic and the diapers, it did not always seem to be such a wonderful experience. For the student who wishes to read a firsthand account of these years, we heartily recommend Shirley Jackson's *Life Among the Savages,*[6] a humorous description of modern parenthood.

3. *The early school years.*

As the child moves out into the neighborhood and the community, *so do the parents.* It is at this point that the young parents begin to be concerned about conditions in their residential area— traffic hazards, for example—and the wider community. They join the PTA, help organize a Girl or Boy Scout troop, and lend their support to other community improvement programs.

This illustrates, in our opinion, the process by which marriage and parenthood push the young couple toward social maturation. Up to this time they have not usually displayed any sustained interest in the community as such, but now they begin to care and to assume responsibility.

This is often the stage at which college graduates return to the church, many of them having left the church during the years of adolescent struggle for emancipation from the parents.

As a rule, for middle-class parents this stage begins at nursery school or when the first child enters kindergarten at five and extends through the Junior High School level. The duration of the stage will depend largely on how many children the couple have and how they are spaced.

In many ways, this stage is one of the easier periods for

parents; at least this is what parents report in our parent discussion groups. From the mother's point of view, the hard work involved in the physical care of the smaller child has lessened, and the worries of the adolescent period have not begun. From the father's point of view, his wife and children are apt to need him somewhat less urgently at this stage, he is further along in his occupation, and the heavy bills of high school and college have not yet reared their ugly heads. In some ways, this is a relatively calm and relaxed stage for parents.

4. *The years of emancipation.*

This stage has also been well described as "the launching stage" by some writers.[7] There are two basic goals, or "developmental tasks," as Havighurst calls them,[8] to be accomplished during this stage: (1) emancipation or release of the children from the control and protection of the parents; and (2) the launching of the child into the competitive struggle of the larger society.

For middle-class parents, this stage spans both the high school and the college years, and sometimes graduate school as well. It is possible that the struggle for emancipation is less intense at the middle-class level than at the lower-class level, for the simple reason that the freeing process is spread over a longer time span for middle-class youngsters. They are not expected or required to be adults when they graduate from high school.

The basic preparation of the child for the adult world at the middle-calss level includes giving him (or her) a good personality, well adjusted, poised, etc., and a good education (training for the competitive struggle). When the parents have accomplished these two goals, their responsibility is essentially over. They may, of course, have to lend a helping hand from time to time, as Sussman's study shows,[9] but this is only temporary. For all practical purposes, the middle-class child is now on his own. This is probably not true at the upper-class level, although there are few studies of the family patterns of this class.

It seems to be true, as Bossard suggests,[10] that this emancipation period can be very difficult at the middle-class level if the family group has been broken by death or marital failure; the parent left with the child (or children) tends to structure his or her life too completely about the child, thus increasing the strain of letting go. One can observe this often in counseling with divorced mothers.

Some observers, including the writer, believe that middle-class mothers may accept the emancipation of their children better if they cultivate outside interests as a partial replacement for the child. This might be a job or some absorbing volunteer work in the community.

It seems likely that the small middle-class family of the 1930's, with only one or two children, experiences more strain in giving up the child than the larger family of the lower economic groups in our society.

It is usually assumed that adolescence is a period of storm and stress in our society, both for parents and children. However, in his classic high school study, *Elmtown's Youth,* Hollingshead did not find that his data supported this view of adolescence.[11] On the contrary, he feels that the high school years are often the glorious years for Americans, the time of their life that they will eventually regard with considerable nostalgia.

The writer is inclined to agree with Hollingshead, but it must be remembered that adolescence and high school can be very different experiences for various subgroups in our population, as the Elmtown study itself makes clear. Our own research with college students indicates that social class mobility has a close relationship to adolescent and postadolescent adjustment.[12] When the child has *social class continuity,* he is socially closer to his parents and experiences a minimum of conflict. But when he lacks this continuity and is moving into a new social world, his conflicts tend to be maximized.

In summary, it can be said that the emancipation stage is very likely to find a great many parents ambivalent; on the one hand, they are relieved that the long child-rearing process is at an end; but on the other hand, they miss their children and often feel lonely with the house quiet and deserted. This brings us to the next stage.

5. *The empty nest.*

In this stage, the children have grown up, completed their schooling, and have moved out into the larger society. Except for the parents, the family home is now deserted. Until the grandchildren begin to appear, the house will hear the sound of youngsters no more.

Glick has shown that as of 1950, the average (median) couple will have 14 years of their marriage left when their last child marries.[13] At that point the wife would be approximately forty-eight and the husband about fifty-one.[14] Glick makes this comment: "The combined effects of earlier marriages, smaller families, and longer average length of life have produced a remarkable change in the length of time that married couples live together after their children have set up homes of their own." [15] Going back to 1890, "the chances were 50-50 that one spouse or the other would die at least two years before their youngest child married." [16]

As yet, it is not very clear what these "empty nest" years hold for married couples. For some middle-class couples, the departure of the children reminds them of their age and makes them feel old, but for other couples this period seems to become a sort of second honeymoon—a time to visit Europe and do all the other things parents cannot afford or do not have time to do. Some couples begin to take regular winter vacations in Florida; others sell the big old house and buy or build a small ranch-style home.

Until the grandchildren put in an appearance, the parents are almost as free as they were in Stage I, the honeymoon period. New interests and hobbies are often necessary at this time to fill the void left by the departure of the last child. In many families, of course, the first grandchild has appeared before the last son or daughter has moved out of the parental home.

On the whole, the writer has the impression that this stage is a rather pleasant one for most middle-class couples, although we are unable to cite any studies to this effect. This *might* be true for the following reasons: (*a*) the couple are not really old by American standards, not until their sixties; (*b*) they should be at their economic peak; and (*c*) their parental responsibilities are at perhaps their lowest point. In addition, the role of grandparent is a satisfying one in our society, a fact that adds to the enjoyment of this stage.

6. *The later decades.*

By now the husband has usually retired; the grandparent role is well established; the couple begin to find themselves referred to as "senior citizens." By this time the children's marriages have either succeeded or failed; the grandchildren themselves are approaching marriage, and in some cases the great-grandchildren are beginning to appear on the scene.

Because of the extreme degree of mobility in our society, parents and their married children are often separated geographi-

Figure 16: Number of Widows in the United States, 1900–1953 and Forecast for 1960 *

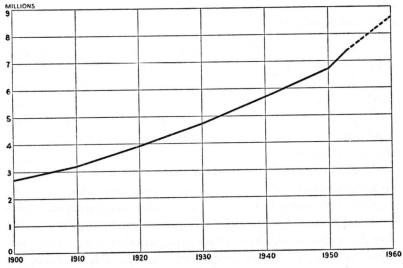

This study reflects the fact that wives in our society usually outlive their husbands. This pattern implies that women may need special preparation for this last cycle of married life.

* Source: Statistical Bureau, Metropolitan Life Insurance Company.

cally. A pattern seems to be emerging whereby the parents, after the father's retirement, move to the community of one of their married children. In one case known to the writer, the parents, after retirement, sold their home in Detroit and moved to Madison, Wisconsin, where a married daughter and her family lived. As the mother said to us: "Once our work was finished in Detroit, and once our children had moved away, we decided there wasn't anything to keep us in Detroit. So we moved here, partly to be near our grandchildren." Two or three times a year they drive to Michigan and visit their other married daughter. It seems to the writer that this plan has considerable merit. This particular couple had found it very satisfactory.

During the last three or four years of this stage, the wife will usually be alone, her marriage having been broken by the death of her husband. This stage appears to be a difficult one, judging by the studies of bereavement by Eliot and Fulcomer.[17]

Some Observations

In summarizing this stage analysis of modern marriage, several general observations seem to be possible:

1. In the 40 to 50 years spanned by the stable American marriage, a tremendous *variety* of social situations has to be met.

2. A good marriage, then, has to be capable of adjusting to all the myriad changes encountered. This destroys any fixed conception of marital adjustment.

3. Poor marriages are those that cannot make these numerous adaptations. In one of our marriage counseling cases, for example, the couple seemed to get along reasonably well during the childless honeymoon stage, but the adjustment gradually deteriorated after the arrival of children. This couple, in other words, could not adjust to Stage II. Other couples may not be able to make the transition to Stage V; once the children are reared, there is really nothing left to hold them together. This accounts for some of the middle-aged divorces, which are otherwise hard to explain.

4. The level of adjustment in any given marriage may vary considerably from one stage to another. Most of the existing research does not permit us to see this because most studies are cross-sectional and not longitudinal: that is, the couples are studied as of a given day and are not observed over a period of years or decades. In the writer's opinion, this is a major deficiency in the marriage and family research to date.

5. Successful marriage in our society, and perhaps in any society—involves the ability of a man and woman to *mature and age together*. To some extent, this means that they must be able to grow up at approximately the same rate of speed.

6. Each of the six stages has its own characteristics, its own stresses and strains, about which we have very little systematic knowledge. Marriage counselors, in particular, need insight into the dominant patterns of the various stages.

7. In considering marriage with any particular person, it may help to try to visualize the person as the partner for the various stages of marriage: the very attractive "sexy" girl, for example, might be pleasant enough for Stage I, the honeymoon period, but would she be as good at Stage II, the diaper patrol stage? The same question might be applied to certain potential husbands as well.

Conclusion

In this chapter we have attempted to give the reader a glimpse, however fleeting, of marriage as a lifelong way of life. It may be, of course, that no one can grasp this conception of marriage in his teens or even his early twenties. And yet this is what one is called upon to do in choosing a marriage partner.

Perhaps it is easier to see the point if it is put this way: choosing a husband or wife is like picking out a date for the next forty or fifty years. Seen in this light, one can only conclude that it is a decision deserving the most mature study and consideration any of us are capable of. It is hoped that this book has made some contribution toward that end.

References

1. See Paul C. Glick, "The Family Cycle," *American Sociological Review*, 12 (1947), 164–174, also his later report, "The Life Cycle of the Family," *Marriage and Family Living*, 17 (1955), 3–9. We will refer to these two different studies by their date of publication.

2. *Statistical Bulletin*, Metropolitan Life Insurance Company, November, 1955, p. 4.

3. Glick, *op. cit.* (1955), 5.

4. Benjamin Spock, *The Pocketbook of Baby and Child Care* (New York, Pocket Books, Inc., 1946).

5. Glick, *op. cit.* (1955).

6. See Shirley Jackson, *Life Among the Savages* (New York, Farrar, Strauss & Young, Inc., 1953).

7. See Reuben Hill and Willard Waller, *The Family* (New York, Dryden Press, 1951), chap. 20.

8. See Robert J. Havighurst, *Human Development and Education* (New York, Longmans, Green & Co., Inc., 1953), chap. 1 for an analysis of the concept of "developmental task."

9. Marvin B. Sussman, "The Help Pattern in the Middle-Class Family," *American Sociological Review*, 18 (1953), 22–28.

10. See James H. S. Bossard, *The Sociology of Child Development* (New York, Harper & Bros., 1948), chap. 18.

11. For a discussion as to whether or not adolescence is a period of storm and stress, see August B. Hollingshead, *Elmtown's Youth* (New York, John Wiley & Sons, 1949), chap. 1.

12. See E. E. LeMasters, "Social Class Mobility and Family Integration," *Marriage and Family Living*, 16 (1954), 226–232.

13. Glick, *op. cit.* (1955).

14. *Ibid.*

15. *Ibid.*, p. 6.

16. *Ibid.*

17. See David Martin Fulcomer, *The Adjustive Behavior of Some Recently Bereaved Spouses,* unpublished Ph.D. dissertation, Northwestern University Library, 1942; the various studies by Eliot in this area are summarized in his excellent article, "Bereavement: Inevitable but Not Insurmountable," in Howard Becker and Reuben Hill (eds.), *Family, Marriage and Parenthood* (Boston, D. C. Heath & Co., Inc., 1955), pp. 641–668.

Suggested Readings

1. Anne Morrow Lindbergh, *Gift from the Sea* (New York, Pantheon Press, 1955). In this best-seller there are some penetrating insights into modern marriage and its relationship to aging and maturation.

2. John Levy and Ruth Monroe, *The Happy Family* (New York, Alfred A. Knopf, Inc., 1938). This has become a classic because of its sane discussion of modern marriage.

3. Reuben Hill and Willard Waller, *The Family* (New York, Dryden Press, 1951), chap. 25, "Proposed Changes in Family Designs." This explores the possibilities for improving marriage and family life in our society.

4. Earl Koos, *Families in Trouble* (New York, Columbia University Press, 1946). Page for page, this little study probably contains more insight into the American family than any other volume.

5. John Sirjamaki, *The American Family in the Twentieth Century* (Cambridge, Harvard University Press, 1953). Contains helpful perspective on marriage and family life as related to modern society.

6. Paul Glick, "The Life Cycle of the Family," *Marriage and Family Living,* 17 (1955), 3–9. The serious student will find this summary of the latest census data very worthwhile.

APPENDIX

OUTLINE FOR TERM PAPER ANALYZING THE STUDENT'S FAMILY

Introduction and Instructions

This paper is intended to give you insight into the family environment out of which you as a person emerged. The underlying assumption of the paper is that you will be better prepared for modern marriage if you have some insight into yourself as a person. Since our parental family is basic in shaping us, a detailed analysis of that family should be helpful.

It should be made clear that this is *not* to be a *history* of your family. What we want is a functional analysis of your family: how it is organized internally and how it fits into our society externally. Credit will not be given for a purely historical paper.

You should know that this paper will be read by no one but the instructor, that it will be returned to you, and that its contents will not be revealed to any other person. Furthermore, these papers will be kept in a locked office while in the instructor's possession. You are, of course, perfectly free to withhold any family information you do not wish to include in your analysis.

This paper will count as one fourth of your final grade in this course. The evaluation will be based on (*a*) the amount of effort that appears to have gone into the paper, and (*b*) the use of course content in analyzing your family.

It may help you to know that out of over 1,000 students who have written this paper, over 95 per cent have reported it to have been a worthwhile project. For most of them, this was the first time they had ever attempted a thorough description and analysis of their parental family.

Students from "traumatic" or "broken" families sometimes have difficulty writing a paper of this nature. Those who have done it, however, are almost unanimous in their belief that the project was helpful to them. Actually, they are the persons most in need of such an analysis.

If you find that you are unable to accept this assignment, consult your instructor concerning alternate projects.

Internal Organization of the Family

1. *Marital adjustment of the parents.*

Most studies of the American family conclude that the marital adjustment of the parents is a crucial fact in family life. Try to rate your parents on the following adjustment scale: Very Poor, Below Average, Average, Above Average, Very Good. Write down specific illustrations of incidents that seem to support your evaluation of their adjustment.

Try to analyze the basic factors that account for their adjustment or lack of adjustment. These might include information about their courtship, the circumstances leading up to their marriage, their personality patterns, their educational backgrounds, the types of families from which they came (in particular the level of adjustment of their parents), their socioeconomic backgrounds, and so forth.

IN THIS SECTION ASK YOURSELF HOW MUCH YOU REALLY KNOW OR DO NOT KNOW ABOUT THE EARLY LIVES OF YOUR PARENTS. Remember that they were not always adults. Try to improve your understanding of your parents as you gather the material for this paper.

2. *Role distribution in the family.*

Most students of the American family analyze families by breaking down the tasks to be performed in the family and calling these activities "roles." Thus, the earning of a living for the family is called the "economic" role or the "breadwinning" role. This can then be analyzed in terms of who does it (man or wife or both, with perhaps some help from children). Other roles often used are: *child-bearing* (how often the wife-mother has gone through pregnancy, also the role of the husband-father in helping her through each pregnancy); *child-rearing* (who assumes the major responsibility for taking care of the children, whether the father or any relatives participate in the child-rearing process, conflicts over child-rearing, etc.); *home management* (cooking, cleaning, shopping, division of labor between parents; roles of children in these tasks; handling of finances, problems if mother works or does not like housework, etc.); *companionship* roles (the sharing of activities between husband and wife, whether or not the family as a unit participates jointly in various activities, ability or failure of one of the parents to play the companionship role with the children, tendency of the father to seek his companionship among other men, etc.); *kinship* roles (relationships with relatives, whether or not relatives have lived with family or close to family; effects of the kinship groups on the family, conflicts with relatives, etc.); *sex partner* (any evidence that might indicate failure of the parents to arrive at an adequate sexual adjustment, not usually known to the child but still very important in trying to understand problems of maladjustment in married couples); *community relationship* role (whether or not the parents have been very active in neighborhood and community affairs, effects of this on the family, club memberships, etc.).

In analyzing roles in the family, keep in mind the following: Have the roles been clearly assigned and accepted by the parents and the children? Have there been serious conflicts over roles (who should do what)? Have there been many changes in roles (for example, during the war)? Have the persons been adequate in the performance of their roles (for example, a father might be very adequate in the performance of the breadwinner role but be very inadequate in the companionship role)? In this way family affairs can be analyzed in terms of specific jobs that must be done in any family if the group is to function well.

3. *Power distribution within the family.*

Theoretically, marital and family systems can be classified into three groups on the basis of power distribution: patricentric, matricentric, and democratic. Most research in the United States tends to show that lower-class families still are basically patricentric, whereas middle- and upper-class families tend to be more democratic. We are interested in knowing how you analyze your family in this context. Please give specific illustrations to support your generalization on this item. Can you see any strengths or weaknesses in your family related to the distribution of power? What do you think has determined the distribution of power in your family? Have there been any changes in this phase of your family's life?

4. *Parent-children and sibling relationships.*

Number of children, your ordinal position (oldest, youngest, etc.), effects of this ordinal position on you, if any; parent relationships with children, lines of attachment (whether closer to mother or father); relationships with brothers and sisters (if any); possible effects of being a member of a large or small family; sibling rivalries; attempts to reach out for substitute parents (grandparents, aunts and uncles, etc.); what you can remember of these relationships when you were very young (preschool level if possible).

Psychiatrists and psychologists believe that such early relationships are of great importance in forming our basic personality structure. You should have a better understanding of yourself if you can get some clear picture of your family environment during these early years.

5. *Effects of father's occupation on family.*

Often, the father's occupation imposes stresses on family life that are of vital importance in understanding the family patterns. This may be related to long hours, absence from home, strains and tensions at the office, financial reverses, and so forth. It is suggested that you consider this angle in studying your family.

If your mother works outside the home, the effects of her employment should also be considered. This might include changes in her relationship to her husband, effects of an independent income, fatigue brought on by her outside work, etc.

6. *Religious patterns of the family.*

In some families religion is a basic factor, while in others it plays a rather minor role. Do you feel that your family is very devout in its religious life? Has religion been a strong supporting influence in your family? Did your parents seem to reflect deep religious values in their daily lives? Has there been any conflict in the family over religion? Do the children reflect the religious teachings of the family? Would you consider marrying outside your family's religion?

7. *Courtship and the family.*

We are very much interested in learning how much, and in what way, modern parents influence their children in dating and courtship practices. Are you aware of any supervision of this sort? If so, can you analyze how it has operated from the beginning of your dating period? Has your father had as much influence on this as your mother? Do your dating and courtship seem to reflect norms internalized in your personality but absorbed from your family experiences? Have you had conflicts with your family over courtship? Do you ever observe ways in which courtship practices have changed since your parents were courting? Can you make these observations specific, with illustrations?

External Relationships of Your Family

1. *Urbanization.*

Most of our families were rural dwellers until recent generations. Sociologists believe this migration from the farm to the city to be one of the basic causes of change in the American family. Try to trace these movements in your family. How many generations have they lived in the city (if your family is now urban)? How has this affected such things as birth rates, educational levels, occupations, standard of living, emancipation of the women, and various other patterns (such as family recreation)? Can you analyze the general effects of the size of community in which your family lives? Would you prefer to rear your children in a different type of community? If so, why?

2. *Social class position.*

The instructor has taken the position in class that one of the big factors in American families is the tendency of the children and the parents to be divided by vertical class mobility—the tendency for the kids to move up a notch in the class structure. Is this happening in your family? If so, try to analyze it. We are especially interested in such moves where the parents are members of the so-called working class (such as skilled manual workers) and the children are the first generation to attend college.

Try to locate your family on Warner's class scale: upper upper, lower upper, upper middle, lower middle, upper lower, and lower lower. In small communities there may be fewer divisions than this (such as upper, middle, and lower). How long has your family occupied its present class position—say during the past two or three generations? Has it been moving up, down, or remaining at the same level? Are the children in the present generation (or the previous one) all living on the same class level? If some are higher or lower, can you see how this has affected family solidarity?

Remember that in Warner's system he takes into account more than just money income. He also evaluates such things as prestige of occupation (such as the ministry), family history in the community, informal cliques (who entertains whom), membership in clubs, etc.

3. *Effects of wars, depressions, etc.*

Your family does not live in a social vacuum. It has been affected by the boom of the 1920's, both world wars, the depression, the new emancipation of women, secularization, etc. Can you place your family in its societal context? Why don't you try? It might give you more understanding of your family (and yourself) than you have ever had before.

INDEX OF AUTHORS

607

608   *Index of Authors*

INDEX OF SUBJECTS